D1610654

Trade Shocks in Developing Countries

SPONSORS

The funding for this project was provided by:
Oxford Institute for Energy Studies
International Centre for Economic Growth [ICEG]
World Bank
The Dutch Government

Trade Shocks in Developing Countries

Volume 2: *Asia and Latin America*

PAUL COLLIER

AND

JAN WILLEM GUNNING

AND

ASSOCIATES

OXFORD

UNIVERSITY PRESS

OXFORD

UNIVERSITY PRESS

Great Clarendon Street, Oxford OX2 6DP

Oxford University Press is a department of the University of Oxford.
It furthers the University's objective of excellence in research, scholarship,
and education by publishing worldwide in

Oxford New York

Athens Auckland Bangkok Bogotá Buenos Aires Calcutta
Cape Town Chennai Dar es Salaam Delhi Florence Hong Kong Istanbul
Karachi Kuala Lumpur Madrid Melbourne Mexico City Mumbai
Nairobi Paris São Paulo Singapore Taipei Tokyo Toronto Warsaw

with associated companies in Berlin Ibadan

Oxford is a registered trade mark of Oxford University Press
in the UK and in certain other countries

Published in the United States
by Oxford University Press Inc., New York

British Library Cataloguing in Publication Data

Data available

Library of Congress Cataloging in Publication Data

Trade shocks in developing countries / Paul Collier and
Jan Willem Gunning and associates.
p. cm.
Includes bibliographical references and indexes.
Contents: v. 1. Africa—v. 2. Asia and Latin America.
ISBN 0–19–829338–0 (Volume 1)
ISBN 0–19–829463–8 (Volume 2)
1. Buffer stocks—Prices—Developing countries. 2. Buffer stocks—
Prices—Africa. 3. Buffer stocks—Prices—Asia. 4. Buffer stocks—
Prices—Latin America. 5. Commodity control—Developing countries.
6. Commodity control—Africa. 7. Commodity control—Asia.
8. Commodity control—Latin America. I. Collier, Paul.
II. Gunning, Jan Willem.
HF1428.T72 1999 332.6'09172'4—dc21 98-47376

1 3 5 7 9 10 8 6 4 2

Typeset in Palatino
by Best-set Typesetter Ltd., Hong Kong
Printed in Great Britain
on acid-free paper by
Biddles Ltd
Guildford & Kings Lynn

PREFACE

This book is the outcome of a project involving many individuals and institutions. Core funding for the project was provided by the International Centre for Economic Growth (ICEG) and the World Bank. The Oxford Institute for Energy Studies funded the case studies of two oil shocks. The Dutch government funded the Asian case studies and two of the workshops. Without this support the project would not have been feasible.

The study grew out of our earlier work on the coffee boom in Kenya. The authors of the country studies were asked to adopt the methodology of the Kenyan study with respect to the estimation of windfall savings rates and the disaggregation into private and public behaviour. The methodology was discussed with the country teams at launch workshops in Washington, DC, Oxford and Colombo (Sri Lanka). Subsequent workshops in Amsterdam and Oxford were used to discuss draft chapters. Interim results of the project were published in *Trade Shocks in Developing Countries* (Institute for Contemporary Studies, for ICEG, 1994) and were presented at the European Economic Association Annual Conference of 1992 (published in the *European Economic Review*, 1993) and the Royal Economic Society Annual Conference of 1996. We would like to thank Angus Deaton for extensive comments on a previous draft.

Paul Collier and Jan Willem Gunning

Washington, January 1998

CONTENTS

Volume 2

14

One Decade of External Coffee Shocks in Colombia, 1975–85

SANTIAGO MONTENEGRO

14.1. Introduction

The aim of this chapter is to study the Colombian coffee shocks in the period 1975–1985.[1] Between 1975 and 1977, the relative price of coffee multiplied 2.6 times, which increased the country's terms of trade by 50%. While the real exchange rate appreciated significantly, the current account of the balance of payments developed a substantial surplus and the budget deficit fell dramaticaly and even presented surpluses in two years of the boom. The boom years (1976–80) were followed by a reverse shock, expressed in the collapse in the value of coffee and non-coffee exports in 1981 and the following three years. Naturally, the economic downturn this brought about was aggravated by the world recession, the high levels of interest rates and the international financial crisis. All of this helped to deteriorate the current account and produced a significant fall in the level of international reserves, which had reached historic levels at the end of the boom. Paradoxically, the economic deceleration did not reverse the real exchange rate appreciation because the authorities engineered a consumption and investment boom at the end of and after the boom. This not only produced a huge budget deficit but also contributed heavily to the current account deterioration. A stabilisation package, therefore, was called for and it began to be introduced in mid-1984, culminating in a massive exchange depreciation in 1985–86.

In the next section of this chapter, we analyse the nature of the shock (as given by real income deviations from trend) faced by Colombia in the period 1970–86. In Section 14.3, we study the savings behaviour of the representative consumer and of the public and private sectors, as well as that of the so-called Coffee Fund. In Section 14.4, we study the goods markets' response. We stress the evolution of relative prices and treat at some length the investment response to the boom, disaggregating the latter into its tradable and non-tradable components as well as assessing the investment behaviour of the public sector during and after the boom. Given that we could not obtain reliable investment figures for sector of destination, in Section 14.5 our factor market analysis centres on the employment response to the boom. In Section 14.6, we turn our attention to the financial markets, stressing the extraordinary monetary control problem brought about by the boom, the evolution of aggregate lending and the interest rate response. Although public consumption and invest-ment behaviour is studied in the Section 14.4, in Section 14.7 we concen-trate on the sensitivity of public revenue to real national income and on the sources of deficit-financing through this period. In Section 14.8, we evaluate additional aspects of the control regime in Colombia. There, we treat, in turn, the management of the internal coffee price; the effects of the crawling-peg exchange rate regime on the black-market exchange rate; and the effects of import controls on resource allocation and on the per-formance of non-coffee exports and the manufacturing sector, as well as the consequences of the exchange controls system on savings rates throughout the economy. Section 14.9 concludes.

14.2. The Nature of the Coffee Shocks

Colombia's economy was subject to several shocks in the period 1975–76, the coffee boom of the second half of the 1970s being by far the most important and the one on which we will centre our attention in this chapter.[2] The world price of coffee began to increase in 1975 as a result of frosts affecting the Brazilian coffee areas. The relative price of coffee in terms of importables increased 2.6 times between 1975 and 1976 and then dropped back to where it basically was in 1975 by 1979. Between 1981 and 1983 it stood at levels which were very low by historical standards. By 1985, it had regained the 1975 real level. The following year, it dramati-cally increased, jumping by more than 60% (Figure 14.1).

Figure 14.2 shows the impact on the country's terms of trade. Between 1975 and 1977, Colombia's terms of trade improved by 50%, falling to a level 20% above the 1975 level in 1979 and 1980. In the period 1981–85, the terms of trade, although below their level during the coffee boom, were above the average level for the first part of the 1970s. The second coffee shock of 1986 brought the overall terms of trade almost to the level they had reached at the peak of the coffee boom in 1977.[3]

To asses the impact of these price changes on the economy's real in-come, it is worth viewing the evolution of the value of exports throughout the period. This is also shown in Figure 14.1. It is quite striking to find that, although the price of coffee increased between 1975 and 1976, the volume of exports fell during those two years and only began to increase when the real price started falling in 1978. As a consequence, the boom was really stretched beyond the price boom proper. Whereas the share of coffee exports in GDP (in nominal terms) was on average lower than 6%

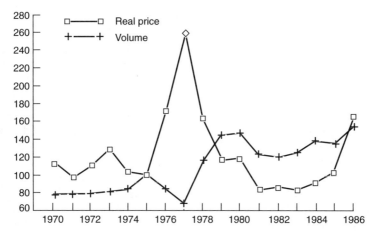

Figure 14.1. Price and volume of coffee exports, 1970–86 (*1975 = 100*)

Note: The real price of coffee is the ratio of the implicit price of coffee exports to the price of importables.

Source: DANE, National Accounts.

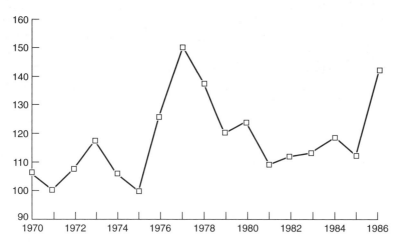

Figure 14.2. Terms of trade, 1970–86 (*1975 = 100*)

Note: Ratio of the implicit price of exports to the implicit price of imports.

Source: DANE, National Accounts.

in 1970–75, it increased to more than 8.5% in 1977–78 and remained above 7% in 1979–80, only to fall dramatically thereafter. In 1986 both the real price and the volume of exports increased. This explains why, despite the lower price increase (compared to the 1977 price rise), the share of coffee exports in GDP recorded the highest figure for the period we are considering. Between 1985 and 1986, the share jumped from 5.5% to 9.5% of GDP.

In order to estimate a measure of windfall income throughout the period 1970–86, it is first necessary to construct a counterfactual level of exports in order to assess the contribution of the external sector to the overall windfall income. Following Bevan *et al.* (Chapter 2), we assume that the level of coffee exports was not affected by variations in the real price of coffee and that without the external shocks the barter terms of trade would have remained at the 1975 level. The counterfactual value of exports is then equal to the actual value divided by the barter terms of trade and the external windfall is calculated as the difference between actual exports and this counterfactual. Deflating this difference by the import price index, then, gives the real value of the external windfall at 1975 prices. To obtain the aggregate windfall income, we then first add this external windfall to real GDP at 1975 prices and get a series of real income, GDY. We then assume that a counterfactual GDY is given by a trend value of GDY.

We construct this trend by running a simple regression of lnGDY (natural log of GDY) on a trend series.[4] If α and β are the estimated coefficients, trend GDY is then obtained by calculating the exponential of $(\alpha + \beta T)$, where T is time. It follows that windfall income is the difference between actual real GDY at 1975 prices and trend GDY. In Figure 14.3 we present this aggregate windfall.[5]

The figure shows that the boom extended well beyond the terms of trade peak and lasted until 1980. This was followed by a clear reverse shock in the first half of the 1980s, which cannot be explained by the

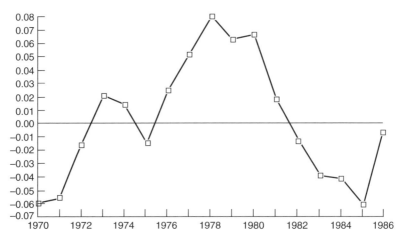

Figure 14.3. Real income deviation from trend, 1970–86 (*1975 = 100*)

Source: GDY figures in Figure 14.4.

overall terms of trade, for they clearly stayed above their 1975 level even in the period 1981–85. This reverse shock is associated with the collapse in the price and value of coffee exports (Figure 14.1). Of course, the world recession and the fall in demand for non-coffee exports, the high world interest rates and the international financial crisis were also responsible for the economic downturn of the first part of the 1980s. In line with most Latin American economies, Colombia then experienced its worst recession since the recession of the 1930s.

Finally, from the very outset of the coffee boom of the second half of the 1970s it was clear that the boom was going to be transitory. This was recognised by the authorities, who constantly reminded the private sector about the transitory nature of the boom (Sarmiento 1982).

14.3. Savings Rates

14.3.1. Estimation of the Aggregate Savings Rate

In this section, we estimate a measure for the aggregate windfall savings rate. The first step is to estimate a series for the level of real savings. This figure was calculated by subtracting from total real GDY aggregate real total consumption expenditure by households and the public administrations at 1975 prices. The difference is necessarily what the 'representative' consumer invested in either capital formation (including inventory accumulation) or acquiring net foreign financial assets.[6] As with aggregate windfall GDY, we calculate aggregate windfall savings as the deviation of actual real savings from trend savings.[7]

Both windfall real income and windfall savings are shown in Figure 14.4. From simple inspection it is clear that, although the two figures are correlated, the windfall savings rate is not constant throughout the period 1970–86. Although it is close to 1 in 1973–74 and very high again in 1976–77, it is on average much smaller in the other years. To compute the average windfall savings rate for the period, we ran a simple regression of windfall savings on windfall income and obtained a propensity to save of 0.43, which could be considered significantly high.[8] Another way to compute the windfall savings rate during some of the periods is simply to sum both total windfall savings and total windfall income and divide one by the other. Using this procedure, we find that the aggregate windfall savings rate during the coffee boom of the 1970s (1976–80) was 48%, that is, almost half the total windfall income. If we consider 1976 and 1977 only, the savings rate was equal to 84.6%. It follows, therefore, that the economy as a whole saved a high proportion of its windfall income throughout the period studied, and, more particularly, during the boom.

In Section 14.4 we show that, given that windfall investment was

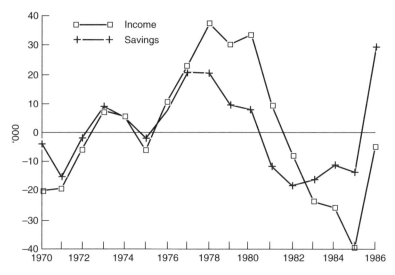

Figure 14.4. Aggregate windfall income and savings, 1970–86 (*1975 prices*)
Source: DANE, National Accounts.

relatively low, most of the aggregate windfall savings were invested in the acquisition of foreign assets, which helps explain the massive increase in foreign reserves experienced by the Colombian economy in the second half of the 1970s. All of these figures would indeed show that the Colombian economy behaved with a relatively high degree of rationality during the coffee boom.

14.3.2. Disaggregation into Private and Public Sectors

In Colombia, it is important to disaggregate not only the private and public sectors, but also the Coffee Fund, the marketing body which manages the coffee industry. Adding this agent's windfall income and savings to either the private or the public sector may vary these sectors' savings figures quite significantly.

First, we calculate the public sector's windfall savings rate. In so doing, we initially compute windfall public income by subtracting actual real revenues from estimated trend revenues.[9] To calculate the level of public savings, we subtract real public consumption from total revenues. Then, we compute windfall savings as the difference between actual and trend savings.[10] These results are shown in Figure 14.5. A quick look at this figure clearly indicates that public windfall savings were extremely high in the period 1970–86. A simple regression of windfall savings on windfall income for the public sector gives a parameter of 1.177, which would

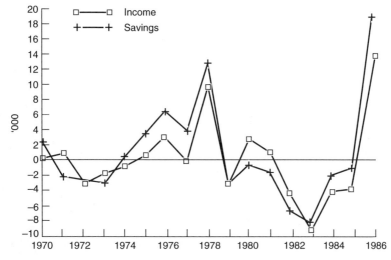

Figure 14.5. Public windfall income and savings, 1970–86 (*1975 prices*)
Source: DANE, National Accounts.

mean that on average the Colombian public sector saved 117% of windfall income in the period 1970–86.[11] Although this is a remarkable result, it only confirms what several studies have already shown for the historical level of public savings vis-à-vis the private sector's savings in Colombia.[12] If we only consider the coffee boom period (1976–80), the accumulated public savings rate is even higher, 148.8%.

Proceeding in a similar way, the windfall savings rate for the Coffee Fund is estimated. We find that this agent's savings rate is unity, as is immediately obvious from Figure 14.7, where we record its actual real revenue and savings figures.[13] Having estimated the overall windfall income and windfall savings rates as well as those of the public sector and the Coffee Fund, we estimated the corresponding rates for the private sector residually. We found that private windfall savings out of windfall income for the period 1970–86 were only 30%. Considering just the coffee-boom period, the accumulated savings figure rises a little over this average, reaching 33% (Figure 14.6).

The economy-wide importance of the latter figure becomes evident when we compute each sector's share in total windfall income: 9.5% of the windfall accrued to the public sector; 81.5% went to the private sector; and the rest, 9%, accrued to the Coffee Fund, almost as much as the amount that went to the public sector. Meanwhile windfall savings were distributed as follows: 29% were generated by the public sector; the private sector's share was 54.8%; and 16.2% accrued to the Coffee Fund.

When the economy faced the negative shock of the first half of the 1980s

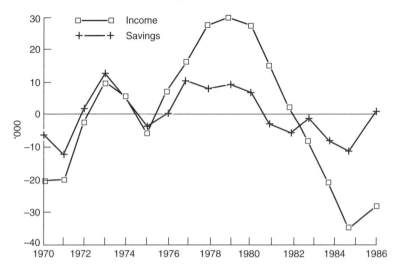

Figure 14.6. Private windfall income and savings, 1970–86 (*1975 prices*)
Source: DANE, National Accounts.

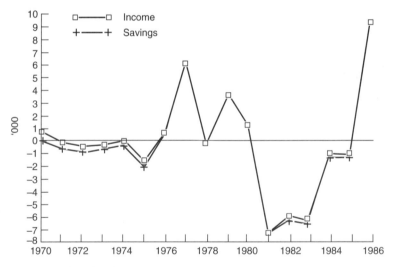

Figure 14.7. Coffee fund income and savings, 1970–86 (*1975 prices*)
Source: DANE, National Accounts.

(1981–85), the accumulated savings rates changed radically compared with those of the previous period. In fact, the aggregated (dis)savings rate rose to 80.4%, up from 48%, thus appearing to indicate that, whereas overall consumption remained on average close to its trend, the fall in real income was largely mirrored by higher (dis)savings (compared to trend). Disaggregating these figures into private and public gives a very interesting result. Whereas the public dissavings figure fell to 82.3%, down from a 148% savings rate during the coffee boom, the private sector's windfall dissavings rate increased to 61.6%, up from a 32.7% savings rate during the boom. Although the public sector was consistently saving more (in absolute terms) than the private sector (out of both total and windfall income) the two sectors' saving behaviour was differently affected by the nature of the shock. Whereas public savings rates moved pro-cyclically, private savings behaved countercyclically (again, in absolute terms). Given the latter's weight in total savings, it was big enough to increase the aggregate windfall dissavings rate during the recession of the 1980s. Meanwhile, the savings behaviour of the Coffee Fund, as given by its windfall savings rate, remained basically the same as during the coffee boom of the 1970s, as Figure 14.7 clearly indicates. That is to say, it remained very close to unity.

To conclude this section, it is worth emphasising that the contribution of the public sector to the generation of these high aggregate windfall savings rates went beyond its own savings effort proper. To control the impressive increase in the monetary base during the period in which international reserves were rocketing, the authorities sterilised the increase in reserves by introducing compulsory savings instruments for exporters in general and coffee exporters in particular. The private sector's windfall savings figures presented above already reflect this policy. This may mean that, had this policy not been carried out, the gap between public and private sector savings rates would have been even higher.

14.4. Goods Markets

14.4.1. Consumption and Investment

First, we assess the impact of the coffee boom in goods markets by looking at actual consumption relative to trend (Figure 14.8).[14] While aggregate consumption had grown very close to trend up to 1975, the coffee shock of the 1970s and then the recession of the 1980s changed this picture. In fact, during the first two years of the coffee boom, real consumption does not depart significantly from trend, so that the consumption rate, measured in relation to windfall income, is only 15.4% in 1976–77.[15] This situation is radically altered in the subperiod starting in the third year of the boom. In 1978–80, the windfall consumption rate jumps to 62.8%, which also implies that consumption was on average above trend by more than 5.5%, a situation which extends well beyond the coffee boom. Actual consumption remains well above trend until 1982.

Santiago Montenegro

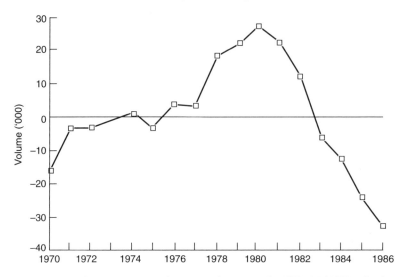

Figure 14.8. Total consumption deviation from trend, 1970–86 (*1975 prices*)

Figure 14.9. Total public real consumption deviation from trend, 1970–86 (*1975 prices*)

    This aggregate consumption behaviour is mainly explained by the evolution of public sector expenditure. Figure 14.9 shows the deviation of real public consumption from trend in 1970–86.[16] The figure neatly shows the effort made by the authorities to control expenditure during the first years of the boom. Although public consumption was already below trend in the two years before the boom, it was drastically reduced in 1976 and 1977, when it was 11% and 12% below trend, respectively. A large part of the adjustment took the form of lower real wages to public sector employees. This measure was contained in the policy package introduced by the Lopez administration (1974–78) to control the inflationary effects of the boom. Despite a lower rate of nominal devaluation of the exchange rate, the peso value of international reserves increased from 16 billion to more than 300 billion pesos between 1975 and 1981, which meant that the annual increase of reserves ranged from 40% to 75% of the previous year's M_1 (Section 14.6).

By 1979, the situation had changed significantly: public consumption was already above trend and remained so until 1984. In 1982, it was more than 12% above its trend level. The stabilisation programme introduced in 1985–86 to correct external and internal imbalances reduced public consumption dramatically, so that by 1986 it was almost 15% below trend.

We now turn our attention to consider capital goods. In Figure 14.10 we indicate the deviation from trend of total gross fixed capital formation for the period 1965–86, which excludes inventory accumulation. According to this figure, with the exception of the last year of the boom (1980), windfall gross fixed capital formation during the boom was negligible, if compared with investment recorded before and immediately after the boom.[17] Accumulated real windfall investment represented only 11.2% of total windfall savings in the period 1976–80.

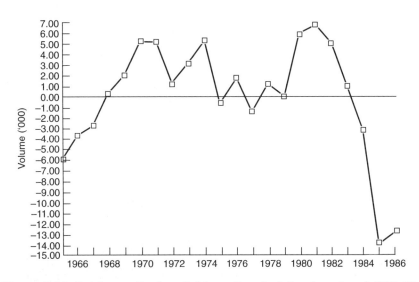

Figure 14.10. Total gross fixed capital formation deviation from trend, 1970–86 (*1975 prices*)

In Figures 14.11 and 14.12 we disaggregate real investment into its traded and non-traded components. The latter includes all forms of construction; traded investment records all investment in transport equipment and machinery. These figures indicate that there was no construction boom. On the contrary, Figure 14.12 shows that overall construction during the boom was significantly below trend, particularly in 1978 and 1979, when total construction was 4.5% and 11.2% below trend,

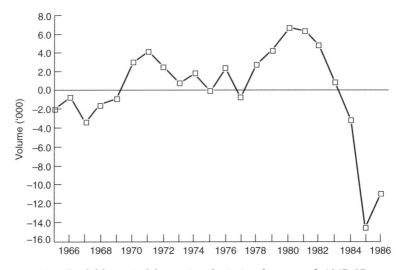

Figure 14.11. Tradable capital formation deviation from trend, 1965–85

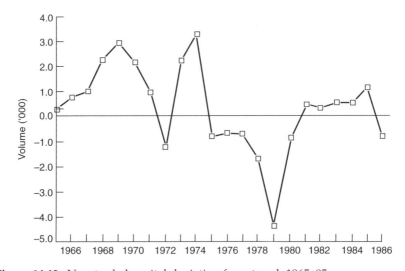

Figure 14.12. Non-traded capital deviation from trend, 1965–85

respectively. This is the more surprising when compared with the evolution of total construction in the pre-boom period. There are two clear construction booms, with their peaks in 1969 and 1974, neither of them related to an external boom. The former implied a total departure from trend of 9.5%; the figure for the latter was 10.5%. Total construction collapsed (as measured in relation to trend) in 1975, and was back above trend only in 1981. Between that year and 1985 it was above trend, peaking in 1985 at 2.2% above its trend level. The investment boom that the economy enjoyed in the period beginning in 1980 was, therefore, led by tradable investment, as Figure 14.11 duly records.[18] Tradable capital formation was depressed overall and steadily falling from its 1971 peak (18.95% above trend) up to 1977; in 1978 it started an expansion which brought the real actual tradable investment to a level 17.5% above trend in 1980 (15.7% in 1981 and 10.9% in 1982). The recession, the widening payments deficit and the stabilisation package introduced by the authorities in 1985–86 finally ended the tradables investment boom. As a consequence, at the end of the period real tradables investment was 27.5% and 19.5% below trend, respectively.

This (tradables) investment boom was fundamentally originated in the public sector. The path followed by public investment, with the exception of 1977, was very similar to the consumption path: during the boom it was depressed; then it dramatically increased, only to collapse (relative to trend) in the last two years of the period. Investment projects which had been planned before the boom were postponed and began to be implemented only in 1980.

Why did no construction boom occur? Perhaps the construction sector was also affected by a multiplicity of factors: the tight conditions of the financial markets in general and the mortgage market in particular; the availability of construction materials such as cement, iron and steel products; the relative availability or scarcity of construction areas, especially in large cities, which could have affected land prices; and government (e.g. monetary) policy, which in one way or another could have influenced the variables just mentioned.

From a different perspective, studying the construction sector (public and private) as a whole may hide significant and differentiated behaviour of some subsectors within this large aggregate. In Figure 14.13, for example, we present the evolution of house-building construction for the period 1965–86.[19] The peak in the second half of the 1970s could be interpreted as a house-building construction boom, which could be corroborated by the path followed by its relative price, as we show in Figure 14.15 below. Whereas the relative price of house-building construction peaked in 1979, when it was above its 1975 level by almost 23%, the relative price for the rest of the construction sector had increased by only 14% in relation to its 1975 level. The possible link between external shocks

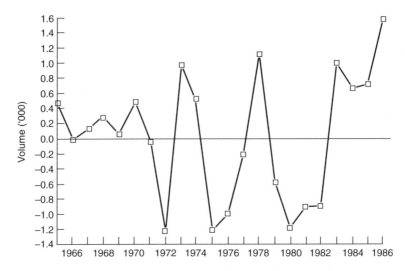

Figure 14.13. House-building construction deviation from trend, 1965–85

and housing booms is, however, obscured by the presence of booms before and after the coffee shock of the 1970s.

Finally, it is important to mention that the evolution of aggregate investment (private and public) during and after the boom in Colombia fits the optimum investment path suggested by the construction booms model. This indicates that a rational response to an external positive shock is to invest part of the windfall abroad, so that the investment boom is extended beyond the terms of trade shock proper. In the case of Colombia, the private sector seems to have played a more passive role than the public sector, which led the savings and investment processes and engineered a massive acquisition of foreign assets during the 1970s.

14.4.2. Relative Price Changes

How did the boom affect the relative prices of consumption and investment goods? With a managed nominal exchange rate, the theory of the Dutch Disease predicts that positive (negative) shocks will increase (decrease) the relative price of non-tradable goods *vis-à-vis* the price of tradables. That is, the exchange rate will appreciate (depreciate) in real terms. If some tradables, such as importables, are protected with binding quantity restrictions on imports, then the model has to be slightly modified, because they behave as non-tradables at the margin. In this case, the relative price of consumer non-tradables in terms of importables need not vary as a consequence of the boom. The Dutch Disease theory predicts,

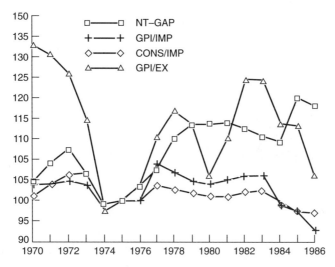

Figure 14.14. Relative prices, 1970–86 (*1970 = 100*)

therefore, that the price of consumer non-tradables in terms of exportables would increase significantly. In this modified version of the model, importables could contract only if import controls were relaxed.

With this in mind, in Figure 14.14 we present the relative price of non-tradable consumer goods in terms of importables for the period 1970–86. According to this figure, the relative price of non-traded consumer goods increased by 9 percentage points with respect to its 1975 level (DP/MP). But, as expected given the private sector's fairly low windfall savings rate, the relative price of consumer goods in terms of non-booming exportables increased much more significantly during the boom. By 1978, this relative price had risen more than 21% in relation to its 1975 level (DP/EX). As the boom subsided, it fell back in 1980. Then, it increased again (29% above its 1975 level) in 1982–83, and collapsed with the massive exchange depreciation of 1986. The fact that this relative price reached such high levels at the beginning of the 1980s, actually exceeding the peak of the coffee-boom years, is perhaps explained by the public sector's expenditure boom of that period, and by the fact that the figures for the 1970s already reflect the strength of the counterinflationary policies which led to the high savings rates during the boom.

There are, therefore, clear signs of the presence of the Dutch Disease following the coffee boom. These effects are also corroborated by the devastation that the boom caused on non-booming exports and on the manufactures sector (Section 14.8).

This crisis may perhaps also explain why the private sector's investment collapse occurred despite the accentuated steady fall of the relative

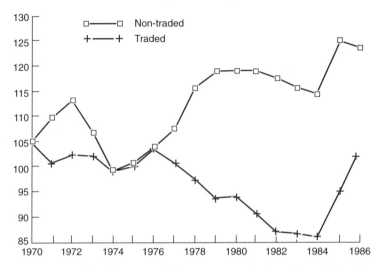

Figure 14.15. Traded and non-traded investment relative prices, 1970–86 (*1970 = 100*)

price of tradable investment between 1977 and 1984 (Figure 14.15). Only when the exchange rate was massively devalued in 1985 and 1986 did this relative price regain its 1975 level. The private sector took no advantage of this low relative price, to which should be added other favourable conditions such as higher savings, the availability of foreign exchange and foreign lending facilities.

The relative price of construction did increase during the boom, as the construction booms theory would suggest (Figure 14.16). However, it did not fall as soon as the boom subsided and even increased once more in 1985. By 1979, this relative price was 18.74% above its level in 1975. How does this price performance fit with the path followed by the volume of total construction, discussed above? That is to say, how could it have been that the relative price of aggregate construction increased so dramatically while the actual volume of construction was significantly below its trend level? We have no convincing explanation to this puzzle. As we mentioned above, there are several variables which simultaneously affect the construction sector. One of them, or a combination of several of them, may explain this paradoxical behaviour. But that goes beyond the scope of this work.

14.5. Labour Markets

Unfortunately, we were not able to obtain reliable investment figures by sector of destination, so that we do not study the sectoral response of

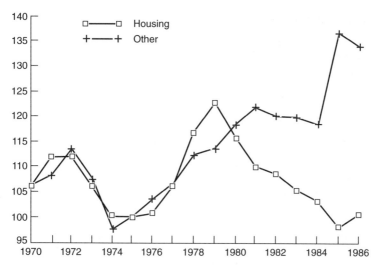

Figure 14.16. Housing and non-building construction prices relative to import substitutes, 1970–86 (*1970 = 100*)

capital markets to the boom. For the analysis of the sectoral evolution of employment, we were able to compute some aggregates based on the best information available so far (Reyes 1987). These figures, however, still have some problems: they do not, for example disaggregate the public sector into its traded and non-traded components (see Tables 14.1–3). But they record the so-called informal sector, which according to Table 14.1 accounted for more than 15% of total employment between 1970 and 1984, a figure which is as large as coffee, construction and the public sector combined.

Table 14.2 shows the evolution of the total and six categories of employ-ment for the period 1970–84. Up to 1978, employment in the coffee and construction sectors showed no significant deviation from the path fol-lowed by total employment, but in 1979 it declined in absolute terms, thus tending to confirm the negative deviation from trend experienced by total construction that year. In 1980, employment in construction began to increase faster than aggregate employment, a reflection of the process that took overall construction above its trend level by 1981. Employment in construction was more dynamic than total employment up to 1982, when it started falling again in absolute terms. By then the economy had slowed down and the unemployment rate began to increase dramatically.

The relative lack of dynamism of the construction sector during most of the years of the boom is also illustrated by this sector's real wage (Table 14.3). The construction sector's real wage fall is second only to the public sector's by 1977, compared with the 1975 level. Only in 1980 is this sector's real wage above the average economy-wide figure. As for the evolution of

Table 14.1. Composition of employment, 1970–84

	Total tradables (other than coffee)	Coffee	Construction	Other non-tradables	Public sector	Informal	Total
	(1)	(2)	(3)	(4)	(5)	(6)	(7)
1970	18.07	5.12	4.75	51.25	5.46	15.35	100.00
1971	17.15	4.94	4.54	52.10	5.63	15.65	100.00
1972	17.75	4.77	4.23	49.78	6.24	17.23	100.00
1973	18.50	5.87	4.48	48.23	6.25	16.66	100.00
1974	19.40	5.65	4.63	47.41	6.45	16.46	100.00
1975	19.73	5.36	4.03	45.98	6.62	18.28	100.00
1976	18.88	5.69	4.02	46.13	7.43	17.84	100.00
1977	19.49	5.43	4.08	45.98	7.42	17.60	100.00
1978	18.87	5.14	4.05	47.51	7.37	17.06	100.00
1979	17.20	4.90	3.89	49.21	7.42	17.39	100.00
1980	16.65	4.65	4.23	48.24	7.46	18.77	100.00
1981	16.43	3.87	4.43	49.08	7.51	18.68	100.00
1982	14.69	3.72	4.55	50.13	7.45	19.45	100.00
1983	13.55	3.62	4.44	50.29	7.88	20.22	100.00
1984	13.66	3.47	4.27	49.11	8.38	21.11	100.00

Notes:
(1) Includes manufacturing industry and modern agriculture
(4) Includes traditional agriculture and 'other' urban employment
(5) Includes all public employment, tradables and non-tradables
(6) Records non-wage urban informal activities

Source: Computed from the chapter by Reyes in Ocampo and Ramirez (1987: table A.1)

employment in the coffee sector, the 'booming' sector, after a 10% increase in 1976 relative to the 1975 level, employment in the coffee sector systematically fell until 1984. This development during the boom is certainly surprising, not only because all theoretical approaches would predict the movement of labour towards the booming sector (which is labour intensive), but also because it is a well-recorded event that coffee production did significantly increase during and after the boom, as did exports.[20]

A possible explanation for this event may lie in the introduction of a new variety, the *caturra* type, in the middle of the 1970s, which increased yields quite significantly, whereas there was no net increase in total land under cultivation during that period. The coffee boom accelerated this process by providing the means for the conversion of coffee-growing areas from the old to the new variety. One reason for the introduction of this technological change could have been the steep increase in real wages in the sector. Although Table 14.3 does not distinguish wages paid in the coffee sector, it is clear that the aggregate tradables shows the sharpest increase during the coffee boom.[21]

If this was so, it was the irreversible factor (investment), rather than the reversible factor (labour), which was attracted towards the booming

Table 14.2. Evolution of total and sectoral employment, 1970–84 (*1975 = 100*)

	Total tradables (other than coffee)	Coffee	Construction	Other non-tradables	Public sector	Informal	Total
	(1)	(2)	(3)	(4)	(5)	(6)	(7)
1970	79.81	83.11	102.86	97.12	71.96	73.17	87.14
1971	77.70	82.31	100.71	101.31	76.09	76.55	89.41
1972	82.94	82.04	96.79	99.84	86.96	86.94	92.22
1973	87.32	101.88	103.57	97.69	88.04	84.89	93.13
1974	94.10	100.80	110.00	98.65	93.26	86.15	95.69
1975	100.00	100.00	100.00	100.00	100.00	100.00	100.00
1976	100.22	110.99	104.64	105.07	117.61	102.20	104.72
1977	107.22	109.92	110.00	108.54	121.74	104.48	108.54
1978	108.67	108.85	114.29	117.39	126.52	106.06	113.62
1979	102.55	107.51	113.57	125.93	131.96	111.96	117.68
1980	103.57	106.43	128.93	128.81	138.48	126.04	122.77
1981	103.72	89.81	137.14	133.00	141.52	127.30	124.59
1982	95.55	89.01	145.00	139.91	144.57	136.51	128.32
1983	89.72	88.20	143.93	142.85	155.65	144.45	130.62
1984	93.22	87.13	142.86	143.88	170.65	155.55	134.70

Notes:
(1) Includes manufacturing industry and modern agriculture
(4) Includes traditional agriculture and 'other' urban employment
(5) Includes all public employment, tradables and non-tradables
(6) Records non-wage urban informal activities

Source: Computed from the chapter by Reyes in Ocampo and Ramirez (1987: table A.1)

sector. This of course, is a non-optimum event, for it increased production by more than necessary in the long run, which, among other things, was reflected in a large accumulation of stocks in the first half of the 1980s.

In 1978, the year in which consumption expenditure departed significantly from trend, employment in non-tradables started increasing relative to overall employment. By contrast, employment in tradables sectors evolved markedly below total employment in the first years of the boom, and after 1978 it fell in absolute terms until 1983. These are additional signs of the presence of the Dutch Disease in the Colombian economy during and after the coffee boom. This hypothesis also tends to be confirmed by the evolution of the tradables real wage *vis-à-vis* the non-tradables wage. Whereas the non-tradables real wage fell until 1975 and then increased by less than the economy-wide real wage, not only did the tradables real wage not fall between 1975 and 1977, but by 1979 it was more than 25% above its 1975 level (in that year, the average wage rate was only 15% higher than its 1975 level).

Did resources move in the right direction during the boom? The more dynamic sectors such as consumer non-tradables did not necessarily

Table 14.3. Sectoral real wages, 1970–84 (*1975 = 100*)

	Total tradables (other than coffee)	Construction	Other non-tradables	Public sector	Informal	Total
	(1)	(2)	(3)	(4)	(5)	(6)
1970	98.98	109.06	84.54	109.60	119.06	89.85
1971	101.06	110.60	89.92	118.87	120.65	94.51
1972	104.10	98.09	97.51	110.45	107.06	97.57
1973	102.73	95.88	98.64	108.90	104.68	99.31
1974	100.98	97.42	98.39	104.56	106.35	100.49
1975	100.00	100.00	100.00	100.00	100.00	100.00
1976	101.49	91.24	97.68	84.54	109.97	98.12
1977	105.35	89.40	95.32	81.18	104.06	98.54
1978	120.45	103.02	101.78	92.97	123.39	109.38
1979	127.11	113.70	109.20	97.18	135.75	114.66
1980	126.84	119.73	113.29	102.52	139.10	116.33
1981	130.32	128.87	119.22	109.03	167.52	120.57
1982	134.83	131.66	118.19	112.22	165.84	119.11
1983	140.00	133.95	118.74	111.79	153.66	119.39
1984	145.43	139.18	117.52	112.79	148.81	118.97

Notes:
(1) Includes manufacturing industry and modern agriculture
(3) Includes traditional agriculture and 'other' urban employment
(4) Includes all public employment, tradables and non-tradables
(5) Records non-wage urban informal activities

Source: Computed from the chapter by Reyes in Ocampo and Ramirez (1987: table A.2).

expand at the expense of tradables or coffee, which were experiencing redundancies, for two possible reasons. The first is that the economy started with a high rate of unemployment. The unemployment rate presents a clear cyclical behaviour, diminishing in the period that real income was above trend and dramatically increasing when real income was below trend, as in the first half of the 1980s (from 8% to almost 14% between 1981 and 1985). Meanwhile, the real wage remained fairly rigid. Whereas the real wage increases after 1976 up to 1981, a period in which the unemployment rate falls by more than 2 percentage points, the average real wage remains practically constant thereafter, when the unemployment rate increased by more than 5.5 percentage points between 1981 and 1985. Real wage rigidities could have induced resources to move in the wrong direction: from being employed to being unemployed and vice versa.

Another reason for resources moving in the wrong direction could have been the pressure of an important informal sector (Hausmann and Montenegro 1988; Montenegro 1991). In an economy with an important informal sector and with wages exhibiting rigidity, resources move to and from the informal sector in a countercyclical manner. Negative (positive) external shocks both increase (decrease) the number of workers in the informal sector and reduce (increase) the real wage accruing to workers employed in informal activities. A quick look at Tables 14.2 and 14.3 supports these conclusions for the Colombian economy in the period we are considering. Informal employment, although growing, evolved very sluggishly compared with overall employment during the coffee boom, a tendency which was completely reversed in 1980 and the years that followed. In fact, when the coffee price collapsed and the economy entered the recession of the first half of the 1980s, employment in the informal sector grew much faster than total employment. But the evolution of the real informal wage is even clearer. It increased by almost 70% between 1975 and 1981 and then it was the only real wage figure that showed a significant fall as the economy entered the recession of the 1980s.

14.6. Financial Markets

14.6.1. The Monetary Control Problem

The coffee boom created a dramatic monetary control problem. The dollar value of reserves multiplied about ten times between 1975 and 1981; despite the lower rate of nominal devaluation of the exchange rate, the peso value of reserves increased from 16 billion to more than 300 billion pesos in the same period. The annual increase in reserves ranged from 40% to 76% of the previous year's M_1. During 1979–81, the level of reserves not only exceeded the monetary base, it was greater than M_1 (Tables 14.4 and 14.5).

The main action that the authorities took to sterilise the higher reserve flows aimed at reducing both the central bank's net domestic credit and the secondary expansion of money. Net domestic credit fell so sharply that between 1978 and 1981 it was actually negative. Net domestic credit to the treasury was negative from 1978 onwards, whereas net credit to the rest of the public sector had been negative since the first part of the decade. By running a budget surplus, the government used fiscal policy not only as a device to reduce aggregate demand but also as a monetary control instrument.

The authorities issued the so-called Open Market Operations to sterilise the increase in foreign reserves. They were particularly significant in 1976–77 and 1979–80, when they sterilised on average 32% and 21% of the increase in reserves. In 1977 alone, this sterilisation represented 54% of the increase in reserves. Total sterilisation, that owing to both open market operations and reductions in net domestic credit, amounted to an

Table 14.4. Money supply and its components, 1970–86 (*current 1975 pesos*)

	Money supply (M_1) (1)	Monetary base (2)	Net international reserves (3)	Total net credit, public sector (4)	Other net credit (5)	Treasury money (6)	Non-monetary liabilities (7)	Secondary expansion (8)
1970	36.71	35.26	17.13	58.09	46.18	37.00	51.02	39.30
1971	40.73	39.14	20.92	66.33	47.72	45.37	54.21	43.56
1972	50.65	48.76	46.74	64.20	51.81	53.08	68.10	54.02
1973	65.47	63.93	74.48	56.75	71.75	59.25	92.49	68.22
1974	78.27	74.37	68.02	76.32	90.02	76.87	100.11	85.23
1975	100.00	100.00	100.00	100.00	100.00	100.00	100.00	100.00
1976	134.74	141.54	248.53	66.70	93.21	128.41	146.23	122.62
1977	175.68	198.34	423.47	39.74	158.36	174.67	344.81	135.28
1978	228.96	268.30	604.67	−11.50	176.45	220.26	370.72	158.80
1979	284.54	349.82	1,076.04	−245.33	136.73	267.40	548.26	168.14
1980	363.72	450.68	1,583.44	−353.24	96.90	389.21	844.07	208.66
1981	440.82	547.17	1,886.46	−371.97	67.01	473.13	906.60	251.18
1982	552.83	644.59	1,936.70	209.38	94.45	768.72	1,273.01	389.20
1983	689.42	733.11	1,424.97	654.09	376.38	1,272.25	1,113.12	611.50
1984	850.57	931.38	984.20	2,199.87	633.84	1,524.67	1,699.56	706.47
1985	1,090.02	1,141.66	1,951.52	2,399.35	680.04	1,791.85	2,881.96	997.93
1986	1,338.32	1,452.02	4,511.43	2,205.96	788.90	2,339.65	6,235.67	1,135.57

Source: Computed from *Revista del Banco de la Republica*

Table 14.5. Change in components relative to whole money supply variation, 1971–86

	Money supply (M₁) (1)	Monetary base (2)	Net international reserves (3)	Total net credit, public sector (4)	Other net credit (5)	Treasury money (6)	Non-monetary liabilities (7)	Secondary expansion (8)
1971	100.00	61.91	26.27	33.15	13.34	1.60	12.46	38.09
1972	100.00	62.13	75.52	−3.47	14.42	0.60	21.93	37.87
1973	100.00	65.58	52.16	−8.13	47.02	0.32	25.80	34.42
1974	100.00	52.23	−14.07	24.72	49.85	1.06	9.32	47.77
1975	100.00	75.58	41.02	17.61	16.05	0.82	−0.08	24.42
1976	100.00	76.60	119.14	−15.49	−6.83	0.63	20.85	23.40
1977	100.00	88.89	119.08	−10.65	55.59	0.87	76.01	11.11
1978	100.00	84.14	94.78	−15.54	11.87	0.66	7.62	15.86
1979	100.00	93.96	236.33	−68.00	−24.97	0.65	50.05	6.04
1980	100.00	81.61	178.57	−22.03	−17.58	1.19	58.54	18.39
1981	100.00	80.19	109.53	−3.93	−13.55	0.84	12.71	19.81
1982	100.00	55.73	12.50	83.89	8.56	2.03	51.26	44.27
1983	100.00	41.52	−104.40	52.63	72.12	2.84	−18.34	58.48
1984	100.00	78.83	−76.22	155.04	55.82	1.21	57.02	21.17
1985	100.00	56.27	112.58	13.47	6.74	0.86	77.38	43.73
1986	100.00	80.08	287.30	−12.59	15.32	1.70	211.65	19.92

Notes: (1) = (2) + (8); (2) = (3) + (4) + (5) + (6) − (7)

Source: Computed from *Revista del Banco de la Republica*

average of 35.4% for the period 1976–81 and to an average of 57.3% in 1979–80.

The second set of monetary measures was directed at avoiding the increase in the secondary expansion of money. The authorities were able to reduce the size of the multiplier by 20% between 1975 and 1981. The central instrument they used to get this result was raising the average reserve requirements on sight deposits to more than 46% in 1977 and the marginal reserve requirement to 100% between 1977 and 1980. Despite these achievements, the overall success of the monetary contraction is not clear. Although both the increase of the base and of M_1 were severely reduced, the set of measures to obtain these objectives, but especially the high levels of reserves requirements, produced two side-effects. First, they induced the development of financial innovations that allowed funds to be transferred from accounts with high reserve requirements to new types of liabilities not subject to those tight measures. Second, the financial repression brought about by the high reserve requirements and interest rate controls, introduced in 1976, induced the development of a curb market for credit. These measures reversed the effects of a financial reform, which, in 1974, had substantially liberalised the financial sector by both legalising several intermediaries and freeing interest rates on deposits.[22]

14.6.2. *Financial Assets and Aggregate Lending*

During the boom, total liquid assets increased significantly. Given that the share of money balances in GDP remained constant and even diminished, the increase in total liquid assets was due to the extraordinary expansion of interest-bearing assets. This was in part due to the legalisation of several intermediaries, and also the result of higher savings generated by the boom, even though interest rates were then controlled by the authorities. In fact, thanks to the interest rate liberalisation in 1980, the share of liquid assets increased even more, so that its share in GDP rose by more than 6% between 1979 and 1981. The fact that such an increase took place after the boom might be an indirect indication of the existence of the curb market as a consequence of the interest rate controls during the boom.

Meanwhile, the share of loans outstanding in GDP remained flat and even decreased during the boom. As a consequence, the liquid assets/ loans ratio increased from 1.12 in 1974 to 1.56 in 1979. Despite the financial liberalisation of the first half of the 1970s and despite the boom itself, which increased both real and financial savings significantly, financial intermediaries were not allowed to increase their lending operations in line with the expansion of their liabilities. As part of the counterinflationary policies, the authorities increased the average reserve requirement ratio on bank deposits and in 1977 imposed a marginal reserve requirement of 100%. Added to this draconian measure, all financial intermediaries were forced to acquire non-monetary liabilities issued by the central bank.

As soon as the boom subsided, the 100% reserve requirement was lifted and the deposit rates were liberalised. As a consequence, total lending expanded dramatically between 1979 and 1983, increasing its share in GDP by more than 6 percentage points. Similarly, the assets/loans ratio fell substantially, but a financial crisis which emerged in 1983, severely affecting several intermediaries, halted this credit expansion in that year.

14.7. The Public Sector's Reaction to the Shocks

14.7.1. Public Revenue Response

The fiscal position of the government followed a clear pro-cyclical path. Table 14.6 shows the pattern of fiscal aggregates, as a percentage of GDP, over the period 1970–86.[23] Four different subperiods are distinguishable: relatively large deficits in the first half of the 1970s; low deficits (even overall surpluses) during the coffee boom up to 1978; an accentuated fiscal deterioration beginning in 1979; and, finally, the period ends with a strong fiscal correction which is evident by 1986. The large deficit that appeared in 1979 was due to both higher consumption and higher investment expenditure. While higher consumption had no apparent justification,[24] higher investment was the product of previously planned projects delayed by the boom as part of counterinflationary policy. Although at the end of the period the share of public consumption had fallen significantly from the peak of the early 1980s, the public investment share in GDP rose markedly in historical terms. In fact, by the end of the period, the share of public investment in total investment was about 50%, up from 30% in the 1970s.

As for the evolution of public receipts, they followed cycles with opposite signs to those observed for investment and consumption, thus inducing clear alternating deficit–surplus periods. Total receipts were above trend in most of the coffee-boom period, with the exception of 1979. However, the figure for 1978 is the only boom year in which total revenue was significantly above its trend level,[25] reaching more than 16% above trend. This significant deviation from trend was in part due to the behaviour of direct taxes in 1978 (Figure 14.17).[26] However, the relatively good fiscal performance observed during the first three years of the boom was basically the result of lower public expenditure.

During the whole coffee boom (1976–80) indirect taxes were above trend (Figure 14.18).[27] This tendency is presented by both traded and non-

Table 14.6. Public sector fiscal pattern as a percentage of GDP (*current prices*)

	Public sector total primary revenue (1)	Final expenditure, public administrations (2)	Gross fixed capital formation (3)	Total exhaustible expenditure (4)	Public sector primary surplus (5)	Net property rent (6)	Total net transfers to residents (7)	Total net transfers abroad (8)	Other asset acquisitions (9)	Overall public sector surplus (10)
1970	12.92	9.25	5.58	14.83	−1.91	0.60	0.00	0.52	0.16	−0.94
1971	13.15	10.97	5.96	16.93	−3.77	0.84	0.43	0.45	0.25	−2.30
1972	11.67	9.57	6.32	15.89	−4.22	0.69	0.33	0.28	0.06	−2.97
1973	11.69	9.46	5.71	15.17	−3.48	0.92	0.35	0.22	0.61	−2.60
1974	12.13	8.75	4.92	13.67	−1.54	0.54	0.33	0.26	0.90	−1.31
1975	12.97	8.93	5.41	14.34	−1.37	0.86	0.52	0.14	0.00	0.14
1976	13.12	8.21	5.60	13.81	−0.69	0.82	0.71	0.08	−0.18	1.09
1977	12.19	7.71	6.61	14.32	−2.13	1.00	0.55	0.03	0.28	−0.82
1978	13.94	8.56	5.48	14.04	−0.10	1.07	0.51	0.12	0.22	1.39
1979	11.65	9.31	5.56	14.87	−3.22	1.06	1.03	0.00	0.38	−1.51
1980	12.86	10.09	7.38	17.48	−4.61	1.53	0.84	0.08	0.49	−2.65
1981	13.24	10.43	7.81	18.25	−5.01	1.64	0.75	0.00	0.42	−3.04
1982	12.79	10.92	8.54	19.47	−6.67	1.05	0.58	0.05	0.62	−5.61
1983	12.40	10.95	9.06	20.01	−7.61	0.88	0.59	0.00	0.36	−6.51
1984	13.53	11.04	8.67	19.70	−6.17	0.04	0.65	0.00	0.42	−5.91
1985	14.01	10.70	9.18	19.88	−5.87	0.17	0.32	0.03	0.62	−5.97
1986	16.03	9.94	8.86	18.79	−2.77	−0.69	0.10	0.09	0.32	−3.60

Notes: (4) = (2) + (3); (5) = (4) − (1); (10) = (5) + (6) − (7) + (8) − (9)

Sources: Computed from DANE, National Accounts

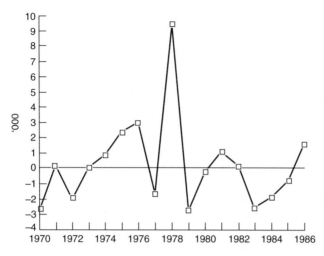

Figure 14.17. Total public direct taxes, 1970–86 (*1975 prices*)
Source: DANE, National Accounts.

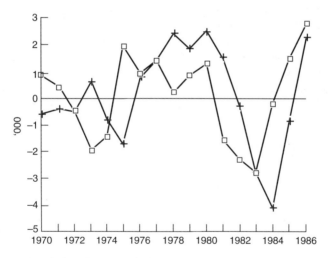

Figure 14.18. Traded and non-traded indirect taxation, 1970–86 (*1975 prices*)

traded indirect taxation, including in the former coffee taxes. In fact, the *ad valorem* tax on coffee exports was drastically reduced throughout the period, and more particularly during the coffee boom of the 1970s. Despite this, the net tax take collected from coffee exports increased owing to the higher value of exports. At the end of the period, public receipts turned back significantly above trend. Although this event is certainly associated with the evolution of the terms of trade and real national income, it is also true that revenues increased as a result of measures intended to increase indirect tax revenue.

14.7.2. Financing the Budget Deficit

Credit from the central bank and foreign borrowing were the two main sources of finance. Non-monetary financing was very limited throughout the period of our study and when used it was introduced in a semi-compulsory manner, mainly as a way to transfer resources from other public sector surplus-generating agencies to the central government. During the coffee boom, central bank credit and external financing were severely diminished, both in absolute terms and in relation to trend, to the point that the central government even repaid some of its domestic and external debts. Lower foreign borrowing was closely linked with the postponement of the planned pre-boom investment projects.

In the longer term, this could have been the most important decision taken by the Colombian authorities at that time. Colombia not only did not borrow too much, but successfully completed the huge investment projects financed with foreign resources. As a consequence, though not without difficulties, the economy managed to raise further external finance during the 1980s and was, at the beginning of the 1990s, one of the few developing economies which had managed to service its financial commitments, without even re-scheduling its external debt.

To finance the investment boom, by 1980 external credit to the central government was already significantly above its trend level. In 1980–84, the period in which the budget deficit soared, the main source of finance was the central bank. The 1982 international financial crisis also hit Colombia, especially in 1983. Given that the (tradables) investment boom continued until 1984, the level of international reserves accumulated in the previous years diminished dramatically, as we have already mentioned. In the last two years of the period of our study, foreign credit was resumed, and, given that the size of the deficit was drastically reduced, the need for monetary financing from the central bank was also drastically reduced.

14.8. Main Features of the 'Control Regime' in Colombia

14.8.1. The Management of the Domestic Coffee Price

The coffee sector has been heavily regulated in Colombia. One of the key policy objectives of the National Coffee Committee has been to try to insulate the coffee sector from short-term fluctuations in world prices, while buying from producers all coffee that is not bought by private exporters.

In general, domestic price policy has had two components. First, not all the variation of the world price has been passed into the domestic price. For example, while the world price increased 162% between 1975 and 1977, the internal price rose by only 64%. More generally, this behaviour is captured by Figures 14.19 and 14.20. The latter records the ratio between these two prices. It is clear that this ratio increases when the external price goes up and comes back to 'normal' levels as soon as the world price falls. Second, the domestic price has been set below the external price in order to allow the Coffee Fund to generate a significant flow of income and savings, as studied in Section 14.3. This does not mean that the Coffee Fund does not face financial deficits. This flow of savings is naturally gross of investment expenditure, including inventory accumulation. The latter may be extremely costly in times of low world prices. The existence of this mechanism transfers these costs from producers (who do not have to keep inventories) to the Coffee Fund.

Producers also benefit from Fedecafe's presence in the coffee regions. At the village level, the federation has developed a number of projects, some directly related to the production of coffee, such as rural infrastructure and technical assistance, but others in areas such as health, education and rural electrification, which are not directly linked to coffee producers.

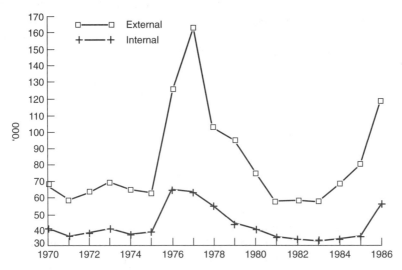

Figure 14.19. External and domestic real coffee prices, 1970–86 (*1980 real pesos/lb*)

Source: Montenegro and Steiner (1987).

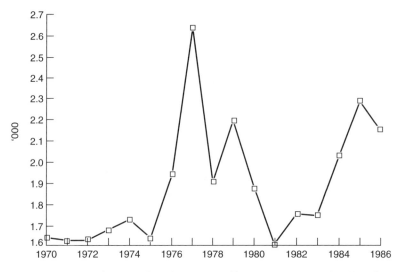

Figure 14.20. Ratio of external to domestic coffee price, 1970–86 (*1980 real pesos*)
Source: Figure 14.19.

14.8.2. *Exchange Rate Regime*

The exchange rate was managed by following a crawling-peg exchange rate system during the period of this study. To make an assessment as to what extent the policy-induced exchange rate departed from its 'free market' equilibrium we assess the black-market exchange rate premium.

In Figure 14.21, we present the premium of the black-market over the official exchange rate in the period 1975.1–1985.4. It is worth stressing that the premium already captures not only the effects of the coffee boom, but also the effects of all other measures introduced by the authorities to tame the effects of the shock, particularly the official exchange rate policy. The fact that there was virtual parity and that the black-market rate was even slightly below the official rate in 1975.1–1977.1 was because the authorities drastically reduced the rate of depreciation of the legal crawling-peg. Actually, the crawl was reduced from 24% in the first quarter of 1975 to less than 1% in 1977.2. For the rest of the boom years, the premium fell, so that the black rate was more than 5% on average below the official rate. In 1980.1, the premium began to increase, slowly at first, but as the external and internal disequilibria accentuated, it rose massively. When the current account and budget deficits were finally corrected, the premium fell again. This figure shows a clear correlation: low premiums when real income is above trend and high premiums when real income is below trend.

By mid-1982, it was clear that there was a serious current account deficit

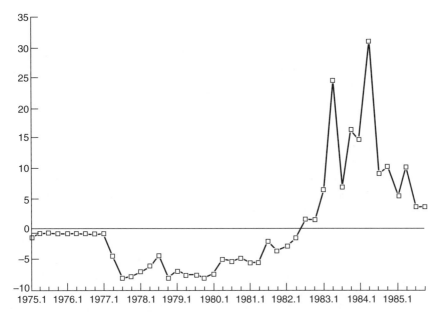

Figure 14.21. Ratio of black-market to official exchange rate, 1975.1–1985.4 (%)
Source: Uricoechea (1987).

and international reserves were falling dramatically from their 1980 peak. The market was, therefore, anticipating an exchange depreciation, which magnified the size of the premium. After the latter peaked in the second quarter of 1984, the premium fell significantly. We interpret this correction as an expectations revision brought about by an additional anticipation that the adjustment package was going to involve a fiscal correction. In fact, in this quarter, a new economic team, which had argued strongly in favour of this approach, took over the finance ministry. Even before the new measures began to be fully implemented, the premium duly responded by falling drastically in the third quarter of 1984.

14.8.3. Foreign Exchange Controls

In this section we study the extent to which the government allowed private agents in aggregate to acquire financial claims upon it.[28] The private sector's financial claims upon the public sector vary with changes in the balance of payments and in the budget balance, or both. These claims are represented by the total net domestic liabilities of the central bank's balance sheet. Total liabilities are, in turn, divided into monetary and non-monetary.[29] To compute how the coffee boom and the subsequent reverse shock affected the private sector's financial claims on the public sector it is necessary to construct a counterfactual. We construct such a counterfactual by assuming that the share of the central bank's total net domestic liabilities in GDP would have stayed constant at its 1975 level throughout the period of analysis. The difference between actual total liabilities and this counterfactual is, therefore, what we could define as an (asset) demand for public financial assets.[30] Consequently, the change in this aggregate is windfall asset demand for public financial assets. We perform the same exercise for the central bank's non-monetary liabilities and reach what we could denominate as windfall demand for non-monetary public financial assets.

   Figure 14.22 records both total and non-monetary financial claims on the central bank for the period 1971–86. There is a clear correspondence with the GDY deviations from trend we have previously recorded. This figure clearly shows that windfall non-monetary claims on the central bank account for most of the variation in total financial claims (in 1975 domestic currency). In 1971–75, the former represented 76.5% of the total; during the coffee boom (1976–80) this figure was 73.8%; between 1981 and 1985, windfall non-monetary claims accounted for 54.8% of total windfall claims, and in 1986 alone this figure jumped up to 132.7%. Comparing these figures with the private sector's windfall savings is something which should be done with great caution, given the different sources. Having said this, we find that the non-monetary windfall financial claims accounted for 48% of the sum of the private sector's and the Coffee Fund's total windfall savings during the coffee boom (1976–80).[31] The magnitude

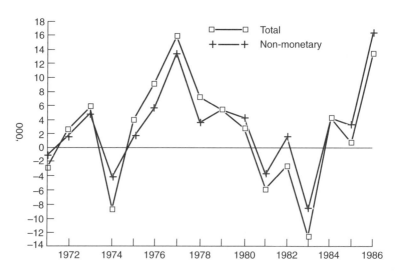

Figure 14.22. Change in financial asset holdings, 1971–86 (*1975 prices*)

of this figure is important, not only because the private sector's windfall savings figure was low compared with the public sector's and the Coffee Fund's, but more importantly because most of the windfall non-monetary claims on the public sector were really forced savings instruments. To encourage private savings (and for monetary control purposes), the authorities introduced Open Market Operations (OMO) by which exchange certificates and Bonds were issued and taken up by exporters, the Coffee Federation and some financial intermediaries. But these operations were not really 'open'. Coffee exporters, for example, had no option other than either keeping the exchange certificates until maturity or being penalised when selling them at a discount. The exchangeable bonds were absorbed via agreements with the Coffee Federation and some financial intermediaries.

To what extent were these financial claims of the private sector and the Coffee Fund honoured by the public sector? The evolution of net foreign assets throughout the period 1971–86, and more particularly after 1976, indicates that the government retained the necessary amount of foreign reserves for meeting private claims. Figure 14.23 shows the annual change in total net international reserves and total windfall financial claims on the central bank. Figure 14.24, in turn, records the corresponding cumulative changes for these two figures (in constant 1975 pesos). Even when the stock of financial assets turned negative in 1983–85, the exchange reserves still represented about 20 billion pesos in 1984, although down from more than 80 billion in 1980.

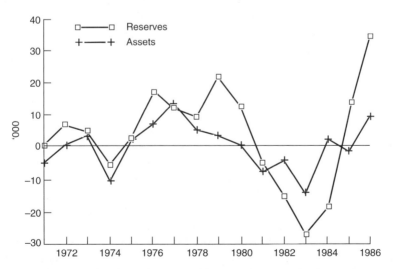

Figure 14.23. Annual change in asset holdings and reserve backing, 1971–86 (*1975 prices*)

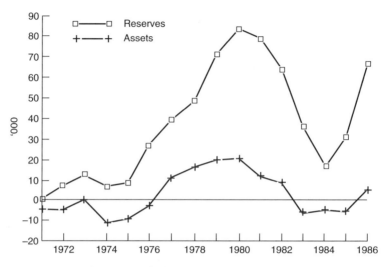

Figure 14.24. Cumulative asset holdings and reserve backing, 1971–86 (*1975 prices*)

14.8.4. Import Controls

Import controls were, until the beginning of the 1990s, a historical constant and were actively modified in response to shocks in Colombia. The main instrument was the use of import licences. Relaxing controls was fundamentally a counterinflation policy, and controls were re-introduced in times of balance of payments deterioration. Consequently, quotas were relaxed in 1973–74, when the number of import items which could be freely imported increased to 30% of the total. In value terms, imports not requiring a licence accounted for more than 40% of the total by 1974, up from less than 20% in 1970. The next stage in the liberalisation came in 1976. The government further relaxed the controls to tame the inflationary effects of the coffee boom. As a result, by 1978, 53% of total import items did not require a licence. In value terms, however, still only about 42% of total imports were freely imported. These liberalisation measures mainly affected capital and consumer goods, and some traditional industries, such as textiles, beverages, food, tobacco and non-metallic manufactures (Ocampo 1989).

The most far-reaching measures in the direction of scrapping the controls were taken after the boom, between 1981 and 1982. As a result, more than 70% of import items were freely imported by 1982. As a percentage of the total value of imports, 45% of imports were, then, freely imported, a share that was higher for the private sector. More than 65% of total private imports required no licence in 1981–82. As a consequence of both the recession and the balance of payments crisis, these measures were drastically reversed in 1983 and 1984. By December 1984, not only did 83% of import items require a licence, but 16.5% of them were in the 'prohibited' category, a category re-introduced after more than a decade. In value terms, only 15% of total imports were being freely imported by June 1985. Finally, as soon as the stabilisation package introduced to correct the budget deficit and the balance of payments disequilibrium showed positive results, controls again began to be lifted. In 1986, 42% of the total value of imports was freely imported and the items in the prohibited category accounted for only 1% of the total.

Hence, relaxing import quotas is a way to dampen the contraction of the exportables and exports sectors. For this to be effective, it is necessary not only to contract the importables sector, which is, basically, manufactures, but also, more critically, to have a flexible labour market. If, for example, the (non-booming) product wage is rigid, as quotas are lifted unemployment only increases. Of course, if the exchange rate is allowed to appreciate, this will contract the exportables sector (and exports). At the end of the day, both import substitutes and exportables are likely to contract. This is precisely what happened in Colombia. Although manufactures grew at more than 8% in the first half of the 1970s, growth fell to less than 4% during the boom and to just 1.22% in 1980–85. In 1980 manufactures growth was less than 1%, and in 1981 and 1982 was even negative: −1.31 and −1.56%, respectively. This performance was also poor relative to the rest of the economy. Both overall and non-tradable output performed much better than tradables and manufactures during and in the period immediately following the boom. The decline in non-coffee and manufactures exports was no less dramatic. Whereas in 1970–75 they grew at 7.3 and 17.2%, respectively, non-coffee and manufactures exports growth fell to 4.0 and 4.9%, respectively, during the boom. In 1980–85 total exports grew on average at only 2.8%, and manufactures exports fell 6% on average.

These figures show the magnitude of the crisis faced by the manufactures sector—one of the worst crises, if not the worst, in its history. The authorities relaxed controls, not to allow efficient resource allocation or to stimulate non-coffee exports, but rather as a counterinflationary policy. In this objective they were relatively successful, for they kept the rate of inflation under control during the boom years. The fact that the relative price of importables *vis-à-vis* the price of consumer goods fell is a sign of such success (see Section 14.4). Consumer imports were dramatically increased; they multiplied 2.5 times between 1975 and 1978. This meant that the share of consumer imports in total imports increased from 1.6% to almost 4% in the same period. The deviation from trend of consumer imports accounted for 30% of total (private and public) windfall consumption during the boom years.

14.9. Conclusions

The Colombian economy showed a relatively high windfall savings rate during the coffee boom of the 1970s, about 50%. The disaggregation between the private and the public sectors and the Coffee Fund shows that this result is fundamentally explained by the performance of the latter two agents. The private sector's rate did not increase significantly above the economy's historical average savings rate. Although public saving was on average high in the boom years, so was its variance. Public saving dramatically deteriorated as soon as the Turbay administration took office in 1978.

Investment also performed very poorly during the boom. While aggregate investment was flat (relative to trend) during the boom years, the construction sector was significantly below trend, thus behaving in the opposite way to that predicted by construction booms theory. In other respects, however, this theory seems to have some explanatory power for the boom. First, despite the sector's contraction, the relative price of aggregate construction increased during the boom, although it remained high when the boom subsided. Second, the housing subsector showed a boom which coincided with the coffee boom. The relevance of the latter is, however, obscured by the fact that before and after the boom there were housing booms not associated with terms of trade shocks. Third, the postponement of the investment boom fits in with the optimum (private sector) investment response indicated by this theory. However, this boom was led by the public sector and had no direct connection with the coffee boom. On the contrary, several projects that had been planned and had obtained foreign financing from multilateral agencies or multinationals before the boom struck, were postponed as part of the fiscal and monetary contraction consequent upon the external shock.

Low private sector savings explain the presence of Dutch Disease effects. Given that importables (manufactures) were protected by quantity restrictions on imports, Dutch Disease effects showed in the path followed by the relative price of non-tradable goods in terms of non-coffee exportables, which increased significantly during the boom. The management of the nominal exchange rate also contributed to this result, in that the rate of devaluation of the crawling-peg was drastically decelerated as part of the counterinflationary package introduced by the authorities. As a consequence, non-coffee exportables and exports contracted severely. Dutch Disease effects also reached the manufactures sector, since quantity restrictions on imports were lifted, thus directly hitting this sector. Both the real exchange rate appreciation and trade policy produced perhaps the worst industrial crisis in history.

Employment figures tend to confirm the presence of the Dutch Disease as well as what we call wrong-direction resource movements. Whereas employment in non-booming tradables declined relative to consumer non-tradables, real wages paid in the former sector rose relative to those paid in the latter. Despite the differences among sectors, the economy-wide real wage paid in the modern sector showed downward inflexibility, which may explain the countercyclical behaviour of the unemployment rate. During the boom, the unemployment rate fell and real wages rose sharply; after the boom and in the recession years, while unemployment increased dramatically, the real wage kept its value and even increased slightly. By contrast, not only the volume of employment but also real wages fluctuated sharply in the informal sector. Relative informal employment declined during, and increased significantly after, the boom. In fact, this sector's real wage was the only one which fell significantly when the boom subsided. Real wage rigidities and the presence of a significant informal sector made resources (employment) move in the wrong direction in Colombia. That is, resources moved from being unemployed to being employed and they shifted in and out of the informal sector.

As soon as the boom struck, financial repression was re-introduced. While newly created intermediaries were kept in place, interest rates were controlled and drastic reserve and deposit requirements were introduced. Given that the exchange rate was not allowed to float (although the rate of depreciation of the crawling-peg was significantly reduced), the monetary base increased dramatically. To sterilise the increase in reserves, the authorities created non-monetary liabilities to be compulsorily absorbed by exporters and the financial system (as deposit requirements). They also diminished net domestic credit to the private and public sectors, increased average reserve requirements and in 1977 introduced the draconian measure of setting the marginal requirement (for new deposits) at 100%.

In a period where the supply of international capital was soaring and most developing countries were borrowing massively, Colombia decided not to borrow abroad. And when the country decided to borrow, the lending party was soon over. This behaviour allowed Colombia to avoid the debt problem that hit most Latin American economies and to experience positive growth in the 1980s. This was perhaps the best legacy of the external coffee shocks of the decade 1975–85.

NOTES

1. This chapter draws on Montenegro (1991: ch. 7). The author appreciates the collaboration of María Claudia Llanes in the preparation of the statistical material of this work.
2. Other shocks were the Euro-dollar credit boom of the 1970s; the 1973–74 and 1979–80 oil shocks; the international financial crisis of the 1980s; the world

recession of the first part of the latter decade. The massive public expenditure expansion (consumption and investment) beginning in 1979 was an important domestic shock. In 1986, there was a second coffee shock, although it was short-lived. In what follows we assume that these changes are already embedded in the variables' deviations from their counterfactuals (trends).

3. At the end of the period of our analysis, that is, by the mid-1980s, the composition of exports had started to change as exports of oil, coal, nickel and other non-traditional exports increased their share in total exports.

4. In the estimation of the counterfactual, the whole 1970–86 period was considered. That is, the estimation of the counterfactual included the boom period. As counterfactuals are normally constructed as extrapolations of the previous period's trend, this procedure may need justification. First, it must be noted that the boom was followed by a bust which we also want to analyse. Had we built the bust period's counterfactual by extrapolating the boom period's trend we would have exagerated the magnitude of the bust. Second, room must also be made for the possibility that booms and busts influence trends, that is the counterfactuals. In calculating the counterfactual for the whole period this problem may be overcome. Third, recognising that all methodologies to construct counterfactuals might be problematic, we believe that what is important is to use the same procedure for the construction of the counterfactuals for all variables, say income, savings and expenditure.

5. The results of the regression of lnGDY on T are the following: $\alpha = -73.83$; $\beta = 0.0439$ (0.002334); R-squared $= 0.9594$. The parenthesis by the β coefficient is the standard error of the coefficient. β records the geometrical rate of GDY growth in the period 1970–1986, which is indeed below the historical post-war figure for GDP, which is about 5%.

6. Strictly speaking, our GDY figure is not the best figure to calculate aggregate savings, for it does nor represent real national disposable income. That is, one must still deduct from GDY net factor payments and net transfers abroad. However, given that we really seek a measure for windfall rather than actual savings, the inclusion of these figures changes very little indeed the estimate of the deviation of savings from trend, which is our way to calculate the windfall.

7. To estimate this trend we run a regression of ln savings on time and compute trend real savings as the exponential of the new estimated independent variable. Windfall savings is then defined as the difference between actual savings and trend savings. The results of the regression of lnS on time are: $\alpha = -82.25$; $\beta = 0.047$ (0.00744); R-squared $= 0.729$. This is *not* a savings function. It is just a counterfactual level of savings. The actual level of savings was relatively high before, during and after the boom. An econometric estimation of a savings function goes beyond the scope of this work.

8. The standard error is 0.12 and R^2 is 0.44. We did not estimate an independent term. Clearly, the R-squared figure is low, which indicates that the parameter obtained is not constant throughout the period of the estimation, that is to say, the savings rate is not constant.

9. As before, we calculate public trend revenues by running a regression of $\ln YP$ on time. The regression results are: $\alpha = 10.5397$; $\beta = 0.0526$ (0.00363); R-squared $= 0.9333$.

10. The results of the regression of $\ln YS$ on time are: $\alpha = 9.1866$; $\beta = 0.0481$ (0.0177); R-squared $= 0.3306$).
11. Regressing dSP on dYP gives: $\beta = 1.1775$ (0.124); R-squared $= 0.8456$.
12. See e.g. Ocampo and Crane (1988).
13. As constructed, these figures show that the Coffee Fund's final consumption expenditure is negligible, which explains why gross savings practically match disposable income. It is worth noting that although almost one hundred percent of disposable income is saved, this does not mean that the Coffee Fund never runs financial deficits. To the extent that investment expenditure, which includes inventory accumulation, exceeds savings, the Coffee Fund shows high financial deficits, as happened in the first half of the 1980s.
14. Windfall consumption was estimated residually from windfall increase and windfall savings. This result is almost similar to estimating windfall consumption directly, that is estimating trend consumption and defining windfall consumption as the difference between actual and trend consumption. The results of the regression of $\ln C$ on T are: $\alpha = -72.249$; $\beta = 0.043$ (0.00198); R-squared $= 0.969$.
15. Alternatively the windfall savings rate was 84.6%.
16. Again, this figure is estimated residually.
17. The results of the regression of $\ln$ gross fixed capital formation on time are: $\alpha = -95.28$; $\beta = 0.0538$ (0.00267); R-squared $= 0.953$.
18. The results of running a regression of $\ln$ gross fixed capital formation on time are: $\alpha = -113.43$; $\beta = 0.0626$ (0.00468); R-squared $= 0.8996$. The coefficient for the trend variable (T) indicates that tradables investment was indeed one of the more dynamic investment variables during the period in consideration. It shows that tradables investment grew on average at 6.26% in the period 1965–86.
19. The result of the regression of $\ln$ real house-building on time are: $\alpha = -56.925$; $\beta = 0.03349$ (0.00262); R-squared $= 0.89$.
20. In the coffee year 1974–75 Colombia produced less than 8 million bags (each bag contains 60 kg); since then production has increased so that as soon as 1978–79 it accounted for more than 12 million bags; by 1984 it had reached 13.5 million bags. In 1974–75 Colombia exported 7.5 million bags. Exports peaked in 1979–80, when they represented 11.5 million bags; since then, until 1984, except in 1981–82, when exports were slightly lower than 9 million bags, they remained around this figure.
21. This is another manifestation of the real exchange rate appreciation of the period.
22. For a comprehensive historical analysis of the Colombian financial sector see the chapter by Avella and Lora in Lora and Ocampo (1989).
23. We distinguish between the overall deficit and the primary deficit. By the latter is meant the excess of exhaustive expenditure (final consumption and gross fixed capital formation) over revenues. That is to say, net transfer payments (either abroad or to domestic residents) are excluded from the primary deficit. Revenues, then, comprise the profits of public sector enterprises as well as direct and indirect taxes.
24. It is widely accepted that the Turbay administration, which took office in 1978, had a more relaxed attitude towards fiscal matters.

25. The results of the regression of ln total revenues on time are: $\alpha = -93.01$; $\beta = 0.0529$ (0.00362); R-squared = 0.933. This shows that the rate of growth of total public revenue (5.29%) was slightly higher than the consumption rate, yet lower than investment's growth rate.
26. GDP recorded the highest growth rate of the whole period, more than 8%. It is unlikely, however, that this completely explains this high revenue tax take, especially of direct taxes. Owing to lags in collection, higher income tax receipts would have appeared in the following year.
27. The results of the regression of lnIT on time are: $\alpha = -102.49$; $\beta = 0.0569$ (0.0044); R-squared = 0.917.
28. The Foreign Exchange Statute, which, among other things, introduced the exchange controls and crawling-peg exchange rate regime, was created in 1967. Without fundamental modifications, it lasted for more than twenty-three years.
29. Total monetary liabilities plus the treasury money is equal to the monetary base or high-powered money.
30. The counterfactual could be seen a as 'transactions' demand for public financial assets. The share of the central bank's total net domestic liabilities in GDP could be interpreted as the inverse of the velocity of circulation of the supply of these public financial assets (base money and non-monetary liabilities).
31. We could not disaggregate between these two sectors' non-monetary financial claims on the central bank.

REFERENCES

Avella, M. and Lora, E. (1989) 'El Dinero y el Sistema Financiero Colombiano', in Lora, E. and Ocampo, J. A. (eds.) *Introduccion a la Macroeconomia Colombiana* (Bogota: Fedesarrollo-Tercer Mundo Editores).
Bevan D., Collier P., Gunning, J. W. (1989) 'The Kenyan Coffee Boom', mimeo. (Oxford: Unit for the Study of African Economies, IES).
Cardenas, M. (1989) 'El Sector Externo', in Lora, E. and Ocampo, J. A. (eds.) *Introduccion a la Macroeconomia Colombiana* (Bogota: Fedesarrollo-Tercer Mundo Editores).
Hausmann, R. and Montenegro, S. (1988) 'External Shocks and Adjustment in a Small Open Economy with an Informal Sector', mimeo. (Oxford).
Lora, E. (1989) 'La Estructura de la Economia Colombiana', in Lora, E. and Ocampo, J. A. (eds.) *Introduccion a la Macroeconomia Colombiana* (Bogota: Fedesarrollo-Tercer Mundo Editores).
Montenegro, S. (1991) *'External Shocks and Macroeconomic Policy in a Small Open Economy'* (D.Phil. Thesis, University of Oxford).
Ocampo, J. A. (1989) 'Efectos de la Liberacion y del Control de Importaciones Sobre la Industria Manufacturera Colombiana, 1976–1986', *Coyuntura Economica*, 1, 121–51.
Ocampo, J. A. and Crane, C. (1988) 'Ahorro, Inversion y Crecimiento Economico

en Colombia' (Informe de Investigacion Presentado al BID, Fedesarrollo, November).

Reyes, A. (1987), 'Tendencias del Empleo y de la Distribucion del Ingreso', in Ocampo, J. A. and Ramirez, M. (eds.) *El Problema Laboral Colombiano. Informe de la Mision Chenery*, I (Bogota, Colombia: Tercer Mundo Editores).

Sarmiento, E. (1982) *Inflacion, Produccion y Comercio Internacional* (Bogota: Procultura S. A. y Fedesarrollo)

Uricoechea, M. (1987), M.A. thesis (Bogota: Universidad de los Andes).

15

Costa Rica: Mismanagement of the Coffee Boom

CLAUDIO GONZALEZ-VEGA

15.1. Introduction

Costa Rica is a small economy. With a population of 3.2 million people, per capita GDP of US$2,050, and total GDP of about US$6.5 billion, by the early 1990s the country's domestic market was still comparatively insignificant. Given a narrow resource base and a limiting domestic market, Costa Rica always perceived that trade must act as the economy's engine of growth. Indeed, much of the impulse for growth during this century was provided by exports of agricultural commodities. The development for export of coffee, bananas, cacao, sugar, and beef raised the levels of domestic output and income, increased the country's capacity to import, and yielded dynamic benefits from specialisation and competition. A wider array of new, non-traditional exports have been key determinants of the country's comparatively rapid recovery after the crisis of the early 1980s.

As a result, Costa Rica is a very open economy. Exports increased from one-third of GDP in the late 1970s to almost two-thirds in the early 1990s, and imports grew to almost three-fifths of GDP. At least two-thirds of the agricultural output have been exported, and trade played an important role in the development of manufacturing. In 1963, Costa Rica joined the Central American Common Market (CACM) and adopted a strategy of regional import substitution. Industrial goods (4% of exports then) grew to 29% of the total by 1979, just before the breakdown of the CACM. About four-fifths of these exports went to protected markets in partner countries in the customs union. Following commercial policy reforms initiated in 1986, non-traditional agricultural and manufactured exports have been the most dynamic sector of the economy (Monge-Gonzalez and Gonzalez-Vega 1994).

Macroeconomic events in this small, open economy have been dominated by the evolution of its international relations: the demand and the prices paid in foreign markets for its main export crops, the opportunities provided and the constraints imposed by its participation in the CACM, and its degree of access to savings from abroad, in order to finance high rates of both consumption and domestic investment (Gonzalez-Vega 1989b).

Prior to the mid-1970s, macroeconomic instability had been primarily a function of fluctuations in the international prices of two exports (coffee and bananas) and of variations in their levels of output in response to natural events and to labour unrest in the banana plantations. Costa Rica then enjoyed increasing access to foreign savings, to finance brisk long-term growth and facilitate required balance-of-payments adjustments, when prices or yields became temporarily low, without an excessive reduction in employment and consumption. A smaller size of its public sector and the pursuit of cautious fiscal and monetary policies, led by a strong and independent central bank, had resulted in remarkable price and exchange rate stability prior to 1973, despite the country's inevitable vulnerability to external shocks.

After 1973, however, Costa Rica experienced several major external shocks, including two international oil crises, the 1976–79 coffee boom followed by a world recession, sudden changes in access to international financial markets, as well as war, insurrection, and political turmoil in Central America and the breakdown of the CACM. This sequence of sizeable external shocks over a relatively short period sharply increased the instability of the economy and magnified problems of adjustment, and the comparatively successful tools for macroeconomic management which the authorities had developed over the years were no longer appropriate to deal with the new situation.

The 1974 oil crisis was faced by the authorities in the traditional way, with a rapid expansion of both domestic and foreign borrowing. The credit flows required were much greater, however, than on earlier occasions, and a large increase in its external debt was not sufficient to prevent Costa Rica's first inflationary experience since the late 1940s, interrupted only by the coffee boom. When, at the end of the boom, the authorities once again attempted to smooth the process of adjustment with domestic and foreign borrowing, this time they were not successful.

Structural rigidities resulting from a protectionist strategy of development contributed to an environment less conducive to rapid and smooth adjustment. Import-substitution policies had not reduced the country's dependence on traditional exports, whose growth facilitated the expansion of protected trade within the CACM. A cascading pattern of nominal protection, with high tariff rates on final consumer goods and low duties on imports of intermediate and capital goods, had fostered import-intensive manufacturing and imparted a strong anti-export bias to industrial development. Since import reductions required after negative external shocks implied the diminished availability of inputs for production, the powerful manufacturing sector was able to block attempted adjustments, forcing an excessive increase in foreign borrowing.

Powerful public sector labour unions prevented, in turn, required reductions in government expenditures. These and similar political economy forces increasingly reduced the degrees of freedom of the authorities and explain, in part, the adoption of incomplete, inconsistent policy measures which magnified, rather than minimised, both the degree of macroeconomic instability and the extent of the adjustments required. These events led, in the early 1980s, to 'the crisis', a blown-up version of similar episodes of recurrent macroeconomic difficulties which intermittently resulted from the economy's vulnerability to changes in external market conditions, but which so far had been more easily manageable (Gonzalez-Vega 1984, 1989a).

In order to deal with temporary trade shocks, after 1973 Costa Rica borrowed heavily abroad. This strategy involved substantial risks, since unexpected deteriorations in the country's terms of trade quickly eroded its ability to service a large external debt (Myers and Thompson 1989). Restricted access to foreign loans not only forced major macroeconomic adjustments but also rendered a strategy of relying on foreign borrowing in the face of future negative trade shocks unfeasible.

An analysis of Costa Rica's macroeconomic history in the second half of the 1970s presents major difficulties in view of this multiplicity of exogenous shocks and their overlapping (either reinforcing or contradictory) consequences. Thus, any attempt to isolate the impact of the coffee boom has to rely on heroic assumptions. Moreover, although the period is frequently described as the 'coffee boom', the prosperity that this expression refers to goes beyond events in the coffee sector.

This chapter explores a few basic questions. Did the 1976 coffee boom contribute to the long-term growth of the Costa Rican economy? How were various sectors affected by the boom? Did macroeconomic management (or mismanagement) of the boom made the crisis of the early 1980s even worse? What lessons can be learned from this experience, exceptional in its magnitude, but not alien to Costa Rica's past and future economic history? The chapter first describes the nature and extent of the shock and measures the resulting windfall. Based on counterfactuals, it explores impacts on components of aggregate demand and supply, asset accumulation, employment, and relative prices. It analyses the consequences of policy decisions and concludes with an interpretation of lessons learned about macroeconomic management during a temporary trade shock.

15.2. Nature and Extent of the Shock

15.2.1. The Coffee Boom

On 18 June 1975 frost severely damaged about one-half of Brazil's 1976–77 coffee harvest. In addition, rain reduced the Colombian coffee crop by

20% and civil war disrupted Angola's production. This reduction in the world's coffee supply dramatically increased prices, from their comparatively low 1975 levels (about US$50 per 46 kg bag) to record levels (US$336 in April 1977 for the sorts typically sold by Costa Rica). Although high prices discouraged consumption and stimulated production all over the world, with the accompanying price reductions, coffee remained unusually expensive for several years, partly in response to the producing countries' efforts to limit supply. On 19 May 1979 there was another, although less severe, frost in Brazil, which further contributed to the high prices of the period.

The annual average prices received by Costa Rican exporters are shown in Table 15.1. By 1977, these prices had reached 3.8 times their 1975 level, and by 1980 a bag of coffee could still buy twice as many imports as in 1975. The relative price of coffee had been at its lowest level since 1950 and it was expected to rise in 1976, even before news of the frost arrived. Had the price of coffee remained at US$58, over five years one bag would have generated US$290. Actual 1976–80 earnings, on the other hand, amounted to 2.8 times that level (US$802). This generated a windfall of US$512 per bag over those five years.[1] Coffee export earnings did not grow as rapidly, because of a reduced volume exported in 1976 and 1977 (Table 15.1).[2]

A smaller coffee export volume was attributed to low levels of fertilisation and chemical inputs in response to low 1975 prices. High boom prices stimulated a strong supply response (with a two-year lag) for 1978 and 1979. Although there was only a slight increase in area planted, in view of policies to restrict supply, there were major yield improvements as a result of better agronomic practices induced by the boom. Increased

Table 15.1. Coffee exports indicators, 1975–81

	1975	1976	1977	1978	1979	1980	1981
Price[a]	58	110	217	167	149	159	115
Real price[b]	58	116	217	158	123	115	78
Real price index	100	200	374	272	212	199	134
Export value[c]	97	154	319	314	316	248	240
Export value index	100	159	330	324	326	256	248
Export volume[d]	77	64	68	85	97	72	69
Area planted[e]	84.6	85.2	85.8	86.4	87.0	87.6	88.1
Yields[f]	43	40	39	47	53	45	55

[a] Price per 46 kg bags in US dollars; annual average
[b] Prices in US dollars deflated by Costa Rica's import price index (1975 = 100)
[c] Millions of current US dollars
[d] Millions of kg
[e] Thousands of hectares
[f] Double hectolitres per hectare

Sources: Banco Central de Costa Rica (1986); United States Department of Agriculture (1989)

output contributed to sustain a boom atmosphere, even after coffee prices began to drop.

Counterfactual coffee exports were estimated here in order to measure the magnitude of the windfall generated by the boom, under two basic assumptions:

1. counterfactual volumes of coffee exports are the same as actual volumes observed, and
2. all coffee price increases above the 1975 level represent a windfall.

These assumptions had opposite influences on the estimation of the windfall. On the one hand, actual volumes include a vigorous boom-induced supply response. Although not all additional production is a windfall, since the extra output has an opportunity cost, in the absence of price increases the exportable volume would have been less than observed. From this perspective, the windfall was underestimated.[3] On the other hand, to the extent to which there were expectations that prices would rise above their unusually low 1975 levels, actual price increases in part represented a return to the trend and in part a true windfall. The second assumption leads to overestimation of the *unexpected* windfall. Price changes were so sharp, in any case, that there is no doubt that a major windfall was earned.

Over the five years (1976–80), the accumulated windfall amounted to US$862 million, as shown in Table 15.2.[4] This was equivalent to the substantial capital inflows of the previous ten years. Indeed, between 1966 and 1975, accumulated capital account balances added up to US$867 million. Moreover, the windfall was equivalent to more than one-and-a-half times the total outstanding balance (US$520 million) of Costa Rica's public external debt by 1975. Substantial access to foreign debt flows during the rest of the decade made it possible to sustain, in the face of a

Table 15.2. Coffee exports windfall, 1975–81

	1975	1976	1977	1978	1979	1980	1981
Coffee exports[a]	97	154	319	314	315	248	240
Counterfactual coffee exports[a]	97	81	85	109	123	90	121
Windfall[a]	0	73	234	205	193	158	119
Windfall in real terms[b]	0	77	234	193	159	114	81
Windfall as a percentage of							
Coffee exports	0	47	73	65	61	64	49
Total exports	0	12	28	24	21	16	12
GDP	0	3.0	7.6	5.8	4.8	3.6	3.6

[a] Millions of US dollars
[b] Windfall in US dollars deflated by the Costa Rican import price index (1975 = 100)

Source: Computed from Banco Central de Costa Rica (1986)

declining real value of the windfall, both the boom atmosphere and the level of aggregate expenditures. The windfall represented a large proportion of coffee exports, total exports of goods, and GDP, and was similar in relative importance to the Mexican oil boom.

Since its introduction in 1820, coffee had shaped the economic and political evolution of the country and it still had a major impact on the Costa Rican economy by the late 1970s. With the boom, its contribution to GDP increased more than three times, from 2.6% in 1975 to 8.3% in 1977. Coffee generated at least twice as large a share (14%) of central government tax revenues during the boom than during earlier periods, and its share in total exports increased to 39% in 1977, an importance it had not had since 1966. Its contribution to value-added in agriculture increased from 13% (1975) to 37% (1977).

15.2.2. The Terms of Trade Shock

Substantial as it was, the coffee boom was not the only macroeconomic event of the period. The Costa Rican economy experienced several other exogenous, partially overlapping shocks (two oil crises, changes in the world markets for other major exports, a foreign debt boom, and civil war in Central America). These events simultaneously influenced expectations and decisions. Some of them were reflected in the evolution of the country's international barter terms of trade, shown in Table 15.3 and in Figure 15.1.

Table 15.3. Export and import prices and barter terms of trade, 1972–82 (*index 1975 = 100*)

	Export prices	Import prices	Terms of trade	Export prices[a]	Import prices[b]	Terms of trade[a,b]
1972	65	60	108			
1973	73	67	110			
1974	88	91	96			
1975	100	100	100	100	100	100
1976	113	95	119	97	95	102
1977	144	100	144	103	100	104
1978	135	106	127	110	106	104
1979	141	122	116	134	120	112
1980	159	138	116	144	134	107
1981	146	147	99			
1982	143	143	100			

[a] Exports without coffee
[b] Imports without oil

Source: Banco Central de Costa Rica (1986)

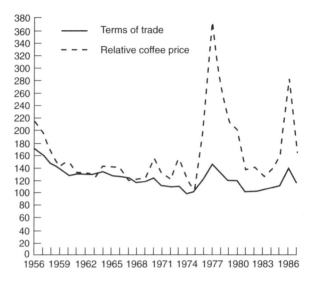

Figure 15.1. Barter terms of trade and relative coffee prices, 1956–87 (*1975 = 100*)

With the sharp increase in import (oil) prices in 1973 and 1974, Costa Rica's international terms of trade deteriorated by about 12%. This was followed by substantial improvements in 1975–77, as a consequence of coffee and other export price increases, and renewed deterioration afterwards, in view of declining coffee prices and new oil price increases. By 1977, the country's barter terms of trade were 44% above their 1975 level and in 1980 they were still 16% above that level. By 1981, they had returned, however, to their 1975 level.[5] Thus, the positive terms of trade shock lasted from 1975 to 1981 (creating a well-defined five-year boom for 1976–80). It was preceded and followed by major negative terms of trade shocks and it coincided with major inflows of foreign savings, which generated a parallel and complementary external debt boom. It is almost impossible to separate the consequences of these two booms.[6]

This positive terms of trade shock was exceptional. The peak value of the index (144 in 1977) had not been observed for twenty years (since 1958, at the end of the Korean War boom). The 1974 level of the terms of trade index, after the first oil shock, had been the lowest observed at least since 1950 and has not been observed again.[7] The level (99) for 1981–82 was also exceptionally low. Costa Rica experienced, therefore, an unusually wide swing in its international terms of trade, and the boom may have loomed larger, by being sandwiched between two major negative shocks.[8]

Over this five-year period (1976–80), a unit of Costa Rican exports commanded 1.24 times as much purchasing power, given a counterfactual with constant barter terms of trade. The increase in real incomes augmented domestic demand, particularly government activity, and it in-creased both the country's creditworthiness in international capital mar-kets and trade with the also-booming Central American Common Market partners, important coffee growers too.

Export values grew at an average annual rate of 15.2% between 1975 and 1980, reflecting both rapid price increases and a sustained growth in export volume (4.9% per year). As a consequence, export earnings gener-ated major real income increases for Costa Ricans and brought about a period of unusual prosperity.

Similar to what was done for the coffee windfall, counterfactual total exports were estimated in order to measure the amount of the windfall generated by the terms of trade shock, given the following assumptions:

1. counterfactual export volumes were the same as actual volumes, and
2. all of the terms of trade changes with respect to their 1975 level repre-sented a windfall.

Coffee and oil dominated these changes. As shown in Table 15.3, the country's barter terms of trade excluding coffee and oil did not change much until 1979.

The windfall from the total terms of trade shock is shown in Table 15.4. Over the period (1976–80), the accumulated windfall amounted to US$800 million. The acceleration of import prices towards the end of the 1970s eroded the real value of this windfall (to US$733 at constant 1975 import prices). The windfall represented a large proportion of total exports (almost one-third in 1977), and of GDP (8.3% in 1977).

During 1976–77, the terms of trade windfall was larger than the coffee windfall, whereas the opposite was true for the rest of the period. In effect, while coffee prices remained comparatively high until 1980, the terms of trade deteriorated towards the end of the decade. As a result, the terms of

Table 15.4. Terms of trade export windfall, 1975–81

	1975	1976	1977	1978	1979	1980	1981
Exports[a]	493	593	828	865	934	1,002	1,008
Counterfactual exports[a]	493	498	574	680	804	867	1,018
Windfall[a]	0	94	254	185	131	135	−10
Real windfall[b]	0	99	254	175	107	98	−7
Windfall as a percentage of							
Total exports	0	16	31	21	14	13	n.a
GDP	0	3.9	8.3	5.3	3.2	3.1	n.a

[a] Millions of US dollars
[b] Windfall in millions of US dollars, deflated by the Costa Rican import price index (1975 = 100)

trade windfall was 7.2% less than the coffee windfall. Because it better captures the nature of the overall prosperity, the analysis in this chapter will correspond to the terms of trade shock rather than to the coffee boom proper.[9]

The other partners in the CACM are major coffee exporters and, as such, experienced a coffee boom as well. This, in turn, fuelled an induced boom in Central American trade, which added to Costa Rica's export growth. Exports from Costa Rica to Central American countries grew at an annual average rate of 20.3%, as shown in Table 15.5. Imports from Central America grew rapidly as well, and Costa Rica generally had a negative trade balance with the rest of the CACM.

Similarly, rapid economic growth and the coffee boom increased Costa Rica's creditworthiness in international markets, already too willing to lend to its public sector. The outstanding balance of its external debt had increased from US$157 million in 1969 to US$520 million in 1975, at an annual rate of 22%. This balance increased during the boom at a rate of 34%, to reach US$2,254 million by 1980, as shown in Table 15.6. Private sector external debt doubled to reach US$1,042 million. During the boom, net resource transfers amounted to US$963 million, more than the windfall. Most of this (89%) was a transfer to the public sector.

Table 15.5. Trade with Central America, 1975–81 (*millions of US$*)

	1975	1976	1977	1978	1979	1980	1981
Exports	107	131	174	179	175	270[a]	238
Imports	115	135	168	203	212	220	152

[a] Unusually large increase of exports to Nicaragua at the end of the Sandinista war
Source: Banco Central de Costa Rica, *Balanza de Pagos*, several years

Table 15.6. Foreign debt during the boom, 1975–81 (*millions of US$*)

	1975	1976	1977	1978	1979	1980	1981
Public sector[a]	520	643	852	1,115	1,492	2,254	2,655
Private sector[a]	n.a.	523	638	758	770	1,043	956
Total debt[a]	n.a.	1,166	1,490	1,873	2,262	3,297	3,611
Net resource transfers[b]	n.a.	124	183	229	247	180	96

[a] Outstanding balances
[b] Measured as the difference between new loans and the flow of amortisation and interest payments on the debt
Source: Quesada (1986)

15.2.3. Nature of the Shock

The event under analysis is a positive five-year terms of trade shock, associated mostly but not entirely with coffee prices. It resulted in a windfall which sharply increased in 1977 and then declined as debt service problems and oil price increases dominated macroeconomic events in the last part of the period (Table 15.4). Most agents attributed the prosperity to coffee and expectations were governed, in the earlier years, by the evolution of coffee markets. The second oil shock changed these expectations, but the consequences were felt only later.

Because it came after a severe negative shock, some of the improvement was perceived as merely a return to a trend, compatible with Costa Rica's satisfactory output and export growth experience through the early 1970s. In this sense, the improvement was expected to be permanent. Access to international capital markets and growing indebtedness further contributed to perceptions that the boom was not as temporary as it turned out to be. Indeed, when eventually the windfall declined towards the end of the decade, sustained real expenditures were financed with increasing debt flows and borrowing dulled visions of an ending prosperity.

The change of administration in May 1978 gave the public sector's behaviour a further boom bias. The incumbent (President Oduber) had wanted to sustain a boom atmosphere, to promote the re-election of the ruling party, and the victorious adversary (President Carazo) felt naïvely compelled to prove that he could deliver as much as the earlier administration had been able to do during the boom.

To the extent to which the 1975 coffee prices were viewed as exceptionally low and were expected to rise, expectations were inclusive. Nobody had predicted, however, the large actual magnitude of the price increase and, to this extent, expectations were mostly exclusive. The largest price increases of the two previous decades (28% in 1970 and 43% in 1974) had been small compared to the boom changes. The day before the frost in Brazil, Costa Rican newspapers had reported that during the earlier year US coffee consumption had declined 6%, and that the world's coffee supply was expected to increase 35%.[10] Coffee growers were mostly concerned with the negotiation of a new international agreement to restrict world supply.

Once the impact of the frost became known, increased earnings were expected for at least two years, after which a supply response was expected to lower prices again.[11] By August, the Costa Rican Coffee Institute announced a price of US$100 for the 1975–76 crop, and private producers expected as much as US$150.[12] The Minister of Agriculture considered these price changes as temporary in justifying his opposition to tax increases.[13] At the National Coffee Congress of February 1976 little attention was devoted to the consequences of the frost. The growers merely requested that, in view of the high prices, the authorities promoted coffee production with technical assistance and credit, so that the country could acquire an entitlement to a larger quota under a new international agreement. The National Coffee Congress of 1977 explicitly recognised that the boom was temporary and emphasised the need for a new international agreement to face the consequences of increasing world supply.[14]

Using 10% as a discount rate, the present value of the 1976–80 windfall was estimated as CR\$5,827 million (at current import prices) and CR\$5,334 million (at constant 1975 import prices).[15] Under this assumption, the present value of the real windfall was equivalent to 32% of 1975 real GDP. Fully invested at an annual rate of return of 10%, the windfall would have resulted in an annual increase of permanent income of CR\$533 million at constant prices. This is equivalent to 3.2% of 1975 GDP. Such an increase in permanent income would have required that the whole windfall be profitably invested. To the extent to which this was not the case (i.e. the windfall was consumed or it was poorly invested), the impact on permanent income would have been smaller than estimated here.

It is mostly from this portion of increased real incomes that consumption would have come in the case of a shock perceived as temporary, since a temporary windfall should have resulted mostly in increased savings and investment. The temporary nature of the coffee boom contrasted with the implications of the earlier oil shock, which was perceived by many as having resulted in a permanent change in relative prices and in a reduction of permanent incomes in the oil-importing countries.

While it is expected that a positive trade shock with unrevised expectations (coffee boom) would mostly increase domestic savings, the parallel, massive debt shock towards the end of the period would be expected to reduce domestic savings, given the high degree of substitution between foreign and domestic savings that has characterised Costa Rica's history (Gonzalez-Vega 1989b; Cáceres 1985). This is in conflict with the result in Raventós (1991) that the boom reduced foreign borrowing and presents a difficulty in the interpretation of the consequences of the coffee boom for savings and investment.

15.3. Aggregate Macroeconomic Impacts

The terms of trade shock and domestic policy responses to the shock dominated Costa Rica's macroeconomic history during the period. After the shock, the Costa Rican economy would never be the same. Counterfactual values for key macroeconomic magnitudes are estimated here and contrasted with actual behaviour.[16] The construction of counterfactuals always presents major challenges. Here, the multiplicity of exogenous influences and the complexity of their interactions makes this task very difficult. Moreover, the magnitude of the deviations turned out to be very sensitive to assumptions about key behavioural parameters in the counterfactuals. As a result, the estimated windfalls are only indicative of their relative importance and do not represent accurate measurements of the impacts.

An additional complication in the construction of counterfactuals resulted from the fact that the base year was not typical; that is 1975 values were not close to long-term trends. Rather, they reflected a process of adjustment to the first oil shock that was still in progress at the onset of the coffee boom. Key parameters were selected on the basis of their trend, rather than 1975 values, in order to correct for this.

15.3.1. Windfall Income

During 1976–80, real income was higher as a consequence of the terms of trade shock, which increased the economy's purchasing power well beyond 'normal' levels. Following Bevan *et al.* (1990) real income was estimated as GDP at constant 1975 prices plus the export windfall, which augmented income in the same way that a discovery of new resources would.

During most of the period, the rate of growth of real GDP was exceptionally high, as shown in Table 15.7. The rate for 1977 (8.9%) was the highest observed since 1965 (9.8%) and it has not been replicated. Clearly, this acceleration of output growth was in part associated with the recovery from the first oil shock and would not have been as pronounced in the absence of the coffee shock, which stimulated domestic demand and trade within the CACM and increased the rate of foreign borrowing. It was not possible to measure the extent to which this output expansion was directly due to the coffee boom, however. The chapter adopts the conservative assumption of not attributing it to the boom (except for a minor portion) and, to this extent, this exercise underestimates the windfall income associated with the boom.

Moreover, real income was higher, in addition to this output expansion, as a consequence of the export windfall. The resulting increase was extraordinary, since income in real terms was at least 6% above counterfactual levels. Real income grew at a rates of over 10% in 1976 and of about 15% in 1977.[17]

Following Bevan *et al.* (1990) counterfactual income can be estimated as actual GDP minus the return on the additional investment induced by the boom. Windfall real income is the sum of windfall exports plus the addition to GDP which can be attributed to the returns from the extra investment out of earlier windfall income, as shown in Table 15.8. The accumulated windfall income (extra exports and extra GDP) was

Table 15.7. Increase in real income as a consequence of the boom, 1975–80

	1975	1976	1977	1978	1979	1980
Actual Gross Domestic Product[a]	16,805	17,733	19,312	20,522	21,536	21,698
Rate of growth	2.1	5.5	8.9	6.3	4.9	0.8
Balance of payments basis						
Export windfall (version I)[b]	0	852	2,177	1,482	921	839
Real income (I)[c]	16,805	18,585	21,489	22,004	22,457	22,537
Rate of growth	2.1	10.6	15.6	2.4	2.1	0.4
Export windfall (Ia)[d]	0	695	1,598	1,067	697	677
Real income (Ia)[d]	16,805	18,428	20,910	21,589	22,223	22,375
Rate of growth	2.1	9.7	13.5	3.2	2.9	0.7
National Income Accounts basis						
Export windfall (II)[e]	0	745	1,665	1,154	766	774
Real income (II)[e]	16,805	18,478	20,977	21,676	22,302	22,472
Rate of growth	2.1	10.0	13.5	3.3	2.9	0.8
Export windfall as a percentage of						
Real income (I)[c]	0	4.6	10.1	6.7	4.1	3.7
Real income (Ia)[d]	0	3.8	7.6	4.9	3.1	3.0
Real income (II)[e]	0	4.0	7.9	5.3	3.4	3.4

[a] Millions of colones at constant 1975 (GDP) prices
[b] Millions of colones at constant 1975 foreign (import) prices and exchange rates. Values in US dollars from Table 15.4 converted to colones and deflated by the import price and exchange rate indexes
[c] Millions of constant 1975 colones, with windfall valued at constant domestic import prices
[d] Windfall measured in millions of colones at constant 1975 GDP prices. Values in US dollars converted to colones and divided by the GDP deflator
[e] In millions of constant 1975 colones. Export values from National Income Accounts (GDP prices of 1975)
Sources: Computed from Banco Central de Costa Rica (1986) and Table 15.4

substantial, amounting to 6,630 million colones when the export windfall is measured in units of imports at constant 1975 prices (Version I) and to 5,331 million colones when the export windfall is measured in units of GDP at constant 1975 prices (Version II). This is equivalent to one-third of 1975 GDP. Windfall real income was substantial in 1977, when it represented between 8% and 10% of real income.

An alternative counterfactual might have been constructed by extrapolating past GDP growth. The following linear regression was used in order to estimate the real GDP trend, for the 1957–75 period:

$$\text{GDP}(t) = -294,371 + 150.86t + 0.829\text{GDP}(t-1) + 0.057\text{AR}(1),$$

with adjusted R^2 of 0.996 and Durbin–Watson of 1.96. Real GDP for 1974 had been 110 million colones above its trend value, whereas 1975 real

Table 15.8. Windfall real income, GDP, and fixed investment, 1975–80

	1975	1976	1977	1978	1979	1980
A. Version (I)						
Observed						
Real income[a]	16,805	18,585	21,489	22,004	22,457	22,537
Propensity to invest[b]	22.0	23.4	22.4	23.0	26.2	23.9
Fixed investment[c]	3,695	4,356	4,806	5,066	5,877	5,386
Rate of growth	n.a.	17.9	10.3	5.4	16.0	−8.4
Counterfactual						
Real income[d]	16,805	17,733	19,287	20,463	21,444	21,515
Fixed investment[e]	3,695	4,105	4,456	4,737	4,964	4,980
Rate of growth	n.a.	11.1	8.6	6.3	4.8	0.3
Windfalls						
Real income	0	852	2,202	1,541	1,013	1,022
Fixed investment	0	251	341	329	913	406
GDP[f]	0	0	25	59	92	183
B. Version II						
Observed						
Real income[g]	16,805	18,478	20,977	21,676	22,302	22,472
Fixed investment[h]	3,695	4,331	4,692	4,991	5,836	5,370
Rate of growth	n.a.	17.2	8.3	6.4	16.9	−8.0
Counterfactual						
Real income[d]	16,805	17,733	19,289	20,477	21,488	21,587
Fixed investment[e]	3,695	4,105	4,465	4,740	4,974	4,997
Rate of growth	n.a.	11.1	8.3	6.2	4.9	0.4
Windfalls						
Real income	0	745	1,688	1,199	814	885
Fixed investment	0	226	226	251	862	373
GDP[f]	0	0	23	45	48	111

[a] Millions of constant 1975 colones, with the export windfall in constant import prices, from Table 15.7 (balance of payments version)

[b] Observed ratios of gross fixed capital formation with respect to GDP, both in current prices

[c] Millions of constant 1975 colones, from applying observed propensities to real income. It is not the volume of investment, since the deflator is import prices rather than capital goods prices

[d] Observed real income (GDP) minus a 10% rate of return on accumulated windfall investment up to the previous year

[e] Computed under the assumption of a fixed propensity to invest out of counterfactual income of 23.149%

[f] Return on accumulated windfall investment in earlier years

[g] Millions of constant 1975 colones, with the export windfall in units of GDP at 1975 prices, from Table 15.7 (National Income Accounts version)

[h] Millions of constant 1975 colones, from applying observed propensities to real income, measured in units of GDP at 1975 prices

Table 15.9. Costa Rica: Gross Domestic Product deviations from trend, 1976–80

	1976	1977	1978	1979	1980
Observed Gross Domestic Product[a]	17,733	19,312	20,522	21,536	21,698
Trend Gross Domestic Product[b]	17,631	18,848	19,352	20,218	21,087
Deviations from trend	102	823	1,170	1,318	611

[a] Millions of colones at constant 1975 prices
[b] From linear regression

GDP had been well below (by about 415 million colones) the forecast trend. At the end of the boom and given a fiscal and foreign debt crisis, observed 1981 real GDP was again well below the trend (by about 750 million colones). The boom constituted, therefore, a period of real GDP values reaching well above the trend, bounded by two years when the actual observations were well below the same trend (Table 15.9).

Clearly, the GDP windfall estimates in Table 15.8 are much smaller than the observed deviations from the trend shown in Table 15.9. A large portion of these deviations was most likely directly or indirectly related to the boom and reflected, in addition to the returns from windfall investment considered here, the output from increased capacity utilisation during the boom as well as other boom-induced impacts. This interpretation is plausible, in view of the rapidly expanded output very soon after the onset of the boom. If this was the case, the conservative procedure adopted in this chapter underestimates windfall GDP and, thereby, windfall income.

15.3.2. Asset and Liability Changes

In order to estimate propensities to save out of windfall income, counterfactuals to the observed asset changes had to be constructed. Actual fixed capital formation was estimated by applying the observed propensities to invest to the real income series for 1976–1980, as shown in Table 15.8. Counterfactual capital formation was obtained, in turn, by assuming a propensity to invest out of counterfactual real income of 23.149% for the boom period (forecast for 1975 from the trend). The difference is windfall investment.

Two periods of rapid fixed capital formation (investment booms) are observed; one in 1976, when investment grew almost 18%, and another one in 1979, when it grew over 16% in real terms. The first boom occurred very soon after the onset of the coffee shock. The second one was mostly related to accelerating borrowing abroad. The investment windfall was particularly large in 1979. Accumulated, this windfall amounted to 2,240 million colones at constant import prices (version I) or to 1,938 million colones at constant GDP prices (version II). This represented 34% or 36% of the real income windfall, respectively.

Although these sharp fluctuations in the marginal propensity to invest out of windfall income may be, in part, related to implementation lags and adjustments in the timing of fixed capital formation to changes in relative prices and other macroeconomic circumstances, the high propensities to invest observed towards the end of the period suggest that capital formation was most likely associated with the explosive expansion of foreign borrowing. The parallel implications of the external debt boom make it very difficult to evaluate the consequences of the coffee boom.

First, it becomes difficult to construct a counterfactual for the country's liabilities abroad. What would the evolution of Costa Rica's foreign borrowing have been in the absence of the terms of trade shock? The international environment of the second half of the 1970s was such that a mere extrapolation of Costa Rica's external borrowing before 1975 would not be appropriate; borrowing would have accelerated even in the absence of the coffee boom. The terms of trade boom increased, in turn, both the country's creditworthiness and the authorities' willingness to borrow abroad. Particularly towards the end of the period, borrowing was the political economy response to the need to finance unsustainable expenditures triggered earlier by the boom. Thus, in the absence of the boom, foreign borrowing would have been less than observed and there was indeed an external debt windfall.

Second, although the windfall in real income is expected to increase savings and, thereby, holdings of foreign assets, exceptional access to foreign savings tends to increase the country's liabilities and it may thus reduce savings. Indeed, there is substantial evidence about a strong substitution effect between foreign and domestic savings in Costa Rica. The final outcome was the net effect of these two opposing influences. Increased savings are expected from the boom, but if the foreign borrowing effect was too strong, the propensity to save out of windfall income may have just been reflected as less dissaving (less debt) than otherwise. It is almost impossible to separate these two effects.

A first approximation to this savings windfall, a combined result of both sets of influences, is presented in Table 15.10. Total savings are defined as the accumulation of foreign and domestic assets (represented, for the time being, by gross fixed capital formation, as estimated in Table 15.8). In order to construct a counterfactual of foreign asset accumulation, a fixed ratio of the current account deficit to GDP, of 8.5%, was assumed.[18] The coffee boom seems to have brought about the windfall accumulation of foreign assets (reduced current account deficit) in the early years (1976 and 1977), but this was followed by windfall borrowing abroad (1979 and 1980) as the terms of trade shock was gradually replaced by the debt shock.

Table 15.10. Windfall foreign assets and savings, 1975–80

Version II	1975	1976	1977	1978	1979	1980
Observed						
Real income[a]	16,805	18,478	20,977	21,676	22,302	22,472
Propensity to borrow abroad[b]	8.5	6.0	5.5	7.9	10.3	10.3
Current account[c]	1,427	1,109	1,147	1,702	2,290	2,324
Counterfactual						
Real income[a]	16,805	17,733	19,289	20,477	21,488	21,587
Current account[d]	1,427	1,507	1,640	1,741	1,826	1,835
Windfalls						
Foreign assets[e]	0	399	492	40	−464	−489
Fixed investment[a]	0	226	226	251	862	373
Total savings[f]	0	625	718	2,991	398	−116
Propensity to save[g]	—	83.9	42.5	24.3	48.9	−13.1

[a] From National Income Accounts, in million colones at constant 1975 GDP prices (Table 15.8)
[b] Observed ratios of the current account with respect to GDP, current prices
[c] Million colones, at constant 1975 GDP prices, from applying observed propensities to real income
[d] Computed under the assumption of a fixed propensity to borrow abroad of 8.5% of GDP
[e] Accumulation of foreign assets as a result of a greater current account surplus (or less deficit) than expected. A negative sign indicates accumulation of liabilities
[f] Foreign asset accumulation windfall plus gross fixed capital formation windfall
[g] Ratio of savings windfall to real income windfall

Under these assumptions, the net result was an addition of 22 million colones, at constant 1975 GDP prices, to the country's foreign debt, as shown in Table 15.10. Given the values chosen for the parameters, on the aggregate the two sets of influences on savings abroad more or less cancelled out, but the accumulation followed a well-defined pattern over time, as shown in Figure 15.2.

Windfall total savings, defined as the sum of the foreign assets and investment windfalls, are shown in Table 15.10. Under present assumptions, only in 1980 was there a decline of savings below counterfactual predictions. Over the five-year period, accumulated windfall savings amounted to 1,916 million colones.[19] This represented 36% of windfall real income. This average masks large differences in savings rates over time and, as discussed below, between the private and the public sectors.

Apparently, over four-fifths of windfall income were saved in 1976, but this propensity to accumulate assets rapidly declined afterwards, except at the time of the new coffee shock in 1979, and it became negative in 1980. If this last year is excluded, the implicit propensity to save out of windfall

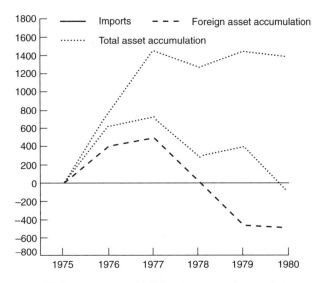

Figure 15.2. Windfall imports windfall foreign asset accumulation and windfall total asset accumulation, 1975–80

income would be 46%. A high fraction of windfall income was saved during the period (comparable to 48% in Kenya), confirming the hypothesis that the shock was essentially perceived as temporary. The accumulation of assets would have been even higher, moreover, in the absence of comparatively favourable terms for borrowing in international markets, particularly since a good portion of the extra debt financed public sector current expenditures, rather than investment.

15.3.3. Aggregate Supply Effects

To examine the macroeconomic consequences of the coffee boom and explore its impact on asset accumulation further, counterfactuals were constructed and deviations were estimated for the components of aggregate supply and demand. The observed ratios of each aggregate with respect to GDP in current prices were applied to real income estimates obtained as in Table 15.7 for each year of the period (Version II). For fixed investment a 22% ratio was used.

The results of these computations were estimates of the observed aggregates, measured in units of GDP at constant 1975 prices. Counterfactuals were then computed for each variable, by multiplying counterfactual GDP by the corresponding ratios, assumed constant over the whole period. The ratios were based on the historical evolution of these magnitudes prior to the shock. Deviations were finally computed, as the difference between the observed and the counterfactual values of each variable. Attempts were made to maintain the consistency of the aggregate supply and demand accounts throughout the exercise.[20]

During the boom total imports increased more rapidly than any other macroeconomic aggregate. Between 1975 and 1980, imports (measured in US dollars) increased 17% per year. These substantial import flows were the consequence of the increased purchasing power of exports and accelerated foreign borrowing. This borrowing made it possible for the current account deficit of the balance of payments to increase steadily from 8.4% of GDP in 1976 to an unsustainable 15.3% in 1980.

An imports counterfactual was built by applying a constant ratio (0.32%) to counterfactual GDP, as shown in Table 15.11. The ratio of imports to GDP had increased steadily over the years, from 26% in the late 1950s, to 37% just before the first oil crisis (1972) and to 48% in 1974. The average value of this ratio for 1957–72 had been 30%. The ratio chosen (32%) is compatible with a sustainable current account balance of 7% to 10% of GDP. Higher ratios would have implied a much greater use of

Table 15.11. Imports and aggregate supply windfalls, 1975–80

Version II	1975	1976	1977	1978	1979	1980
Imports[a]	694	770	1,022	1,166	1,397	1,524
Rate of growth	−3.6	11.0	32.6	14.1	36.7	9.1
Observed						
Real income[b]	16,805	18,478	20,977	21,676	22,302	22,472
Propensity to import[c]	38.6	34.9	36.3	36.0	37.2	36.8
Imports[d]	6,478	6,451	7,622	7,810	8,295	8,274
Counterfactual						
Real income[e]	16,805	17,733	19,269	20,434	21,441	21,537
Imports[f]		5,675	6,166	6,539	6,861	6,892
Deviations						
Imports	0	776	1,456	1,271	1,434	1,382
Gross Domestic Product[g]	0	0	42	88	95	161
Aggregate supply	0	776	1,499	1,360	1,528	1,544
Excess imports as a percentage of imports	—	12.0	19.7	16.2	17.3	16.7

[a] Millions of US dollars, in current prices, according to balance of payments statistics
[b] GDP plus export windfall, in million colones at constant 1975 GDP prices
[c] Ratio of imports to GDP, in current prices
[d] From multiplying observed real income by the propensity to import
[e] Computed by subtracting the returns from windfall investment from real GDP, assuming a rate of return of 10% and a ratio of investment to GDP of 22%
[f] Counterfactual income times 32%
[g] Returns on accumulated windfall investment

foreign savings, not credible in the absence of the coffee boom and of boom-induced increases in borrowing.

Excess imports were particularly substantial in 1977 and 1979, financed with large inflows of foreign savings and by the drawing down of assets (reserves) accumulated earlier. Over the period, this windfall amounted to 6,319 million, as shown in Table 15.11.[21] The windfall accounted for no less than 12% and up to 20% of total imports each year. This last proportion was even higher towards the end of the period, since borrowing abroad accelerated. From this perspective, therefore, the coffee boom was gradually transformed into a foreign-debt-induced import boom. Restrictions on access to international capital markets curtailed imports by 1980 and, when access was finally lost, the imports to GDP ratio declined sharply.

Excess aggregate supply, measured as the sum of windfall imports and windfall GDP, indicates the increased availability of goods for domestic absorption and for export as a consequence of the trade shock. The accumulated windfall amounted to 6,707 million for the period.

15.3.4. Domestic Absorption Effects

This section explores the extent to which windfall real income may have been used to expand private and public consumption and investment. The share of government consumption in aggregate domestic absorption increased from 11% in the late 1960s to over 15% in 1982, at the worst moment of the fiscal crisis. The share of private consumption steadily declined, from 71% in 1966 to 66% in 1974 and 62% at the end of the decade. Investment grew twice as rapidly as private consumption during 1966–79 and its share became particularly high during the boom. Counterfactuals were constructed under the assumption of a ratio of private consumption to GDP of 70%, of government consumption to GDP of 16%, and of fixed investment to GDP of 22%.

The resulting deviations are shown in Table 15.12. Windfall investment amounted to 3,128 million for the period. The share of government consumption (36% of windfall income) was high and grew rapidly over time. Accumulated government consumption windfall amounted to 2,000 million. These estimates imply, on the other hand, that there was practically no private consumption windfall. This suggests that the private sector perceived the shock as temporary and saved most of its windfall income. Negative private consumption windfalls for the last years may reflect a crowding-out of private consumption by overexpanded government activities.

The small (even negative) estimated private consumption windfalls are consistent with the observed reduction in the ratio of private consumption with respect to GDP, well below historical levels. The rising importance of

Table 15.12. Private and government consumption and fixed investment, 1975–80

	1975	1976	1977	1978	1979	1980
Observed ratios with respect to GDP[a]						
Private consumption	71.6	66.4	65.2	67.6	66.9	65.6
Government consumption	15.2	16.0	16.0	16.8	18.1	18.2
Total consumption	86.8	82.3	81.2	84.4	85.0	83.8
Fixed investment	22.0	23.4	22.4	23.0	26.2	23.9
Observed[b]						
Private consumption	12,306	12,260	13,680	14,653	14,921	14,730
Government consumption	2,558	2,955	3,353	3,639	4,026	4,095
Total consumption	14,864	15,215	17,033	18,292	18,947	18,825
Fixed investment	3,695	4,331	4,692	4,991	5,836	5,370
Counterfactual[c]						
Private consumption	12,306	12,413	13,488	14,304	15,009	15,076
Government consumption	2,558	2,837	3,083	3,269	3,431	3,446
Total consumption	14,864	15,250	16,571	17,573	18,440	18,522
Fixed investment	3,695	3,901	4,239	4,495	4,717	4,738
Deviations						
Private consumption	0	−154	192	350	−88	−346
Government consumption	0	118	269	369	595	649
Total consumption	0	−36	461	719	507	303
Fixed investment	0	430	452	496	1,119	632

[a] Percentages from magnitudes in current prices
[b] From the multiplication of observed real income by the observed ratios with respect to GDP. Million colones at constant 1975 GDP prices
[c] From the multiplication of counterfactual real income by a constant propensity for private consumption of 70%, for government consumption of 16%, and for fixed investment of 22% of GDP

the windfall in the case of government consumption reflects the contrasting behaviour of these two sectors. This windfall was associated with an increase in the ratio of government consumption with respect to GDP.

The absolute magnitudes of the estimated windfalls are sensitive to assumptions about key parameters. One of them is the ratio of imports to GDP, assumed to be 32%, which implies moderate access to foreign savings and a current account deficit of 7% to 10% of GDP in the counterfactual (no boom) situation. If 30% is assumed instead, implying even less access to foreign savings, the import windfall becomes 8,328 million. Had the country's counterfactual access to foreign borrowing been low, therefore, the experience of the period would have been associated with substantially larger current account deficits and lower propensities to save than otherwise.

If, instead, it is assumed that in the absence of the boom access to foreign savings would still have been fairly high, a 34% ratio of imports to GDP would have been possible. In this case, windfall imports would have been less, since there would have been high imports anyway, and over the period there would have been an accumulation of foreign assets of 14% of windfall income, suggesting a very high propensity to save. The range of credible foreign asset accumulations would go from 15% of windfall income, with high savings rates, to an extra debt equivalent to 60% of windfall income, in the case of liability accumulation.

Such an increase in savings was extraordinary, by historical standards. Costa Rica's domestic savings effort has not been impressive. Although the reasons are not well established, there are indications of a strong substitution effect due to ample access to foreign savings. There is also evidence of a dampening impact on savings of the expanded social security system and of the enlargement of the bureaucratic middle classes. There has been, however, investment in health and education, not recognised as domestic savings in the National Income accounts. If at least a portion of these expenses in human capital formation was added to savings and investment flows, the resulting totals would look higher.

Net domestic savings declined from about 9% of disposable national income in the 1950s and early 1960s to about 6% in the late 1960s and early 1970s. This ratio increased during the second half of the 1970s, to a peak of 13% in 1977, at the time of the coffee boom. This reinforces the claim of significant savings windfalls. Moreover, while private consumption hardly increased, government consumption gains were substantial. This suggests a very high propensity to save in the case of the private sector, as predicted for transitory income increases, and a very high propensity to consume in the public sector, which thus behaved *as if* the increase in real income was permanent. This behaviour, explained mostly by political economy pressures, led to unsustainable government expenditure levels and to the fiscal crisis of the early 1980s. That is, private agents behaved as expected of rational decision-makers, given available information about the *temporary* nature of the trade shock. The government, instead, ignored the temporariness of the shock and brought about macroeconomic instability.

15.3.5. Investment Windfalls

In order to obtain observed values for the components of gross fixed capital formation (private and public sector investment, tradable and non-tradable capital goods), the observed ratios to GDP in current prices were multiplied by annual real income values. Counterfactuals were computed by assuming a share of private investment of 68% of the total and a share of tradable capital goods of 48%. Deviations are reported in Table 15.13.

Almost 60% of windfall capital formation was undertaken by the public sector, compared to a historical share of 25%. The public sector's investment windfall exceeded the private sector's in the early stages of the boom (1976–77) as well as in 1980, when the boom was almost over. Most of the

Table 15.13. Private and public investment and tradable and non-tradable capital windfalls, 1976–80

	1976	1977	1978	1979	1980
Observed shares of investment[a]					
Private	64.3	63.5	67.7	66.0	61.3
Public	35.8	36.5	32.3	34.0	38.7
Tradable	47.3	50.0	52.0	47.8	42.6
Non-tradable	52.7	50.0	48.0	52.2	57.4
Windfalls					
Total investment:	430	452	496	1,119	632
Private[b]	130	98	321	646	72
Public[c]	300	354	175	473	560
share (%)	69.8	78.3	35.3	42.3	88.6
Tradables[d]	177	312	439	523	16
Non-tradables[e]	252	140	57	596	616
share (%)	58.6	31.0	11.5	53.3	97.5

[a] Observed proportions of total investment, in current prices
[b] Assuming a counterfactual share of 68%
[c] Assuming a counterfactual share of 32%
[d] Assuming a counterfactual share of 48%
[e] Assuming a counterfactual share of 52%

private sector's windfall investment came, on the other hand, in 1978 and 1979, after a two-year lag.

It appears that private sector investment was crowded out in 1980, as the economy's budget constraint became even more binding. Again, private agents behaved as expected, postponing investment from one to two years, to obtain higher rates of return, while the public sector invested immediately after the onset of the boom, more concerned with politics than with economic optimisation. To sustain these investment levels, the public sector used the proceeds from accelerating foreign borrowing.

The larger share (53%) of non-tradable capital (buildings and other construction) reflected the predominant role of the public sector. Most of this non-tradable investment took place towards the end of the period and was financed mostly with foreign borrowing. Tradable capital goods (machinery and equipment) accounted for 47% of the investment windfall and were mostly associated with private investment. This was reflected in an increase in the share of capital goods in total imports, from 23% in 1974 to 32% in 1979.

Adding private capital formation to private consumption and public investment to government consumption, channels for the utilisation of windfall income are identified. Three-quarters were spent by the public sector, both in its current and capital accounts. That is, while private sector consumption hardly increased, both public sector consumption and investment attracted the lion's share of windfall income and, thereby, the utilisation of the exceptional resources was mostly the result of bureaucratic decisions. The social profitability of these uses of resources appears to have been low and not conducive to stability or economic growth.

15.3.6. Financial Windfalls

Given exchange rate stability and low rates of domestic inflation as well as high rates of income growth, during the 1960s and most of the 1970s Costa Rica experienced significant financial deepening. The ratio of the money supply in the broad sense of currency and demand, savings, and time deposits (M_2) to GDP increased from 20% in the late 1950s to 30% in the mid-1970s.

The increased real incomes sharply augmented the demand for money and other financial assets during the boom. To estimate counterfactual money holdings, trends for ratios of money in a strict sense (M_1), quasi-money, and money balances in a broad sense (M_2), all with respect to GDP, were estimated by using regression analysis. Values for 1975 were forecast and then held constant during the boom period. These ratios were 31% for total liquidity (M_2), 18.6% for money (M_1), and 12.4% for quasi-money. Windfall money holdings were estimated as the difference between observed and counterfactual values, as shown in Table 15.14.

The accumulation of excess domestic financial assets during the boom was substantial. The total liquidity windfall amounted to 11,630 million (over two times the export windfall). Although there was a stagnant demand for money in the narrow sense (or even a slight decline, particularly towards the end of the period, as inflation accelerated), most of this accumulation took the form of quasi-money, namely interest-bearing deposits in both domestic and foreign currency. This suggests that money balances were accumulated as stores of value rather than for transaction purposes and were one mechanism used by the private sector to postpone either consumption or investment.

The trends for the ratios of total domestic credit and credit for the private and public sectors, with respect to GDP, were estimated by using regression analysis and values for 1975 were forecast and held constant. These ratios were 34.4% for total domestic credit, 28% for private sector credit, and 6.4% for public sector credit. Excess credit was then computed as the difference between observed and counterfactual values, as shown in Table 15.14.

The estimated excess of domestic credit amounted to 11,035 million (about two times the income windfall). While in the past the private sector had received about 85% of total domestic credit, this changed with the boom. The private sector received only one-quarter of additional domestic credit, whereas the public sector enjoyed access to increasing shares of

Table 15.14. Money, credit, and fiscal windfalls, 1975–80

	1975	1976	1977	1978	1979	1980
Observed ratios with respect to GDP (%)[a]						
Total liquidity (M₂)	33	36	37	42	44	42
Money (M₁)	17	18	18	19	18	17
Quasi-money	16	18	19	23	26	25
Domestic credit	37	37	36	40	79	51
Private sector	30	29	27	29	31	29
Public sector	7	7	9	11	18	22
Central government tax						
Revenues	12	12	12	13	12	11
Expenditures	18	19	18	20	21	22
Deficit	5	7	5	7	9	11
Windfalls						
Total liquidity (M₂)[b]	0	1,151	1,798	2,713	3,113	2,855
Money (M₁)[c]	0	−2	130	264	3	−150
Quasi-money[d]	0	1,153	1,669	2,449	3,110	3,004
Domestic credit[e]	0	699	1,017	1,778	3,565	3,974
Private sector[f]	0	465	340	665	872	510
Public sector[g]	0	235	677	1,113	2,693	3,464
Central government						
Revenues[h]	0	78	24	246	−24	−87
Expenditures[i]	0	466	365	688	849	1,133
Deficit	0	388	81	443	873	1,219

[a] Ratios of financial magnitudes (stocks outstanding at the end of the year) with respect to GDP, in current prices
[b] On the assumption of a counterfactual total liquidity to GDP ratio of 31%
[c] On the assumption of a counterfactual money to GDP ratio of 18.6%
[d] On the assumption of a counterfactual quasi-money to GDP ratio of 12.4%
[e] On the assumption of a counterfactual domestic credit to GDP ratio of 34.4%
[f] On the assumption of a counterfactual credit for the private sector to GDP ratio of 28%
[g] On the assumption of a counterfactual credit for the public sector to GDP ratio of 6.4%
[h] On the assumption of a counterfactual tax revenues to GDP ratio of 12.2%
[i] On the assumption of a counterfactual government expenditures to GDP ratio of 17.5%

total credit. It was through this access to credit that the public sector was able to finance windfall expenditures well above additional tax revenues, including a proliferation of state-owned enterprises (e.g. CODESA). This eventually led to financial repression, inflation, and the contraction of the financial system in real terms. The substantial accumulation of extra money balances by the private sector did not result, therefore, in increased credit for this sector, but rather it helped finance government consumption and investment as well as several implicit subsidies.

The evolution of the financial system's portfolio during the boom thus corroborates the emerging story. In the presence of temporarily increased incomes, private agents saved most of the windfall, partly in the form of foreign assets, but mostly as domestic financial assets. Eventually, some of these savings were transformed into private investment. A large portion was transferred, however, to the public sector, through its increasing share in domestic credit portfolios and, by 1980, through the inflation tax. Inflation eroded, in turn, a substantial portion of the purchasing power saved by the private sector in the form of financial assets. Potentially postponed private investment thus never materialised, since private savings were shifted to finance public sector current and capital account expenditures. Both uses generated low social returns in terms of future growth opportunities.

15.3.7. Fiscal Effects

Information about public sector revenues and expenditures is not available for construction of counterfactuals. Only central government tax revenues and expenditures (less than half of the total for the sector) could be used, leaving the parastatal organisations out. A comparatively small tax revenue windfall (497 million) resulted from the boom, which fell far below the extraordinary expansion of central government expenditures (Table 15.14). Indeed, while the tax revenue windfall was equivalent to 9% of the real income windfall, the central government excess expenditures amounted to 64% of windfall income. Historically, however, central government expenditures had been equal to 17.5% of GDP.

With additional expenditures higher than windfall revenues, the coffee-cum-debt boom caused an increasing excess deficit. Over the period, this deficit was equivalent to 55% of windfall income. This, in contrast with historic pre-boom deficits of less than 3% of GDP, implies an extraordinary expansion of the public sector. The central government budget represented less than one-half of total public sector expenditures. The decentralised agencies and government enterprises expanded rapidly during this period. The resulting public sector deficit was financed with both domestic credit and foreign borrowing.

15.4. Dutch Disease and Construction Booms

15.4.1. Changes in the Pattern of Production

Within the tradables sector, manufacturing was more dynamic than agriculture, as shown in Table 15.15, possibly as a consequence of the Central American trade boom induced by high coffee prices. To some extent, given high degrees of protection, these commodities may be treated as

Table 15.15. Real rates of growth of value-added in several productive sectors, 1975–81

	1975	1976	1977	1978	1979	1980	1981
Gross Domestic Product	2.1	5.6	8.9	6.2	5.0	0.8	−2.3
1. Tradable goods[a]	3.1	3.2	7.6	7.5	1.7	0.2	2.0
1.1 Agriculture	3.0	0.5	2.2	6.6	0.5	−0.5	5.1
1.2 Coffee	−8.2	−4.0	6.6	13.0	0.1	7.9	6.3
1.3 Agriculture without coffee	6.4	1.7	1.1	5.0	0.6	−2.8	4.7
1.4 Other traditional exports[b]	3.3	−2.9	−0.3	6.1	−3.4	−7.3	8.8
1.5 Other agriculture	10.8	7.6	2.8	3.6	5.4	2.0	0.7
1.6 Manufacturing	3.2	5.8	12.7	8.2	2.7	0.8	−0.5
2. Tradables without coffee	4.6	4.0	7.7	6.9	1.8	−0.6	1.5
3. Non-tradables	1.4	7.3	9.8	5.4	7.3	1.1	−5.1
3.1 Construction	5.7	20.8	3.9	5.8	19.3	−1.1	−21.7

[a] Tradables are proxied by agriculture and manufacturing
[b] Bananas, sugar, and beef

Source: Banco Central de Costa Rica

non-tradables. For this reason, their production expanded at the expense of exports beyond the CACM.

Traditional agricultural exports (bananas, sugar, and beef) did poorly, suggesting also a Dutch Disease effect, through overvaluation of the domestic currency, which became substantial towards the end of the period. By 1981, however, sufficient devaluation contributed to the swift recuperation of traditional exports. Agriculture for domestic consumption, which in several ways is a non-tradable sector (perishable vegetables and fruits, basic grain production protected by import quotas) grew briskly, stimulated by the growth of domestic demand.

The share of tradable production in GDP (in nominal terms) dropped from 41% to 36% during the boom, as shown in Table 15.16. If coffee is excluded, the share of tradables declined from 38% to 32%, a substantial drop in five years, with most of the reduction taking place towards the end, given a growing overvaluation of the colon, followed by a massive devaluation in 1981. The share of non-tradable production increased from 59% to 64% of GDP.

15.4.2. Employment and Real Wages

The boom accelerated the rate of growth of employment and rapidly increased real wages. From June 1975 to June 1980 total employment increased at an average annual rate of 6.6% (Table 15.17). As a result,

Table 15.16. Shares in value-added of several productive sectors in current prices, 1975–81

	1975	1976	1977	1978	1979	1980	1981
1. Tradable goods[a]	40.7	40.1	40.9	39.1	36.8	36.4	42.0
1.1 Agriculture	20.3	20.4	21.9	20.4	18.5	17.8	23.0
1.2 Coffee	2.6	4.7	8.3	6.1	4.5	4.5	5.4
1.3 Agriculture without coffee	17.7	15.7	13.6	14.3	14.0	13.3	17.6
1.4 Other traditional exports[b]	9.6	7.8	6.7	7.1	7.1	6.6	10.9
1.5 Other agriculture	8.1	7.9	7.0	7.2	6.9	6.8	6.7
1.6 Manufacturing	20.4	19.7	19.0	18.7	18.3	18.6	18.9
2. Tradables without coffee	38.1	35.4	32.6	33.0	32.3	31.9	36.6
3. Non-tradables	59.3	59.9	59.7	60.9	63.2	63.6	58.0
3.1 Construction	5.2	5.8	5.2	5.5	6.4	6.2	5.2

[a] Tradables are proxied by agriculture and manufacturing
[b] Bananas, sugar, and beef

Source: Banco Central de Costa Rica

43,606 more persons had been added to the employed labour force of 440,942 by 1980, compared to a situation in which the number of jobs would have grown at the 1975 rate of 4.4% (already high by historical standards). On average, employment increased more rapidly in the non-tradable sectors, at a rate of 7.4% per year, compared to 5.3% for employment in the tradable sectors.

While private sector employment increased by 5.7% per year, public sector jobs increased by 8.5% annually. This growth of public sector employment was one of the implicit policies to keep unemployment low, particularly for qualified and professional workers, in the presence of commercial and factor price policies that reduced incentives to hire them in the modern private sectors. Growing public sector employment reflected, as well, the increasing intervention of the state in the economy and the accumulation of entitlements to public services. Boosted by the coffee boom, this expansion of the public sector was not sustainable in the long run and was at the root of the fiscal disequilibria of the early 1980s. Moreover, given the importance of wages in public sector expenditures, it became politically difficult to reduce government spending once the boom was over. The concentration of workers in large institutions allowed their unionisation. These unions blocked, in turn, any attempts at fiscal austerity.

The boom was accompanied by rapid growth of real wages, at an average rate of 7.9% per year from December 1975 to December 1979, followed by a slight decline in 1980, as inflation accelerated with the fiscal crisis. The increases were exceptional in 1976 and 1977 (over 11%), as shown in Table 15.18. The impact on agricultural wages is evident. For

Table 15.17. Annual rates of growth of employment, 1975–80

	1975	1976	1977	1978	1979	1980
Total employment						
June[a]	4.4	6.2	10.2	6.3	7.0	3.3
December[a]	6.1	8.6	7.7	5.1	8.0	−0.4
Tradables[b]						
June	3.2	5.4	10.4	5.3	3.7	2.1
December	2.6	10.5	5.6	3.9	3.6	2.6
Agriculture						
June	2.5	−1.4	14.4	2.3	1.1	3.4
December	−0.5	11.8	3.3	1.9	1.6	5.4
Manufacturing						
June	3.8	10.9	7.5	7.5	5.6	1.2
December	4.9	9.5	7.2	5.3	4.9	0.7
Non-tradables						
June	5.2	6.7	10.1	7.1	9.1	4.1
December	8.4	7.4	9.1	5.8	10.7	−2.0
Construction						
June	−3.1	−3.9	4.1	9.9	14.2	−4.2
December	0.1	3.8	13.4	2.8	9.5	−11.1
Other non-tradables						
June	6.5	8.2	10.9	6.7	8.5	5.2
December	9.4	7.8	8.6	6.2	10.9	−1.1
Private sector						
June	3.4	3.6	10.6	7.6	4.6	2.3
December	2.7	6.6	10.3	4.3	4.7	1.4
Public sector						
June	6.7	12.0	9.4	3.7	12.0	5.5
December	13.7	12.5	2.8	6.6	14.6	−3.5

[a] June to June; December to December
[b] Agriculture and manufacturing
Source: Academia de Centroamerica

1975–79, real agricultural wages grew by 12.1% per year. The increase was almost 30% in 1976 and 22% in 1977. As a result, the ratio of agricultural wages to the economy's average wage increased from 53% in 1975 to 63% in 1979. Real wages in manufacturing increased by 6.2% per year, still a significant increase. The construction boom resulted in 10.1% annual increases in real wages in this sector. Although the coffee windfall was first received by a subsector of agriculture, its consequences resulted in major real wage increases throughout the economy.

15.4.3. Domestic Terms of Trade

Both growth in domestic demand for non-tradable consumer goods and the construction boom, which increased the demand for domestically-

Table 15.18. Annual rates of change of average real wages, 1975–80

	1975	1976	1977	1978	1979	1980
Total employment						
June[a]	−2.9	4.1	11.4	8.6	5.6	−2.2
December[a]	1.7	11.8	9.8	6.5	3.8	−0.4
Tradables[b]						
June	−6.1	7.5	11.7	8.4	6.1	−2.0
December	−0.3	15.1	6.5	6.3	6.2	3.4
Agriculture						
June	−4.3	6.6	21.8	9.9	10.0	−5.1
December	−1.4	29.2	6.1	7.3	7.5	9.4
Manufacturing						
June	−7.2	5.6	8.2	6.9	3.7	−0.2
December	−0.1	7.2	7.8	5.0	5.0	1.0
Non-tradables						
June	−1.7	2.4	11.3	8.4	4.8	−2.6
December	2.2	10.3	11.2	6.4	2.2	−2.1
Construction						
June	−1.8	5.3	11.2	6.4	6.3	1.9
December	4.9	15.6	22.3	2.9	1.1	−7.3
Other non-tradables						
June	−2.2	1.7	11.1	8.7	4.9	−3.3
December	1.4	9.2	10.2	6.8	2.5	−2.2
Private sector						
June	−7.1	4.7	10.1	8.5	5.5	−2.7
December	−2.4	11.3	11.9	3.5	5.2	−1.1
Public sector						
June	1.3	0.8	13.2	10.0	3.3	−2.8
December	5.4	9.4	8.0	11.2	0.1	−0.7

[a] June to June; December to December
[b] Agriculture and manufacturing

Source: Academia de Centroamerica

produced capital goods, changed relative prices. The evolution of value-added deflators for various productive sectors shown in Table 15.19 indicates an improvement in the relative price of non-tradable with respect to tradable goods.

While the GDP deflator increased by 91%, the prices of tradables (including coffee) increased by 81% and the prices of non-tradables increased by 96%. If coffee is excluded, the prices of tradables increased by only 70%. The prices of agricultural goods (excluding coffee) increased by 75%, whereas the prices of manufactured commodities increased by only 68%, reflecting, in addition to the Dutch Disease effect, an endogenous trade liberalisation effect as a consequence of the boom.

While the relative price of tradables with respect to GDP, excluding coffee, declined to 89% by 1980, the relative price of non-tradables

Table 15.19. Value-added deflators for several productive sectors, 1975–81

	1975	1976	1977	1978	1979	1980	1981
Gross Domestic Product	100	117	136	147	161	191	269
1. Tradable goods[a]	100	117	142	145	153	181	282
1.1 Agriculture	100	123	164	165	170	197	334
1.2 Coffee	100	229	483	363	307	338	526
1.3 Agriculture without coffee	100	107	117	134	150	175	306
1.4 Other traditional exports[b]	100	103	112	130	153	182	385
1.5 Other agriculture	100	111	122	139	145	167	227
1.6 Manufacturing	100	112	122	128	139	168	238
2. Tradables without coffee	100	110	120	130	143	170	265
3. Non-tradables	100	116	133	176	165	196	260
3.1 Construction	100	114	125	144	161	190	278
3.2 Services	100	114	128	148	169	197	254
3.3 General government	100	124	150	177	206	240	286

[a] Tradables are proxied by agriculture and manufacturing
[b] Bananas, sugar, and beef

increased to 103%. As a consequence, the relative price of non-tradables with respect to tradables, excluding coffee, increased 14% throughout the period.

The terms of trade of manufacturing rapidly and steadily declined as a consequence of induced trade liberalisation. Import restrictions had been imposed in 1974 in response to the first oil shock. These included temporary surcharges on imports, selective consumption taxes on typically imported commodities, and restrictions on credit terms on the sales of imported durable goods. Beginning in 1976, these temporary import restrictions were progressively reduced.

Windfall incomes were then spent on imports of the restricted commodities, particularly consumer durables. The share of consumer durables in total imports increased from 6.7% in 1975 to over 10% in 1978–79.[22] The share of non-durable consumer goods increased from 14.1% in 1975 to 16.1% in 1980. Combined, by the end of the period, the shares of imports of consumer goods had gained 5 percentage points.

An outstanding change was the increase in the relative price of government services, of 26% with respect to the GDP deflator and of 41% with respect to the price of tradables excluding coffee. Since the price of government services is essentially a proxy for government wages, this indicates that among the major beneficiaries of the coffee boom, and particularly of the debt boom, were public servants, whose numbers and salaries rapidly increased.

15.5. Distribution of the Coffee Windfall

The sharply higher international coffee prices of the second half of the 1970s substantially augmented incomes for all participants in the Costa Rican coffee sector. This section explores the distribution of the windfall among the participants, which include twenty-six exporting houses, a few domestic toasters (*torrefactores*), who account for 4% of value-added in the sector, over a hundred *beneficios* (hullers and processors for export), thousands of growers, wage labourers, input suppliers, and the public sector.

There is little concentration of coffee production in Costa Rica. At the time of the 1973 Agricultural Census, 32,353 coffee farms were identified, which represented 39% of the total number of farms in the country. They grew coffee on 83,407 hectares of land, equivalent to 17% of the country's cultivated area. The average size of a coffee farm was 2.6 hectares. About three-quarters of the farms had fewer than 50 hectares. These are small but precious family exploitations, frequently located near urban centres. At the time of the 1984 Agricultural Census, there were 34,464 coffee farms, producing on 97,000 hectares of land. By then, the average size of a farm was 2.8 hectares.

Exporting houses are highly specialised and ten of them have dominated exporting activities. At the time of the boom there were 106 *beneficios*, 29 of which were cooperatives. About one-half of them both grew and processed coffee, but 87% of the crop was purchased from individual producers. There is substantial competition among *beneficios* for the crop of independent producers. Labour comes both from the growing household and from wage earners, 40% of whom are permanent, and the rest hired as pickers during the harvest. About 170,000 workers participated in the crop in the late 1970s; of these, one-quarter worked in the plantations, two-thirds worked as pickers, and the rest in the *beneficios*. They represented one-fifth of the Costa Rican labour force and enjoyed steadily increasing real wages.

There is strong government control of the coffee sector and the relationships among these participants are strictly regulated. *Beneficios* must sell the coffee of a given year (picked from June to April) by September of the following year and turn the corresponding documents over to the Coffee Institute (ICAFE) for the estimation of the final price to be paid to growers. Partial payments during the year are not required, but the *beneficios* make advances to maintain a competitive edge. Exporters' costs and regulated profits are deducted from actual f.o.b. prices, and adjustments are made for coffee devoted to domestic consumption. The *beneficios* are allowed deductions of taxes, milling charges (variable but not fixed costs), and profits of 9% of total sales revenues. The rest must be paid, by law, to

producers. The *beneficio* operates as a trustee and is subject to clear ac-
countability to the grower. Despite these government regulations, the
system is very competitive at all levels (Stewart 1989).

In his analysis of income distribution in the coffee sector, Bornemisza-
Paschka (1986) estimated the shares of these participants in total export
revenues. Given the insignificant value added by coffee roasters and
export companies, these two groups are not considered for these purposes. Table 15.20 shows the shares of the various groups for the boom
period 1975–80. The coffee export windfall (computed in Table 15.2)
was assigned to the various participants in the sector, under the assumption that the distribution observed in 1975 represents a reasonable
counterfactual.

All participants obtained substantial windfall incomes from the boom,
as shown in Table 15.21. Among them, labourers and independent growers obtained the largest shares of the windfall. Indeed, the gains that
accrued to labour, of US$218 million, represented 25% of the five-year
windfall. Almost three-quarters of the labour windfall was received in
1977 and 1978. Growers, on the other hand, received a windfall of US$290
million, or 34% of the extra revenue. In the first year of high prices (1976)
coffee growers were the most favoured group, extracting 73% of the
additional revenues. Afterwards, the government (via taxes), labour (via
wage increases), and input suppliers (through derived demand) increased
their participation in the windfall.

The share of input suppliers amounted to US$164 million (almost one-
fifth of the windfall). This sum represents gross income, however, since
their costs are not known. Their participation was high in 1977 and 1978,
when high coffee prices induced an increased supply of the crop and
induced demand for inputs. Input prices also increased.

The share of the public sector, amounting to US$135 million, repre-
sented 16% of the total windfall and was therefore comparatively small.
This share included, in addition to taxes, payments for the use of public
utilities and other government services. *Beneficios*, finally, received only

Table 15.20. Distribution of total revenues in the coffee sector, 1975–80

	1975	1976	1977	1978	1979	1980
Labour	31.7	19.6	31.9	37.7	27.3	15.4
Coffee growers	19.7	45.0	25.7	14.7	31.0	36.7
Input suppliers	25.8	14.0	23.8	24.8	21.7	18.5
Public sector	22.4	16.9	17.0	20.0	16.4	19.8
Beneficios	0.4	4.5	1.6	2.8	3.6	9.6

Source: Bornemisza-Paschka (1986)

Table 15.21. Distribution of coffee export revenue and coffee windfall, 1975–80 (*million US$*)

	1975	1976	1977	1978	1979	1980
Observed						
Labour	30	30	102	118	86	38
Coffee growers	19	69	82	46	98	91
Providers of inputs	25	22	76	78	68	46
Government	21	26	54	63	52	49
Beneficios	0	7	5	9	11	24
Total	95	154	319	314	315	248
Counterfactual						
Labour	30	26	27	35	39	29
Coffee growers	19	16	17	21	24	18
Providers of inputs	25	21	22	28	32	23
Government	21	18	19	24	28	20
Beneficios	0	0	0	1	0	0
Total	95	81	85	109	123	90
Windfall						
Labour	0	4	75	83	47	9
Coffee growers	0	53	65	25	74	73
Providers of inputs	0	1	54	50	36	23
Government	0	8	35	39	24	29
Beneficios	0	7	5	8	11	24
Total	0	73	234	205	192	158

6% of the windfall (US$55 million), given strict regulations about profit margins. Over the five years, on average, the coffee windfall amounted to about US$1,300 per worker, US$9,000 per grower, and US$500,000 per *beneficio*.

15.6. The Political Economy of Trade Shocks and Fiscal Crises

Among Latin American countries, Costa Rica has been unique in terms of its political stability and the strength of its democratic institutions. Sustained stability has promoted economic growth: it has favoured investment, attracted foreign savings, and reduced the risks and transaction costs of economic activity, by promoting an institutional infrastructure that efficiently defines property rights and facilitates the enforcement of contracts. Absence of an army released resources for education, health, and physical infrastructure. Emphasis on equity reinforced human capital formation. As a result, for a long time Costa Rica enjoyed rapid economic growth and a better quality of life than would be predicted for its per capita income levels. Through the mid-1970s, the country was an example of growth-cum-equity (Gonzalez-Vega and Cespedes 1993).

Indeed, between 1961 and 1979, an average rate of growth of GDP of 6.5% per year allowed a 3.4% increase in per capita GDP. Growth took place despite the country's vulnerability to external shocks and cautious macroeconomic management made it possible successfully to isolate the economy from external fluctuations. From 1950 to just before the first oil shock, the average rate of inflation had been less than 2% per year and the fixed exchange rate system had been successfully sustained by an independent central bank.

In sharp contrast, in the 1980s Costa Rica experienced major economic difficulties. An economy which for over two decades had become used to rapid growth faced declining output and trade flows. The rate of growth of GDP dropped from 8.9% in 1977 to −7.3% in 1982. Exports and imports declined and the country's trade deficit, which had grown from US$92 million in 1972 to US$522 million in 1980, had to be curtailed to US$23 million by 1982.

Before the 1980s, Costa Rica had been successful in generating employment and in using labour markets to distribute the fruits of growth. It had been the country in Latin America with the highest rate of growth of employment in modern non-agricultural activities (García and Tockman 1985). With the crisis, open unemployment rates at least doubled, from 4.5% of the labour force in 1979 to 9.5% in 1982, while underemployment increased substantially.

Inflation accelerated. In 1981, the wholesale price index increased by 65% and it rose by another 108% in 1982; by then average real wages had dropped to 46% of their 1979 levels. Inflationary pressures also resulted in the rapid devaluation of the domestic currency, from 8.57 colónes per US dollar in late 1979 to over 65 colónes per US dollar in mid-1982. A sharp contraction of the real size of the financial system resulted from attempts to finance fiscal deficits with domestic credit and the inflation tax.

Given the exceptional record of steady growth and price stability of the pre-boom period, the difficulties of the early 1980s may seem surprising. Several trade shocks and the unfortunate policies adopted in response separate the two periods. The crisis cannot be explained, however, by negative shocks alone. The difficulties resulted from a complex combination of unfavourable long-term trends and short-term circumstances (Céspedes, et al. 1990).

Structural determinants of the crisis reflected a contradiction between the country's basic characteristics (a small domestic market, relative labour abundance, and very specialised natural resources) and features of the protectionist strategy of industrialisation adopted in the late 1950s (Gonzalez-Vega 1984). High costs and distortions resulted from the penalisation of agriculture and the anti-export bias of policies. By the mid-

1970s, shortcomings of the strategy were evident and major policy reforms were required. Unfortunately, rather than use the opportunity provided by the boom for this purpose, the authorities decided to postpone any reforms.

Political stability and democratic participation had contributed to the consolidation of a multitude of interest groups and the institutionalisation of numerous growth-reducing transfer payments. The accumulation of fiscal entitlements added to existing distortions, enlarged the public sector, and promoted bureaucratic controls and regulations. Decentralised agencies and state-owned firms became pressure groups in their own right and claimed substantial shares of available resources.

The negative effects of the first oil shock were dissipated at the onset of the coffee boom, with its overwhelming windfalls and as increased real incomes were further supplemented by unusual access to foreign savings. Policy reforms were postponed; instead, the period was characterised by an accelerating expansion of the public sector and of entitlements to fiscal transfers. The public sector treated the coffee windfall as a new, permanently higher level of income and celebrated this with spending euphoria. The already interventionist government became a major entrepreneur (via CODESA) and paid little attention to the revision of tax structures or the mobilisation of domestic savings.[23]

By the turn of the decade, because of the mismanagement of the coffee boom, the Costa Rican economy was ill-prepared for the adjustments required after a new negative shock. The Carazo administration (1978–82) found it difficult to bring the rate of growth of aggregate expenditures down to a level consistent with the new circumstances. Import capacity was curtailed by the reduction in export earnings and capital flows, but the required austerity encountered political opposition. The powerful manufacturing sector, dependent on imported inputs, was prepared to defend its entitlements. Strong public sector unions were ready to block any attempts at fiscal control and numerous organised groups struggled to maintain their standard of living, aided by the government's expansionary credit policies.

Based on a weak coalition, the Carazo administration chose to postpone the adjustment by borrowing heavily abroad. Costa Rica's public external debt increased to US$3,419 million by 1984. The stock of accumulated fiscal deficits financed abroad eventually reached the limit which foreign lenders were willing to accept. The authorities expanded domestic credit even more rapidly, in order to sustain the spending of the public sector at the levels it had become used to during the coffee boom. The resulting inflationary pressures led to the loss of the stock of international monetary reserves. Once these reserves were exhausted and access to foreign funds ceased, domestic inflation accelerated. When revenues from the inflation tax declined, as a result of currency substitution and other mechanisms of evasion, the private sector was crowded out from domestic credit portfolios. The proportion of domestic credit for the private sector declined from 81% in 1975 to 55% in 1982. This crowding-out accentuated the decline in output. Instability and impoverishment followed.

The increased government expenditures and income transfers which resulted from the coffee boom were not sustainable over the long run. Although there is a possibility that the authorities simply misjudged the size of future foreign exchange flows and committed themselves to unsustainable consumption-support programmes, the bulk of the overexpansion must be attributed to political economy pressures. Given the legal formality of the Costa Rican system, entitlements to current and future income streams for a multitude of interest groups (industrialists, public sector workers, social security beneficiaries, small farmer borrowers, rice growers, and cattle ranchers) had been institutionalised as specific property rights. This institutionalisation, in the form of revenue earmarking and legal spending requirements, had in turn reduced the discretionary powers of the authorities to adjust to changes in the environment. In addition, the predominance of the nationalised banks made it possible to direct domestic credit to the financing of public sector activities and income transfers.

With the coffee boom, a particularly large set of new programmes and transfers had been created, but retrenchment looked politically costly when the boom was over. Social peace was perceived as being highly dependent on the preservation of entitlements to public sector services and income transfers. This not only made policy reforms difficult, but also guaranteed that the impact of the crisis would be suffered the most by the politically least powerful segments of society.

The experience of Costa Rica during the coffee-cum-debt boom highlights the need for cautious macroeconomic management during a positive temporary trade shock and suggests that, given political economy pressures and the behaviour of the authorities, the availability of export windfalls or large flows of borrowed foreign funds may not always be welfare improving.

During the coffee boom of the 1970s, the Costa Rican private sector correctly predicted the transitory nature of the windfall and saved a substantial portion of the excess real income. In addition to investing the windfall, private savers increased their holdings of domestic financial assets. A large portion of this purchasing power was captured, however, by the public sector, through increasing shares of domestic credit and the inflation tax. The potential private investment represented by those financial assets thus never materialised, since such resources were eventually shifted to the public sector, not through increased explicit taxation, but through financial repression. Most of the windfall was thus spent by the public sector, which behaved (given the nature of the political economy scenario) as if the increase in income was permanent. The resulting unsustainable level of government expenditures led, in the early 1980s, to the crisis, to instability and to impoverishment.

NOTES

1. Since some increase in prices was expected, not all excess earnings are a true windfall. If the expected price was US$65, the corresponding windfall would be US$477 (60% of earnings), and if the expected price was US$90, the windfall would be US$352 (45% of actual earnings).
2. The *quantum* exported showed less variability than both prices and revenues, and *quantum* and prices showed a positive but small correlation each year.
3. This procedure was adopted to make the results comparable to those obtained for Kenya (Chapter 2 of this book).
4. The acceleration of import prices towards the end of the 1970s (second oil shock) eroded the real value of this windfall (to US$777 million at constant 1975 import prices). Based on an expectations model, Muñoz-Giró (1993) found a windfall of US$582 million.
5. That is, the downturn was essentially a return to the average terms of trade, rather than an unusually low level of this price. The question then is how to manage an *improvement* which is not expected to last.
6. Moreover, to the extent to which the coffee boom increased Costa Rica's creditworthiness, it most likely increased the volume of foreign lending to the country.
7. The values observed in 1953–58 were by far the highest for the 1920–90 period. Between 1920 and 1990, only two times (1954 and 1956) were the terms of trade higher than in 1977 (Bulmer-Thomas 1987: 334).
8. In this sense, the Costa Rican coffee boom differed from a typical commodity boom, where peaks are sandwiched by shallow troughs (Gilbert 1985).
9. For simplicity, the term 'coffee boom' will be used to describe the whole set of events of the period.
10. *La Nacion*, 18 June 1975.
11. *The San Jose News*, 8 August 1975.
12. *Excelsior*, 5 August 1975 and *The San Jose News*, 8 August 1975. It was recognised that 'Costa Rica will not be able to benefit as much from the new prices as it would like, since production has been off in recent years owing to dropping prices.'
13. Hernan Garron, in *La Nacion*, 6 August 1975.
14. *Congreso Nacional Cafetalero*, February 1976 and February 1977.
15. The exchange rate for 1975 was CR$8.57 per US dollar.
16. For convenience, the deviations of observed macroeconomic magnitudes from their counterfactual values are referred to as 'windfalls'. Clearly, these differences do not represent a true windfall in all cases, but they are associated with or result from the windfall income generated by the boom.

17. Table 15.7 contains three estimates of real income. The first two are based on balance of payments statistics. One (I) adds to real GDP the export windfall, measured in constant import prices, as in Bevan *et al.* (1990). The other adds, instead, the export windfall measured in constant GDP prices, in order to use a common numeraire. The third estimate is based on the National Income Accounts and measures the export windfall in constant GDP prices. These results follow identical patterns, with real income rates of growth above those for GDP in 1976 and 1977, and below afterwards.

18. This is the observed 1975 value of the ratio. The forecast for 1975, on the basis of a linear regression trend, was 11.9%, a reflection of accelerating foreign borrowing during the first oil shock, but not sustainable. The 1974 value (9.7%) was also considered to be too high.

19. From now on, unless otherwise noted, all figures are in colónes, at constant 1975 GDP prices.

20. Changes in inventories were computed as the residuals in the identity. This variable incorporated, therefore, any errors in the procedure.

21. This windfall is very sensitive to assumptions about the imports to GDP ratio. Its accumulated amount would have been 4,311 million for a 34% ratio and 8,328 million for a 30% ratio.

22. To the extent to which accumulation of consumer durables may be interpreted as capital formation at the household level, a good portion of what has been called private sector windfall consumption actually represented this form of investment. This suggests that private agents behaved as expected, with their decisions modified by changes in the policy regime.

23. Under Oduber (1974–78), CODESA, the public investment corporation, became an instrument for state intervention in productive activities in direct competition with the private sector. Its non-restricted access to central bank credit was a major element of the deterioration of public sector finances. In the early 1980s, CODESA's enterprises used 18% of domestic credit, but contributed only 1.8% of GDP and 0.3% of employment. The coffee windfall financed its unprofitable activities. Similarly, Oduber continued the earlier initiatives of Figueres in creating welfare agencies, such as the family allowances programme, and promising streams of future income transfers not sustainable beyond the boom.

REFERENCES

Banco Central de Costa Rica (1981) *Balanza de Pagos*, San José: Banco Central de Costa Rica.
——(1986) *Estadísticas 1950–1985*, San José: Banco Central de Costa Rica.
Bevan, D., P. Collier and J.W. Gunning (1990) *Controlled Open Economies. A Neoclassical Approach to Structuralism*, Oxford: Clarendon Press.
Bornemisza-Paschka, P. (1986) 'Evolución de la Distribución del Ingreso en el Sistema Cafetero Costarricense desde 1974 hasta 1984', unpublished thesis, San José: Universidad de Costa Rica.

Bulmer-Thomas, V. (1987) *The Political Economy of Central America Since 1920*, Cambridge: Cambridge University Press.

Cáceres, L.R. (1985) 'Ahorro, Inversión, Deuda Externa y Catástrofe', *El Trimestre Económico*, Vol. 52, July–September.

Céspedes, V.H., C. Gonzalez-Vega and R. Jiménez (1990) *Costa Rica frente a la Crisis: Políticas y Resultados*. San José: Academia de Centroamérica.

García, N. and V.E. Tockman (1985) *Acumulación, Empleo y Crisis*, Santiago: PREALC.

Gilbert, C.L. (1985) 'Efficient Market Commodity Price Dynamics', Washington, DC: World Bank, Country Policy Department Working Paper.

Gonzalez-Vega, C. (1984) 'Fear of Adjusting: The Social Costs of Economic Policies in Costa Rica in the 1970s', in Donald E. Schulz and Douglas H. Graham (eds.) *Revolution and Counterrevolution in Central America and the Caribbean*, Boulder: Westview Press.

——(1989a) 'Debt, Stabilization, and Liberalization in Costa Rica: Political Economy Responses to a Fiscal Crisis', in P.L. Brock, M.B. Connolly and C.O. Gonzalez-Vega (eds.) *Latin American Debt and Adjustment: External Shocks and Macroeconomic Policies*, New York: Praeger, pp. 197–209.

——(1989b) 'Costa Rica: Macroeconomic Policies, Crises, and Long-Term Growth', unpublished monograph prepared for the World Bank's Project on Macroeconomic Policies, Crises, and Long-Term Growth.

Gonzalez-Vega, C. and V.H. Cespedes (1993) 'Costa Rica: The Political Economy of Growth, Equity, and Poverty: 1950–1985', in S. Rottenberg, C. Gonzalez-Vega *et al.* (eds.) *The Political Economy of Growth, Equity, and Poverty: Costa Rica and Uruguay*, Oxford: Oxford University Press.

Monge-Gonzalez, R. and C. Gonzalez-Vega (1994) *Política Comercial, Exportaciones y Bienestar en Costa Rica*, San José: Academia de Centroamérica and Centro Internacional para el Desarrollo Económico.

Muñoz-Giró, J.E. (1993) 'A General Equilibrium Analysis of Temporary Terms-of-Trade Shocks in a Developing Economy: Coffee in Costa Rica', Ph.D. dissertation, Columbus, Ohio: The Ohio State University.

Myers, R.J. and S.R. Thompson (1989) 'Optimal Portfolios of External Debt in Developing Countries: The Potential Role of Commodity-Linked Bonds', *American Journal of Agricultural Economics*, Vol. 71, No. 2, May, pp. 517–22.

Quesada, R. (1986) 'Deuda Externa de Costa Rica', San José: Banco Central de Costa Rica.

Raventós, P. (1991) 'Shocks and Economic Policy in Costa Rica in the 1970s', Ph.D. dissertation, Cambridge: Harvard University.

Stewart, R. (1989) 'A Study of Costa Rica's Coffee Marketing System', unpublished report.

United States Department of Agriculture (1989) 'World Coffee Situation', August.

16

Bolivia's Tin and Natural Gas Crises, 1985–89

JUAN ANTONIO MORALES

16.1. Introduction

This chapter is concerned with the negative price shock that affected Bolivia's two main exports, tin and natural gas, in the second half of the 1980s, and with its effects throughout the economy. The shock started shortly after a drastic stabilisation programme that the government had launched to tame a devastating hyperinflation (unrelated to the trade shock). The interaction of the shock with the anti-inflationary policies gives distinctive features to the Bolivian case. An additional element that distinguishes the Bolivian experience from others is that an ample liberalisation of markets accompanied the stabilisation programme.

Tin and natural gas are produced by both the public and the private sectors. The production of the former sector was, in the years preceding the crisis, far more important than the production of the latter. The state-owned enterprises relevant to our study are the mining company Corporación Minera de Bolivia (COMIBOL), the tin-smelting company Empresa Nacional de Fundiciones (ENAF), and the petroleum company Yacimientos Petrolíferos Fiscales Bolivianos (YPFB). ENAF was consolidated with COMIBOL in the last quarter of 1985. YPFB has production-sharing arrangements with private companies but is the sole exporter of natural gas.

The main results to emerge of our analysis are as follows. The income losses caused by the shock, cumulated over 1986–89, are estimated to be in present value 10% of 1985 GDP. The estimated average annual loss over that period is of 2.9% of 1985 GDP. The output losses were especially important in the first two years after the shock; in 1988, the production indicators started to show a modest recovery. Notwithstanding the output losses, control over inflation was maintained throughout the period, except during a few weeks after the tin crash in 1985.

Three factors, in order of importance, explain the inflation performance: (1) the huge fiscal adjustment that took place; (2) the regaining of access to international loans, some of them to smooth consumption; and (3) the liberalised markets, which generally dampened the domestic effects of the shock. In particular, the flexible exchange rate regime and the flexible prices in most markets avoided the development of a persistent inflation, after the once-and-for-all upward adjustment in the price level on impact of the trade shock.

The adjustment in consumption that took place after the negative shock was important, but not to the full extent of the slump. So there was a negative savings effect. Yet gross fixed capital formation (GFKF) expanded, but obviously not at the rate that it would have in absence of the shock.

The shock has produced major resource movements. The shift has been mainly from the busted tin-mining sector to new sectors of exportable production, mainly gold, zinc, and soyabeans. Our data also show a very significant shift to the sector of agricultural exports. Employment in construction also increased from 1987 on.

Tin and natural gas were not only important because of the foreign exchange and national income that they generated; they were also a very significant direct source of income for the public sector, since the most important exporters at the time of the shock were state-owned enterprises. The indirect income, coming from taxes collected from the private tin mines, was important but not as large as the direct one. The income impact of the negative shock was proportionally larger in the public sector than in the private sector.

Also, the adjustment in the consumption of the private sector was less significant than that of the public sector. It seems that the private sector, which had a more indirect perception of the magnitude of the slump than the government, tended therefore to consider it as more transitory. The government perceived that the very low prices after the shock would revert to more normal values only very slowly. In line with this perception major adjustments in consumption and public sector employment took place.

The external shock caused recurrent menaces to Bolivia's foreign exchange reserves during 1986–89. Monetary policy had to be tighter than otherwise. There are solid grounds for thinking that the very high real interest rates of that period resulted from the excess demand for money, which in turn is explained by the tight policy. The excess demand for money also explains the persistent phenomenon of dollarisation.

The trade shock occurred in the midst of a trade liberalisation process. The liberalisation was maintained in spite of the negative shock. The shock actually helped to sustain the liberalisation process, since it attenuated the fall in the price of import substitutes relative to the price of exportables.

The chapter is organised as follows. Section 16.2 deals with the nature of the shock and the expectations that were formed about it. Section 16.3

gives a description of the economic policy environment when the shock occurred. In Section 16.4 we evaluate the responses of the economy, in terms of investment and savings and of the reallocation of resources that followed the price changes caused by the shock. In Section 16.5 we make a disaggregation of the transmission of the shock to the public and private sectors. In Section 16.6 we examine the interactions between the policy reforms of 1985, which accompanied the stabilisation programme, and the shock. Section 16.7 provides the concluding remarks.

16.2. The Nature of the Shock

16.2.1. Tin

The long-term evolution of the real price of tin is shown in Figure 16.1. We observe an upward trend between 1900 and 1980 and cyclical deviations from it with variable frequencies and amplitudes. If the period 1981–89 is added the upward trend disappears. After the very favourable tin prices between 1974 and 1980 there was a slow decline until the crisis in the last quarter of 1985.

The separation of the transitory fluctuations from the trend is central to our analysis. Morales *et al.* (1993), in their econometric analysis with annual values from 1900 to 1989, find mixed results on the hypothesis that the logarithm of the price level of tin follows a random walk. With

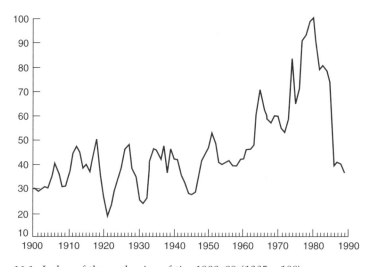

Figure 16.1. Index of the real price of tin, 1900–89 (*1985 = 100*)

Source: New York price deflated by the Manufacturing Unit Value Index (MUV) of the World Bank (see Grilli and Yang 1988).

quarterly and monthly values they found it always impossible to reject the random walk hypothesis.[1] Acceptance of the random walk hypothesis would lead to the conclusion that all price changes are permanent.

A closer examination of the tin market between 1956 and 1985 would suggest high persistence, probably going to the limit of a random walk. There is no doubt that the functioning of the International Tin Agreements (ITAs) gave inertia to the positive price shocks in that period. On the other hand, the tin sales by the General Services Administration (GSA) of the United States often shook the market, producing discontinuous, downward jumps of random size in prices.[2]

The feature of asymmetric inertia in the ITAs needs a closer examination. The asymmetry arose from the ITAs prolonging favourable states for producers more often than unfavourable ones. The scheme was unsustainable in the medium run, as the October 1985 bust proved.[3]

The ITAs and the GSA's sales had a very important informational content for all participants in the market. High-cost producer countries, including Bolivia, exerted all the pressure they could to raise the price fork of the ITAs and to prevent the sales of the GSA. Well before the crash of October 1985, prices were expected to fall. The uncertainty was about the timing and, especially, the magnitude of the slump.

An examination of the attitude of the domestic producers towards price risks adds information on the nature of expectations. First, the government typically does not choose the depletion rates, not even in the state-owned mines. This does not mean that government's policy does not influence the depletion rate, rather that this effect is frequently unintentional. The rule in the state-owned mines is, even now, to maximise output, whatever market conditions, unless current producer prices are extraordinarily low (CEMYD 1990: 19). Privately owned mines are more sensitive to market conditions but there is no evidence that they follow Hotelling rates of depletion. Interestingly, some private enterprises anticipated the price bust of 1985 but they did not increase production nor sales.

Second, just before the crisis, Bolivian tin producers had accumulated stocks in expectation of major domestic policy changes. Moreover, the stocks could be financed at very negative real interest rates. Producers bet on a sharp devaluation of the Bolivian peso, either officially or *de facto*, following a liberalisation of the foreign exchange market. This would have meant extra profits even in the event of a moderate drop in world prices.

Finally, large producers, traders, and international lenders, with a direct knowledge of the market and its arbitrage opportunities, probably had different expectations from those of the national government and the common citizen. Difference in expectations led to different adjustment speeds. The government's perceptions followed, with a small lag, the perceptions of producers and other directly concerned agents. The adjustment lag in the private sector's expectations was longer. The public formed its expectations with the information provided by the government on the nature of the crisis and on the cuts in public expenditure and employment needed to cope with it. Major public announcements made by cabinet members and frequent press releases conveyed the government's perception of the shock to the private sector at large. The actual cuts in public expenditure sent an even more telling signal.

16.2.2 Natural Gas

Argentina has been the sole buyer of Bolivian natural gas. Sales took place under several contracts of variable duration and scope. The real natural gas price reached a maximum in 1984, declined slightly in 1985, and showed a gradual but profound descent until 1988 (Figure 16.2). Natural gas prices were not initially indexed to petroleum prices, although the latter frequently served as reference in the negotiations on the former. As Figure 16.3 shows, the rise in natural gas prices lagged the rise in petroleum prices after the first oil shock in 1973. Between 1981 and 1985, after the second oil shock, natural gas prices continued increasing, even when oil prices were already falling. With the oil crisis of 1986, the natural gas price had to be revised downward.

Only in 1988 was the natural gas price (partially) indexed to a moving

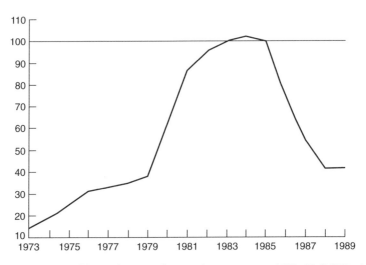

Figure 16.2. Index of he real price of natural gas exports, 1973–89 (*1985 = 100*)

Source: Natural gas prices from Central Bank of Bolivia (1991); the deflator is the World Bank's MUV.

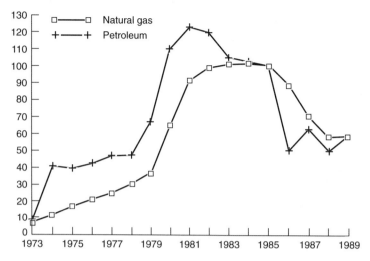

Figure 16.3. Price indices of natural gas and petroleum, 1973–89 (*1985 = 100*)

Source: Petroleum prices from World Bank (1988) and updatings; natural gas prices from Central Bank of Bolivia (1991).

average of quarterly prices (inclusive of the costs of transportation to Argentina from overseas ports) of a basket of fuels. Persistent variations in the price of oil are fully translated into natural gas income with a lag of six months.

Bolivia was forced in 1984 to accept payment in Argentinian goods and services for 50% of the natural gas bill. This percentage was lowered afterwards. To the extent that the austral (and the Argentinian peso before) was overvalued, prices in Figure 16.2, before the fall in 1986, are overstated. Also, after 1986, the fall in purchasing power of the gas exports was higher than shown in Figure 16.2. The fall in prices was accompanied moreover by frequent delays in payment by Argentina. For a long period Bolivia did not receive the expected income from its natural gas sales.

Bolivia had little experience and exposure to the international energy market. Natural gas exports to Argentina started only in 1973. The developments in 1986 came as surprises since there was no memory of this type of event.

In the months preceding the fall, as happened with tin, Bolivian policymakers believed (although they never admitted publicly) that natural gas prices were at too-high levels. They also knew that the fall in petroleum prices in early 1986 would almost surely force a reduction in the contract prices to Argentina. The extent of the fall was not, however, fully anticipated.

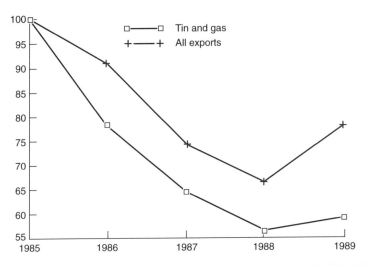

Figure 16.4. Price indices of exports relative to imports, 1985–89 *(1985 = 100)*

Note: All exports = all merchandise exports.

Source: Export and import price indices from Central Bank of Bolivia (1990).

16.2.3. *Changes in the Terms of Trade*

Tin and natural gas exports represented 74% of total legal[4] merchandise export revenues in the five years preceding the crisis. Figure 16.4 depicts the ratio of tin and natural gas export prices to imports and the ratio of all (merchandise) export prices to import prices (the barter terms of trade). Despite the weight of tin and natural gas, note that the fall in their prices relative to the price of imports was significantly more pronounced than the fall in the overall terms of trade. Obviously, the prices of exports other than tin and natural gas were experiencing strong improvements.

   Measured changes in the terms of trade by themselves give an incomplete idea of the effect of the shock, since the price movements in the export bundle went in different directions. The point to underscore is that the tin and natural gas shocks had an important informational content in Bolivia's short-term economic prospects. This aspect is missed if the analysis is confined to the terms of trade. Furthermore, the shock directly influenced public sector expectations, and more significantly than in the private sector.

16.2.4. *Characterisation of Expectations*

The account given above of the expectations-formation leads unambiguously to a diagnostic of exclusive expectations. Neither the producers, nor the government, nor the public had included in their prior expectations an export crisis of such magnitude and duration. The characterisation of the shock as revised or unrevised is less clear. For a long period before the shock, prices for tin, more than for natural gas, were thought to be unsustainable high. After the shock, expectations were: (1) that the situation of very low prices was transitory; but (2) that the recovery could not lead to their previous levels for a very long time. The perception was that prices had abruptly passed from too-high levels to too-low levels.

The price shocks also implied a strong and more lasting income shock in the sense that they made some production decisions irreversible. For instance, mines that were barely breaking even at the pre-shock prices were either closed or ceded to cooperatives of their dismissed workers, who tried to exploit the little metal that remained.[5] It is unlikely that these mines will be commercially operated again.

The tin crisis, especially, led to a rethinking of Bolivia's development prospects and to important changes in resource allocation that are far from complete. Policymakers are aiming now at lower rates of growth of the economy for the next ten years than the average between 1962 and 1978, which used to be considered normal. The spirit around 1986–87 is reflected in the very influential report prepared for the World Bank by David Morawetz (1986) with the title 'Beyond Tin and Natural Gas, What?' This report suggests that a (partial) revision downwards of permanent income occurred. We would then be facing a case of exclusive, partially revised expectations.

The case can also be made for exclusive unrevised expectations. Before the shock the more informed agents had discounted a part of the fall in prices. Even the closing of some mines was probably discounted, because the ores had had very low metal contents for years and the mines were profitable only at very high prices. The price shock of 1985 only ended a very long agony. Permanent income was revised only to the extent that some losses and expenditures were brought forward, a minor considera- tion in view of the magnitude of the shock.

16.2.5. A Counterfactual to the Shock

The construction of the counterfactual to the trade shock needs some elaboration, in view of the following observations:

1. As said above, the price of tin was considered too high on the eve of the shock. Long conversations with Bolivian specialists of the tin market revealed that the price observed in 1989, one-third lower than in 1985, was considered close to a 'normal' price. More important, many private mines could again obtain normal profits at that price.
2. Similarly, the high 1985 price of natural gas was unsustainable given the developments in the energy market. The fact that domestic

investment decisions were made on the assumption of a price close to the one of 1986 helps us in defining a benchmark price.
3. The hyperinflation had caused severe disruptions in the production of tin. Once economic order was restored output and exports immediately increased. The duration of the fall in tin prices obliged, shortly after, sharp reductions in output.

The construction of the counterfactual uses the information above.

1. Tin prices are assumed constant over 1986–89 and are set at their 1989 level.
2. Natural gas prices are similarly assumed constant over 1986–89 and are set at the 1986 level.
3. The volume of tin exports is assumed to remain constant at its 1986 level.
4. Other exports are considered to be unaffected by the shock.

Our estimate of counterfactual exports appears in column (10) of Table 16.1. The shortfall in export revenue in 1986 was exclusively due to the fall in prices; between 1987 and 1989, there were also quantity responses in tin. Over the whole period 1986–89 the estimated shortfall in export revenue was a little over U$500 million (col. 11 in Table 16.1).

16.3. The Economic Context

In August 1985, the government announced a very ambitious (and successful) stabilisation programme.[6] The stabilisation programme also included very important reforms to liberalise the economy. The combination of stabilisation and liberalisation was called the New Economic Policy (NEP) by the government.

The stabilisation plan relied on exchange rate unification supported by very tight fiscal and monetary policies. The domestic components of the stabilisation policies were completed with the suspension of debt service payments to private foreign creditors until a definite agreement could be reached with them.

The stabilisation programme included an almost complete liberalisation of the market for foreign exchange. All exchange rate controls were lifted except the obligation imposed on exporters to surrender all their foreign exchange proceeds to the central bank. This latter regulation is in fact binding only for public sector export enterprises, since private exporters can buy back their surrendered foreign exchange almost immediately.

The NEP rapidly controlled inflation. Most importantly, the NEP was credible with official international lenders. Bolivia not only received

Table 16.1. Magnitude of the export slump

	Value of exports				Price indices exports				Counterfactual		Windfall	
	Tin (1)	Natural gas (2)	Other (3)	Total (4)	Tin (5)	Natural gas (6)	Other (7)	Total (8)	Imports (9)	Exports (10)	Current prices (11)	1985 Prices (12)
1985	186.6	372.6	113.3	672.5	100.0	100.0	100.0	100.0	100.0	672.5	0.0	0.0
1986	104.1	328.6	205.1	637.8	53.6	88.3	99.6	86.8	95.7	679.8	−42.0	−43.9
1987	68.9	248.6	252.0	569.5	58.9	69.7	85.0	75.3	102.1	713.2	−143.7	−140.8
1988	76.9	214.9	308.4	600.2	61.5	57.4	79.2	69.4	105.0	785.3	−185.1	−176.3
1989	126.5	213.8	480.9	821.2	75.2	57.5	103.9	85.0	109.5	955.2	−134.0	−122.4
Total										3,133.5	−504.8	−483.4
Present value										2,694.9	−426.3	−409.6

Sources and notes: Export values in millions of US$; price indices derived from prices in US$
Col (1) to col. (4), from Central Bank of Bolivia (1990)
Col. (5) to col. (9), price indices of exports and imports from Central Bank of Bolivia (1990)
Col. (10) includes quantity effects (see text)
Col. (11) = col. (4) – col. (10)
Col. (12) = col. (11) divided by col. (9)

substantial debt alleviation from its creditors but was also able to obtain new loans from multilateral agencies, as well as from foreign governments willing to cooperate with the national effort.

The stabilisation programme liberalised almost all markets for goods and factors. All price controls on the products of private producers, except public utilities, were lifted.

Foreign trade was also liberalised. The NEP dismantled the system of foreign trade controls that had been in place for many years. Quantitative restrictions on exports and imports were abolished. Tariffs were also substantially lowered towards a unified rate. There was no endogenous trade policy: the trade liberalisation was not reversed in response to the negative shock. Financial markets were also virtually completely liberalised. The deregulation of the labour market was also significant. The principle of 'free contracting'—which had been superseded by administrative regulations on job security—was re-established. With free contracting, enterprises can, more easily than before, dismiss workers. Wage indexation was also abolished. It is also worth adding that the strength of the labour unions, which used to be considerable especially in the mining sector, was greatly eroded by the trade shock and the NEP.

16.4. Responses of the Economy to the Shock

16.4.1. Asset Changes and Savings Rates

The numbers in Table 16.2 help us to construct an estimate of the losses in Gross Domestic Income (GDY) and in GFKF caused by the trade shock. Actual GDY (col. 2) is the sum of actual GDP at constant 1985 prices and the overall terms of trade effect, TOTE, converted to 1985 Bolivian pesos (Bs).

Three assumptions are crucial in the determination of counterfactual GDY (col. 4) and GFKF (col. 6). First, actual GDP is corrected for quantity changes, following hypothesis 3 above. To this corrected GDP we added a counterfactual TOTE derived from our assumed prices in hypotheses 2 and 3. To the GDY so obtained we further add the (negative) returns of the investment forgone by the negative savings effect of the trade shock. Note that actual TOTE less counterfactual TOTE less the quantity effects (all in US$, 1985 prices) is equal to the windfall export income reported in col. (12) of Table 16.1.

Second, the investment ratios used in the counterfactual differ from the actual investment rates. The assumption is that as result of the economic reforms of the last quarter of 1985 the investment rates could have gradually recovered their levels of 1980–82 from 1987 on.

Third, we assume a conservative rate of return of 10% on investment.

Table 16.2. Counterfactual growth and capital formation

	Actuals			Counterfactuals			Windfall GFKF		
	GFKF/GDP	GDY (1985 prices)	GFKF	GDY (1985 prices)	GFKF/GDY	GFKF	Annual	Cumulative	Return at 10%
	(1)	(2)	(3)	(4)	(5)	(6)	(7)	(8)	(9)
1980	14.4								
1981	11.0								
1982	13.8								
1983	8.6								
1984	8.6								
1985	7.2	2,866.7	207.5	2,866.7	7.2	207.5	0.0	0.0	0.0
1986	9.5	2,746.8	260.9	2,777.7	9.5	263.9	−2.9	−2.9	−0.3
1987	10.3	2,728.4	281.0	2,827.8	10.7	302.3	−21.2	−24.2	−2.4
1988	11.5	2,746.7	315.9	2,873.2	11.9	341.3	−25.4	−49.6	−5.0
1989	11.5	2,881.1	331.3	2,972.2	13.1	388.4	−57.0	−106.6	−10.7
Average 1980–82	13.1								
Total 1986–89		11,102.9		11,450.9			−106.6		−18.3
Present value 1986–89		9,661.7		9,956.0			−86.1		−14.6

Sources and notes:

Col. (1): Investment ratios (%) at current prices from World Bank (1990a), except for 1989

Col. (2): Gross Domestic Income (GDY) is the sum of Gross Domestic Product (GDP) and the terms of trade effect (TOTE). GDP data come from the NIS as reported by the Central Bank of Bolivia (1991), converted to 1985 prices. TOTE data come from author's computations with data of the Central Bank of Bolivia (1990). The TOTE data is converted to 1985 Bs at the rate of exchange of Bs 0.704 per US$

Col. (3) = col. (1) times col. (2)

Col. (4): Counterfactual GDY is actual GDP, in 1985 prices, plus the quantity effect of the trade shock in col. (13) in table B2 of Morales (1994) plus the counterfactual price effect in col. (12) in the same table, converted to 1985 Bs; in 1987–89 also corrects for lost returns returns on shortfall investment as shown in col. (9), lagged one year

Col. (5): Linear reversion to 1980–82 average by 1988

Col. (6) = Col. (4) times col. (5)

Col. (7) = Col. (3) minus col. (6)

Col. (8) = Col. (7) summed

Col. (9) = Col. (8) times 0.1 (10% return on capital)

The trade shock plus the forgone investment produced income losses that cumulated over 1986–89 and taken in present value represented 10.3% of 1985 GDP $((9,956 - 9,662)/2,867 = 0.103)$. The average annual loss over that period was 2.9% of 1985 GDP.[7] Investment was 106.6 million 1985 Bs (Bs 86.1 million in present value terms) less than if the trade shock had not happened. A fraction of this small forgone gross investment probably implied disinvestment, since replacement investment and maintenance were no longer made in some tin mines. Some of them even closed as mentioned in Section 16.2.4.

Bolivia resumed its access to international loans from official creditors following the stabilisation plan of 1985. It is very difficult to figure out the proportion of those loans aimed at smoothing the effects of the trade shock. The International Monetary Fund (IMF) came forth with two Compensatory Financing Loans, US$77.6 million in 1986 and US$59.2 million in 1988. Other loans, although not explicitly intended for the same purpose, had similar effects.

It is reasonable to think that the shift in the direction of the net resource transfers from 1985 to 1988 was produced by the foreign support to the stabilisation programme and not by the trade shock. Therefore, the counterfactual in Table 16.3 is constructed on the assumption that the 'foreign

Table 16.3. Actual and counterfactual foreign savings

	Foreign Savings (million 1985 Bs)			IMF compensatory financing (million US$, current 1985 prices)		Foreign savings ratios (%)	
	Actual	Counterfactual	Windfall			Actual	Counterfactual
	(1)	(2)	(3)	(4)	(5)	(6)	(7)
1980						−4.0	
1981						2.1	
1982						−4.0	
1983						−2.9	
1984						−3.3	
1985						1.7	1.7
1986	79.7	23.5	56.2	77.6	81.1	2.9	0.8
1987	174.6	181.0	−6.4	0.0	0.0	6.4	6.4
1988	151.1	118.3	32.7	59.2	56.4	5.5	4.1
1989	−66.3	−68.4	2.1	0.0	0.0	−2.3	−2.3
Total			84.6				
Present value			79.0				

Sources and notes:
Col. (1) = col. (2) of Table 16.2 times col. (6) divided by 100
Col. (2) = col. (4) of Table 16.2 times col. (6) divided by 100 – Col. (5) converted to Bs at an exchange rate of 0.704
Col. (3) = col. (1) − col. (2)
Col. (4): information provided by the Central Bank of Bolivia
Col. (5) = col. (4) deflated by col. (1) of Table 16.1
Col. (6) = col. (2) divided by col. (4) of Table 16.2 times 100

Table 16.4. Savings and transient income (*million 1985 Bs*)

Present values	
1. Windfall export income	−288.3
2. Windfall GFKF	−86.1
3. Savings of extra permanent income	−1.7
4. Windfall foreign savings	79.0
5. Savings from transient income	−163.4
Propensities	
6. Propensity to save	56.7
7. Propensity to consume	43.3

Sources and notes:
Line 1: from col. (12) of Table 16.1 converted to Bs at the exchange rate of Bs 0.704 per US$
Line 2: from col. (7) of Table 16.2
Line 3 = (col. 5 of Table 16.2 minus col. 7 of Table 16.3) × col. (9) of Table 16.2
Line 4: from col. (3) of Table 16.3
Line 5 = line 2 minus line 3 minus line 4
Line 6 = line 5 over line 1 (%)
Line 7 = 100% minus line 6

saving propensities' would not have differed from the actual propensities, except for the incidence of the IMF loans. This correction in the foreign savings propensities is reflected in col. (7) in Table 16.3. Those propensities are applied to counterfactual GDY in col. (4) of Table 16.2.

The net resource transfer from abroad would have been Bs 84.6 million lower (around US$120.2 million) had the shock not happened. This is a relatively small amount in comparison with the income loss of slightly over US$500 millions caused by the shock.

Table 16.4 summarises the findings on forgone income and savings caused by the trade shock (in present value). Line 5 shows the negative savings effect of the shock amounting to Bs 163.4 million. Also, we find that the propensity to (dis)save out of (negative) transient income was close to 56.7%.

16.4.2. Goods Markets

The relative price changes after the trade shock are shown in Figure 16.5. Observe there: (1) an increase in the price of non-tradable (NT) consumer goods *vis-à-vis* the price of import substitutes; (2) a strong fall in the price of NT capital goods relative to the price of import substitutes in 1986, but a rapid recovery thereafter; and, (3) a fall in the price of NT capital relative to the price of NT consumer goods during the whole period 1986–89.[8] The price of import substitutes is equal to the Bs international price of

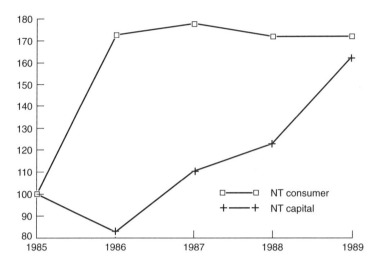

Figure 16.5. Price of non-tradables relative to import substitutes, 1985–89
(*1985 = 100*)

Source: Based on author's computations with unpublished data from the National
Institute of Statistics.

importables, plus its tariff and the tariff equivalent of its quantitative
restrictions.

Figure 16.5 needs to be interpreted with caution given the contempora-
neousness of the stabilisation and trade liberalisation programmes with
the shock. Observe that most of the relative price changes took place in
1986. Initially, the effects of stabilisation, trade liberalisation, and the less
restrictive credit conditions more than compensated for the income effects
of the trade shock on the demand for NT consumer goods. Also note that
the yearly values in Figure 16.5 overstate the increase because 1985 was
still a year of high inflation.[9]

From 1987 on, the price of NT consumer goods declined relative to the
price of import substitutes. The fall was especially strong in 1988 and 1989.
We may conclude that it is only then that the short-run effects of the trade
shock started to be felt.

In regard to the price of NT capital goods, was not its fall *vis-à-vis* the
price of import substitutes and the price of NT consumer goods more
likely due to the liberalisation programme than to the shock? The answer
is mixed. Liberalisation may explain the fall in the price of NT capital
relative to the price of NT consumer goods, but the 1986 fall in the price
of NT capital relative to the price of import substitutes is doubtless
explained by a strong savings effect.[10]

Three indicators of the quantitative evolution of NT capital goods are
used in our analysis (Figure 16.6): (1) an index of the stock of NT capital

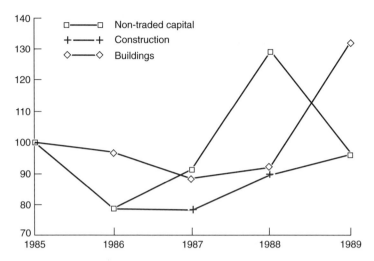

Figure 16.6. Indices of non-traded capital goods output, construction value-added and square metres of approved buildings in La Paz, 1985–89 (*1985 = 100*)
Source: Morales (1994)

goods; (2) an index of value-added (in 1985 prices) in construction; and, (3) an index of square meters of approved buildings by the municipality of La Paz.[11]

The indicators in Figure 16.6 point to a sharp decline in the volume of NT capital goods in 1986 and 1987. The indicators differ from 1988 on. A strong recovery occurred in 1988, caused by the active policy of public works of that year. The unexpectedly low values for NT capital and value-added in construction of 1989 are difficult to reconcile with the strong demand for residential construction of 1989, at least in La Paz.

Investment in NT capital goods (in 1985 prices) significantly lagged the investment in tradable (T) capital goods in all years except 1988 (Figure 16.7). Investment in T capital goods rapidly increased in 1986–87. This was probably because replacement of equipment was badly needed after the losses in the capital stock during the hyperinflation years.

Thus, it appears that the construction slump was short-lived, at most two years, 1986 and 1987. In addition to more loans obtained abroad, other factors, not related to the external sector but to policy impulses to domestic demand, were instrumental in the recovery of non-traded GFKF.[12]

The path of the relative price of NT capital is consistent with the dynamics of the theory of construction booms. There was initially a sharp reduction in construction activity, but once the government obtained the international loans and donations (and therefore the actual and shadow rate of interest decreased for government projects), construction resumed.

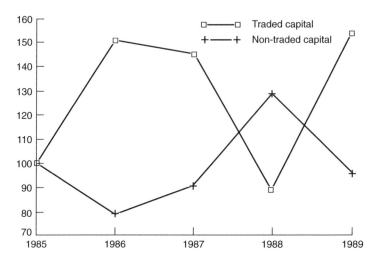

Figure 16.7. Capital goods at 1985 prices, 1985–89

16.4.3. Factor Markets

Natural gas is a very capital-intensive activity and therefore we can expect little resource movements in that sector. In the large tin mines, most investments are irreversible but the technology is significantly less capital intensive than in petroleum. Changes in their capital stock (ignoring the wealth accumulated as natural deposits) result, in the absence of positive investments, from slow wear and tear or, more dramatically, from closing the mines. The amount of capital released by the closing of the mines was almost negligible, but the number of workers freed was very substantial.

Given the discussion above, investigation of the new destinations for released capital does not seem very fruitful. On the other hand, the identification of the sectors where fresh investments went after the slump can be very informative. Unfortunately, investment figures disaggregated by sector of destination for such a recent period as 1985–89 are not available. The indirect information (based on output growth) suggests that many new investments have been undertaken since 1988 in the new, capital-intensive mining sectors of gold and zinc, and in the sectors of production of agricultural exports.

The trade slump not only affected tin mining and natural gas but was transmitted to the non-tradable sectors. Table 16.5 shows a substantial labour movement between the sectors of tradables and non-tradables and within each sector. The most noticeable feature is the big reduction in employment, both in absolute and relative terms, in the mining (and petroleum) sectors. This clearly is a resource-movement effect. Employment in the tradable sector of commercial agriculture increased from 1987

Table 16.5. Employment by sector indices (*1987 = 100*)

Tradables			Non-Tradables		Whole urban economy
Mining and petroleum	Commercial agriculture	Import-substitution sectors	Construction	Consumer goods	plus commercial agriculture
(1)	(2)	(3)	(4)	(5)	(6)
A. Index					
1985 234.7	80.1	127.8	113.0	89.4	93.3
1986 137.3	72.0	100.0	100.0	98.2	98.6
1987 100.0	100.0	100.0	100.0	100.0	100.0
1988 123.9	119.3	120.0	146.5	100.6	102.4
1989 127.4	157.7	130.8	288.4	103.4	107.7
B. Share relative to whole economy					
1985 251.5	85.9	136.9	121.1	95.8	100.0
1986 139.2	73.0	101.4	101.4	99.6	100.0
1987 100.0	100.0	100.0	100.0	100.0	100.0
1988 121.0	116.5	117.1	143.0	98.2	100.0
1989 118.3	146.4	121.4	267.7	96.0	100.0

Notes:
Col. (3): employment proxied by formal employment in the manufacturing sector
Col. (5): employment proxied by formal employment in the sectors of electricity, gas, water, commerce, transport, storage, communications, financial services, other services and the whole informal urban sector
Source: Author's computations based on data from UDAPE (1991)

on, as many workers displaced from other sectors moved to the production of soyabeans and other agricultural exportables. Employment in the import-substitution sector initially suffered a decline, mainly as a consequence of the policy reforms of 1985, but then it rapidly and steadily recovered. Employment in the sector of NT consumer goods increased in 1986 and has remained almost constant since then. Its share relative to the rest of the economy in 1989 was closer to the one of 1985.

After a strong decline in the first two years after the slump employment in the construction sector recovered at a very rapid pace with construction output. The number for 1989 seems, all the same, to be anomalous.

Real wages declined sharply in the aftermath of the stabilisation programme, but they recovered steadily during 1986–89, at least in the private sector (Table 16.6).[13] Construction wages fell sharply relative to mean wages as a whole between the third quarter of 1985 and the second quarter of 1986; afterwards their evolution was close to the mean wage as a whole. Wages in the manufacturing sector and the wholesale and retail trade sector increased less rapidly than those in both the construction sector and the whole economy. There are no disaggregated data for import substitutes and NT manufactures.

Table 16.6. Mean real wage earnings in the private sector *(1987 = 100)*[a]

	(1)	(2)	(3)	(4)	(5)	(6)	(7)
1985.3	33.2	54.9	46.7	49.2	62.2	43.6	54.6
4	99.2	73.4	69.3	59.9	88.8	46.4	79.2
1986.1	73.0	62.4	58.1	69.0	87.3	58.7	73.6
2	68.3	70.6	47.6	77.2	84.9	68.0	77.0
3	70.9	72.5	84.5	82.0	82.8	88.4	79.8
4	85.9	80.3	82.5	79.6	82.7	81.8	82.1
1987.1	92.8	90.8	87.0	101.8	89.6	97.9	92.3
2	81.5	99.0	101.9	93.4	103.2	100.6	99.3
3	126.4	108.1	105.9	105.4	108.8	107.9	108.2
4	109.3	114.1	117.6	111.3	107.5	101.3	110.4
1988.1	112.4	119.4	130.1	117.1	140.4	110.1	126.1
2	122.9	124.6	122.1	114.8	137.8	126.2	132.2
3	132.1	119.1	124.7	111.2	153.6	115.8	130.7
4	129.4	120.3	129.6	104.3	153.1	116.3	130.3
1989.1	125.9	132.6	129.0	111.6	155.2	124.2	137.4
2	138.7	135.4	141.2	114.0	153.9	133.6	141.6
3	133.1	123.3	128.7	112.9	155.8	134.1	136.2
4	127.4	125.7	127.2	115.3	159.3	141.3	139.6

[a] Data at end of quarter; real wages are nominal wages deflated by the CPI

Source: Author's computations based on data from UDAPE (1991)

It appears that in mining, the sector directly affected by the shock, the adjustment was in employment and not in wages. In construction, which typically requires fewer skills and where unions are not strong, there was a strong adjustment downwards in both wages and employment on the impact of the shock. The employment level recovered first and then, with a lag, wages narrowed the gap that they had with wages as a whole.

16.5. The Transmission of the Shock to the Public and Private Sectors

16.5.1. Main Changes in the Fiscal Aggregates

The trade bust strongly destabilised the budget initially but the government swiftly reacted to redress this situation. Table 16.7 shows the main changes that occurred in the non-financial public sector (NFPS) accounts (as percentages of GDP) in the 1980s. The NFPS accounts consolidate the accounts of the general government (central and local governments) and those of the public enterprises.

Our first observation concerns the very significant change in the NFPS revenues between the beginning and end of the 1980s. The Olivera–Tanzi

Table 16.7. Non-financial public sector operations (*percentage of GDP*)

	1980	1981	1982	1983	1984	1985	1986	1987	1988	1989
A. Total revenue	40.5	35.2	31.9	23.5	19.7	25.2	27.5	24.5	26.8	26.4
1. Tax revenue	9.7	9.1	4.7	2.6	2.6	6.7	9.4	11.1	11.0	12.5
2. Other revenues	30.8	26.1	27.2	20.9	17.1	18.5	18.1	13.4	15.8	13.9
B. Total expenditure	37.4	32.2	29.5	24.9	27.2	23.1	21.5	21.7	25.2	25.0
1. Current expenditures (excluding interest and unrequited transfers)	30.5	26.3	23.8	21.5	23.6	19.4	16.5	15.9	17.2	18.1
2. Capital expenditures		6.9	5.9	5.7	3.4	3.6	3.7	5.0	5.9	8.0
C. Primary surplus (line A − line B)	3.1	3.0	2.4	−1.4	−7.5	2.1	6.0	2.8	1.6	1.4
D. Interest	5.5	3.6	4.4	5.0	3.5	7.4	6.7	4.9	4.4	3.7
1. Domestic interest		2.5	0.8	0.7	1.2	0.6	0.7	1.3	0.8	0.2
2. Foreign interest	3.0	2.8	3.7	3.8	2.9	6.6	5.4	4.1	4.2	3.5
E. Unrequited transfers	5.4	5.7	4.7	4.8	4.0	2.3	1.9	5.3	3.2	2.8
F. Total transfers (line D + line E)	10.9	9.3	9.1	9.8	7.5	9.7	8.5	10.2	7.6	6.5
G. Other expenditures	0.0	1.3	7.5	6.7	8.6	2.3	0.0	0.0	0.5	0.0
H. Overall surplus/deficit (line C − line F − line G)	−7.8	−7.6	−14.2	−17.9	−23.6	−9.8	−2.5	−7.4	−6.5	−5.1
I. Net domestic borrowing	2.5	3.6	13.6	19.3	21.1	5.4	−3.4	5.0	1.7	2.0
J. Net foreign borrowing	5.3	3.9	0.7	−1.4	2.5	4.4	6.0	2.4	4.8	3.1

Source: Otálora (1990) for 1980–88 and author's computations for 1989 based on data from the Ministry of Planning, Unit for Policy Analysis, La Paz

effect explains the fall in tax revenues during the high-inflation years 1982–85. After the stabilisation programme of late 1985 and the tax reform of 1986, a substantial recovery of tax collections occurred. The drop in income in the public enterprises, triggered by the adverse trade shock, explains the diminution in the item 'Other revenues' (see also Table 16.9).

The adjustment in exhaustible expenditure (lines B.1 and B.2 in Table 16.7) was also substantial. Note that the main adjustment took place in current expenditure (excluding interest and transfers); by contrast, capital expenditure increased after the slump *vis-à-vis* the levels immediately preceding the slump and, surprisingly, *vis-à-vis* the levels of the earlier period 1980–82.

The severance benefits to the dismissed workers of COMIBOL accounted for a large share of the unrequited transfer of 1987. Remember that the dismissal of miners was a direct consequence of the tin crisis. The item 'Other expenditures', with large values during 1982–85, covers an array of ill-defined accounts, mainly related to counterpart items of revaluations of the NFPS (net) foreign liabilities.[14]

The difference between revenue and exhaustible expenditure defines the primary surplus.[15] In the aftermath of the launch of the stabilisation programme a primary surplus emerged that was mostly reduced in the following years.

Increases in capital expenditure and the resulting global deficit were mainly financed with foreign credits and the reduction of foreign assets involuntarily held in Argentina (discussed in Section 16.2). Little recourse was made to seignorage: the central bank's credits to the NFPS mainly implied a reduction in its holdings of foreign reserves. Thus the deficits were financed almost entirely with an increase in the net foreign debt.[16]

Table 16.8 presents our fiscal counterfactual based on the following assumptions:

1. The counterfactual revenue/GDY ratio (27.6%) is set at the revenue/ GDP value of 1986 for the whole period 1986–89. This ratio is very close to the average ratio of 1983–85 corrected for a reverse Olivera–Tanzi effect and for the effect of the increase in petroleum taxes, which partially substituted the revenue loss caused by the trade shock.[17]
2. The counterfactual exhaustible consumption/GDY ratio was set at 19.0%, its average value in 1988–89 (in terms of GDP), on the assumption that this was close to a lower limit without major exogenous shocks.
3. The counterfactual public GFKF/GDY ratio was set at its GFKF/GDP value for 1986. Afterwards it was augmented to 5.8%, its average value for the pre-crisis years 1981–82.

The numbers in columns (1) to (3) in Table 16.8 give the difference between the actual and the counterfactual values.

Table 16.8. Fiscal changes owing to the slump (*million 1985 Bs*)

	Total revenue (1)	Consumption (2)	GFKF (3)	Total exhaustive expenditure (4)	Primary surplus (5)
1985	0.0	0.0	0.0	0.0	0.0
1986	−8.5	−74.5	−1.5	−76.1	67.6
1987	−112.0	−10.7	−3.0	−13.8	−98.3
1988	−56.9	−24.0	53.1	29.1	−85.9
1989	−59.7	−17.3	26.4	9.1	−68.8
Total	−237.2	−126.6	74.9	−51.7	−185.5
Present value	−202.3	−117.2	−59.4	−57.7	−144.5
Ratio of actual/conterfactual revenue				0.92	
Same as above in present value				0.93	
Ratio of total shortfall revenue/shortfall (%)				68.16	

Sources and notes:
Cols. (1) to (3), see text
Col. (4) = col. (2) + col. (3)
Col. (5) = col. (1) − col. (4)

The fall in NFPS total revenue is surprisingly large, averaging 68.2% of the shortfall revenue over the period 1986–89 (237.2/(11,450.9 − 11,102.9) = 0.682). The fall in NFPS consumption expenditure is smaller than the fall in revenue, as expected, but still large. The positive public sector GFKF was larger than expected owing to the important foreign aid to finance investments (especially those of the ESF). The NFPS accumulated both assets (in the form of GFKF) and liabilities to finance the primary deficit.

It is interesting that the ESF was financed almost entirely with donations from the international community. The inflow of foreign exchange for the ESF, of slightly more than US$117 million between 1987 and 1989, represented more than one-fifth of the losses caused by the trade shock.

16.5.2. Public Revenue and Expenditure and Private Incomes

Table 16.9 shows the change in revenue from the average pattern of 1981–82 set as our benchmark.[18] Taxes levied on minerals decreased as expected, so did income from the foreign sales of goods and services. Note that in this second case the fall is very substantial. Also, observe that the public enterprises (especially YPFB) were obliged to increase their transfers to the general government.

Unfortunately, a disaggregation of changes in the composition of the NFPS revenues into tradables and non-tradables is not feasible and we

Table 16.9. Revenue composition of the non-financial public sector (*percentage of GDP*)

	Average 1981–82	Average change from 1981–82 pattern	
		1983–85	1986–89
A. Central government revenues	7.0	−3.0	4.0
1. Mining taxes	0.5	−0.2	−0.4
2. Petroleum taxes	2.0	−0.2	3.9
a. On natural gas	0.6	0.8	0.9
b. Other petroleum	1.4	−1.1	3.0
3. Import tariffs	2.0	−1.2	−0.7
4. Internal revenue	2.5	−1.5	0.7
5. Other	0.1	0.0	0.5
NB Mining and natural gas taxes	1.1	0.7	0.4
B. Revenue of other general government agencies	4.1	−0.7	1.0
C. Total general government revenues	11.2	−3.7	5.0
D. Public enterprises	20.9	−8.5	−14.2
1. Foreign sales of goods and services	14.3	−3.5	−7.8
a. Three main exporters	13.0	−3.1	−7.2
b. Other	1.3	−0.5	−0.6
2. Domestic sales of goods and services	9.9	−4.1	−1.0
3. Other current income	1.1	−0.4	−0.1
4. Less adjustment for transfers to general government	−4.3	−0.5	−5.2
E. Other	1.5	1.4	2.0
F. Total	33.6	−10.7	−7.3

Source: Author's computations based on unpublished data from the Ministry of Planning, Unit for Policy Analysis (UDAPE), La Paz

have to limit ourselves to qualitative remarks. Note that the fall in NFPS income (direct revenue and taxes on exports and imports) owing to the export downswing was partially offset by taxes falling more on other tradables (petroleum products sold in the domestic market) than on property or income. The fall in the NFPS income and the changes in its composition implied a transfer of resources from the domestic private sector to the public sector. This amount cannot be evaluated.

What happened to expenditure? This point will be examined by considering three sources of transfers from the NFPS to the private sector. The first source is employment and the wage bill. Table 16.10 shows that there was an initial strong reduction in the number of workers after, and as a consequence of, the trade shock. Also, the proportion of public sector workers among formal wage earners declined. The initial

Table 16.10. Slump-induced foregone investment (*million 1985 Bs*)

	Total (1)	Government GFKF (2)	Government share (%) (3)
1985	0.0	0.0	
1986	−2.9	−1.5	52.6
1987	−21.2	−3.0	14.3
1988	−25.4	53.1	−209.0
1989	−57.0	26.4	−46.3
Cumulative 1986–89	−106.6	74.9	
Present value 1986–89	−86.1	59.4	

Sources and notes:
Col. (1): col. (7) of Table 16.2
Col. (2): col. (3) of Table 16.8
Col. (3) = col. (2) divided by col. (1) times 100

dismissal of workers produced large savings to the NFPS. Also, the wage bill of the public sector, as percentage of GDP, decreased strongly on the impact of the shock but returned to levels similar to those of 1982 during 1987–89.

Second, private sector real wages steadily recovered after their strong fall in the last quarter of 1985 (as shown in Table 16.6). Has this had an effect on real wages in the NFPS? By 1987 most of the adjustments of the stabilisation programme had probably ended. After that year, differences in real wage increases can be assumed to be largely determined either by the evolution of the external sector or by the measures taken domestically to cope with it. We can infer from the comparison of Tables 16.6 and 16.13 that wages in the overall public sector have lagged wages in the private sector since 1987. By the end of 1989, wages in the public sector were even behind the wages in the traditionally low-paying sector of commerce.

Third, regarding changes in the commodity markets, we made the point before that the initial increase in the price of NT consumer goods relative to the price of import substitutes was a consequence of the stabilisation programme; afterwards this relative price barely moved.

The price of NT capital goods decreased relative to the price of import substitutes in 1986, causing a negative transfer to the private sector. From 1987 on, and especially in 1988 and 1989, the active NFPS investment programme strongly increased the price of NT capital, and therefore the transfers to the private sector became large and positive.

This transfer to the private sector, via the NT capital goods markets, can be attributed only indirectly to the slump. We should not overlook the fact that the trade shock (and the stabilisation programme) induced compensatory financing and other foreign credits for distress alleviation. It is these loans to the government that produced an increment in NFPS expenditure on NT capital goods and, hence, the transfers.

To summarise, although it is true that the trade shock primarily influenced the NFPS, the private sector was significantly affected by it. The shock was transmitted from the public sector to the private sector through two main mechanisms: first, major changes in the tax structure that shifted the burden from trade taxes to domestic taxes (albeit of tradables) and, second, through expenditure, with major cuts in the public payroll and in NT consumer goods. NFPS expenditure on NT capital goods became the main transfer mechanism of foreign aid to the private sector, especially after 1987. A non-negligible fraction of this foreign aid was intended for consumption-smoothing after the shock.

16.5.3. Changes Caused by the Slump

Assets We recall that the trade shock does not seem to have impaired the NFPS investment programme in the aggregate, unlike what happened with private sector investment. GFKF in the NFPS was lower than expected only in 1986 and 1987 (Table 16.10). In those two years, the forgone NFPS investment represented 52.6% and 14.3% of total forgone investment. In 1988 a turnaround occurred. It is worth noting that even if the ESF contribution of around 77.5 million 1975 Bs (around U$117.2 million) is deducted from the cumulative GFKF of Bs 75.3 million, only Bs 2.2 million less than the counterfactual will be obtained. This lends support to our hypothesis of a huge policy-induced adjustment in the investment programme of the public sector.

Table 16.11 summarises the main results on the changes in income, assets, and savings. We can see that the NFPS suffered a greater income loss than the private sector because of the trade shock, as expected from the nature of the Bolivian export sector in 1985–89. The NFPS had to cope with 68.2% of the total GDY loss, whereas the private sector took the remaining 31.8%. The public sector reduced its consumption proportionately more than the private sector. This is reflected in the substantial differences in the savings rates between the public and private sectors. This probably reflects differences in perceptions. The government—and the international organisations that supported the stabilisation programme—thought of the reversal of the price shock towards a more normal price as a slow process; anyway, more so than the public.

We may conclude that the government partially revised its permanent income and, therefore, reduced its consumption, although by less than its fall in income. Again, the effects on the budget of the trade shock are intertwined with those of the inflation stabilisation. The latter hardened,

Table 16.11. Distribution of changes in assets and savings rates (*million 1985 Bs*)

1. Change in public assets	−110.6
2. Change in private assets	−80.7
3. Total value of windfall	−348.0
4. Gross windfall income of public sector	−237.2
5. Gross windfall income of private sector	−110.8
6. Gross windfall income of public sector (% of total)	68.2
7. Gross windfall income of private sector (% of total)	31.8
8. Overall savings rate (%)	55.0
9. Savings rate in public sector (%)	46.6
10. Savings rate in private sector (%)	72.8

Sources and notes:
Line 1: from col. (3) plus col. (5) of Table 16.8
Line 2 = col. (7) of Table 16.2 minus col. (3) of Table 16.3 minus line 1 of this table
Line 3 = col. (2) minus col. (4) of table 16.2
Line 4: from col. (1) of table 16.8
Line 5 = line 3 minus line 4
Line 6 = line 4 over line 3
Line 7 = line 5 over line 3
Line 8 = (line 1 plus line 2) over line 3
Line 9 = line 1 over line 4
Line 10 = line 2 over line 5

as it had to, the government's budget. So, most of the reduction in consumption took place in the first year of implementation of the stabilisation programme. There was even a primary surplus! The initial drastic adjustment smoothed the way for further adjustments to cope with the trade shock.

Expenditure on tradables and non-tradables Figure 16.8 shows a decomposition of the expenditure of the NFPS (as a proportion of GDP) into tradables and non-tradables. The pre-shock years are included in the figure for comparative purposes.

The most striking feature in Figure 16.8 is the decline in NFPS consumption of non-tradables. Observe that NFPS consumption of tradables was, during 1985–89, only slightly below the consumption of the pre-shock years.

Regarding the GFKF of the NFPS a mild recovery in its tradable content (as a percentage of GDP) occurred after the shock of 1985. NFPS expenditure on NT capital goods increased by less than the one on T capital in 1986 but in 1987 and 1988 it grew more rapidly. The resumption of the government's construction programme explains this. Although the negative trade shock did not have a strong impact on the level of GFKF in the NFPS (if anything it was positive), it had an impact on its composition. NT investment received more weight.

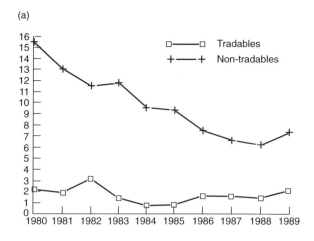

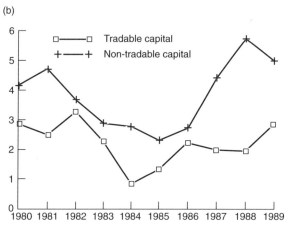

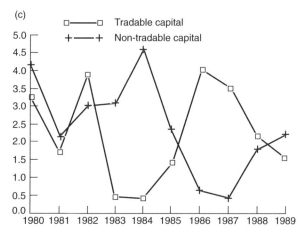

Figure 16.8. Composition of consumption and investment in terms of tradables and non-tradables (% of GDP): (a) public consumption (b) public investment (c) private investment

Private NT GFKF (as a share of GDP) initially suffered a strong fall. This decline continued in 1987 but at a slower rate, and there was a recovery from 1988 on. In contrast, there was a rapid rise in T GFKF in the private sector on the impact of the shock, but it declined afterwards. The combination of the stabilisation programme, the opening of the economy, and the trade shock, which prompted investments in the private sector to replace capital equipment, explains this feature.

Labour allocation between the public and private sectors As shown in Table 16.12, the shock caused a reduction in the number of workers in the public

Table 16.12. Labour and wages in the public sector

	No. of workers (thousands) (1)	As a percentage of formal wage earners (2)	Wage bill as a percentage of GDP (3)
1980	170.1	49.7	12.8
1981	174.6	48.1	11.3
1982	182.6	46.0	9.2
1983	190.2	47.8	8.4
1984	202.0	48.4	13.4
1985	211.5	47.0	9.4
1986	180.9	46.6	6.6
1987	174.9	44.6	7.8
1988	175.5	42.3	9.7
1989	179.4	39.7	8.9

Sources: Col. (1) and col. (2): UDAPE (1989)
Col. (3): Otálora (1990), except for 1989, where preliminary estimate of author is used

Table 16.13. Real wages in the public sector
(1987 = 100)

	Public enterprises (1)	Overall public sector (2)
1988.1	130.9	116.1
2	127.5	117.6
3	120.2	119.1
4	122.7	122.3
1989.1	111.1	121.0
2	130.7	120.0
3	121.9	110.8
4	106.3	105.9

Sources and notes: National Institute of Statistics; real wages are nominal wages deflated by the CPI of final month of quarter

sector. The most dramatic case occurred in the state-owned mining corporation COMIBOL, where 21,000 out of 27,600 miners were laid off. In the
same table we observe a strong decline in the public sector wage bill (as a
percentages of GDP) in the first year after the shock; afterwards, the share
substantially recovered. Employment in the public sector has reduced its
participation in the whole of waged employment and in the distribution
of income. This was an important consequence of the shock. Real wages in
the sector fell sharply (Table 16.13).

16.5.4. *Financing the Budget Deficit*

The ways of financing the overall budget deficit are shown in lines I and J of
Table 16.7 (as percentages of GDP) and in Table 16.14 in million current Bs.
If unrequited transfers and 'other expenditures' (lines E and G in Table
16.7) are deducted from the primary surplus (line C in Table 16.7), a net
positive resource transfer to the NFPS appears, for all years between 1987
and 1989. Domestic and foreign sources financed this resource transfer.

Regarding foreign financing, long- and medium-term flows generally
took the form of development loans, arrears in interest payments, and
reduction of Bolivia's asset holdings in Argentina. It can be argued that
the long- and medium-term financing was used for GFKF and interest
service. Short-term foreign loans and the depletion of foreign exchange
assets, including the foreign exchange reserves (usually misclassified as
domestic financing) were used to finance a significant part of the unrequited transfers and the temporary gaps between tax revenues and
current exhaustible expenditures.

The discussion above cannot easily be translated into a counterfactual
given the difficulty in identifying the sources of additional finance of the

Table 16.14. Financing the budget deficit *(million current Bs)*

	Domestic	Foreign	Overall deficit	Inferred change in primary deficit	
				Million Bs	As a percentage of overall deficit
	(1)	(2)	(3)	(4)	(5)
1986	−282.1	491.3	209.2	−219.5	−104.9
1987	461.8	221.6	683.4	366.7	53.7
1988	180.3	495.6	675.9	384.9	57.0
1989	355.8	257.9	613.7	352.2	57.4

Sources and notes: Col. (1) to col. (3): UDAPE (1991)
Col. (4): from col. (5) in Table 16.8, converted to current Bs with implicit GDP deflators
Col. (5) = col. (4) divided by col. (3) times 100

shock-induced deficit. We can only say that the inferred change in the primary deficit fluctuated around 56% of the overall deficit if one leaves out 1986 (col. 5 in Table 16.14). We could assume, without a strong base however, that the financing of the inferred deficit was mostly foreign (including in this concept the losses in foreign exchange reserves). The limited domestic financing of the overall deficit, and the even more limited financing of the induced deficit with monetary emission, explain why Bolivia could maintain its stabilisation programme despite the very adverse shock.

16.6. The Shock and the Policy Reforms of 1985

16.6.1. The Trade Slump and the Management of the Foreign Exchange Reserves

Shortly after the tin crash of October 1985, an attack on the reserves of the central bank occurred. Private agents feared either: (1) a weakening of the NFPS budget that would again induce excessive seignorage; or (2) that not enough dollars would be available later, should they need them for imports or to hedge themselves against accelerating inflation.

In the first weeks after the tin crisis the central bank drastically reduced the amount of foreign exchange reserves that it supplied to the public. A big jump devaluation of the Bolivian peso ensued. Altered expectations depreciated the exchange rate beyond what the reserve position justified and the monetary authorities expected. Again, as during the hyper-inflation, private agents reduced their cash holdings of domestic money to a minimum and inflation seemed to rekindle.

In reaction the authorities tightened fiscal and monetary policies even more to stabilise the exchange rate. The stabilisation of inflation followed. In the first weeks of February 1986 inflation was again under control. The jump devaluation of the exchange rate, after the trade shock, produced a jump increase in the price level. With flexible prices in most of the markets and, therefore, little potential for inertial inflation, the initial price-level jump was not followed by other price increases. It sufficed to restrain fiscal and monetary expansion to regain control.

The control of inflation and depreciation did not imply that the foreign exchange situation had come to rest. The huge trade deficits produced by the fall in export revenues, followed besides by an expansion of consumption after years of repression, compounded balance of payments problems that were already severe because of the interest charges on the external debt (Table 16.15). The current account deficits were particularly high in 1986 and 1987. From 1987 to 1989, the net unrestricted foreign exchange reserves dwindled.

Table 16.15. Balance of payments: current account balance and net foreign exchange reserves (*million US$*)

	Current account balance (1)	Net reserves (2)	Net unrestricted reserves (3)
1985	−444.5	136.2	51.2
1986	−385.4	246.6	22.6
1987	−507.7	168.4	−79.5
1988	−316.0	160.9	−5.7
1989	−149.9	18.6	−38.0

Source and Notes: Central Bank of Bolivia (1990)
Col. (3): reserves excluding gold and reserves held at Central Bank of Argentina earmarked for imports of Argentinian goods and services

16.6.2. Equilibrium in the Money Market

Following Bevan *et al.* in Chapter 2 we assume that the transactions demand for money relates to permanent income and that the assets demand for money follows the transient component of income. At the risk of some simplification, we can assimilate the demand for currency and demand deposits in the banking system, i.e. M_1, with the transactions component of demand. On the other hand, we assume that the assets demand for money is satisfied by time deposits and certificates of deposit (CDs) issued by the central bank.

In view of Bolivia's recent history, the expected inflation rate is also a major determinant of both transactions and assets demand for domestic money. The very high degree of dollarisation is a main feature of the Bolivian monetary landscape. Most time deposits and CDs are in dollars or dollar-indexed. Little of the money stock in Bs can be considered as responding to the asset demand for money. As a consequence, the transient component of liability with the domestic private sector in the foreign exchange reserves is limited to the required banking reserves on time deposits and the stock of CDs.

The events of the last quarter of 1985 created the informational problem of where the demand for money stood. To play on the safe side the monetary authorities continued their tight control of the money supply. Thus, the NFPS accumulated more deposits than loans with the central bank between 1986 and 1988.[19] This policy preserved the bank's foreign exchange reserves. In addition, the policy, working through interest rates, induced a very significant repatriation of private capital. The radical fall in inflation had to augment the transactions demand for money. Yet, the money supply did not follow, for the reasons given above. This led to a temporary disequilibrium in the money market, which was conducive to very high real interest rates that choked a faster recovery. The recovery in the NT capital goods sector and of income was slower than otherwise and mostly spanned by fiscal policy.[20]

16.6.3. Trade Policy and the Slump

The trade shock did not lead to a reversal of the NEP's trade liberalisation. Was the trade liberalisation more easily sustainable because of the negative shock? The answer seems to be yes. To see this, let us assume that the negative trade shock did not happen. With immobile capital in the short run, the trade liberalisation would have released labour from the sector of import substitutes to the sector of non-tradables and traditional exportables (mining and natural gas). Wages would have decreased relative to the return of capital in the sectors of non-tradables and exportables, and increased in the sector of importables. Therefore, with fixed capital, employment and output would have increased in the sectors of non-tradables and exportables, and declined in importables. Since the export sector is very capital intensive, the increase in employment and output there would have been small and surely less than in the non-tradable sector.[21]

The negative trade shock produced a deterioration in the price of traditional exports relative to the domestic price of importables. Also, it reduced the foreign exchange accruing to the government. This caused speculative behaviour among the public that threatened to deplete the weakened central bank's foreign reserves even more. The reduction in the demand for domestic money while private income was not significantly impaired by the impact of the shock had to be faced with a strong devaluation, which only then lowered the private sector's real income. The cut in private income reduced its demand for non-traded goods.

The negative trade shock and liberalisation thus produced movements in relative prices in opposite directions. The shock somewhat shielded the sector of importables (and induced a shift of resources to new export sectors). Without the shock liberalisation would have been more difficult to sustain.

The opening of the economy put recurrent pressures on the current account of the balance of payments. The repatriated capital, induced by the high interest rates, avoided the full translation of this additional pressure into pressure on the reserves. Domestic banks, the direct recipients of repatriated capital, provided the required funds to finance imports.

Did the growth of imports, mostly of consumer goods, pre-empt private sector investment demand and, hence, slow the reallocation process and the attainment of the new long-run equilibrium? The description above suggests an affirmative answer. Indeed, the flow of repatriated capital substituted export income, but this change in the composition of the import capacity was accompanied by an increase in the cost of capital for the private sector.[22] The conjecture that the interaction of very tight monetary policy (partially but significantly owing to the price bust) and trade liberalisation caused higher interest rates than otherwise seems plausible. Through this indirect channel imports crowded out private investment, at least of those domestic firms that could not finance themselves abroad.

16.7. Concluding Remarks

In this chapter we have applied the theory of construction booms. The theory has given us a systematic approach to the implications of the shock on Gross Domestic Income, on savings and investment decisions, on resource reallocations, on changes in relative prices, and on the balance between the private and the public sectors. We referred also to the control of inflation, a major Bolivian concern, and how it was maintained despite the shock.

Rich as the theory of construction booms is, it was sometimes insufficient for our objective of separating out the effects of the shock from other effects caused by major policy changes. The construction of counterfactuals is always problematic, but in the Bolivian case it was especially so. In particular, it has been very difficult to isolate the substitution effects in production and consumption caused by the shock from those arising from the inflation-stabilisation and trade-reform programmes.

Despite the criticisms that can be levelled against the methodology of this chapter, the very general conclusion stands, that after the negative shock Bolivia could smooth the transition to a new equilibrium rather well. The unwavering application of the policy reforms, undertaken just before the shock, and the resumption of foreign credits largely explain this outcome. The dramatic conditions when the shock hit the economy did not preclude the adjustment.

The huge adjustment in the public sector is a major explanatory factor of the situation after the shock. The government's management of the shock, which benefited from the support (financial and with advice) of the official international creditors, explains the substantial shifts in resource allocation and in the structure of production observed now. The exchange rate regime, which allowed a significant devaluation without dramatic public announcements, is another major explanatory factor. It is also possible—though it is not documented in our study—that illegal cocaine exports eased the adjustment.

Appendix
Data Sources for the Decompositions in Figure 16.8

Data	Source
GDP in current and in 1980 prices, in domestic currency	NIS as reported in Central Bank of Bolivia (1991)
GFKF/GDP (derived from current Bs)	World Bank (1990a), except for 1989, which is based on NIS data as reported in Central Bank of Bolivia (1991)
Public GFKF/GDP ratio Private GFKF/GDP ratio (derived from current Bs)	World Bank (1990a), except for 1989, which comes from unpublished data from UDAPE
Non Traded GFKF/GFKF ratio (derived from 1980 Bs)	ECLA (1990), corresponds to ratio of construction investment in total GFKF
Traded GFKF/GFKF ratio	One less the non-traded GFKF/GFKF ratio
GFKF data in Bs (in current prices and in 1985 prices)	NIS as reported in Central Bank of Bolivia (1991)
Value-added in construction (in Bs, 1985 prices)	NIS as reported in Central Bank of Bolivia (1991)
Implicit deflators of value-added in construction	Unpublished data of NIS until 1987, thereafter author's estimate based on an index of construction costs
Imports in US$ decomposed into: Consumer imports Consumer non-durables Consumer durables Intermediate goods imports Capital goods	Central Bank of Bolivia (1990)
Imports in US$ decomposed into: Public sector imports Private sector imports	Central Bank of Bolivia (1990)

Notes: NIS is the Bolivian National Institute of Statistics

NOTES

I would like to thank David Bevan, Paul Collier, Jan Gunning, Rolando Jordán, Ernesto Sheriff, and Rosemary Thorp for very helpful comments on earlier drafts. Rafael Boyán provided research assistance.

1. Note, however, that the power of the available tests on the random walk hypothesis is weak (Kletzer *et al.* 1990).

2. The ITAs were price-stabilisation schemes negotiated between the majority of producer countries and most of the main consumers of tin. Six ITAs were agreed between 1956 and 1985. The GSA stockpile was built up in the 1950s; in the following two decades it was (partially) depleted. The depletion followed a discontinuous path, mixing rapid sales with long periods of inactivity.
3. Calabre (1991: 103–11) gives a very informative background of the tin crisis of 1985.
4. The illegal cocaine exports, considered to be important, are not included in the computation of the terms of trade. We shall ignore these exports in this study because of the lack of reliable data.
5. It is true that many mines would have not been closed had not the economy been in the midst of a stabilisation effort.
6. More complete descriptions of the Bolivian stabilisation programme can be found in Sachs (1987) and Morales (1988).
7. These estimates of forgone income, as a percentage of GDP, are smaller by around 1.2% than the estimate found in Morales (1992), who uses the methodology of World Bank (1990b: 14).
8. The numbers in Table B5 of Morales (1994), on which Figure 16.6 is based, need to be interpreted with caution since the quality of the data on the prices for non-tradables is weak. However, the direction of the changes in relative prices seems correct and is consistent with other information.
9. Quarterly values would have been more informative. Unfortunately, there are no data of this frequency for NT capital goods. After the shock, contrary to expectations, the prices of NT consumer goods relative to the price of import substitutes experienced a jump which lasted until the third quarter of 1986. We argue that the short-run effects of the stabilisation and liberalisation programmes explain the initial rise in the relative price of NT consumer goods more than the shock. The argument runs as follows. During the hyperinflation consumer importables were also demanded as assets. For a given real rate of interest, increases in the expected (real) rate of exchange depreciation raised the demand for importables and its domestic price relative to the price of NT goods. After stabilisation, expected depreciation decreased and so did the demand and the relative price of importables. The trade liberalisation and the larger availability of credits to finance consumer imports further reduced this relative price. In more conventional terms, the real exchange rate appreciated after the stabilisation programme. This appreciation in the aftermath of a stabilisation programme is a common feature of many high-inflation countries (Bruno *et al.* 1988).
10. The long-run changes in relative prices after the trade shock and the liberalisation will be very different from the short-run effects. They will depend on the capital/labour intensities. The information available suggests that the capital/labour ratio in the production of non-tradables is lower than in the production of importables, and the capital/labour ratio in importables is lower than in exportables. This pattern of capital/labour ratios is typical of mining countries. With full factor mobility, for the price of non-tradables to increase relative to the price of import substitutes, there must be a fall in the price of exports relative to import substitutes.

11. The index of non-traded capital goods should follow the construction value-added index. This is not, however, the case because the National Accounts data register changes over time in the technical coefficients of value-added to final output.

12. Namely, the tax-sharing arrangements between the central government, the decentralised regional development corporations and the municipalities, brought about by the tax reform of 1986, and the Emergency Social Fund (ESF). The ESF, a public works programme, was created to mitigate the severe hardships imposed by the stabilisation programme and the trade shocks on the poorest urban groups.

13. The Bolivian data on employment and wages are of a very poor quality. Therefore, we need extreme caution in making inferences based on them. Note, for instance, that mean wages for the whole are in almost all quarters higher than wages in all sectors, except financial establishments. Since workers in financial establishments constitute a small share of all formal workers there is the suspicion that Table 16.6 is not consistent, even if one allows for much higher wages in the former than in the latter.

14. The item informs us more on the difficulties associated with high-inflation accounting and on the lack of adequate treatment of the exchange rate depreciations, than on resource movements. Because the item does not imply resource movements, it was added to the 'unrequited transfer' account in our previous versions.

15. This definition differs from the more conventional one where only interest payments are excluded from the overall surplus/deficit to yield the primary surplus.

16. A reduction in foreign exchange reserves implies an increase in the net foreign debt.

17. From Table 16.9, line C, we obtain the reverse Olivera–Tanzi effect plus the 1986 tax reform effect, as a percentage of GDP, $3.7 + 5.0 = 8.7$. From this we subtract the incidence of petroleum taxes, 3.9 (line A2), to obtain 4.8. This value added to 22.9, which was the revenue/GDP ratio of 1983–85, yields 27.7.

18. Comparisons with the bizarre years of the hyperinflation may be misleading.

19. The mandatory deposits of the public enterprises in the Central Bank were the main instrument to control the expansion of the money base. Also note that Central Bank credit to the private sector was almost entirely financed with foreign loans and did not give rise to significant money creation. The foreign loans are included in the counterpart account in 'Other' in Table 16.18.

20. A fuller description of the monetary events in the aftermath of the trade shock is given in Morales (1994).

21. Note that the long-run effects would be entirely different, as discussed in note 10.

22. The supply curve of foreign funds can be thought as a kinked curve, with a horizontal segment at (or below) world interest rates going up to the availability of funds from official lenders, followed by an upward-sloping segment fed by private lenders. Since access to international commercial banks was not possible, the upward-sloping segment mainly, but not exclusively, captures the supply of repatriated capital.

REFERENCES

Bruno, M., G. Di Tella, R. Dornbusch and S. Fischer (eds) (1988) *Inflation Stabilization: The Experience of Israel, Argentina, Brazil, Bolivia. and Mexico*, Cambridge, MA: MIT Press.

Calabre, Serge (1991) *L'Etain* (Tin), Paris: Economica.

CEMYD (Centro de Estudios Minería y Desarrollo) (1990) *Desempeño y Colapso de la Minería Nacionalizada en Bolivia* (Performance and Colapse of the Nationalized Mines in Bolivia), La Paz.

Central Bank of Bolivia of (1990) 'Boletín del Sector Externo' (External Sector Bulletin), No. 4, 1980-90, La Paz (December).

——(1991) 'Boletín Estadístico' (Statistical Bulletin), No. 269, La Paz (March).

ECLA (United Nations Economic Commission for Latin America) (1990) 'Statistical Yearbook for Latin America and the Caribbean', Santiago de Chile: ECLA.

Grilli, E. and M.C. Yang (1988) 'Primary Commodity Prices, Manufactured Good Prices, and the Terms of Trade of Developing Countries: What the Long Run Shows', *The World Bank Economic Review*, 2 (1): 1–47.

Kletzer, K.M., D.M. Newbery and B.D. Wright (1990) 'Alternative Instruments for Smoothing the Consumption of Primary Commodity Exporters', World Bank, International Economics Department, WPS 558 (December).

Morales, J.A. (1988) 'Inflation Stabilization in Bolivia', in M. Bruno *et al.* (eds), *Inflation Stabilization: The Experience of Israel, Argentina, Brazil, Bolivia and Mexico*, Cambridge, MA: MIT Press, 307–60.

——(1992) 'Reformas Estructurales y Crecimiento Económico en Bolivia' (Structural Reforms and Economic Growth in Bolivia), in J. Vial (ed.) *¿Adonde va América Latina? Balance de las Reformas Económicas*, Santiago de Chile: CIEPLAN, 103–34.

——(1994) 'The Vulnerability of Inflation Stabilization to External Shocks: A Case Study of Bolivia', in E. Bacha (ed.), *Economics in a Changing World: Development, Trade and the Environment*, New York: St Martin's Press, 171–94.

Morales, J.A., J. Espejo and G. Chavez (1993) 'Temporary External Shocks and Stabilization Policies for Bolivia', in E. Engel and P. Meller (eds), *External Shocks and Stabilization Mechanisms*, Washington, DC: Inter-American Development Bank, 173–220.

Morawetz, D. (1986) 'Beyond Tin and Natural Gas, What?', World Bank Latin American and Caribbean Regional Office, mimeo.

Otálora, C.R. (1990) 'La Política Fiscal Boliviana de 1975 a 1988', Universidad Católica Boliviana, Instituto de Investigaciones Socio-Económicas DT 90/02 (February).

Sachs, J. (1987) 'The Bolivian Hyperinflation and Stabilization', *American Economic Review*, 77 (2): 279–83.

UDAPE (Bolivia, Ministry of Planning, Unit for Policy Analysis) (1989) 'Dossier Estadístico' (Statistical Dossier), La Paz (Septermber).

——(1991) 'Estadísticas Económicas de Bolivia' (Economic Statistics of Bolivia), No. 2, La Paz (June).

World Bank (1988) 'Commodity Trade and Price Trends', 1987–88 Edition. Washington, DC: World Bank.

——(1990a) 'Bolivia: Updating Economic Memorandum', Report No. 8623–BO, Washington DC: World Bank.
——(1990b) 'Adjustment Lending Policies for Sustainable Growth', Country Economics Department, Policy and Research Series, No. 14.

17

Dealing with Negative Oil Shocks: The Venezuelan Experience in the 1980s

RICARDO HAUSMANN

17.1. The Venezuelan Mess: Dancing out of Step or Stepping out of Line?

The 1980s were, by all accounts, a terrible decade for Venezuelan development. GDP per capita, which increased by 234% from 1950 to 1980, or 4.0% per year, had a cumulative fall of 18.1% between 1980 and 1989. The currency, which had only been (moderately) devalued once in over a century, depreciated tenfold between 1983 and 1989. The yearly inflation rate, which had averaged 3.4% for the period 1950–80, reached 84% in 1989. The foreign debt, which was negligible in 1974, totalled 54% of GDP or more than three years of exports by 1989. Was this havoc due to particularly incompetent or irresponsible management of economic policy—i.e. stepping out of line—or to the difficulties found in keeping pace with a very unstable and unpredictable source of revenue—i.e. dancing out of step? After all, the world petroleum market, to which the country traditionally directed over 90% of its exports, passed through very unsettled waters. As shown in Figure 17.1, oil exports at 1990 prices reached US$24 billion in 1980 and fell to 10.2 billion in 1989, a decline of 66.4% in real per capita terms, or of 17.7% of 1980 GDP.

The fall in external income followed the two well-known positive shocks of the 1970s and also came in two steps. The first one, in 1982–83, was linked to OPEC's attempts to defend oil prices by cutting output. It reduced the real value of exports (at 1990 prices) from US$22.4 billion a year for 1979–81 to US$15.9 billion for 1983–85. The second one took place when prices collapsed in 1986 and cut real exports down to US$9.5 billion for 1986–89. Relative to 1980 GDP, these two negative shocks amounted to 8.5% and 8.2%, respectively.

Furthermore, there were important similarities between the two shocks. In both cases, the shocks hit the economy just after it had gone through a stabilisation effort which had left the economy with significant external surpluses and with high international reserves. The fiscal accounts were also brought into surplus. In both cases, just before the shock it was felt

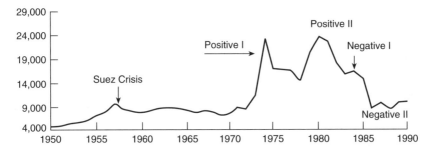

Figure 17.1. Oil exports at constant 1990 prices

that the economic situation had been stabilised, prompting the government to increase its public spending in order to reduce rising unemployment. When the negative shock came, thus wiping out the existing surplus and leaving a significant deficit, the government had already committed itself to fiscal expansion and was also well into its five-year term, when hard decisions are difficult to make.

Hence, economic policy did not react with sufficient swiftness to these two negative shocks, causing, each time, a collapse in the policy regime. In 1983, in the wake of a massive attack against the currency, the traditional fixed exchange rate system was abandoned and a multiple exchange regime was adopted. After the second negative shock, the foreign exchange premium rose to a point where the government decided to abandon that exchange system in 1989 and replace it with a unified float. Hence, the two shocks took place under rather different control regimes and led to important changes in the regimes themselves. Summary data on the macroeconomic adjustment to the two shocks are presented in Table 17.1.

The study of external or trade shocks has tended to focus on the windfall side.[1] The general theme has concentrated on the fact that the additional resources have not usually been put to the best use while they have seriously distorted optimal long-run resource allocation. The Dutch Disease literature[2] developed this argument into a coherent theoretical framework. Policy discussions dealt mainly with the issue of how best to allocate the windfall, which in most cases meant how to save it.[3]

This emphasis was to be expected in light of the positive commodity shocks of the 1970s. However, during the 1980s, negative shocks tended to dominate. Obviously, the models built to explain positive shocks can shed much light on what happens on the down side, but there is an important feature specific to negative shocks: they affect the solvency of the government. Private agents may come to realise or believe that the current policy framework is no longer viable and may attempt to secure their assets through speculative attacks in anticipation of debt repudiation,

Table 17.1. Summary data on the two shocks

	1981	1985	1989	1985–81	1989–85
Balance of payments (bn. US$)					
Oil exports	19.1	12.8	9.9	−6.3	−2.9[a]
Import of goods FOB	12.4	7.5	7.1	−4.9	−0.4[a]
Trade balance	7.8	6.8	5.9	−1.0	−0.9[a]
Current account	2.1	3.3	2.5	1.2	−0.8[a]
Net international reserves (excl. gold)	16.3	12.0	2.5	−4.3	−9.5[a]
Non-oil GDP	336.7	3,626.9	350.5	−0.7%	1.8%
Absorption	444.3	376.2	370.8	−4.1%	−0.4%
Public sector deficit (% of GDP)	−1.6	0.1	−1.7		
Unemployment[b]	6.1	12.1	9.8	6.0	−2.3[a]
Inflation (consumer prices)[c]	11.4	9.1	81.0	13.6	43.4[d]
Nominal exchange rates (bolivars per US$)					
Official exchange rate[e]	4.3	7.5	43.8	14.9%	55.5%[d]
Parallel rate	—	14.7	—		
Exchange premium	—	96.0	—		
Relative prices					
Tradables *vs.* non-tradables	100.0	103.6	102.2	3.6%	−1.4%[f]
Non-tradable capital *vs.* non-tradable conrumer goods	100.0	94.6	94.7	−5.4%	0.0%[f]

[a] Arithmetic difference
[b] Second semester of each year
[c] December to December
[d] Annual rate of change
[e] December of each year
[f] Accumulated percentage change

Source: Central Bank of Venezuela

devaluation or regime change. This may lead to capital flight or large inventory shifts or may severely limit the availability of external financing needed to cushion the blow. Moreover, these anticipatory reactions of economic agents against future changes in policy may be self-fulfilling (Obstfeld 1986a) and may severely constrain public policy. A central message of this chapter is that such behaviour may become dominant at the macroeconomic level, dwarfing other responses which would other-wise be expected. Moreover, the precise nature of the private sector's anticipatory reaction is highly dependent on the nature of the control regime in place, since it will tend to determine the avenues which are open for attack.

The Venezuelan experience in the 1980s is a particularly fertile ground for the analysis of negative shocks. Two large shocks took place under very different control regimes, thus highlighting the role which the institutional setting plays in determining the response. Moreover, the experience can shed a different light on the suitability of alternative exchange rate regimes for countries subject to large and frequent trade shocks. In addition, the analysis can be simplified for two reasons: first, oil shocks only have direct effects on the public sector, thus implying that it is the policy reaction to the shock that will affect households and firms. Second, the supply response of the oil industry is not of macroeconomic interest.[4]

The chapter is structured as follows. Section 17.2 presents a brief summary of theoretical literature on the impacts negative shocks have under alternative exchange rate regimes. Section 17.3 provides a brief description of macroeconomic developments in Venezuela and their relationship to oil market events. Section 17.4 discusses the nature of the two negative oil shocks which will be analysed in this chapter, proving their permanent nature. Section 17.5 presents some aspects of the methodology used to quantify the shocks and the macroeconomic adjustment to them. Sections 17.6 and 17.7 present the detailed analysis of the two negative shocks of the 1980s. In Section 17.8 we try to derive the main conclusions and lessons.

17.2. Adjustment to Negative Permanent Shocks: A Quick Theoretical Overview

In this section we review the theoretical literature so as to have some *a priori* assumptions on what we should find when looking at the Venezuelan data. We start by analysing the optimal adjustment to a negative oil shock as can be derived from the standard small open economy model. We will then turn to some of the complications which arise under fixed, multiple and flexible exchange rate systems.

A negative oil shock in the Venezuelan context is simultaneously an external and a fiscal shock. As an external shock, optimal adjustment requires a real depreciation and a fall in absorption. Output should remain at full employment (Salter 1959 and Swan 1960). Now, since the shock is fiscal, something must be done about the increased public deficit. Inaction is dangerous, although the precise nature of the costs involved depends on the type of exchange rate regime. If the deficit is cut through a reduction in purchases of tradables, the economy will remain unaffected. If instead, fiscal adjustment is done through an increase in taxes or through a reduction in expenditure on non-tradables then the shock will be transmitted to the private sector, causing a reduction in private spending. Not much else can be said unless we clarify the nature of the exchange rate regime.

Under a fixed exchange rate regime, reserves will be drawn down (or external debt accumulated) unless other policies are changed. If the government attempts to reduce the deficit by means of either a cut in spending on non-tradables or an increase in taxes, and assuming nominal wages adjust sluggishly, there will be a recession, which will cause unemployment to rise, private real wealth to be drawn down and nominal wages to fall, leading gradually to a real depreciation.

If instead the government devalues the currency then (assuming sluggish nominal wage adjustment) there will be an immediate fall in the external and fiscal deficits. This is due to several effects. First, the devaluation will increase the output of and reduce the demand for tradables, causing the resource gap to fall. These effects will tend to have an expansionary influence on output. Second, real financial wealth of the private sector will fall owing to the jump in the average price level, causing a cut in spending and an increase in savings needed to restore desired levels of financial wealth. Third, there will be an important income effect owing to the rise in real value of oil exports and of imports. Since the government is a net exporter and the private sector is a net importer, a transfer of income will take place, reducing private revenue and the public deficit. These last two effects will have a contractionary impact on output, provided the government does not spend the additional devaluation-induced revenue. The Venezuelan experience during the 1980s suggests that contractionary effects dominate in the short run. However, in the long run, these changes will be reversed and the economy will go back to a balance of payments crisis. Devaluations by themselves have only temporary effects.

These results assume that agents do not foresee a collapse in the policy regime. However, much more interesting results appear if this assumption is relaxed. In one possible framework, agents will be assessing the solvency of the government, that is, its inter-temporal budget constraint.[5] If they feel that future action on the deficit will not be forthcoming or that the ability to borrow may be insufficient,[6] they will guess that the government will be forced to default on the real value of its obligations. One way is to default on the nominal value of its liabilities, as Mexico did in 1982 with the Mex-dollars or as Argentina and Brazil did in early 1990 with banking deposits.[7] A simpler way to default is through a devaluation, which reduces the real value of the monetary base and of domestic bonds. Recognising these possibilities, domestic agents will try to convert their wealth into foreign assets through capital flight, prompting a balance of payments crisis.

Also, as discussed in Chapter 1, inventory accumulation of tradable goods in anticipation of the collapse may take place, with stocks falling to normal levels thereafter. This will accentuate the loss of reserves through the current account and may have important output effects, since demand for non-tradables is likely to fall. Also, if domestic tradables are less than perfect substitutes of foreign goods, their output may rise. After the collapse, these effects will be reversed, meaning that crises may cause signifi-cant output effects.

Private fixed capital investment is likely to fall (except for speculative accumulation of tradable equipment in anticipation of the devaluation) because the public expects an eventual recession and does not know the nature of the new regulatory framework.[8] Even if the agents know that there will be a rise in the relative price of tradables, they do not know whether this will be brought about through more protection or through devaluation, making it difficult to choose between specific projects. Given the option value of waiting, investors will stand by until the dust settles.

17.2.1. Adjustment under Multiple Exchange Rates

The standard models of multiple exchange rates (Dornbusch 1976; Edwards 1989) assume that all commercial transactions take place at a single official exchange rate and that all financial transactions occur at a free-floating parallel rate. It is further assumed that imports are demand determined, making the internal price of tradables equal to the foreign price calculated at the official exchange rate.

A slightly different model assumes that official-rate imports are rationed by the government (Hausmann 1990b: ch. 7). This is a plausible hypothesis since it seems unlikely that, in the presence of large exchange premia, official-rate imports could be demand determined.[9] In any case, rationing was important in the Venezuelan case. In this model, the internal price of tradables is endogenous, with importers appropriating a rent.

This model has very different stability properties. First of all, it is unstable: if the government runs a surplus, the parallel rate will gradually fall back to the official rate until the system becomes a fixed exchange rate regime. If the government runs a deficit, the increased money supply will cause prices to rise and the official exchange rate to appreciate in real terms. If the fiscal accounts are such that an appreciation increases the deficit,[10] then the induced monetary expansion will lead to a further real appreciation and a further increase in the deficit. In this process, the premium will be rising until a point where the official exchange rate loses all credibility, prompting the government to devalue it. This may be called a *leaping-peg* system with large maxi-devaluations taking place periodi-cally. What causes this instability is that agents are unable to reduce the supply of money through a deterioration of the balance of payments, since both the current and the capital accounts are now exogenous. If there is a public sector deficit, a money-overhang problem will arise and it will require ever-rising exchange premia.

Interestingly, within a certain range, official-rate devaluations do not affect the domestic price of tradables and may lower inflation since they transfer import rents to the government, thus reducing the fiscal deficit.

Moreover, faced with a negative shock, the government has an additional degree of freedom. It may cut the import ration so as to defend the level of reserves administratively. This policy will have an expansionary impact on output in the short run. It will also increase the premium and speed the rate at which it rises, bringing forward the next official devaluation. Inventories also play an even more destabilising role here than in the fixed exchange rate case. Since agents are not free to increase imports, hoarding will affect any storable good whose price is likely to rise after the collapse, making the demand for internal output much more affected by the inventory cycle.

The standard model of a small open economy with a floating exchange rate generally shows long-run global stability, with the inflation tax covering the unfinanced portion of the fiscal deficit (see Kiguel and Lizondo 1989; Hausmann 1990b). Consequently, there is in principle no possibility of regime collapse.[11]

If we assume that the reserve target of the central bank is exogenous, then a negative shock will have effects on the economy even if there is no explicit fiscal reaction. The shock will cause the net public sector supply of foreign currency to the exchange markets to fall. This will produce an immediate depreciation of the exchange rate, which will overshoot its long-run real level. The jump will be greater if the public sector does not act to reduce the underlying fiscal deficit since, this being the case, economic agents will interpret the fall in external income as having eventually to be financed through the inflation tax. In order to avoid the tax, agents will shift their portfolios towards foreign assets, precipitating the jump in the exchange rate. Thus, the causes of the overshooting are very different from those which arise in the Dornbusch (1976) model.

This jump will have the standard effects of a devaluation: wealth will fall and the fiscal deficit will be reduced (both contractionary effects), and the structure of output and demand will change in reaction to the shift in relative prices (expansionary). The net short-run effect on output is uncertain. Interestingly, in spite of the shock, the current account will move to a surplus. This is the result of agents trying to accumulate foreign assets in order to restore wealth and change its structure, given the expected rise in inflation.

If, on the other hand, the government fully reacts by adjusting the underlying deficit, then expected inflation will not be affected and the exchange rate will not move, but the economy will react with a short-run recession caused by the fall in absorption, with the balance of payments remaining in equilibrium. Hence, the expected reaction of the economy to a negative oil shock is crucially dependent on two aspects. First, the nature of the exchange rate regime; second, the fiscal reaction to the shock. Fortunately, the Venezuelan experience is able to highlight some of these elements, since the period which will be analysed covers all three exchange regimes and all types of fiscal reaction. Nevertheless, it will be important to address the issue of how efficient the adjustment process was. In order to do this we shall distinguish between three concepts of adjustment costs.[12]

The *primary adjustment cost* is the optimal and unavoidable decline in absorption required to return to equilibrium. If all domestic output was perfectly tradable then primary costs would simply equal the external shock minus whatever excess of income over absorption existed prior to the shock. However, since not all output is perfectly tradable, part of the fall in absorption may go not to improve the trade balance but to reduce non-tradable output. If this decline is not compensated by an expansion in tradable production, the economy will remain at full employment and output will fall below trend, generating a further cut in absorption. We refer to this additional effect as the *secondary adjustment cost*. Finally, we should distinguish these two costs from the *actual adjustment costs* paid each year, which may be above or below the sum of the two previous effects depending on whether the economy has over- or underadjusted, leaving an unwarranted surplus or deficit. We will measure these costs in Tables 17.14 and 17.25.

17.3. Some Background on Venezuela

The 1960s were characterised by stagnant oil revenues but growth of 6.5% was maintained through the impulse of import-substitution industrialisation. However, as the decade ended the growth rate started to fall, reaching 4.5% in 1968–69.

The traditional policy regime prior to the oil shocks of the 1970s can be characterised by four major principles: a fixed and unified exchange rate, fixed and rather rigid interest rates, fiscal discipline and protectionist trade policy.[13] This regime appeared to guarantee high growth and a very low inflation rate (1.9% for the period 1950–70). Fiscal balance implied that the exchange rate was viable and interest rates were fixed above world levels, thus securing demand for the instruments offered by the rapidly expanding financial system.

When the first oil shock occurred in 1973, policy discussions dealt almost exclusively with the issue of what to do with the additional fiscal resources. The newly elected government of Carlos Andrés Pérez[14] initially decided to sterilise the windfall revenue abroad 'until profitable investments appeared locally'. However, as the five-year presidency progressed, expenditures, mainly on public sector companies, rose very quickly and oil revenues declined, so that fiscal balance was reached in 1976 and a deficit of 14% of GDP developed by 1978. Growth initially accelerated to over 10% in 1975 and then began to fall, reaching

3.5% in 1978, as shortages of labour and infrastructure became dominant.[15]

By early 1979, the newly elected government faced a rapidly falling reserve level, an exploding foreign debt[16] and repressed inflation. It did not foresee the second oil shock, which occurred just a few months later. It adopted a policy of fiscal cutbacks, mainly on imported goods, and it freed most prices.[17] The economy went into a recession led by a contraction in the construction sector and by a fall in importable output owing to the rapidly appreciating real exchange rate, caused by the gradual return of the overheated economy to its natural rate of unemployment through a rise in real wages. Moreover, political difficulties in adjusting the controlled local interest rates to the jump in international rates led to some capital outflows.

After two years of spending cutbacks (1979–80) and given the apparently permanent character of the second positive oil shock, the government decided to adopt in 1981 an expansionary fiscal policy based on a projected increase in oil revenues of 12% per year. As the policy got under way, the first negative shock of the 1980s appeared, generating current account and fiscal deficits, accompanied by a massive attack on the currency by 1982. In February 1983, after a loss of more than 10 billion US dollars in international reserves, the central bank decided to abandon the traditional unified and fixed exchange rate system and to adopt multiple rates. Capital account transactions were left to a floating exchange market which depreciated by almost 300% in the following six months. Fiscal policy turned contractionary and trade policy became more protectionist.

By 1984–85 the balance of payments and fiscal accounts were showing impressive surpluses, unemployment had doubled and inflation had remained surprisingly low, prompting the government to adopt an expansionary fiscal policy for 1986. Again, just as the policy got under way, the second negative oil shock took place, almost halving oil exports. In 1986–88, the government attempted to maintain its expansionary policy with increasing difficulty. During 1986, lack of fiscal restraint caused the foreign exchange premium to explode, forcing the government to make a 'credible' devaluation of the official rate (93% in December 1986). However, since fiscal policy remained expansionary, the premium increased again and reached unsustainable levels by 1988. Throughout, international reserves were plummeting. Given that elections were scheduled for December 1988, the policy was maintained in spite of the deteriorating macroeconomic balance, until the new government took over in February 1989. By that time, little could be done to avoid an explosion of the underlying tensions and the economy went into its worst recession ever with a major jump in the price level as the government decided to unify the exchange rate through a floating arrangement.

Table 17.2 summarises these macroeconomic events in Venezuela.

Table 17.2. A summary of macroeconomic events in Venezuela

Period	External situation	Policy orientation	Principal results
1964–73	Stagnant oil income	1. Fixed unified exchange rates 2. Fiscal discipline 3. Import-substitution industrialisation	1. High but falling rate of growth (average 6.8%) 2. Very low inflation (1.7%) 3. External balance
1974–76	1. First oil shock 2. Higher world inflation	1. Expansionary fiscal policy 2. Emphasis on publicly owned basic industries 3. Nationalisations and restrictions on foreign investment	1. Acceleration in growth (9%) 2. Higher inflation but lower than world levels (9%) 3. Large and declining surpluses in fiscal and external accounts. Balance achieved in 1976.
1977–78	Declining oil income	1. Increase in public spending mainly in state enterprises 2. Some attempts to cut back spending and credit	1. Decline in growth (3.5% in 1978) 2. Major external and fiscal deficits 3. Extensive supply bottlenecks: labour and installed capacity
1979–80	1. Second oil shock 2. Jump in world interest rates	1. Strong fiscal contraction (mainly in imports) 2. Price liberalisation 3. Wage increase law 4. Some trade liberalisation 5. Interest ceilings do not adjust fully for the rise in world rates	1. Growth falls to zero 2. Unemployment grows slowly 3. Inflation accelerates to record levels (21% in 1980) 4. Real exchange rate appreciates strongly 5. External and fiscal balance achieved 6. Capital outflows begin
1981–82	Oil income very high, starts to fall	1. Fiscal expansion in public works 2. Interest rates are freed but monetary policy is expansionary 3. Large deficits in public enterprise sector financed through foreign borrowing	1. Mediocre growth (1%) 2. High but falling inflation (16%) 3. Large current account deficit and massive capital outflow (US$8 bn. in 1982)
1983	1. Fall in oil income 2. Start of debt crisis	1. Adoption of a multiple exchange rate regime, average devaluation 30% 2. Import controls 3. Contractionary fiscal policy 4. Monetary policy expansionary 5. Generalised price controls are adopted	1. GDP falls 5% 2. Inflation kept at 7% 3. Large balance of payments surplus (US$4 bn.) 4. Still important fiscal deficit 5. Large expansion in money supply 6. Floating rate depreciates over 200%
1984–85	Oil income stable at lower level (US$13 bn.)	1. Devaluation of official rate 2. Maintenance of import controls 3. Fiscal cuts 4. Interest rate controls adopted 5. Price controls are relaxed 6. Debt strategy: simple rescheduling	1. After an additional contraction in 1984 (−2%), economy starts to grow in 1985 (3.5%); unemployment reaches peak 2. Inflation increases to moderate levels (15%) 3. Large fiscal and balance of payments surpluses

Table 17.2. *Continued*

Period	External Situation	Policy orientation	Principal results
1986–88	Oil income collapses (US$8 bn.)	1. Fiscal expansion adopted 2. Forced financing of imports 3. Major devaluation when situation becomes untenable 4. No change in interest rate ceilings	1. Economy grows at 5% average; unemployment falls back to 7% 2. Major balance of payments and fiscal deficit 3. Acceleration of inflation to over 30% 4. Floating rate depreciates by almost 200% over the period
1989	Small oil income increase	1. Exchange rate system unified in a floating arrangement 2. Interest rates and prices freed 3. Trade and foreign investment liberalised 4. Subsidies cut, public sector prices increased	1. GDP drops by almost 10 points and inflation exceeds 80% 2. Exchange rate unified close to parallel rate 3. Current account surplus and small fiscal deficit

17.4. The Nature of the Shocks

In this section we analyse the nature of the negative shocks of the 1980s and argue that they were permanent in nature. We further claim that they were exclusive, in the sense that they were fundamentally inconsistent with prior anticipations, and revised, in that they led to a major change in income expectations.

Oil projections are made regularly in Venezuela for planning and budgetary purposes by the national petroleum company PDVSA (pronounced 'PeDeVeSa') and are revised by the Ministries of Energy and Finance. Since they affect major political decisions, these projections are the object of intense scrutiny and bickering between government agencies, political parties and the press. Hence, they must obey a legitimacy constraint which usually implies adopting some sort of international standard: expectations must be consistent with the conventional wisdom in the world oil market. In this section we present data produced for the medium-term plans and the yearly national budgets. The sixth medium-term National Plan (covering the period 1981–85) was presented in September 1981; the seventh Plan (covering 1984–88) was made public in November 1984.

Table 17.3 contrasts the projected oil exports of the sixth Plan with the actual values. Notice that a stable increase was expected instead of the marked decline observed. The difference represents 40.4% of expected income in 1983 and 54.3% in 1985. Moreover, exports never returned to forecast levels. Since all the resources available had been assigned by the Plan, which also included some borrowing, the shortfall was bound to make fiscal policy unsustainable.

Table 17.3. Oil exports: actual and projected by the sixth National Plan, 1981–85 (*US$m.*)

	1981	1982	1983	1984	1985
Projected exports	18,273	20,466	22,922	25,672	28,753
Actual exports	19,094	15,659	13,667	14,634	13,144
Percentage difference	4.5	−23.5	−40.4	−43.0	−54.3

Source: Sixth National Plan, CORDIPLAN (1981) and Central Bank of Venezuela

Table 17.4. Oil exports: actual and projected by the seventh National Plan, 1985–88 (*US$m.*)

	1985	1986	1987	1988
High scenario	15,280	16,800	19,180	21,400
Baseline scenario	14,800	15,740	17,360	19,300
Low scenario	13,060	13,740	14,580	16,120
Actual	13,144	7,592	9,104	8,158
Percentage difference				
High	−14.0	−54.8	−52.5	−61.9
Baseline	−11.2	−51.8	−47.6	−57.7
Low	0.6	−44.7	−37.6	−49.4

Source: Seventh National Plan, CORDIPLAN (1984) and Central Bank of Venezuela

The seventh National Plan was written after the dramatic forecasting error of its predecessor, which was severely criticised for the inadequacy of its planning techniques (Matus 1985). Consequently, the government decided to allow for contingencies by presenting three scenarios of oil exports. Table 17.4 shows the data for the planning period 1985–88 and compares them with actual developments. Again, we notice that real income was about 40% below the levels expected by the worst scenario. Furthermore, income never returned to the projected trend. Notice also that in every projection, exports are expected to rise smoothly in value. This is consistent with Hotelling's rule, since otherwise it would be profitable for suppliers with different expectations to change their desired level of output.

Table 17.5 shows yearly projections for Venezuelan oil exports. The projected data, presented in column (1), are taken from the yearly budget laws approved by Congress in the last quarter of each year. These numbers are also based on projections made by PDVSA and approved by the Ministry of Energy and by the Presidential Budget Office. They are used to estimate oil tax revenues, which averaged around 60% of central

Table 17.5. Estimated and actual oil exports (*US$m.*)

	Predicted exports	Actual exports	Percentage difference	Predicted growth (%)	Growth error (%)
1978	10,737	8,535	−20.5		
1979	9,941	13,517	36.0	16.5	16.7
1980	13,482	17,959	33.2	−0.3	33.6
1981	20,189	18,863	−6.6	12.4	−16.9
1982	20,894	15,395	−26.3	10.8	−33.5
1983	16,013	13,714	−14.4	4.0	−17.7
1984	13,912	14,670	5.4	1.4	4.0
1985	14,824	12,820	−13.5	1.1	−14.4
1986	12,774	7,117	−44.3	−0.4	−44.1
1987	8,700	9,054	4.1	22.2	−14.9
1988	9,265	8,136	−12.2	2.3	−14.2
1989	8,877	9,862	11.1	9.1	1.8
Average			−4.0	7.2	−9.0
Standard			23.9	7.6	21.9

Source: *Exposición de Motivos del Proyecto de Ley de Presupuesto*, various years, Oficina Central de Presupuesto and *Petróleo y Otros Datos Estadísticos*, Ministerio de Energía y Minas, various issues

government current income during this period. Column (2) shows the actual value of exports. Column (3) calculates the percentage difference between the first two columns. Column (4) computes the implied rate of growth between the actual value of exports of the present year and the predicted value for the next year. Column (5) indicates the difference between the actual rate of growth and the predicted rate of growth.

As can be seen, predicted exports tend to be similar and on average somewhat higher than actual exports of the previous year. This is indicated by the positive average expected growth and by the low standard deviation for the series as a whole. Part of the deviations can be explained by the fact that the information available in the fourth quarter of the year may differ from the yearly average. This is particularly important for the two years where the predicted growth was highest (1979 and 1986). In 1979, the oil shock took place in September–October and thus affected estimates for the following year. In July 1986 OPEC reacted strongly to the sharp fall in prices, so that by October, prices were well above the low levels reached in May–July. Thus it appears as if each year, or more specifically, each month of October, becomes the basis of the following year's estimate. This is what one would expect if the underlying stochastic process was a martingale instead of trend-stationary.

As is well known, in martingales all shocks are interpreted as permanent since the current price becomes the best estimate of future prices, thus leading to a full revision of expectations. If the process was trend-stationary, today's price rise (above a certain level) would imply expectations of a decline in next year's price. So, part of the instability in the series would be predicted. However, this does not happen in Table 17.5, as can be seen by noticing that the level and growth rate prediction errors of the series (columns 3 and 5) have similar standard deviations.

Moreover, the data clearly show that the three shocks which took place between 1978 and 1989 were not predicted, that they were inconsistent with previous expectations and that they caused these expectations to be altered. In the terminology of Bevan *et al.* (Chapter 2), they would qualify as *exclusive* and *revised*. Thus, for instance, exports in 1978 were below predicted levels, and generated a bearish view of the market for the following year. Thus, during the 1979–80 oil shock, major underprediction errors were made. Notice that the 1980 predicted level was very similar to the actual 1979 level and 33.2% below the actual value. This induced the agents in the oil markets to revise their expectations upwards and a rapid positive trend of 12% per year became the new conventional wisdom, which was reflected in the sixth National Plan.[18] However, major over-prediction errors were made in 1981–83, thus indicating that the first negative oil shock came as a surprise. Nevertheless, after each fall it was expected that prices would remain on their upward trend, but starting from a lower base.

After 1983, the market seemed to have determined a new, much lower plateau and expectations of more moderate nominal increases became the norm. The oil market, however, surprised everyone again by falling significantly and causing huge overprediction errors in 1985 and 1986. Again, each new year's actual data became the basis for next year's prediction, just as in a martingale.

It is interesting to contrast this view of the stochastic process with the arguments used at the time to justify both expectations and policies. As mentioned above, the sixth National Plan of September 1981 projected an increase in the real price of crude oil of 12% per year for the planning period. As the Plan was being printed, the oil market turned bearish. It suddenly became clear that anticipation of future price rises, linked to the Iran–Iraq war had caused heavy speculative accumulation of inventories during 1979–80. This behaviour, more than any other factor, effectively caused the rise in prices, which averaged 29.7 dollars per barrel in 1981 for the Venezuelan mix, up from 12.0 dollars per barrel in 1978. As inventories reached a ceiling and interest rates increased to the highest levels ever, the market weakened dramatically.

After this event took place, four aspects changed the medium-term outlook of experts.[19] First, it was argued that the price elasticity of demand, which had remained very low after the 1973 shock, increased significantly as thermo-electric plants switched quickly to coal and gas. Second, apparent income elasticity of demand fell dramatically and experts associated this fall with the delayed impact of investments in conservation, prompted by the first oil shock, and with a change in the technological pattern of world growth. Third, the world entered into the 1981–82 recession and, fourth, major new, non-OPEC sources of supply had appeared in Mexico and the North Sea.

To contain the fall in prices, OPEC adopted the strategy of output cuts. OPEC output, which had reached 30 million barrels a day in 1980, was reduced almost by half. This strategy meant that the volume of Venezuelan oil output in 1983 was 29% below 1979 levels.

Conventional wisdom during 1983–84 held that, as the world economy recovered from the 1981–82 recession, demand for oil would grow, allowing OPEC progressively to relax its control on output. The experience during 1984 appeared to justify this optimism, since prices strengthened. Consequently, when the Venezuelan government again asked the oil company, in 1984, to produce new medium-term projections for the seventh National Plan, PDVSA presented the three scenarios shown in Table 17.4 characterised by stable real prices for oil and growing OPEC quotas.

However, during 1985 world demand for oil fell and non-OPEC supply increased, forcing Saudi Arabia to cut its output to under 3 million barrels a day in order to defend the price structure. This appeared as too much of a sacrifice to the Saudi government given that its production potential, which had been effectively reached in 1980, was still at 10 million barrels a day. Hence it decided to abandon its role as swing producer in the second semester of 1985 and increased its output to its established 'notional' quota of 4.5 million barrels a day. Soon after, in January 1986, prices crashed, causing Venezuelan oil income to fall to almost half the level projected by the worst scenario provided by the oil industry.[20]

After the shock, the new conventional wisdom argued that OPEC's strategy during 1981–85, which was based on defending prices through quotas, had collapsed because oil had priced itself out of the energy market and because high-cost non-OPEC producers were filling the gap created by the output cutbacks. The new strategy had to be based on recapturing market share both within the oil market and in the broader energy market. Consequently, a much lower price level had to be maintained for a significant period of time.

In conclusion, the negative shocks were unpredicted and caused expectations to change in line with the new information set. A consistent *ex post* interpretation of events was always developed to explain the new price level and to guide policy. From then on, prices were always expected to rise smoothly, until the next shock.

17.5. Some Methodological Considerations

In this section we present some methodological aspects behind the tables that are analysed below. We start with a technique to measure the oil shocks in terms of domestic non-oil GDP and then develop it further to express domestic adjustment in similar units.

The oil sector can be taken to be an enclave with its final demand forming part of public sector spending and its production requiring only specific factors of production. Exports, then, are analytically equivalent to an international transfer, and the relevant GDP indicator is non-oil GDP.[21] The ratio of oil exports to non-oil GDP, call it ϕ, can be written as:

$$\phi = (eP^* X)/(PQ), \qquad (17.1)$$

where e is the nominal exchange rate, P^* is the foreign price of oil, X is the volume of exports, P is the non-oil GDP deflator and Q is non-oil GDP.

For reasons that will become obvious below, it is convenient to multiply and divide by a relevant world price index. We shall use the US wholesale price index (*WPI*):

$$\phi = (eP^* X WPI)/(PQWPI). \qquad (17.2)$$

The percentage change in ϕ can be decomposed by log differentiation of equation (17.2):

$$\hat{\phi}_t = \phi_{t-1}^* \left(\hat{e} + \hat{P}^* + \hat{X} + \hat{WPI} - \hat{P} - \hat{Q} - \hat{WPI} \right), \qquad (17.3)$$

where the symbol $\wedge$ over a letter indicates the percentage change of the variable.

Reorganising the previous expression we have:

$$\hat{\Phi}_t = \phi_{t-1} \left\{ \left[\left(\hat{P}^* + \hat{X} - \hat{WPI} \right) - \hat{Q} \right] + \left[\left(\hat{WPI} - \hat{P} \right) + \hat{e} \right] \right\}. \qquad (17.4)$$

The first term in square brackets of equation (17.4) measures the *relative external shock* as a share of GDP. This term has two components: the *absolute external shock*, in round brackets, measures the impact of changes in export volume and real price; the second one takes account of the fact that non-oil GDP changes, thus affecting the denominator of ϕ. In an expanding economy, homothetic growth will require a constant increase in oil revenue so that its relative share remains constant. The relative external shock measures how much faster or slower than non-oil GDP real oil revenue has been changing.

The second term in square brackets of equation (17.4) takes account of the real depreciation effect which affects the domestic value of oil exports. For convenience we divide it into two components: the 'underlying' depreciation (in round brackets), which consists of the inflation differential, and the change in the nominal exchange rate.

Figure 17.2 shows the accumulated changes since 1968 in both the absolute and the relative external shock.[22] As can be seen, the first positive oil shock of the 1970s had an initial absolute magnitude of over 50% of GDP. The government quickly reacted to it by imposing a major cut in oil output in order to conserve the resource. Production in 1975 was 34% below its 1973 level and kept falling slowly thereafter. From 1975 to 1978, the first oil shock represented on average 30% of GDP in absolute terms. However, given the large acceleration in GDP growth, by 1978 its relative size with respect to the economy had gone back to its pre-shock level. By contrast, the second oil shock represented some 20 percentage points of GDP in 1980–81 with respect to 1978 in absolute terms and a slightly smaller amount in relative terms owing to the stagnation in growth which occurred in this period.

The size of the first and second negative oil shocks is presented in Tables 17.6 and 17.16 and will be analysed below.

One way to describe the economy's adjustment to the shock is to start from the national accounting identities. Nominal GDP must equal aggregate expenditure:

$$PQ + eP^* X WPI/WPI = P_A A + TB, \qquad (17.5)$$

where A is real absorption, P_A is the price of absorption and TB is the trade balance. This expression is only approximately accurate since we have substituted oil GDP by oil exports.

Dividing this expression by nominal non-oil GDP ($P\ Q$), log-differentiating and rearranging terms we obtain:

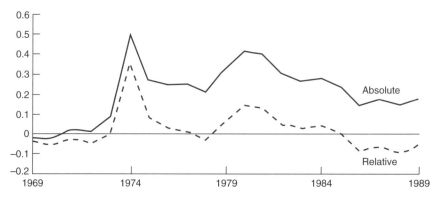

Figure 17.2. Absolute and relative cumulative effects of external oil shocks, 1969–89 (share of non-oil GDP)

$$\phi_t\left(\hat{P}* + \hat{X} - W\hat{P}I - \hat{Q}\right) = \alpha_{t-1}\left(\hat{A} - \hat{Q}\right) + \left(\frac{TB}{PQ}\right)^t - \left(\frac{TB}{PQ}\right)^{t-1} + \left[\alpha_{t-1}\left(\hat{P}_A - \hat{P}\right)\right.$$

$$\left. - \phi_{t-1}\left(W\hat{P}I + \hat{e} - \hat{P}\right)\right]. \qquad (17.6)$$

The term on the left-hand side is the relative real external shock. The first term on the right-hand side, which we call the *relative absorption effect*, measures the excess growth of absorption relative to output, as a share of non-oil GDP. The second term is the shift in the *nominal* trade balance, also as a share of GDP. The change in the *real* or constant price trade balance is simply the difference between the real relative external shock and the relative absorption growth. The gap between the current price and the constant price measure of the trade balance is due to relative price shifts. For instance, a real depreciation will increase the value of a trade surplus measured in units of non-oil GDP.

The third term takes into account these relative price effects. It indicates how much of the shock has been converted into a negative income effect generated by shifts in relative prices. A real depreciation has two effects: it increases the real value of exports and of imports. We call the first effect the *real depreciation effect*. We call the second one the *relative absorption price effect*, which indirectly measures the impact of the devaluation on imports since these explain the difference between the price of absorption and the price of non-oil GDP. In general terms, a negative shock is transformed into either reduced relative absorption, a deteriorated nominal trade balance or a change in relative prices.

Using this approach, data for the two shocks are presented in Tables 17.7 and 17.17. The real relative absorption effect is further decomposed in Tables 17.9 and 17.21. Savings and investment by agents are presented in Tables 17.8 and 17.18. Changes in relative prices are studied in Tables 17.13 and 17.24. The impact of real depreciation on the domestic value of the oil surplus is estimated in Tables 17.10 and 17.19. Transfers of resources to the public sector through real depreciation, exchange profits and seignorage are studied in Tables 17.11 and 17.20. Changes in output are analysed in Tables 17.12 and 17.23. Relative prices are presented in Tables 17.13 and 17.24. The overall efficiency of adjustment is estimated in Tables 17.14 and 17.25.

17.6. The Analysis of the First Negative Shock, 1982–85

In this section we analyse the first negative oil shock. We will start by studying the medium-term changes. Then we will turn to the study of the adjustment path, distinguishing between the period of non-adjustment (1982), the initial reaction to the regime collapse (1983) and the further adjustment effort (1984–85).

Ricardo Hausmann

Table 17.6. The decomposition of the first oil shock: accumulated effects as shares of non-oil GDP (*percentage*)

	1982	1983	1984	1985
Relative real external shock	−8.9	−11.3	−9.8	−14.1
Absolute real external shock	−8.4	−11.8	−10.6	−14.1
Export volume effect	−4.7	−5.7	−5.3	−7.3
Real price effect	−3.8	−6.4	−5.6	−7.3
Oil Price effect	−3.0	−5.3	−3.8	−5.1
Import Price effect	0.8	1.2	1.9	2.4
GDP growth effect	0.6	−0.6	−0.9	0.0
Real depreciation	−2.0	−0.7	6.1	5.0
Inflation differential	−2.0	−4.0	−6.6	−8.6
Nominal devaluation	0.0	3.4	13.5	14.8
Total decomposed effect	−10.7	−11.9	−4.4	−9.9
Actual change	−10.1	−11.5	−4.2	−9.5
Statistical discrepancy	−0.7	−0.5	−0.1	0.2

Table 17.7. Macroeconomic adjustment to the first oil shock: cumulative effects as shares of non-oil GDP (*percentage*)

	1982	1983	1984	1985
Relative real external shock	−8.9	−11.3	−9.8	−14.1
Change in trade balance	−12.3	12.8	16.1	11.9
Relative absorption growth	1.2	−26.6	−20.3	−22.6
Relative price effects	3.4	8.0	−2.0	0.7
Real depreciation effect	−2.0	−0.7	6.1	5.0
Relative absorption price effect	1.3	7.2	3.9	5.7
Statistical discrepancy	−0.7	−0.8	−0.5	−1.5

Compared to the levels reached by the oil income in 1981, the real relative external shock amounted to 14.1% of non-oil GDP by 1985 (Table 17.6). Aggregate adjustment mainly took the form of a cut in real absorption, which fell 22.6% of GDP more than output (Table 17.7), determining a substantial improvement in the real trade balance.

Decomposing the real relative absorption effect (Table 17.9) we notice that the cut in spending affected mainly investment (12.5%) but also private consumption (3.7%). Public consumption was barely cut (0.9%). It also affected mainly tradables, which fell by 19.9% of GDP, whereas private non-tradables declined by only 4.7%, indicating strong demand shifts.

From the viewpoint of the savings and investment balance (Table 17.8), the cut in absorption mainly took the form of a decline in the gross fixed

Table 17.8. Savings and investment by type of agent, as shares of non-oil GDP (*percentage*)

	1980	1981	1982	1983	1984	1985
Domestic savings	46.0	39.3	29.6	21.0	31.0	28.2
Public	26.9	21.5	12.6	12.9	15.6	13.3
Private	19.1	17.8	17.0	8.1	15.3	14.9
Total investment	35.1	32.4	35.7	13.6	22.9	23.4
Fixed investment	35.8	34.4	33.5	22.7	21.0	21.9
Public	17.5	21.0	23.6	17.1	7.3	8.6
Private	18.3	13.4	9.8	5.6	13.7	13.3
Inventories	−0.7	−2.1	2.3	−9.1	1.9	1.5
Foreign savings	−10.9	−7.0	6.1	−7.4	−8.1	−4.8

Source: International Monetary Fund and Central Bank of Venezuela

Table 17.9. Decomposition of the relative absorption effect: cumulative changes as shares of non-oil GDP (*percentage*)

	1982	1983	1984	1985
Total absorption	1.2	−26.6	−20.3	−22.6
Non-tradables	−0.5	−1.1	−2.6	−3.4
Public	0.4	1.0	1.5	0.9
Private	−1.0	−2.3	−4.5	−4.7
Tradables	1.7	−25.7	−18.2	−19.9
Consumption	−0.2	−4.1	−4.4	−7.8
Public	−0.8	−0.4	−0.9	−0.9
Private	0.6	−3.8	−3.7	−3.7
Tradables	−1.3	−7.0	−9.1	−12.1
Non-tradables	1.2	2.9	5.6	5.2
Investment	−1.8	−9.1	−13.1	−12.5
Tradables	−0.1	−4.4	−4.6	−3.5
Local	0.0	−1.5	−1.5	−1.2
Imported	−0.3	−2.3	−2.7	−1.9
Non-tradables	−1.9	−4.5	−9.0	−9.4
Inventories	3.2	−15.8	−4.1	−4.1

investment rate, which dropped by 12.5 percentage points of GDP, in line with domestic savings (11.1% of GDP). Accordingly, neither inventories nor foreign savings played a major role in the process.[23] Most of the savings and investment cuts between 1981 and 1985 were public (8.2% and 12.4%, respectively), whereas little change took place in private rates (2.9% and 0.1%, respectively), which is consistent with our previous finding that most of the consumption cut was private.

Table 17.10. Calculation of the oil exchange tax 1981–85

	1981	1982	1983	1984	1985
1. Oil operating surplus (Bs)	71,194	57,069	50,989	80,292	72,879
2. Oil exports (US$)	19,094	15,659	13,778	14,627	12,761
Implicit surplus share (1/2) (Bs/US$)	3.73	3.64	3.70	5.49	5.71
3. Constant real surplus share (Bs.US$)	3.73	3.93	4.20	4.64	5.16
4. Corresponding oil surplus (2 × 3.)	71,194	61,490	57,925	67,908	65,803
5. Oil exchange tax (1 − 4)	0	−4,421	−6,936	12,384	7,076
as a share of non-oil GDP (%)	0.0	−1.6	−2.4	3.9	2.0

Note: Calculated by multiplying the implicit surplus share by the non-oil GDP deflator and dividing by the US Wholesale price index

Source: International Monetary Fund

Table 17.11. Estimated real transfers to the public sector, as shares of non-oil GDP (*percentage*)

	1982	1983	1984	1985
Seigniorage	−1.2	4.0	−0.5	2.3
Exchange profits	0.0	3.6	4.2	4.3
Oil exchange tax	−1.6	−2.4	3.9	2.0
Total transfers	−2.8	5.1	7.6	8.6

Source: International Monetary Fund for base money, exchange profits and non-oil GDP; Table 17.10 for oil exchange tax

Even though the external shock directly affected only the public sector, since the oil industry was fully nationalised, there were significant income transfers during this period. By devaluing the real exchange rate, the public sector's external surplus increased in domestic value, causing a transfer of real income from the private sector. Depending on the exchange rate given to the oil industry relative to other rates, this effect may appear either as an increase in the operating surplus of PDVSA or as exchange profits at the central bank. Tables 17.10 and 17.11 calculate these effects and show that they amounted to 6.3 percentage points of GDP.[24] In addition, in 1985 the public sector was able to appropriate 2.3 percentage points of GDP through seignorage.[25] These income transfers explain in part the decline in private consumption.

With respect to output[26] (Table 17.12), the tradable sector grew much more than non-tradables. In fact, between 1982 and 1984 private non-

Table 17.12. GDP growth by sector, percentage change as shares of non-oil GDP

	1981	1982	1983	1984	1985
Non-oil GDP	0.4	1.8	−3.7	−1.2	3.3
Private	−0.3	0.3	−3.8	−1.9	3.0
Tradables	−0.3	0.5	−0.5	0.7	1.4
Non-tradables	0.0	−0.2	−3.3	−2.7	1.6
Construction	−0.2	−0.6	−0.8	−1.4	−0.4
Other	0.2	0.4	−2.5	−0.8	2.0
Public	0.7	1.5	0.1	0.6	0.3
Tradables	−0.2	0.8	0.5	0.6	0.5
Non-tradables	1.0	0.7	−0.2	0.2	−0.2

Table 17.13. Relative price shifts, 1981–1985 (*Index 1980 = 100*)

	1981	1982	1983	1984	1985
Tradables vs non-tradables[a]	98.0	94.7	90.7	95.7	101.5
Real exchange rate[b]	89.3	79.6	82.3	96.2	97.8
Construction vs non-tradables[c]	94.6	94.4	80.1	88.5	89.5

[a] Ratio of GDP for tradables (agriculture and manufacturing) vs non-tradables (construction, commerce, transport, services)
[b] IMF definition of real exchange rate, trade weighted average
[c] Ration of construction GDP deflator to total non-tradable deflator

Source: CORDIPLAN/LPES database (for deflators) and Central Bank for the real exchange rate

tradables showed a negative growth rate, whereas tradables declined only in 1983. In 1985 tradables grew at more than double the rate of non-tradables, explaining more than half of the aggregate growth.

This result is in line with the movements in relative prices (Table 17.13). There was a real depreciation after 1982 measured both as the relative price of tradables with respect to non-tradables and as the IMF definition of the real exchange rate. This change in relative prices is also consistent with the shift in demand from tradables towards non-tradables.

A major construction bust took place throughout the period, as can be seen from the fact that demand for non-traded capital goods declined by 9.4% of GDP more than output (Table 17.9) between 1981 and 1985. Moreover, as shown in Table 17.12, the construction sector declined every year between 1981 and 1985, falling by a cumulative 76%. In addition, the relative price of construction with respect to total non-traded goods declined (Table 17.13).

The efficiency of adjustment is analysed in Table 17.14. To do so, we compare the actual values to a counterfactual in which the economy exhibits homothetic growth of 3% per year, including its real oil revenue. We chose a low growth rate because the economy was very close to full employment in 1981 and productivity trends had been negative. Anyway, a more optimistic counterfactual would only make the adjustment more inefficient.

Table 17.14 shows the results of our calculation. The first row measures the external oil shock with respect to its 3% growth trend, in units of trend non-oil GDP. The second row deducts from the external shock an amount equal to the initial output absorption gap (i.e. the excess current account surplus), which we take to be equal to 2 percentage points of GDP in 1981. This row indicates the unavoidable disabsorption costs of the shock.

The third row shows the difference between actual non-oil GDP and trend GDP in units of trend GDP. This represents the loss of potential output given the path taken by the economy and we call it *secondary adjustment costs*. In an optimal adjustment process, these would be avoided. The sum of primary and secondary adjustment costs is called *total adjustment costs*.

In the fifth row we indicate how much actual absorption differed from the 3% trend, measured in units of trend GDP. The final row indicates the difference between total adjustment costs and the actual adjustment which took place. If the difference is positive, then there is excess adjustment expressed in terms of an excessive balance of payments surplus. If the difference is negative, then the economy is reducing its net foreign assets in order to finance absorption, and has consequently adjusted insufficiently.

By 1985 the economy had incurred adjustment costs of 28.2% of GDP, composed of 15.4% in primary absorption costs, 11.1% in secondary adjustment costs and 3.7% in excess adjustment. The secondary adjustment

Table 17.14. How efficient was the adjustment to the first shock? (*percentage of trend non-oil GDP*)

	1982	1983	1984	1985
External shock	9.8	12.8	11.6	15.9
Primary absorption costs	7.8	11.8	10.4	15.4
Secondary adjustment costs	1.5	7.9	11.7	11.1
Total adjustment costs	9.4	20.7	23.3	28.2
Actual adjustment	0.8	33.9	30.8	32.9
Excess adjustment	−7.9	11.0	6.1	3.7

Note: Primary adjustment cost is equal to the external shock minus the initial output absorption gap

costs are broadly consistent with Okun's Law given the rise in the unemployment rate of 6.0% (Table 17.1).

Let us summarise our findings. An external shock of 14.1% of GDP was adjusted by means of a fall in absorption and a real depreciation. The composition of absorption shifted towards non-tradables, that of output towards tradables. All these findings are in line with the (negative) Dutch Disease effect.

Moreover, a major construction bust took place, with a significant drop in demand for non-traded capital goods and a decline in their relative price. This bust occurred in the context of a negative permanent shock.

These relatively standard results for the medium-term adjustment contrast markedly with the initial path taken by the economy. In 1982 there was a real relative negative shock of 8.9% of GDP (Table 17.6). Instead of adjusting through a reduction in relative absorption and a real depreciation, the economy increased absorption by 1.2% more than output and appreciated the real exchange rate.[27] The trade balance, as a result, deteriorated by 12.3% of GDP (Table 17.7). Domestic savings fell by 9.7% of GDP, mainly because of a decline in public savings of 8.9% of GDP. To make matters worse, public investment increased 9.6% in real terms or 2.6% of GDP. Furthermore, real appreciation produced a negative oil exchange tax of 1.6% (Table 17.11) owing to the decline in the domestic value of oil output, thus deteriorating further the public sector accounts.

This clear pattern of non-adjustment was to give significant signals to the private sector. The expectation that the policy regime would have to be reformed and that changes would include a nominal devaluation, (i.e. a default on the real value of money and other government liabilities) caused the private sector to react through three channels: capital flight, inventory accumulation of tradable goods (imports) and a reduction in the purchase of non-tradable capital goods.

In effect, as shown in Table 17.15, capital flight, defined as private non-financial short-term capital outflows plus errors and omissions, reached 6.5 billion US dollars, which explain most of the 8.2 billion dollars in international reserve losses. These were financed only in a small proportion by a reduction in base money (756 million dollars). Most of the resources came through an increase in the private flow of financial savings generated by a cut in demand for fixed investment. Private gross fixed capital formation declined by 3.6% of GDP (Table 17.8), a fall of 23.6% in its own terms. In fact, aggregate fixed investment fell, thwarting the expansionary designs of government policy.

There was a also positive inventory swing equal to 3.2% of GDP (Table 17.9). In fact, all of the increase in absorption is explained by inventories (consumption and fixed investment fell by 2 percentage points of GDP). Furthermore, all of the increase in absorption was in tradables, since non-tradables declined by 0.5%.

Table 17.15. Assets changes during the first oil shock (*US$m*)

	1980	1981	1982	1983	1984	1985
Levels						
International reserves[a]	15,849	16,309	8,121	8,399	10,284	11,976
Dollar value of base money[b]	6,329	7,354	6,598	3,069	3,002	3,112
Yearly changes						
International reserves	3,889	457	−8,185	278	1,885	1,692
Dollar value of base money	448	1,025	−756	−3,529	−67	110
Dollar value of seigniorage[c]	448	1,025	−756	940	−111	583
Capital flight	−2,366	−3,550	−6,469	−1,656	−39	−548
Private short-term capital	−1,362	−2,651	−4,784	−1,370	−720	−810
Errors and omissions	−1,004	−899	−1,685	−286	681	262

[a] Excluding gold
[b] Year-end nominal value of the base money dividend by the year-end financial exchange rate
[c] Year-end nominal increase in base money dividend by the yearly average financial exchange rate

Hence, private behaviour can be explained as an anticipated response to regime collapse because of insufficient fiscal adjustment to the shock. The construction bust, on the other hand, was the consequence not of a decline in absorption but of a change in the pattern of private asset accumulation.

In 1983, the year of the balance of payments crisis, there was a further deterioration of real relative oil income (2.4% of GDP). However, the real trade balance showed a positive swing (25.1%) through a major decline in absorption (27.8%, Table 17.7). In nominal terms, the swing in foreign savings amounted to 13.5 percentage points of GDP (Table 17.8). How did such a drastic cut in absorption take place?

More remarkably, this drop in absorption happened in spite of a fall in aggregate savings of 8.6% of GDP. Thus, the whole adjustment took the form of a fall in total investment: 10.8% in fixed capital formation and 13.5% in inventories. Decomposing the real relative absorption effect we notice that the declines in consumption, investment and inventories amounted to 3.9%, 7.3% and 19.2%, respectively. Hence, inventories explain the bulk of the adjustment. Also, demand for tradables fell by 25.7% more than GDP compared to the 1.1% decline for non-tradables.

On this occasion, the drop in savings was mainly private (8.9% of GDP). This can be explained by the sudden shift of resources to the public sector through the real depreciation and seignorage mechanisms described in Table 17.11, a swing of 7.9% of GDP.

Seignorage was possible because the abandonment of the fixed exchange rate regime eliminated the central bank's obligation to sell its foreign reserves at a fixed price. By renouncing this commitment it was possible to increase domestic credit to the public sector without the offsetting effect of a decline in reserves. In fact, as the private sector tried to convert its excess holdings of money into foreign assets, the exchange rate in the parallel market depreciated by 223% between 18 February 1983 (the day of the balance of payments collapse) and 31 December of that year.

This depreciation implied a 3.5 billion dollar decline in the value of the money base (Table 17.15). Furthermore, since the nominal supply of base money was allowed to increase rapidly, the government was able to appropriate a further 940 million dollars through seignorage. It is these sorts of default costs which agents were trying to avoid.

As mentioned above, the decline in absorption of 27.8% fell disproportionately on tradables (26.7%). This explains not only the drastic improvement in the trade balance but also the relatively moderate recession: non-oil GDP fell by 'only' 3.7%. However this swing in the composition of demand happened in spite of small and contradictory changes in relative prices. As Table 17.13 shows, the real exchange rate (IMF definition) *depreciated* by scarcely 3.4% whereas the relative price of tradables *appreciated* by 4.2%.

Hence there are two questions to be addressed. First, why did the composition of demand change so drastically without a large shift in relative price? Second, why did the relative domestic price of tradables not increase in spite of a nominal exchange rate depreciation and a large increase in the level of implicit protection?

The following interpretation is advanced. Assume inventories depreciate because of perishability or other reasons. This implies that the stocks accumulated in 1982 had to be consumed in 1983. Hence, in spite of a 50% drop in imports, the decline in demand and the dishoarding of stocks effectively created an excess domestic supply of tradables. This forced down their relative price. The new protective system set up with the adoption of multiple exchange rates, therefore, was not a binding constraint for most goods during 1983. In fact, the volume of dishoarding was such that demand for domestically produced importables fell, explaining the decline in the output of tradables (Table 17.12). In this explanation, private behaviour is rational, but did not fully anticipate the decline in domestic demand.

Summing up, in 1983 the balance of payments crisis was followed by a major improvement in the trade balance which was generated not by a rise in savings but mainly by a massive decline in inventories and, to a lesser degree, in investment. The adoption of multiple rates implied that the government defaulted on the dollar value of its monetary liabilities

with the private sector, by 3.5 billion dollars. Moreover, under this exchange regime the government could use seignorage to finance its deficit.
In addition, exchange profits further increased the transfer of real resources to the public sector. Consequently, the cut in spending was mostly
private. Given the previous accumulation of inventories, the decline in
absorption was highly concentrated in tradables, thus explaining the large
improvement in the trade balance without a major decline in output.

Inventory change is not a durable form of demand reduction since it is
limited by a non-negativity constraint on stocks. Hence, the balance of
trade improvement of 1983 was unsustainable. Other adjustments to absorption were needed in 1984 since the inventory effect would now provide an important demand push. Moreover, the reliance on seignorage as
a major source of public finance would lead to an even larger exchange
premium. In February 1984, one year after the balance of payments crisis,
the newly elected government adopted additional and more lasting adjustment measures consisting mainly of a further devaluation and a major
cut in public spending. They were to generate a relatively smooth aggregate transition but with major changes in its composition.

There was a 10% jump in the aggregate savings rate (Table 17.8), owing
mainly to internal reasons since the oil picture showed only a very slight
improvement (1.5% of GDP, Table 17.6). Savings were used mainly to
finance the now positive swing in inventories of 11% of GDP, caused by
the end of dishoarding. Fixed investment declined in real relative terms
by 4 percentage points of GDP (Table 17.9). The nominal trade balance as
a share of GDP actually improved, but this was mostly due to relative
price effects,[28] since real absorption increased.

The rise in savings was mainly a private phenomenon (7.2%), but public
savings increased also (by 2.7) owing to the improvement in oil income,
the transfer of resources through depreciation (see Table 17.11) and a cut
in consumption (0.5% of GDP). However, most of the amelioration in the
fiscal deficit came from a decline in investment (9.8% of GDP or 41.5% in
its own terms). This improvement led to a stop in the use of seignorage,
allowing the parallel rate to stabilise in nominal terms and the premium
to fall. It is in these circumstances that the increase in private savings,
the end of capital flight and the recovery of private investment must be
understood.

In fact, fixed private investment increased by 8.1% of GDP or 47.6% in
its own terms, but still remained 13% below its already low 1982 levels.
Moreover, since aggregate investment fell, there was a further decline
in non-traded capital goods output and relative price (Tables 17.12 and
17.13), confirming the durability of the construction bust.

With the end of dishoarding and the additional nominal devaluation,
there was a real depreciation and a rise in the relative price of tradables,
as would be expected under the adjustment to a permanent negative

shock. Resources shifted towards the production of tradables, but so did demand, given the inventory swing.

The situation was to remain very similar in 1985, except that a negative oil shock was allowed to reduce public savings and the trade balance, without much internal impact. By then, the fiscal and external accounts were in surplus, inflation was at 9.1% and unemployment had risen to 12.1%. The government was convinced that stability had been achieved and that there was room for growth through additional public investment. However, the second oil shock was to change matters dramatically.

17.7. The Analysis of the Second Negative Oil Shock, 1986–89

Although it took about a year for the balance of payments to collapse after prices declined in 1982, it took three years for reserves to run out once prices crashed in 1986. This much longer period of non-adjustment was made possible by the presence of multiple exchange rates, which limited the volume of capital flight. In fact, whereas, under fixed exchange rates, in the single year of 1982 reserve losses amounted to 8.2 billion US dollars, mostly through capital outflows, in the multiple exchange rate interval of 1986–88 the loss reached even higher figures (9.6 billion), but spread out over a much longer period and linked mostly to current account deficits (see Tables 17.15 and 17.26). The balance of payments finally collapsed in 1989.

Real relative oil income declined by 13.4% in the period 1986–88 (Table 17.16). At the macroeconomic level, most of the adjustment took

Table 17.16. The decomposition of the second oil shock: accumulated effects as shares of non-oil GDP (*percentage*)

	1986	1987	1988	1989
Relative real external shock	−10.3	−9.1	−13.4	−9.8
Absolute real external shock	−9.1	−7.2	−10.8	−8.5
Export volume effect	2.6	2.5	4.3	4.1
Real price effect	−11.4	−9.5	−14.5	−12.1
Oil price effect	−10.8	−7.7	−10.7	−7.2
Import price effect	0.7	1.9	4.4	5.5
GDP growth effect	1.3	2.0	3.0	1.5
Real depreciation	3.7	8.2	12.3	27.5
Inflation differential	1.5	−3.1	−4.6	−11.3
Nominal devaluation	5.2	11.7	17.8	43.7
Total decomposed effect	−7.0	−1.6	−2.8	14.9
Actual change	−8.8	−4.1	−6.0	8.2
Statistical discrepancy	−1.8	−2.5	−3.2	−5.8

place through a deterioration of the nominal trade balance of 11.9% (Table 17.17). Real absorption grew less than output in 1986, but this trend was reversed from 1987 onwards, so that by 1988 it had expanded in line with non-oil GDP. In other words, internal demand had not adjusted to the shock.

At the aggregate level, savings in 1988 were only 4.5% of GDP below their 1985 levels (Table 17.18), and fixed investment actually increased by 5.2%, so that foreign savings declined by 13.1% of GDP. Again, we notice a significant accumulation of inventories in the period prior to the balance of payments collapse.

These aggregate figures hide very different behaviour by the public and private sectors. Savings declined by 8.7% of GDP in the public sector whereas they increased 4.2% in the private sector. Public investment

Table 17.17. Macroeconomic adjustment to the second oil shock: cumulative effects as shares of non-oil GDP (*percentage*)

	1986	1987	1988	1989
Relative real external shock	−10.3	−9.1	−13.4	−9.8
Change in trade balance	−8.0	−6.7	−11.9	9.6
Relative absorption growth	−2.7	−2.2	0.3	−10.4
Relative price effects	−1.3	−0.2	−3.5	−13.8
Real depreciation effect	3.7	8.2	12.3	27.5
Relative absorption price effect	2.3	8.1	8.4	9.9
Statistical discrepancy	1.6	−0.2	1.4	6.5

Table 17.18. Savings and investment by type of agent, as shares of non-oil GDP (*percentage*)

	1984	1985	1986	1987	1988	1989
Domestic savings	31.0	28.2	22.3	27.6	23.7	26.4
Public[a]	15.6	13.3	6.4	7.2	4.6	12.4
Private	15.3	14.9	15.8	20.3	19.1	14.0
Total investment	22.9	23.4	23.6	29.7	31.9	17.0
Fixed investment	21.0	21.9	23.0	25.4	26.1	22.4
Public	7.3	8.6	10.7	10.9	12.0	11.9
Private	13.7	13.3	12.3	14.5	14.1	10.5
Inventories	1.9	1.5	0.6	4.3	5.9	−5.4
Foreign savings	−8.1	−4.8	1.3	2.2	8.3	−9.4
Resource balance	−10.2	−7.4	0.5	2.3	7.6	−16.1
Current transfers	2.1	2.6	0.9	−0.1	0.6	6.7

[a] As calculated by the Central Bank's Public Finance Division

Source: Central Bank of Venezuela, National Accounts for 1984–89

increased by 3.4% of GDP, indicating a complete absence of fiscal adjustment.

Confronted by this absence of response, the private sector deduced that the situation could not be maintained, meaning that, when fiscal adjustment eventually took place, private income would fall. Consequently, current income was thought to be above sustainable levels, warranting an increase in savings, instead of the decline that would be expected under a negative shock.

In fact, the lack of fiscal response had already become evident in 1986, when public savings declined by 6.9% and investment increased by 2.1%, causing a major deterioration in the fiscal and external account. The private sector attempted to convert its portfolio into foreign assets, which, given the presence of multiple exchange rates, generated a 71% depreciation of the parallel rate between December 1985 and November 1986, causing the dollar value of the monetary base to fall by 1 billion dollars (Table 17.26) and the exchange premium to reach 235%. This prompted the December 1986 depreciation of the official exchange rate by 93%.

However, this devaluation did not have the same fiscal consequences as those of 1983 and 1984. Since the government's external surplus was now much smaller, the income appropriated through real depreciation was now smaller. Nevertheless, as indicated in Table 17.20, in 1987 the oil exchange tax increased by 2.6% of GDP relative to 1986. However, since the government maintained a subsidised rate for food, medicines and registered debt, much of that rise was returned to the economy through

Table 17.19. Calculation of the oil exchange tax, 1985–1989

	1985	1986	1987	1988	1989
(1) Oil operating surplus (barrels)	72,879	51,130	92,472	99,631	305,606
(2) Oil exports (US$)	12,761	7,049	8,927	8,023	9,862
Implicit surplus share $(1/2)^a$ (barrels/US$)	5.71	7.25	10.36	12.42	30.99
(3) Constant real surplus share	5.71	6.49	7.88	9.41	15.10
(4) Corresponding oil surplus	72,879	45,782	70,385	75,528	148,903
(5) Oil exchange tax	0	5,348	22,087	24,103	156,703
(6) As a share of non-oil GDP (%)	0.0	1.3	3.9	3.2	13.9

[a] Calculated by multiplying the implicit surplus share by the non-oil GDP deflator and dividing by the US Wholesale price index

Source: International Monetary Fund

Note: Row 5: row 1 − row 4

Table 17.20. Estimated real transfers to the public sector (*as shares of non-oil GDP*)

	1985	1986	1987	1988	1989
Real value of seigniorage	2.3	1.1	1.8	1.7	2.2
Real value of exchange profits	4.3	1.6	−2.1	−2.9	−2.7
Oil exchange tax	0.0	1.3	3.9	3.2	13.9
Total transfers	6.6	4.0	3.6	2.0	13.4

Source: International Monetary Fund for Base Money, Exchange Profits and non-oil GDP. Table 17.19 for oil exchange tax

foreign exchange losses at the central bank, leaving a negligible fiscal effect.

During 1987 and 1988, fiscal policy was clearly expansionary. Public savings fell and investment increased from 8.6% of GDP in 1985 to 12% in 1988. This was an important element in determining private behaviour. The representative agent must have interpreted the absence of fiscal adjustment to a large oil shock to mean that the policy regime was unsustainable.

Agents tried to move away from domestic currency, as can be seen by examining the dollar value of the money base, which continued to fall in 1987 and 1988, through parallel rate depreciation. Given the prevailing exchange regime, this did not prevent the government from using seignorage to finance the fiscal deficit (see Tables 17.20 and 17.26).[29]

Again, inventories were a crucial channel through which the private sector could adjust to the expected collapse. Stock accumulation averaged 5.1% of GDP in 1987–88, indicating an anticipation of a jump in the price level. Finally, private investment remained high throughout the period.

The composition of absorption stayed remarkably stable throughout the 1986–88 period (Tables 17.21 and 17.22). Output growth accelerated in 1986 because of the public investment expansion, but consumption lagged behind. However, the situation tended to be reversed from 1987 onwards, so that by 1988 both consumption and investment had expanded in line with output.

There are also no significant differences in the composition of absorption between tradables and non-tradables, even though the first increased slightly more than the second, indicating the lack of adjustment. This result is consistent with the observed decline in the relative price of tradables *vs.* non-tradables throughout the period (Table 17.24). Part of this fall is explained by the fact that in the December 1986 reform, non-traditional exports, which had previously been assigned to the parallel exchange rate, were transferred to the new depreciated official rate. This

Table 17.21. Decomposition of the absolute absorption effect (*yearly changes as shares of non-oil GDP*)

	1985	1986	1987	1988	1989
Relative absorption effect	−2.9	−2.7	0.5	2.6	−10.5
Absolute absorption effect	1.0	4.2	7.1	0.9	−20.9
Public	1.6	3.5	0.1	3.0	−2.4
Consumption	−0.2	0.7	0.4	1.4	−0.2
Investment	1.8	2.7	−0.3	1.7	−2.4
Private	−0.6	0.6	6.9	6.7	−18.9
Consumption	0.2	2.4	3.2	4.0	−5.1
Investment	−0.4	−0.9	0.5	0.5	−4.7
Inventories	−0.4	−0.9	3.2	2.4	−10.1
Statistical discrepancy	0.0	0.0	−0.1	−0.1	−0.3

Table 17.22. Decomposition of the absolute absorption effect by type of good (*yearly changes as shares of non-oil GDP*)

	1985	1986	1987	1988	1989
Total absorption	1.0	4.1	6.7	9.0	−19.4
Non-tradables	1.4	3.0	3.2	4.7	−5.4
Publicly produced	−0.2	0.5	0.4	0.2	0.6
Privately produced	1.6	2.5	2.8	4.5	−6.0
Tradables	−0.4	1.1	3.5	4.3	−14.0
Locally produced	0.2	1.9	2.7	0.8	−6.2
Imported	−0.6	−0.8	0.8	3.5	−7.8
Consumption	−0.4	2.2	6.6	7.1	−13.6
Tradables	−1.8	0.2	3.8	3.4	−11.9
Locally produced	−0.2	1.6	2.9	0.6	−4.7
Imported	−1.6	−1.4	0.8	2.9	−7.2
Non-tradables	1.4	2.0	2.9	3.7	−1.7
Investment	1.4	1.9	0.1	1.9	−5.8
Tradables	1.4	0.9	−0.2	0.9	−2.1
Locally produced	0.4	0.3	−0.2	0.3	−1.5
Imported	0.9	0.6	0.0	0.6	−0.6
Non-tradables	0.0	1.0	0.4	1.0	−3.7
Construction	−0.4	0.9	0.3	0.9	−3.1
Other	0.4	0.2	0.1	0.2	−0.6

Note: In our disaggregation of consumption and investment into tradables and non-tradables, we used data on the composition of fixed investment to allocate spending in capital goods, while we left consumption as the residual between total absorption by type of good and investment. Consequently, inventory accumulation will appear as increased consumption of tradables

Table 17.23. GDP growth by sector (*percentage change as share of non-oil GDP*)

	1985	1986	1987	1988	1989
Non-oil GDP	3.4	5.9	5.4	5.7	−9.7
Private	3.0	5.0	4.5	4.9	−9.8
Tradables	1.4	2.6	1.8	0.4	−3.7
Non-tradables	1.6	2.5	2.8	4.6	−6.4
Construction	−0.4	0.9	0.3	0.9	−3.3
Other	2.0	1.6	2.5	3.7	−3.1
Public	0.3	0.8	0.8	0.6	0.2
Tradables	0.5	0.4	0.6	0.5	−0.2
Non-tradables	−0.2	−0.5	0.4	0.2	0.5

Table 17.24. Relative price shifts, 1985–1989 (*Index: 1984 = 100*)

	1985	1986	1987	1988	1989
Tradables vs non-tradables[a]	104.2	104.2	97.9	95.4	102.7
Real exchange rate[b]	101.7	103.7	169.2	157.9	178.6
Construction vs non-tradables[c]	101.5	99.7	100.4	101.1	101.5
WPI (imported) vs CPI[d]	106.1	110.1	123.2	114.0	120.9

[a] Ratio of GDP deflators for tradables (agriculture and manufacturing) vs non-tradables (construction, commerce, transport, services)
[b] IMF definition of the real exchange rate, trade weighted average
[c] Ratio of construction GDP deflator to total non-tradable deflator
[d] Ratio of wholesale price index of imported goods to consumer price index
Source: Central Bank of Venezuela

implied a significant nominal and real appreciation for exports of non-oil tradables.[30] However, the real exchange rate (IMF definition) for imports shows a major depreciation in 1987, as a consequence of the December 1986 devaluation.

We have already advanced one reason why this shift did not affect the domestic relative price of tradables: the new regime appreciated the exchange rate for non-traditional exports. One more cause is the fact that, under multiple exchange rates and import controls, a devaluation will reduce the implicit tariff appropriated by importers, thus lessening the effect on domestic prices. Partial support for this explanation comes from analysing the ratio of the wholesale (domestic) price of imported goods to the CPI. Since the first is mainly composed of tradables, whereas the second measures mostly non-tradables, this relative price is a proxy for the real exchange rate at domestic prices. As can be seen in Table 17.24, this ratio increases much less in 1987 than the IMF definition and falls much faster in 1988, indicating that the December 1986 devaluation did not significantly increase the relative price of importables. Hence, since it reduced the relative price of non-oil exportables and did not significantly increase the domestic price of importables, the overall impact on tradables (importables plus non-oil exportables) was negative.

In spite of the negative oil shock, there was no construction bust in the non-adjustment period 1986–88. The construction sector averaged a rate of growth of 5.2% over the period, in line with the rise of GDP. Its relative price remained fairly stable. This result contrasts with that observed in 1982, when the government also tried to prop up the economy through public investment, but the private investment declined by more, leaving an important aggregate slump in construction. In 1982, the reaction of the private sector was geared to increase its financial savings and transform them into capital flight. However, in 1986–88 the presence of multiple exchange rates left private agents with real goods as the only hedges against the eventual jump in the price level. In this context, construction competed with inventories as a store of value.[31]

Also, the presence of the multiple exchange rate regime affected the nature of the inventory build-up. If a devaluation is expected and capital flight is limited, then the best investment is to buy imports, given that their domestic price will rise in line with the depreciation. However, since agents were unable to satisfy their demand for foreign goods given quantitative restrictions on imports, they accumulated any storable domestic good. This shows up in Table 17.22 as a strong demand for domestically produced tradables.

Hence, the flight out of money had an expansionary impact on demand for domestic goods, which, given the prevailing high rates of unemployment left by the adjustment to the first shock, generated an important expansion in output. As shown in Table 17.23, GDP grew at rates in excess of 5% throughout the period. As a consequence of this growth, the unemployment rate fell by 5.2 percentage points between the end of 1985 and 1988.

To analyse the efficiency of adjustment, we assume a counterfactual in which output, absorption and real external oil income follow a 4% homothetic growth rate.[32] We also assume an initial output absorption gap of 2 percentage points of GDP given the size of the current account surplus in 1985.

Table 17.25 shows that, by 1988, primary absorption costs were 11.3 percentage points of trend non-oil GDP. Interestingly, secondary adjustment costs were negative, since the economy grew at rates higher than 4%. Hence, total adjustment costs were only 5.5% of trend GDP by 1988. However, since absorption grew more than in the counterfactual, actual adjustment costs were negative. This meant that by 1988 the adjustment was insufficient by the amount of the primary absorption costs. Excess growth in output compensated for excess expansion of absorption.

Table 17.25. How efficient was the adjustment to the second shock? (*percentage shares of trend non-oil GDP*)

	1986	1987	1988	1989
External shock	9.9	8.5	12.6	9.0
Primary absorption costs	7.9	6.2	11.3	6.8
Secondary adjustment costs	−2.0	−3.5	−5.2	8.3
Total adjustment costs	5.8	2.5	5.5	15.7
Actual adjustment	0.5	−1.7	−6.1	17.9
Excess adjustment	−5.0	−4.1	−11.0	1.9

Note: Primary adjustment cost is equal to the external shock minus the initial output absorption gap

Consequently, contrary to the first shock, non-adjustment did not have output costs.

As in 1983, when the balance of payments finally collapsed, drastic improvements did take place in the current account through a major fall in absorption. As shown in Table 17.16, there was a 2.3% improvement in the absolute real external shock (3.6% in relative terms given the decline in output of 9.7%). Absorption fell by 19% in real terms (i.e. 10.4% more than output, Table 17.17). This meant that the real trade balance improved by 14.4% of GDP. However, the improvement in the nominal trade balance was much greater given the important real depreciation which took place when the exchange rate was unified in March 1989.

The improvement in the trade balance can be accounted for by a rise in savings (7.8%), a fall in fixed investment (3.7%) and a major swing in inventories (11.3%, see Table 17.18). The rise in savings was exclusively due to the public sector (7.8%), since private savings actually fell (5.1%). Furthermore, most of the investment cut also took place in the private sector (3.6%).[33]

The jump in public sector savings is explained mainly by the 10.2% increase in the oil exchange tax (Tables 17.19 and 17.20), caused by devaluation.[34] Faced with such a drastic reduction in income, the private sector reduced both savings and consumption, each by an amount equal to 5.1% of GDP. Moreover, investment and inventories were cut by 4.7% and 10.1%, respectively, leaving a total decline in private absorption of 18.9% compared to only 2.4% for the public sector (Table 17.21).

The decline in private absorption exceeded the fall in income, generating an increase in financial savings. These resources were used by the private sector to purchase base money[35] (2.2% of GDP or 636 million dollars, see Tables 17.20 and 17.26) and to cancel import letters of credit for 3.3 billion dollars.[36]

The decline in absorption fell mostly on tradables (14% of GDP) but also

Table 17.26. Assets changes during the second oil shock (*US$m*)

	1985	1986	1987	1988	1989	1990
Levels						
International reserves	11,976	8,206	7,280	2,385	2,452	4,506
Dollar value of base money[a]	3,112	2,156	1,998	1,880	2,251	3,913
Yearly changes						
International reserves	1,692	−3,770	−926	−4,895	67	2,054
Dollar value of base money	110	−956	−157	−119	371	1,662
Dollar value of seignorage[b]	583	223	356	371	636	2,057

[a] Year-end nominal value of the base money divided by the year-end financial exchange rate
[b] Year-end nominal increase in base money divided by the yearly average financial exchange rate
Source: IMF, *Recent Economic Developments*, various years

affected non-tradables (5.4%). Within tradables, it fell by 7.8% on imports and 6.2% on domestic goods. Within non-tradables, it fell by 1.7% in consumer goods and by 3.7% in investment goods, indicating the presence of a major construction bust. These figures contrast with those of 1983. Then, the drop in absorption of non-tradables was marginal and the fall in tradables was mostly concentrated on imports. Hence, in 1989 the much larger downturn in domestic demand caused a much greater fall in GDP (9.7%). As Table 17.23 shows, the decline was evenly split between tradables, non-tradable consumer goods and construction.[37]

The drop in tradable output took place in spite of a major real depreciation. The IMF-style real exchange rate rose by 13.1%, the relative price of tradables *vs.* non-tradables by 7.7% and the ratio of the WPI for imports to the CPI by 6.1% (Table 17.24). The decline in output can be explained by the fact that inventory dishoarding increased the effective supply of goods at a moment when final demand was crumpling. This effect was further amplified by the fact that inventories were mostly composed of domestic goods and not imports, owing to the presence of controls during the period of non-adjustment. Moreover, trade liberalisation and the unification and devaluation of the nominal exchange rate reduced the value of implicit tariffs, thus causing domestic relative prices to shift less than border prices, which are those measured in the IMF definition of the real exchange rate.

Even though the proportional decline in construction was much larger than the fall in other private non-tradables (25% *vs.* 7%), its relative price was not affected. However, both sectors did fall with respect to tradables given real depreciation. However, the construction bust cannot be explained by a fall in aggregate savings, since these actually increased.

Turning now to the issue of the efficiency of adjustment (Table 17.25) we see an increase in the secondary costs of adjustment of 13.5% of GDP, leaving output 8.3% below the trend. Underadjustment was eliminated, leaving a small excess adjustment of 1.9% of GDP. Actual adjustment costs amounted to 17.9%, 46.4% of which were secondary (i.e. inefficient). This contrasts markedly with the figures for 1983, when less than one-quarter of the much larger actual adjustment costs were secondary. Thus, it can be concluded that adjustment in 1989 was more inefficient than in 1983.[38]

17.8. Lessons and Conclusions

We have analysed two permanent negative oil shocks and concentrated on the feature which distinguishes them from positive shocks: the fact that the solvency of the government is questioned, making the policy regime unsustainable unless prompt fiscal action is taken. The two shocks were similar in many respects: they were unexpected, of comparable magnitudes and they struck the economy just after the completion of stabilisation efforts which had left the public and external accounts in surplus and had increased unemployment. Moreover, the shocks appeared at similar points in the five-year political cycle and with the government committed to fiscal expansion. In both cases, the arrival of the shock was followed by a period of non-adjustment: real relative absorption was not cut, leaving the trade balance to bear the brunt of the fall in external income.

Owing to the lack of fiscal adjustment, the reaction of private agents was dominated by strategies designed to avoid the costs associated with the eventual public default. However, since the two shocks took place under very different exchange rate regimes, the strategies open to private agents and the policy instruments available to the government were quite different. In 1982, under a single fixed exchange rate, private agents could protect the value of their domestic financial assets by converting them into US dollars at the set peg. They did so to the tune of 6.5 billion dollars in 1982. Moreover, they could stockpile imported goods. By contrast, in 1986 the multiple exchange rate regime severely limited the efficacy of these strategies. The attempt to transform domestic assets into foreign assets led to a rise in the exchange rate premium and to a fall in the dollar value of domestic assets, rather than to an increase in the stock of dollars. Thus, in spite of more than 1 billion dollars of seignorage issued between 1986 and 1988, the dollar value of base money fell by 1.2 billion dollars. Furthermore, since imports were rationed, speculative stockpiling had to take place through the purchase of domestic storable goods.

This more restricted set of defensive strategies on the part of private agents explains why the government was able to maintain the period of non-adjustment for three years before being forced to take corrective measures, a fact which is in stark contrast to the swiftness of the collapse in 1982–83. From the macroeconomic point of view, this would imply that multiple exchange rate regimes are more robust to external shocks than single predetermined pegs.

There are other characteristics which make non-adjustment under multiple regimes politically more attractive. Since inventory accumulation is directed towards domestic goods, it has a positive impact on output. Also, since imports are restricted, the relative price of domestic tradables is protected from severe real appreciation as implicit tariffs rise with excess demand for foreign exchange. By contrast, under fixed exchange rates, stockpiling affects mostly imports and is financed through a reduction in spending on non-tradables and on domestically produced tradables, thus having a contractionary impact on output. This effect is enhanced by the fact that the fixed exchange rate does not provide a compensating stimulus to tradable output. In the Venezuelan case, there was significant real appreciation in 1982. Hence, non-adjustment is expansionary under multiple exchange rates and contractionary under fixed rates.

Many of these advantages work in the opposite direction as soon as the balance of payments collapse forces the government to act. As agents now try to restructure their wealth portfolios, they quickly run down their inventories. In the case of fixed exchange rates, these are made up mostly of imported goods; with multiple rates they are composed of domestic goods. Therefore, dishoarding has rather different effects: it mostly improves the balance of payments in the first case, whereas it brings down domestic output in the second. This explains in part why the recession was much more severe and the adjustment more inefficient in 1989 than in 1983, even though the cut in absorption was smaller.

The inventory cycle plays itself out in three periods: stockpiling during non-adjustment, dishoarding immediately after the collapse and a return to balance thereafter. This means that part of the sudden improvement in the trade balance during the year of the collapse is not sustainable, since it is based on dishoarding, but that inventory change will not remain negative for long. Hence, although the negative swing in 1983 reduced real relative absorption by 19% of GDP, explaining about two-thirds of the improvement in the trade balance, in 1984 there was a positive inventory swing of 11.7% of GDP, as dishoarding ended. This expansionary effect took place in the context of a major fiscal adjustment which reduced other forms of absorption.

During the second shock, the decline in inventories in 1989 amounted to 12.5% of GDP (Table 17.21). This means that in 1990 the end of dishoarding must have had an important positive impact on absorption. How that effect was accommodated is not discussed for lack of data, but evidence of GDP growth of approximately 4% and stagnant imports suggests that domestic output accommodated the increase in demand. Hence, the fall in GDP during the first year of adjustment may be mostly a short-run phenomenon that will disappear in the next phase of the inventory cycle.

Also, during the years of balance of payments crisis (i.e. 1983 and 1989), dishoarding generated excess domestic supply of tradables, causing output in this sector to drop, despite an important depreciation in the IMF measure of the real exchange rate. Domestic relative prices changed by much less than border prices or in fact moved in opposite directions, as happened in 1983. Only in the year following the collapse does one get a supply response of tradables, which takes place in the context of an increase in demand given the now positive swing in inventories.

The analysis presented leads to some insights into the issue of construction busts. Although both shocks were eventually followed by a decline in construction activity, the start of the collapse was very different in each case. During the first shock, construction output declined in 1982 (i.e. the period of non-adjustment) in spite of an important increase in public investment. By contrast, the construction sector grew in line with aggregate output during the 1986–88 period of non-adjustment, in spite of an important decline in domestic savings. We have explained this disparity by noting that different exchange regimes affect the relative attractiveness of real estate as a form of safeguarding assets when a regime collapse is expected. Under fixed exchange rates, foreign assets and imported goods are preferred. Under multiple rates, real estate competes mostly with domestically produced stocks of goods as a store of value. In this context, it has the advantage of a lower rate of depreciation.

From a political economy viewpoint, it is not at all clear that the ability of multiple exchange regimes to prevent capital flight makes for better policymaking. It is reasonable to expect politicians faced with a negative shock to put off decisions until after the next election. In our two cases, the government attempted to do just that. In 1983, it fell short of the target in spite of the short distances involved. By contrast, the multiple exchange rate regime permitted, by allowing a postponement of adjustment through a limitation of the ability of economic agents to protect themselves against the eventual default losses, the government to drag its feet for three years in 1986–88. Hence, robustness may limit the degree to which markets discipline governments into responsible behaviour. Furthermore, we find evidence that the collapse under multiple exchange rates may lead to more inefficient adjustment, with heavier costs in terms of output.

Finally, we may now turn to the initial question: was the Venezuelan mess a case of dancing out of step or of stepping out of line? Clearly, there was a bit of both. With shocks appearing just as the government had committed itself to fiscal expansion, there was clearly a lack of the needed synchrony that makes for elegant dancing. But putting off adjustment must count at least as a misdemeanour. Government spending is too rigid a process to make it an adequate partner to the frivolous oil revenue. In its attempt to dance to such a boisterous tune, the government is bound to find itself stepping out of line.

NOTES

1. Gelb (1988) presents an international study of the two positive oil shocks of the 1970s.
2. see Corden and Neary (1982), Corden (1984), Neary and Wijnbergen (1986).
3. Wijnbergen (1984) discusses also the use of production subsidies for non-booming manufactures subject to learning-by-doing.
4. Basically, there was no supply response. Output was determined either by OPEC quotas, as was the case most of the time, or by installed capacity. Usually, the marginal cost of output is well below price, so increases in price do not bring in new production.
5. See, for example, Obstfeld (1986a), Buiter (1986b). Froot and Obstfeld (1989) analyse the case in which the regime change is known only with uncertainty.
6. Buiter (1986a) analyses the case in which an economy is allowed to borrow in order to defend the exchange rate. He argues that since borrowing is costly, it may actually increase the size of the speculative attack.
7. The implications of this type of repudiation risk have been used by Ize and Ortiz (1989) and Khan and Ul-Haque (1985) to account for the simultaneous occurrence of capital flight and external borrowing.
8. Irreversibility and uncertainty have been introduced in investment models yielding an option price for waiting. See Dixit (1989), Krugman (1989) and Pindyck (1989).
9. With large exchange premia, overinvoicing reduces the real effective price of imports, causing an increase in demand.
10. This condition will be met if government oil revenues exceed spending in tradables and in external debt service. See Hausman (1990b: 244–7).
11. If demand for money is assumed to be negatively related to the inflation rate, then the possibility of multiple equilibria exists with at least two very different inflation rates generating the same inflation tax. In this case, the economy may jump from one inflation rate to the other.
12. Our framework elaborates on Corden (1988) and Meller (1990).
13. Venezuelan policy in this period has been analysed by Baptista (1989) and Hausmann (1990b: ch. 10).
14. Presidential elections take place in Venezuela in early December every five years. The new government takes office in the first quarter of the following year. The reader should keep in mind the recurring coincidence of the political and economic cycles: 1979, 1984 and 1989 are years in which newly elected governments took over and also periods in which stabilisation programmes were adopted.

15. On the impact of the oil windfall see Pazos (1979), Rodríguez (1987a), Bourguignon and Gelb (1989) and Hausmann (1990b: ch. 5).
16. It is interesting to note that on his inaugural address in 1979, President Luis Herrera Campins announced that he was receiving an over-indebted country and named a commission to study the problem and propose solutions. As a consequence of this initative the Public Credit Organic Law was made stricter in 1981 and short-term debt of decentralised agencies was restructured. However, this did not stop the fall into the debt crisis which would hit Venezuela in 1983. On this period see Palma (1985), Rodríguez (1987a) and Hausmann (1990b).
17. Even though total public sector spending increased by only 0.5% in 1979–80, expenditures on non-tradables rose by 5.1% and those on tradables fell by 11.1%. Consequently, the policy alleviated the balance of payments more than it did the internal imbalance.
18. If the process was trend-stationary the prediction would have implied a price fall.
19. Wack (1985) recounts the way in which Royal Dutch Shell interpreted these changes in their strategic planning process.
20. Not even Saudi Arabia expected this turn of events, as was made clear by the dismissal of the Oil Minister and architect of Saudi oil strategy, Sheikh Ahmed Zaki el-Yamani, in November 1986.
21. Throughout the text, unless otherwise specified, GDP will simply refer to non-oil GDP.
22. Unless otherwise specified, all numbers for the 1968–84 period come from the CORDIPLAN/ILPES database. Information for the 1984–89 period is taken from the National Accounts Statistics for 1989.
23. This conclusion is only valid when comparing the two end-points, 1981 and 1985. In the process of adjustment both foreign savings and inventories play a major role.
24. The real depreciation effect of Table 17.6 captures this same phenomenon since it corresponds to the change in the relative price of oil income in terms of domestic output. It estimates it at 5 percentage points of GDP.
25. Given the multiple exchange rate system in place, seignorage could be increased but at the cost of a rise in the foreign exchange premium. In December 1985 the premium was 96% (see Table 17.1).
26. Notice that Table 17.12 presents the sectoral growth rates weighted by the share of each sector in total non-oil output. It represents the contribution of each sector to the aggregate growth rate. Since the tradable sector is less than half the size of the non-tradable sector, the same contribution implies a much higher growth rate.
27. The relative price of tradables declined 4.2% while the IMF-style real exchange rate appreciated 10.9% (Table 17.13).
28. Real depreciation increased the value of the trade surplus measured in units of non-oil GDP.
29. The simultaneous presence of positive seignorage and of a fall in the dollar value of base money indicates that the public did not demand the additional supply of money and tried to convert it into foreign assets.

30. At the time of the December 1986 devaluation the parallel rate had reached 25.2 Bs/US$, while the new official rate was devalued from 7.5 to 14.5 Bs/US$.
31. One could venture the hypothesis that real estate, *vis-à-vis* inventories, has a lower correlation with the exchange rate but a smaller rate of depreciation (perishability). Hence, as the date of the collapse nears, there should be a declining emphasis in construction and a heightened demand for inventories. This trend appears to be present in Tables 17.18 and 17.21.
32. The fact that unemployment was higher in 1985 than in 1981 leads us to assume a slightly higher counterfactual growth rate.
33. These numbers refer to savings and investment rates as they appear in Table 17.18. In real terms, i.e. not including changes in relative prices or in GDP, public and private investment fell by 2.4% and 4.7% of GDP, respectively. See Table 17.21.
34. Part of this increase had to be transferred abroad through the increase in the value of debt service measured in units of domestic non-oil GDP. Notice that exchange subsidies remained stable at around 2% of GDP. Another contributing factor to the increase in public savings was the rise in oil income.
35. As shown in Table 17.26, in 1989, for the first time since the start of the second oil shock, seignorage was not accompanied by a decline in the dollar value of the money base, indicating that a good portion of it was actually demanded given the sudden increase in the price level.
36. Under the multiple exchange rate system in place, imports had to be financed for a minimum period of 180 days and were guaranteed a fixed official rate. When the balance of payments collapsed in 1989, the government gave only partial coverage for this exchange rate guarantee. Moreover, the minimum-financing-period requirement for imports was lifted. Both changes induced private agents to reduce their short-term foreign liabilities.
37. Given that construction has the smallest share in output, it showed the largest proportional decline, falling by 25%. This compares to a drop of 7% for other private non-traded goods and to a descent of 12.9% in private tradables.
38. Said differently, more of the actual adjustment costs went to reduce output and less to improve the balance of payments.

REFERENCES

Baptista, A. (1989) 'Tiempo de Mengua: Los Años Finales de una Estructura Económica', in Cunill-Grau *et al.* (eds.) *Venezuela Contemporánea 1974–89*, Caracas: Fundación Mendoza.

Bourguignon, F. and A. Gelb (1989) 'Venezuela' in Gelb (ed.) *Oil Windfalls: A Blessing or a Curse?*, Oxford: Oxford University Press.

Buiter, W.H. (1986a) 'Borrowing to Defend the Exchange Rate and the Timing and Magnitude of Speculative Attacks', NBER Working Paper No. 1844 (February).

——(1986b) 'Fiscal Prerequisites for a Viable Managed Exchange Rate Regime: A Non-technical Eclectic Introduction', NBER Working Paper No. 2041 (October).

Corden, W.M. (1984) 'Booming Sector and Dutch Disease Economics: Survey and Consolidation', *Oxford Economic Papers*, 36: 359–80.

——(1988) 'Macroeconomic Adjustment in Developing Countries', IMF Working Paper Series 88/13, Washington, DC: International Monetary Fund (February).

——and J.P. Neary (1982) 'Booming Sector and De-Industrialisation in a Small Open Economy', *Economic Journal*, 92: 825–48.

CORDIPLAN (1981) *El Sexto Plan de la Nación 1981–85*, Caracas: Cordiplán.

——(1984) *El Séptimo Plan de la Nación 1984–88*, Caracas: Cordiplán.

Dixit, Avinash K. (1989) 'Intersectoral Capital Reallocation under Price Uncertainty', *Journal of International Economics*, 26(3/4): 309–25.

Dornbusch, R. (1976) 'Expectations and Exchange Rate Dynamics', *Journal of Political Economy* (December) 84(6): 1161–76.

Edwards S. (1989) *Real Exchange Rates, Devaluation and Adjustment: Exchange Rate Policy for Developing Countries*, Cambridge, MA: MIT Press.

Francés, A. (1990) *Venezuela Posible*, Caracas: Ediciones IESA.

Froot, K.A. and M. Obstfeld (1989) 'Exchange Rate Dynamics under Stochastic Regime Shifts: A Unified Approach', NBER Working Paper No. 2835.

Gelb, A. (1988) *Oil Windfalls: A Blessing or a Curse?*, Oxford: Oxford University Press.

Hausmann, R. (1981) *Oil Rents and Capital Accumulation in the Venezuelan Economy*, Cornell University (unpublished Ph.D dissertation).

——(1990a) 'Venezuela' in J. Williamson (ed.) *Latin American Adjustment: How Much Has Happened?*, Washington, DC: Institute for International Economics, pp. 224–44.

——(1990b) *Shocks Externos y Ajuste Macroeconómico*, Caracas: Banco Central de Venezuela.

——(1990c) 'The Big Bang Approach to Macro Balance in Venezuela', paper presented at the World Bank's Economic Development Institute Senior Policy Seminar: 'Latin America: Facing the Challenge of Adjustment and Growth', held at IESA, Caracas, 19–22 July.

Hull, J. (1989) *Options, Futures and other Derivative Securities*, Prentice-Hall International Editions.

IBRD (1961) *The Economic Development of Venezuela: A Report by Mission from the International Bank for Reconstruction and Development*, Baltimore, MD: Johns Hopkins University Press.

Ize, A. and G. Ortiz (1989) 'Fiscal Rigidities, Public Debt and Capital Flight', in M. Blejer and K. Chu (eds) *Fiscal Policy, Stabilization and Growth in Developing Countries*, Washington, DC: International Monetary Fund.

Khan, M. and N. Ul-Haque (1985) 'Foreign Borrowing, and Capital Flight: A Formal Analysis', International Monetary Fund Staff Papers 32: 608–28.

Kiguel, M. and S. Lizondo (1989) 'Adoption and Abandonment of Exchange Controls Regimes', Washington, DC: World Bank (unpublished manuscript).

Krugman, P. (1989) *Exchange Rate Instability*, Cambridge, MA: MIT Press.

Krugman, P. and L. Taylor (1978) 'Contractionary Effects of Devaluation', *Journal of International Economics*, 8: 445–56.

Matus, C. (1985) *Política y Plan*, Caracas: Ediciones IVEPLAN.

Meller P. (1990) 'Chile' in J. Williamson (ed.) *Latin American Adjusmtent: How Much*

Has Happened?, Washington, DC: Institute for International Economics, pp. 54–84.

Merton, R.C. (1976) 'Option Pricing when Underlying Stock Returns Are Discontinuous' *Journal of Financial Economics*, 3(1/2) Jan/March: 124–44.

Montenegro, S. (1990) 'Stabilization Policy in Open Developing Economies: The Case of Colombia', Oxford (unpublished Ph.D. dissertation).

Neary, J.P. and S. van Wijnbergen (1986) *Natural Resources and the Macroeconomy*, Oxford: Basil Blackwell.

Obstfeld, M. (1984) 'Balance of Payments Crises and Devaluation', *Journal of Money, Credit and Banking*, 16: 208–17.

——(1986a) 'Rational and Self-Fulfilling Balance of Payments Crises', *American Economic Review*, 76: 72–81.

——(1986b) 'Capital Controls, the Dual Exchange Rate and Devaluation', *Journal of International Economics*, 20: 1–20.

Palma, P. (1985) '1974–83: Una Década de Contrastes en la Economía Venezolana', Caracas: Academia Nacional de Ciencias Económicas, Cuaderno 11 (Second Edition, November).

Pazos, F. (1979) 'Efectos de un Aumento Súbito en los Ingresos Externos: La Economía de Venezuela en el Quinquenio 1974–78', Caracas: Banco Central de Venezuela (mimeo).

Park, D. and J. Sachs (1987) 'Capital Controls and the Timing of Exchange Regime Collapse', NBER Working Paper No. 2250 (May).

Pindyck, R. (1989) 'Irreversibility, Uncertainty, and Investment, Policy, Research and External Affairs', Working Paper Series No. 294, International Economics Department, World Bank (October).

Rodríguez, M. (1987a) 'La Estrategia del Crecimiento Económico para Venezuela', Caracas: Academia Nacional de Ciencias Económicas, Cuaderno 19.

——(1987b) 'Consequences of Capital Flight for Latin American Debtor Countries', in D.R. Lessard and J. Williamson (eds) *Capital Flight and Third World Debt*, Washington Institute for International Economics, pp. 129–44.

Salter, W. (1959) 'Internal and External Balance: the Role of Price and Expenditure Effects', *Economic Record*, 35: 226–38.

Swan, T. (1960) 'Economic Control in a Dependent Economy', *Economic Record*, 36: 51–66.

Wack, P. (1985) 'Scenarios: Shooting the Rapids', *Harvard Business Review*, 63: 139–50.

Wijnbergen, S. van (1984) 'Inflation, Employment and the Dutch Disease in Oil-Exporting countries', *Quarterly Journal of Economics*, 99: 233–50.

18

The Mexican Oil Boom, 1977–85

MICHAEL GAVIN

18.1. Introduction

Throughout the twentieth century petroleum has played a prominent, and occasionally decisive, role in Mexico's political and economic development, and the 1970s and early 1980s were no exception. Mexico was profoundly shaken by the oil market disturbances that rocked the world economy during that period, and only with great difficulty did Mexico emerge from the macroeconomic cloud left by the shocks.

This chapter assesses the impact of these shocks on the Mexican economy. The principal difficulty in doing so lies in disentangling their effects from the effects of other external and domestic economic policy disturbances. On the one hand, macroeconomic policy was importantly influenced by the oil shock; on the other, the petroleum sector policies that made the boom possible were themselves heavily influenced by the need to extract the economy from the difficulties in which previous macroeconomic excesses had left it. Similarly, the rise in world interest rates that followed the United States and European disinflation after 1978 was a separate factor that had as much to do with the Mexican economic collapse—and much more to do with its timing—than did developments in petroleum markets, which were on balance favourable until well into the period of macroeconomic crisis after August 1982. But the rise in world interest rates would not have had such severe repercussions if economic policy had been more conservative during the 1970s, as it would necessarily have been in the absence of the oil boom. Indeed, a respectable argument can be made that the most important channel through which the Mexican oil boom was transmitted to the economy was by relaxing—for a time—fiscal and external constraints, thus permitting continuation of extravagant fiscal and monetary policies and, in short, providing the Mexican authorities with financial rope for the eventual macroeconomic hanging.

It would be futile, in light of these interactions between policy and petroleum markets, to try to analyse the Mexican oil boom outside a broad, macroeconomic context. Having said this, the oil boom was the dominant event of the period. Even if it had not been accompanied by self-inflicted macroeconomic wounds, the shock would nevertheless have rocked the economy severely. The fact that the effects of the oil boom were significantly altered, and in important ways amplified, by government policy responses makes the episode no less interesting. In particular, the episode is a particularly vivid illustration of the fact that not only trade policy, but also macroeconomic policy more generally can respond endogenously to resource booms, and of the unfortunate consequences that emerge when the induced policy response is perverse.

The chapter is organised as follows. Section 18.2 lays out some salient aspects of the structure and development of the Mexican economy up to about 1976, just before the oil boom may be said to have begun, and discusses key aspects of the control regime in place during the boom. This background is relevant because it sets the stage for the public sector responses that, we argue, constituted the most important mechanism through which the oil boom was transmitted—in the end disastrously—to the economy as a whole.

Section 18.3 discusses the nature and magnitude of the oil boom itself, quantifying the impact of the boom on the economy as a whole and on the distribution of the income between the public sector, which receives almost all of Mexico's petroleum-related income, and the private sector. We discuss here plausible expectations about the boom, as well as actual outcomes, taking up in particular the question of whether the boom was considered temporary.

Section 18.4 describes the response of the economy to the boom, as well as the crash that followed the onset of the debt crisis in mid-1982 and the dramatic softening of oil markets in late 1985. The most dramatic features of the aggregate developments are the phenomenal investment boom that accompanied the oil boom and the equally dramatic crash after external financing dried up in mid-1982.

This investment boom raises the two key questions of this chapter: first, what caused the investment boom? And second, since the high rates of external borrowing of the late 1970s were accompanied by high domestic savings and investment, why did they lead to insolvency and economic crisis in August 1982? These questions cannot satisfactorily be answered without considering the fiscal authorities' response to the oil boom. Accordingly, Section 18.5 disaggregates the economy into public and private sectors. We find that the private sector did in fact save a high fraction of the windfall income during the boom leading up to 1982, whereas the public sector was dissaving. This section also clarifies the means by which the public sector transferred the oil windfall to the private sector. Finally, Section 18.6 concludes with a summary and some tentative answers to the key questions raised by the Mexican experience.

18.2. Macroeconomic Background

18.2.1. Overview: From 'Stabilising Development' to 'Shared Development'

After a period of some substantial economic turbulence, which ended with a large devaluation and fiscal adjustment in the early 1950s, the Mexican economy entered a two-decade period of rapid economic growth, financial stability, and relatively robust external accounts that has come to be known as the time of 'stabilising development'. Real GDP growth, at roughly 6% per year, was substantially in excess of Mexico's 3% population growth. With inflation approximately equal to that of its major trading partners, Mexico was able to maintain an exchange rate of 12.5 pesos to the dollar from mid-1954 until August 1976.

Thus, when President Luis Echeverría came to power in 1971, the Mexican economy had experienced nearly twenty years of macroeconomic stability and growth. However, proving that at least one cloud can be found around every silver lining, the Echeverría administration came to office convinced that the preceding economic development had in several important respects fallen short of potential, and that economic policy required significant changes. In particular, the new administration emphasised the need to address apparently worsening problems of unemployment and income distribution, and to solve these problems it announced an era of 'shared development', embracing a strategy that focused on public sector expansion, with the aim of rectifying social inequalities through provision of subsidised public services, and reducing unemployment by placing workers on government payrolls.

In the five years leading up to 1976 public sector employment doubled, and total public spending rose from 20.5% to 30% of GDP. A failed 1972 attempt to reform the tax system left tax revenues stagnant, with the result that the public sector deficit rose dramatically. The government covered excess expenditure in part by money creation, and inflation accelerated dramatically. External deficits associated with government borrowing and an increasingly overvalued exchange rate led to a large increase in Mexico's foreign debt, which rose from US$6.3 billion in 1971 to US$28 billion by 1976. By that time the bankruptcy of the Echeverría model of development was apparent; capital fled the country, and domestic real investment fell from 14% of GDP in the early 1970s to 12.7% in 1975. In 1977 the incoming López-Portillo administration found itself constrained by an agreement with the IMF that called for devaluation, limits on external debt accumulation, and very substantial fiscal retrenchment.

Mexico's history during these six years was perhaps exaggerated, but hardly unique. During 1976 and 1977 the IMF also had major rescue operations underway in the United Kingdom, Portugal, and Italy, where budgetary excess had similarly led to external crisis, necessitating IMF intervention and resulting, ultimately, in stabilisation. The difference lies in the subsequent years, when the Mexican authorities were enabled by a sudden rush of oil revenue to terminate the recently negotiated IMF programme and to choose their own macroeconomic course for another four-and-a-half fateful years. This oil revenue was due, in part, to high oil prices and recent, surprisingly large oil discoveries in southern Mexico. But it also reflected an explicit decision by the government to exploit these reserves by producing for export, a decision that was itself a response to the financial and macroeconomic constraints that bound the incoming López-Portillo administration at the end of 1976.

18.2.2. The Oil Industry in Mexico

Petroleum has been produced in Mexico since 1901, and the country was in fact the world's second largest producer in 1921, when it supplied nearly 25% of world demand. But as the economy developed the petroleum sector became of decreasing relative significance. By the early 1970s, the petroleum sector accounted for less than 2.5% of GNP, and the state-owned oil company, Pemex, accounted for less than 3.5% of federal tax revenue. Employment, at roughly 75,000 individuals, was a trivial fraction of Mexico's total employment—which then numbered about 13 million[1]— though a significantly higher fraction of the economy's physical capital was employed in the sector.[2]

Thus, in the early 1970s the petroleum sector was important to Mexico, but in no sense dominant. Indeed, by the early 1970s Mexico was for the first time a small net importer of petroleum products. Thus it was that in late 1973, when the first oil shock washed over the world economy, Mexico was in the short run adversely affected. However, developments had been set in train that would transform these high prices from burden into bonanza.

18.2.3. The Control Regime

Three aspects of the control regime are particularly salient here, commercial policy, exchange rate policy and exchange controls.

Since the 1940s the government of Mexico had operated under the assumption that it was necessary for the public sector to take the lead in shaping the nation's economic development. The 1941 First Law of Manufacturing Industries set the nation solidly on a course of import-substituting industrialisation, towards which end the government utilised subsidies, tax incentives, tariff and quota protection, and in particular cheap energy. Import protection was applied more rigorously to finished industrial goods, with 'productive' imports of industrial raw materials receiving more relaxed treatment. As external balances intensified during the 1971–76 period of 'shared development', import controls were tightened. However, as we shall see below, imports of final goods were not rigidly controlled, and fluctuations in the level of imports served partially to satisfy variations in domestic demand. But though quotas were not rigidly binding, the trade regime provided some protection for domestic production, and the relative price of domestic production clearly increased with domestic demand.

The second key feature of the control regime was a commitment to fixed exchange rates. Recall that Mexico maintained until 1976 the same US dollar parity that had prevailed since 1954. In the midst of economic crisis the outgoing Echeverría administration had devalued, but this experience was remembered as a painful one, and the incoming López-Portillo administration was much more reluctant to abandon the exchange-rate parity than it was to abandon the policies required to make the rate sustainable.

The third, and arguably most important, feature of the control regime was the relative openness of Mexico's capital account. This left great scope for the private sector to place its savings abroad, safe from high inflation and domestic taxation.

18.3. Nature and Magnitude of the Oil Boom

18.3.1. The Oil Boom: Ex Post

Figure 18.1 illustrates the world price of Mexican petroleum in 1988 dollars.[3] By this measure, the world price of Mexico's petroleum rose fourfold from about US$5.00 per barrel in the 1960s and early 1970s to over US$20.00 per barrel in 1974, and remained at roughly that level until the fourth quarter of 1979. At that point it rose even more dramatically, averaging nearly US$40.00 per barrel in 1980, and declining gradually to roughly US$27.00 per barrel in 1982–85. In 1986 the price fell dramatically, and during 1986–88 it averaged about US$14.00 per barrel—a catastrophic fall compared with the previous twelve years, but still far more favourable than before the first oil shock.

In terms of prices, therefore, the oil boom would appear to span the twelve-year period 1974–85. However, the Mexican oil boom should really be dated from approximately 1977 to 1985, with most of the revenue accruing during the 1980–85 period. This is because, during the period 1974–76, Mexico was roughly self-sufficient in petroleum, and not an exporter of any significance. It is only after 1976, when petroleum production exploded and Mexico became once again a major oil exporter, that high oil prices conferred major benefits on Mexico. Unlike for many other

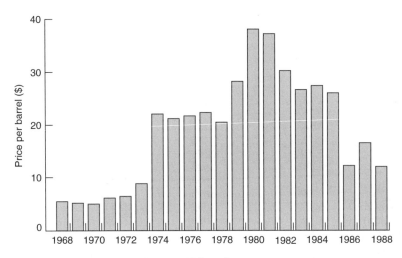

Figure 18.1. World oil price (*1988 US$/barrel*)

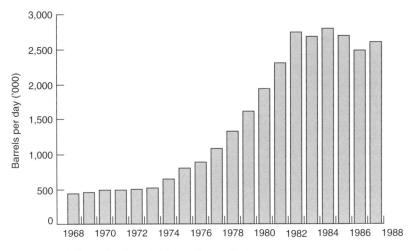

Figure 18.2. Oil production (*'000 barrels per day*)

oil-exporting economies, then, income effects from the oil boom were due largely to increases in production. We turn now to a documentation of developments in the petroleum sector, and a quantification of their effects on Mexico's national income.

Table 18.1 documents the growth in Mexican oil production, along with some other data on the petroleum industry, and Figure 18.2 illustrates the rapid increase in production that occurred after 1976. Perhaps the most striking feature of Table 18.1 is the increase in the official estimate of

Table 18.1. The oil industry

	Proven reserves (bn. bbl)	Production (m. bbd)	World price (1988 US$)	Net exports (m. bbd)
1960	4.787	0.298	5.00	0.011
1965	5.357	0.362	5.75	0.051
1970	5.567	0.487	5.00	0.036
1971	5.428	0.486	6.19	0.001
1972	5.388	0.506	6.44	−0.019
1973	5.432	0.525	8.85	−0.042
1974	5.773	0.653	22.12	−0.011
1975	6.338	0.806	21.20	0.052
1976 (end)	6.350	0.897	21.71	0.072
1977 (Jan)	11.160	1.086	22.37	0.197
(1977 end)	16.001			
1978	40.192	1.330	20.49	0.338
1979	45.803	1.618	28.26	0.516
1980	60.126	1.941	38.18	0.863
1981	72.008	2.313	37.20	1.154
1982	72.008	2.748	30.30	1.526
1983	72.500	2.688	26.77	1.604
1984	71.500	2.806	27.46	1.608
1985	70.900	2.703	26.14	1.519
1986	70.000	2.500	12.38	1.345
1987	69.000	2.616	16.75	1.370
1988			12.18	

Note: bbl = barrels; bbd = barrels per day

Sources: For estimated reserves, Gentleman (1984) and *La Economia Mexicana en Cifras*, various issues. Other data from *La Economia Mexicana en Cifras, International Financial Statistics*, and US Dept. of Energy *Monthly Energy Review*, various issues

petroleum reserves from 6.35 billion barrels at the end of 1976 to over 11 billion in January 1977, and 16 billion barrels at the end of 1977. In interpreting these data, it is useful to bear in mind some political aspects of the officially estimated reserves and the associated constraints on petroleum production.[4]

Beginning around 1970, efforts by Pemex to locate and extract more oil had intensified as the spectre of substantial oil imports loomed on the more-or-less immediate horizon. However, these efforts were oriented entirely towards satisfaction of domestic demand at the customary, heavily subsidised prices, and not towards renewal of Mexico's export potential. Indeed, the magnitude of the big discoveries that were made during 1972 was intentionally understated,[5] allegedly to forestall domestic and US pressure for big increases in production and exports; and as late as 1973 the director general of Pemex voiced his strong opposition to Mexican oil exports.

It was not until the end of 1976, when newly inaugurated President José López-Portillo appointed the aggressive, export-oriented Díaz Serrano to be director general of Pemex, that Mexican policy turned towards rapid expansion of output and exports. The leap in the officially estimated petroleum reserves, which was announced by Díaz Serrano some weeks after his appointment, should therefore be taken as a signal of the López-Portillo administration's determination aggressively to develop Mexico's oil fields for immediate export rather than pursue the previous administration's policy of conservation for future domestic use. The altered estimate of reserves was at least as much news about government policy as it was about geological reality. This policy decision was, in turn, motivated by the macroeconomic crisis that the López-Portillo administration inherited.

Hence, the true dimensions of the boom could not have become apparent to informed observers until some time in mid- or late 1976, before which neither the huge potential nor the official inclination to become an exporter was generally known. By December 1976, however, the government's plans to cash in Mexico's oil reserves had become crystal clear, since Díaz Serrano then announced a six-year plan to increase production to 2.25 million barrels per day by 1982. Table 18.1 and Figure 18.2 show that actual output was in fact slightly higher than contemplated in this plan, but actual output was roughly as announced in the 1976 six-year plan, and should therefore correspond roughly to expectations as of late 1976.

We now estimate the magnitude of the windfall generated by the high world prices and the production boom documented above. We begin by defining a counterfactual baseline, which is intended to represent a reasonable expectation for the sector as of about 1976. As noted above, Mexico's oil trade was in small deficit in the early 1970s. But attempts had been underway to increase domestic production and reduce domestic consumption to avoid becoming a significant importer of oil. The sector was receiving substantially higher investment, production was rising, and domestic prices had been increased somewhat to dampen demand. In short, it would have been reasonable to anticipate production increases roughly in line with overall economic growth, if only because the government had displayed a determination to avoid large imports or exports of petroleum.

We therefore take a baseline scenario in which both production and consumption of petroleum grows at 5% per year; slower than during the 'Mexican miracle' before 1970, but more rapid than during the 1970–75 period. This counterfactual level of production is given in column (2) of Table 18.2, in which the windfall is computed. Windfall production, then, is actual production (column 1) minus the 1975 expectation (column 2). The gross value of the production windfall is this quantity times the world price.

Table 18.2. The petroleum windfall

	Actual production (1)	Baseline production (2)	Price (1988 US$) (3)	Windfall (bn. 1988 US$) (4)	Windfall (% GNP) (5)	GNP (bn. 1988 US$) (6)
1975	806	806	21.20	0.0	0.0	163.1
1976	897	846	21.71	0.3	0.2	158.1
1977	1,086	888	22,37	1.3	1.0	136.4
1978	1,330	933	20.49	2.4	1.5	158.6
1979	1,618	979	28.26	5.6	3.0	187.4
1980	1,941	1,028	38.18	11.4	4.8	238.5
1981	2,313	1,080	37.20	14.9	5.3	280.9
1982	2,748	1,134	30.30	15.5	8.3	187.5
1983	2,688	1,191	26.77	12.4	7.9	158.2
1984	2,806	1,250	27.46	13.3	7.3	182.9
1985	2,703	1,313	26.14	11.2	5.9	190.4
1986	2,500	1,378	12.38	3.4	2.5	135.8
1987	2,616	1,447	16.75	5.4	3.8	143.3

Present value of the windfall income as of 1977 (bn. 1988 US$) $59.0

Note: Petroleum production is in thousands of barrels per day. Present value calculation uses a discount rate of 10%

Sources: Table 18.1 and author's estimates, as described in the text

Of course this increase in production was achieved at a cost, and we must subtract this cost from gross revenues to obtain an estimate of the windfall. We face three difficulties in the use of Pemex data to obtain an estimate of the economic cost of extracting petroleum. First, the oil workers' union was considered to be the most powerful union in Mexico, and wage payments certainly included a substantial element of monopsony rent. This rent is, of course, a means of distributing oil sector revenue and not an element of cost. Second, data are lacking on the value of the capital stock employed in the petroleum sector, and on the rental return to capital so employed. And finally, Pemex is an integrated firm; domestic sales are of refined petroleum products, and exports are (almost entirely) of crude, but Pemex data do not separate the costs of extraction from those of refining crude. After allowing for these factors, the available data suggest an extraction cost of roughly US$4.00 per barrel (in 1988 prices).[6] With this estimate of the cost of extracting the crude, we can compute the net increment to national income of the 'surprise' in petroleum production: this is given in column (4) of Table 18.2.

The estimated windfall rises with Mexican production and world oil prices to a maximum of about US$15 billion (1988 prices) in 1981 and 1982, when it reaches about 8% of GDP. It then declines somewhat in 1983–85,

Table 18.3. The petroleum windfall, public and private sectors

	1988 US$		Percentage of GDP	
	Public (1)	Private (2)	Public (3)	Private (4)
1975	0.00	0.00	0.00	0.00
1976	0.47	−0.16	0.29	−0.10
1977	1.70	−0.38	1.25	−0.28
1978	2.14	0.24	1.35	0.15
1979	8.18	−2.53	4.36	−1.35
1980	17.76	−6.38	7.45	−2.67
1981	21.25	−6.31	7.57	−2.25
1982	19.26	−3.77	10.27	−2.01
1983	14.87	−2.42	9.40	−1.53
1984	16.18	−2.86	8.85	−1.56
1985	13.60	−2.37	7.15	−1.24
1986	−1.01	4.44	−0.74	3.27
1987	3.09	2.35	2.15	1.64

Sources: Table 18.1 and author's estimates, as described in text

and more sharply in 1986 and 1987. Another way of gauging the magnitude of the disturbance is to note that the windfall in 1981 was equal to more than 2.5 times Mexico's 1976 merchandise exports. The present value of the windfall, from the perspective of 1977, is about US$59 billion (in 1988 prices). The corresponding 'permanent income' is of the order of US$6 billion per year, or about 4% of Mexico's 1977 GDP.

The above estimates pertain to the economy as a whole, not distinguishing between the public and the private sectors. However, an important feature of the oil boom is that all revenue accrued in the first instance to the government, and in the absence of some budgetary mechanism for transferring the revenue to individuals, private sector income would actually have declined as a result of the higher petroleum product prices implied by the oil boom.[7] We now estimate the impact of the oil boom on private-sector and public-sector incomes separately.

Columns (2) and (4) of Table 18.3 answer the question: what would have happened to private sector incomes if domestic petroleum product prices had moved in line with world petroleum prices? This change in income is given by the change in petroleum prices, relative to the 1975 level, times the baseline rate of petroleum consumption, described above.

We see that until 1980 the reduction in private sector income owing to higher oil prices was small, because the price was in those years fairly close to the 1975 price. With the large increase in oil prices after 1979, however, we see that there would have been a very substantial transfer of income from the private to the public sector—assuming, of course, that domestic petroleum prices followed world prices and the absence of other transfers. Indeed, in 1980 and 1981, when oil prices were at their peak, the transfer of income would have resulted in a reduction in private sector income equal to nearly 2.5% of GDP, with the public sector benefiting correspondingly. This means that, while the *national* income rose by 5% to 8% of GDP during 1980–85, income at the disposal of the public sector rose by 7% to 8% of GDP. There is, therefore, an element of irony in the fact that, by the time the oil boom had played itself out, it was the government rather than the private sector that was insolvent.

18.3.2. The Oil Boom: Ex Ante

The previous section discussed outcomes; in this section we turn to the more difficult task of evaluating plausible expectations about the boom. This is important because expectations—particularly about the duration of the boom—would have been a crucial determinant of both private and public responses.

We argued above that the boom in petroleum output was largely predictable—indeed, the path for output was essentially announced by the director general of Pemex in December 1976—so we will work with the hypothesis here that individuals had perfect foresight about the evolution of petroleum production. Prices were, on the other hand, subject to much more uncertainty, and in particular the 1980 price increase and the 1985 decline were not forecastable in 1976. We try to get some perspective by asking how the windfall would have looked to an observer able to predict production, but with static expectations about prices. Table 18.4 contains the computations from the perspective of two key dates: 1976, when the oil boom began, and 1979–80, when it intensified with the further large increase in world oil prices. They are also illustrated in Figure 18.3.

Notice that an observer who extrapolated the 1975 price into the future would have predicted the boom through 1978 very well; this is because the price was in fact relatively constant during those years. And although he would have missed the magnitude of the boom, and its sharp decline in 1986 and 1987, the prediction would have been surprisingly good.

In late 1979 prices changed dramatically, and observers would of course have changed their expectations. Table 18.4 and Figure 18.3 show how expectations about the boom would have changed if observers had forecast a price of US$30.00 into the indefinite future. Again, the general outline of the boom is similar to the *ex post* figures, but the abrupt decline in 1986 and 1987 is of course not forecast. In summary, the general profile of the boom would have been correctly forecast by observers using these simple price forecasts, though the magnitude of the boom would not have

Table 18.4. The petroleum windfall: *ex ante*

	1975 oil price		1979–80 oil price	
	1988 US$	percentage of GDP	1988 US$	percentage of GDP
1975	0.00	0.00		
1976	0.30	0.19		
1977	1.24	0.91		
1978	2.49	1.57		
1979	4.01	2.14	6.06	3.23
1980	5.73	2.40	8.66	3.63
1981	7.74	2.76	11.70	4.16
1982	10.13	5.40	15.31	8.17
1983	9.40	5.94	14.21	8.98
1984	9.77	5.34	14.76	8.07
1985	8.73	4.58	13.19	6.93
1986	7.04	5.19	10.64	7.84
1987	7.34	5.12	11.09	7.74

Sources: Table 18.1 and author's estimates, as described in text

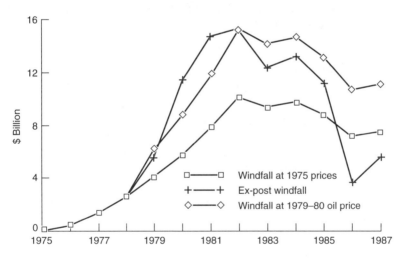

Figure 18.3. Petroleum windfall (*bn. 1988 US$*)

been forecastable at the beginning, and the sharpness with which it disappeared would not have been apparent in the early 1980s.

We can say a little more about the public sector's expectations, at least if their statements can be taken at face value, for officials in the López-Portillo administration used the transitoriness of the oil boom as an explicit justification for their oil policies. In 1979, for example, Díaz Serrano

stated: 'Petroleum is like tomatoes or pineapples. Either they are consumed or lost.'[8] This perception that the oil boom was temporary, and
should therefore be exploited aggressively, was even more explicitly
enunciated by Díaz Serrano in 1977:

the world can be sure of some twenty more years living in the petroleum era, and
Mexico has this time to generate wealth by taking advantage of high demand
levels, and the high prices paid at present . . . Without losing a sense of proportion,
we may point to other good businesses which have been lost to us in other areas,
when artificial substitutes were found for cochineal, dogwood, natural rubber,
and in recent years cotton and sisal. There are only about twenty years when we
can be sure to benefit from hydrocarbons to such an extent that we can cover the
country's necessities for a much longer period than that . . . but we should not
forget that this is a race against the clock.[9]

This statement makes it clear that at least part—and a very influential
part—of the Mexican government saw the oil boom as a temporary phenomenon, though they did not of course forecast its brevity. And furthermore the necessity for setting aside some of the oil proceeds to sustain the
economy after the oil boom had passed is clearly recognised; it is against
this realisation and these intentions that the government's later performance has to be judged.

18.3.3. Summary

In this section we have quantified the magnitude of the oil boom that hit
Mexico during 1977–85. At its peak the petroleum windfall amounted
to approximately 8% of GNP, and the present value of the boom was, in
1977, equivalent to a permanent increase in income of nearly US$6 billion,
or 4% of Mexico's 1977 GNP. This is probably a somewhat larger windfall
than would have been perceived in 1977, because the 1980 oil price increases would not have been predictable then. Because in Mexico all
petroleum revenue accrues to the government, the oil boom involved a
large transfer of income from domestic petroleum consumers to the public
sector.

   The oil boom was perceived as temporary, though the authorities expected that it would last rather longer than it actually did. At least some
authorities understood that the transitory nature of the boom implied
the desirability of high savings and investment, in order to provide for a
future without oil revenue. On the other hand, another more profligate
tendency was apparent in the public sector, and was well illustrated when
President López-Portillo said: 'We have freed expenditure from the slav-
ery of revenues and we have linked such expenditure to national objectives and economic planning' (cited in Randall 1989: 15). Although the oil
boom may have created a reason for saving by the public, as well as the

private sector, it also lifted a binding borrowing constraint and made possible the opposite, more exuberant, fiscal response.

18.4. Economic Response: The Economy in Aggregate

18.4.1. The Output Boom

As discussed above, the López-Portillo administration came to power at the end of 1976 in the midst of a major economic crisis. A major devaluation had already been undertaken by the outgoing Echeverría administration and an IMF programme negotiated, but it fell to López-Portillo to administer the restrictive IMF agreement and stabilise the economy. The result was slow growth in 1977, when real GDP rose by only 3.4%. The contractionary measures hit the cyclical construction industry hardest, and GDP in that sector fell by more than 5%. But the programme was having its intended effects—fiscal imbalances and external deficits were gradually declining, and capital flight slowing.

In 1978 the high rates of investment in the petroleum sector—which were in 1974–75 nearly 50% higher than in 1970–71—combined with the new administration's determination to play the petroleum card, and they began to pay off in a big way. In that year petroleum production rose by 14.3%, and annual increases were even larger in each of the next three years. By 1981 production in the petroleum industry was 85% higher than in 1977, having risen almost 17% per year. This rapid growth in petroleum production, and associated growth in oil exports, relieved Mexico's external payments problems, and in 1978 the government was able to terminate the 1976 IMF adjustment programme. Prospective oil riches also danced in front of foreign bankers' eyes, and for the next four years Mexico had very easy access to foreign capital markets. Thus, from early 1978 until the middle of 1982 the Mexican government could make economic policy in an essentially unconstrained environment.

The rapid growth in the petroleum sector coincided with an overall economic boom of breathtaking proportions, which is documented in Table 18.5. Real GDP increased by an average of 8.4% per year in the four boom years 1977–81; growth in the mining sector was exceptional, and output growth in the non-mining sector averaged 8.2% per year. Only in the state-dominated electricity industry and in the financial services sector was economic growth slower than in the 1960s.

Apart from mining, the sectors that grew most rapidly during the 1977–81 boom were transport and construction. The boom in construction is attributable to the investment boom that was going on in these years, and about which we will have more to say below. But although growth was most rapid in the mining, construction, and transportation sectors, growth

Table 18.5. Economic growth (*percentage change per year*)

	1960–70	1970–77	1977–81	1981–85
Agriculture	3.0	3.3	4.2	2.1
Mining	4.3	6.2	16.6	1.8
Manufacturing	8.1	6.3	8.6	0.0
Construction	8.1	4.7	12.4	−4.6
Electricity	13.5	9.8	8.3	5.7
Commerce, etc.	7.2	5.4	9.0	−1.9
Transport, etc.	6.4	10.3	13.2	−0.1
Finance, insurance, etc.	5.2	5.2	4.8	2.6
Personal services etc.	7.1	6.1	7.4	1.8
Total	6.5	5.8	8.4	0.1

Source: *La Economia Mexicana en Cifras*, various issues

Table 18.6. Employment (*million workers*)

	1970	1977	1981	1985
Agriculture	4.466	4.897	5.189	5.400
Mining	0.155	0.197	0.263	0.275
Manufacturing	1.726	2.051	2.542	2.400
Construction	0.810	1.163	1.881	15.50
Commerce, etc.	2.011	2.345	2.762	2.800
Personal services etc.	2.985	4.557	5.927	6.510
Total	12.863	16.238	20.043	20.500

Source: *La Economia Mexicana en Cifras*, 1986

in other sectors was rapid as well, averaging 7.5% per year, a full percentage point higher than the rapid growth experienced during the 1960s, and 2.6 percentage points higher than in the 1970–77 period.

The general contraction in economic activity during the second phase of the oil boom, 1982–85, is just as broad as was the expansion of 1977–81. The sector that declined most dramatically during this period is construction, which declined by more than 4% per year. But every sector in the economy grew substantially more slowly even than during the relatively troubled 1970–77 period.

During the early stage of the oil boom the sectors in which employment grew most rapidly were, unsurprisingly, the sectors in which output grew most rapidly (see Table 18.6). These were mining, with a 33% increase in employment, and construction, with a 62% increase. The next largest rate of increase is the sector comprising personal, community and social services, in which employment grew more than 30% during 1977–81. This

presumably reflects the rapid growth of non-tradables production generally, since the real exchange rate became increasingly overvalued during
this period. Similarly, the changes in employment during the second stage
of the boom correlate well with changes in sectoral production; most
notable is the large decline in employment in the construction sector from
1981 to 1985.

What emerges from these data, then, is a generalised production boom
during the early stages of the petroleum windfall, which was cut short
by the international payments crisis of 1982. After 1982 the experience is
of generalised economic weakness. Two points warrant emphasis at this
point. First, what is *not* apparent from the production data is anything
resembling the crowding out of non-booming sectors depicted in 'Dutch
Disease' theories; in the early stages of the oil boom the entire economy
grew rapidly, and in 1981–85 the entire economy was correspondingly
depressed. It is, in particular, very hard to make the case that the 1977–81
expansion of the petroleum and construction sectors was at the expense of
other sectors. Second, the macroeconomic boom that began with the oil
boom ended much earlier than did the oil boom itself. World petroleum
prices were high by historical standards until late in 1985. In fact, we
estimated above that the petroleum windfall averaged roughly 7% of GDP
during the 1983–85 period—yet those years were as disastrous for Mexico
as the previous years were prosperous.

18.4.2. Savings, Investment and Foreign Borrowing

The outstanding feature of the 1977–81 boom is the immense increase in
domestic investment, which is documented in Figure 18.4. While total real
GDP rose by roughly 40% in those four years, real gross fixed investment

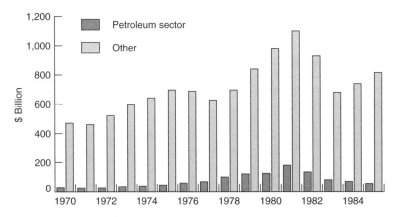

Figure 18.4. Real investment (*1980 pesos*)

was in 1981 more than 95% above the (admittedly somewhat depressed) 1977 rate. This investment boom was almost entirely in the non-residential sector; residential investment rose by only 18% during these boom years and actually declined from 5.3% of GDP in 1977 to 4.5% in 1981. Non-residential fixed investment, on the other hand, rose by almost 125% in this four-year period, increasing from 14.3% of GDP in 1977 to almost 22% in 1981.

Figure 18.4 also shows that, although investment in the petroleum sector rose more dramatically in proportional terms, the greater part of the increase was in the non-petroleum sector.[10]

Whereas investment boomed, consumption grew more or less in line with national income—public consumption growing somewhat more rapidly and private consumption less rapidly than GDP. Thus, national savings averaged nearly 22% of GDP during the four-year boom period, up from 19% during 1970–76. This increase in national savings would, of course, have been perfectly rational if consumers believed that the boom was transitory, though it is also compatible with an explanation based upon myopic consumers with a Keynesian consumption function. Trends in savings and investment are depicted in Figure 18.5.

The investment boom that took place in the early phase of the petroleum boom is clearly visible in that figure, with investment rising from less than 23% of GDP in 1977 to 27.4% in 1981. The savings rate increased substantially during this period as well, from less than 20% of GDP before the oil boom to roughly 22% during the peak of the boom. But because the increase in savings was smaller than the increase in investment, the

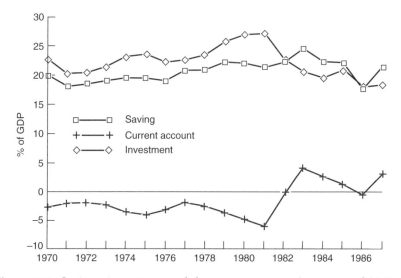

Figure 18.5. Savings, investment and the current account (*percentage of GDP*)

current account deficit grew inexorably, from 70 billion 1980 pesos in 1977, until it finally reached almost 300 billion 1980 pesos (almost 6% of GDP) in 1981. After 1981 these trends changed dramatically, and investment declined from over 27% of GDP to 20% in 1984. Savings rose somewhat, with the result that the current account swung abruptly into surplus.

We now construct a counterfactual for Mexican savings and investment and compare it to outcomes. It would make little sense to construct a counterfactual that simply subtracts the petroleum windfall income from national income; savings and investment were affected not only by that disturbance, but also by the macroeconomic fallout from expansionary government policies (policies that would have been unfinanceable in the absence of the windfall). On the other hand, construction of a complete macroeconomic model of the economy that tries to simulate what would have happened if the petroleum boom had not happened and government policy had been more restrained is clearly beyond the scope of this chapter. Instead we construct a simple scenario, based on the presumption that, in the absence of the petroleum boom, the Mexican authorities would have been forced to respect the 1976 IMF programme, that the fiscal deficit would have been accordingly reduced, and that real GDP growth would have returned to roughly the levels that prevailed before the mid-1960s.

In particular, we assume that, in the absence of the petroleum shock, real GDP would have grown 6% per year after 1977. This is slower than in the 1960s, and approximately the rate achieved during the troubled 1970–77 period. We further assume that the savings rate would have drifted up very slightly, from 20.8% of GDP to 21% in 1978 and thereafter. Some increase in the savings rate would be expected because the IMF programme demanded a reduction in the public sector deficit. Finally, we assume that the investment rate would have declined from 22.8% of GDP in 1977 to 22.5% in 1978, and 22.0% thereafter. Some reduction in domestic investment would have been called for if Mexico was to respect the restrictive limits on foreign borrowing that were included in the 1976 agreement with the IMF. The 22% figure is equal to the rate of investment during the seven years leading up to the petroleum boom, 1970–76.

Table 18.7 lays out the implications of these assumptions. Notice that actual savings substantially exceed counterfactual savings during the early phase of the oil boom. This is both because actual income exceeds counterfactual income and because the actual savings rate was higher during those years. If we take the 1977–81 period as a whole, actual savings exceeded counterfactual savings by 345 billion 1980 pesos. Actual GDP exceeded counterfactual GDP by 1,045 billion 1980 pesos. This implies a windfall savings rate of about 33%—not extremely high, but substantially higher than the roughly 20% average rate that is typical for Mexico. Thus, for the economy as a whole, savings behaviour seems to be

Table 18.7. Savings, investment and foreign borrowing: summary (*bn. 1980 pesos*)

	Actual			Counterfactual		
	Saving	Investment	CAS	Saving	Investment	CAS
1977	727	797	−70	727	797	−70
1978	793	893	−100	777	833	−56
1979	921	1,071	−149	824	863	−39
1980	991	1,215	−224	874	915	−42
1981	1,041	1,331	−290	926	970	−44
1982	1,082	1,107	−25	981	1,028	−47
1983	1,143	961	182	1,040	1,090	−50
1984	1,077	953	124	1,103	1,155	−53
1985	1,106	1,042	64	1,169	1,225	−56

Note: For some years the US dollar current account figures implicit in these data differ noticeably from the balance of payments data. Counterfactuals are author's calculations as described in the text. 'CAS' refers to 'current account surplus'

Sources: Actual data are from *Sistema de Cuentas Nacionales de Mexico, 1960–85* and *La Economia Mexicana en Cifras*, various issues

consistent with the idea that the petroleum boom was perceived to be transitory.

The results for investment are more dramatic; during the 1977–81 period actual investment exceeded counterfactual investment by 929 billion 1980 pesos, implying a propensity to invest out of windfall income of nearly 90%. With the propensity to invest out of the windfall so much higher than was the propensity to save, foreign borrowing was necessarily very high. The difference between the actual and the counterfactual current account sums to 583 billion 1980 pesos, 56% of the windfall, and roughly 13% of annual GDP.

During the second part of the petroleum boom, 1982–85, the picture is again dramatically different. Actual investment declines well below the counterfactual level, while savings are actually somewhat higher than in the counterfactual. The result is a major improvement in the current account deficit, relative to the counterfactual level. Whereas the counterfactual implied current account deficits of roughly 1% of GDP, the actual current account was in surplus by roughly 2% of GDP during 1982–85. This sharp swing into surplus should not of course be interpreted as resulting from unconstrained inter-temporal choice; during this period Mexico, along with many other developing countries, was simply unable to borrow to finance any excess of investment over savings.

Two features of these developments stand out and will require further discussion below. The first is the dissociation of the 1982 crisis from developments in the petroleum sector. True, in 1982 the oil market had weakened somewhat compared with 1981, but it was still strong by any historical measure, and would not weaken measurably for almost two years. Second, examination of the aggregate data on savings and investment raise a genuine puzzle about how Mexico's payments crisis emerged. The data clearly indicate that Mexico's large external deficits were associated with high rates of domestic investment; during 1977–81 windfall investment is estimated, however crudely, at 929 billion 1980 pesos, whereas windfall external borrowing, at 583 billion pesos, was roughly 63% as large. As long as the return on domestic investment was at least 63% of the world interest rate, servicing the foreign debt should have posed no problems. Why, then, the debt crisis? We take up these issues in more detail below. Before doing so we take a closer look at developments in Mexico's external accounts, and at the evolution of relative prices.

18.4.3. External Accounts

Table 18.8 summarises Mexico's external payments during this period. Notice that, although real exports nearly tripled between 1977 and 1981,

Table 18.8. Summary of the balance of payments (*bn. 1988 US$*)

	Current account				Capital account		
	Merch. exports	Merch. imports	Trade balance	Current account	Recorded capital	Errors and omissions	Balance[a]
1970	3.54	6.39	−2.85	−3.26	2.33	1.09	0.16
1971	3.64	6.02	−2.37	−2.48	2.39	0.52	0.43
1972	4.31	7.14	−2.83	−2.60	1.12	2.07	0.58
1973	4.90	9.21	−4.31	−3.62	4.85	−0.95	0.29
1974	5.87	12.64	−6.78	−6.63	7.86	−1.15	0.07
1975	5.67	12.41	−6.74	−8.23	10.11	−1.58	0.31
1976	6.49	11.19	−4.70	−6.54	9.01	−4.25	−1.78
1977	7.75	9.51	−1.76	−2.66	3.79	−0.04	1.10
1978	9.38	12.25	−2.87	−4.17	5.03	−0.20	0.67
1979	12.28	16.68	−4.40	−6.78	6.31	0.96	0.49
1980	19.03	23.19	−4.15	−13.18	14.04	0.12	0.98
1981	22.57	26.89	−4.32	−18.03	30.82	−10.14	2.65
1982	22.92	15.58	7.33	−6.72	8.84	−7.38	−5.25
1983	23.71	9.09	14.63	5.76	−1.36	−0.94	3.46
1984	25.20	11.72	13.48	4.41	0.04	−0.96	3.49
1985	22.36	13.63	8.72	1.28	−1.58	−2.20	−2.50

[a] Including exceptional financing (IMF loans), which are excluded from the recorded capital account

Sources: *La Economia Mexicana en Cifras* (1988), *International Financial Statistics*, and *Balance of Payments Statistics*

the real value of imports rose by even more, leading to a worsening of the trade balance. At the same time, and owing largely to a severely and increasingly overvalued exchange rate, net tourism receipts declined from roughly US$1 billion in 1978–79 to US$0.2 billion in 1981. And of course it was exactly during these years that the US and European disinflations led to large increases in world interest rates, with a massively adverse effect on Mexico's debt-service obligations. Thus, the service account worsened as well, and the current account deficit grew to nearly US$20 billion at 1988 prices.

Table 18.8 reveals an important aspect of Mexico's 1981 payments imbalance that is not apparent from the previous discussion of the goods market. Beginning in 1981 there is evidence of a massive flight of capital from Mexico, with the entry for 'errors and omissions' recording a US$10 billion deficit in 1981, and a further US$7 billion debit in 1982.

More careful estimates of capital flight during the 1977–82 period yield estimates ranging from roughly US$15 billion to US$30 billion, depending upon the method of estimation.[11] This apparent capital flight represented a clear vote of no-confidence in Mexico's financial stability; what is somewhat puzzling is the fact that it took place during the peak of the business investment boom. In the next section we resolve this puzzle by showing that private investment declined in 1981, so that the strength of total investment during that year reflects public sector activity alone.

In any event, the apparent capital outflow signifies a desire by the private sector to accumulate foreign assets. The public sector, then, needed to borrow not only to finance the excess of national expenditure over income, but also indirectly to finance the private sector's foreign asset accumulation. This is one reason why the debt crisis in Mexico was a crisis of public sector, rather than national solvency.[12] This massive capital flight demonstrates the ease with which private savings could leave Mexico and, as we shall discuss below, undermines explanations of the 1977–81 investment boom that are predicated upon a substantial degree of capital immobility.

Turning back to the goods market, Table 18.9 provides some detail on the composition of imports and exports that will be of interest below. The increase in consumer goods imports is, in proportional terms, striking, and far exceeds the growth of aggregate consumption. However, as noted above, Mexico's import-substitution policies had focused upon the consumer goods industry, and consumer goods imports remained in absolute terms relatively low.

Capital goods imports roughly doubled during the 1977–81 boom, which is not surprising in light of the growth in investment during this period. But the most dramatic growth occurred in imports of intermediate goods, which increased nearly fivefold during the boom, out of all proportion to the growth in demand, or in production. And there is another sense

Table 18.9. Merchandise imports by type of good (*bn. 1988 US$*)

	Consumer goods	Intermediate goods	Capital goods	Total
1976	0.547	2.654	4.252	7.454
1977	0.700	3.163	4.665	8.528
1978	1.215	4.420	5.803	11.437
1979	1.369	5.548	8.935	15.852
1980	2.967	14.046	6.175	23.187
1981	3.154	15.231	8.506	26.892
1982	1.638	9.087	4.861	15.586
1983	0.652	6.102	2.334	9.087
1984	0.884	8.157	2.678	11.720
1985	1.117	9.253	3.266	13.636
1986	0.885	7.980	3.090	11.954
1987	0.786	9.035	2.693	12.514

Sources: *La Economia Mexicana en Cifras*, various issues

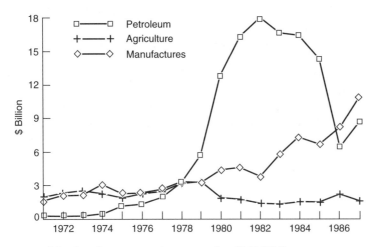

Figure 18.6. Merchandise exports by sector (*bn. 1988 US$*)

in which imports of intermediate goods behave rather differently from the other categories of import. After the 1977–81 boom, imports of capital goods and consumer goods decline roughly to pre-boom levels, and capital goods decline by even more. But imports of intermediate inputs remain nearly three times their 1977 level for most of the 1983–87 period. We shall return to this point in the conclusion.

Figure 18.6 depicts the performance of Mexico's exports during the boom. We noted above that there is little evidence of Dutch Disease in response to the oil boom—at least not if we mean declines or very slow growth of output in non-oil productive sectors. However, Figure 18.6

shows that the oil boom was, especially in 1981 and 1982, associated with slow growth in manufacturing exports and an absolute decline in real revenues from agricultural exports—a decline from which the sector had not recovered by 1987. Thus, not only had the economy become increasingly dependent upon imported intermediate inputs during the oil boom, but the growth in agricultural and manufacturing output that was documented above seems to have been devoted almost exclusively to satisfaction of domestic demand, to the detriment of export performance. After the 1982 economic crisis, which was associated with a very large depreciation of the real exchange rate, manufacturing exports recovered rapidly, and by 1986 they were larger than oil exports.

18.4.4. *Relative Prices*

We turn now to the evolution of relative prices during the oil boom. The most dramatic change is, of course, in the relative price of petroleum, which was documented above. As Figure 18.7 illustrates, the first stage of the oil boom was also associated with a huge appreciation of the Mexican real exchange rate, signifying a major increase in the price of non-traded goods relative to that of tradables.[13]

The 1976 depreciation is clearly visible in Figure 18.7, as is the fact that the real exchange rate appreciated consistently during the early stage of the oil boom. By 1981 the real exchange rate had appreciated some 30% from the 1977 rate, largely as a result of the high inflation during those years, which was unaccompanied by nominal exchange rate depreciation.

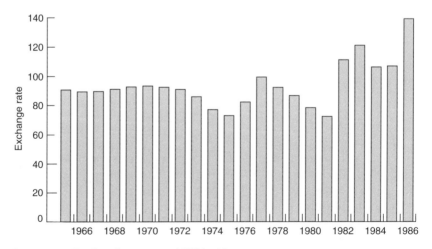

Figure 18.7. Real exchange rate (*CPI basis*)

After the 1982 crisis, when external financing evaporated, the real exchange rate depreciated to historically unprecedented levels. The real exchange rate, then, does not follow oil price fluctuations very closely, being affected much more by monetary factors before the 1982 crisis, and by the sudden unavailability of external credit after that crisis.

There were other, somewhat more subtle but nevertheless significant changes in domestic relative prices. Here we focus on the prices of the construction and manufacturing sectors. Figure 18.8 depicts the relative prices of value-added in the construction, manufacturing, and agricultural sectors, relative to the overall GDP deflator. Notice that from 1977 to 1981 the relative price of construction goods rises roughly 5%, and the relative price of manufacturing declines by roughly the same amount. This makes sense if we remember the investment boom that was under way during that period and we recognise that domestic manufactures were only partially insulated from international competition.[14] The relative price of output in the agriculture sector, which participated much less in the 1977–81 boom, declined sharply during the 1977–81 boom.[15]

During the subsequent phase of the petroleum boom these relative price trends are reversed. Between 1981 and 1985 the relative price of output in the construction sector declines dramatically, whereas the price of manufactures rises substantially. This can be explained by the collapse of investment during the 1981–85 period, which sharply reduced the demand for construction services, and by the substantial depreciation after 1982, which reduced the intensity of foreign price competition faced by manufacturers.

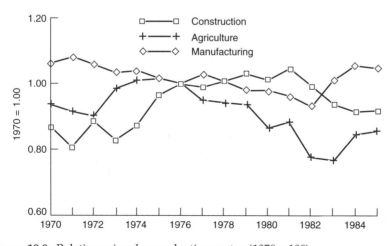

Figure 18.8. Relative prices by production sector (*1970 = 100*)

18.4.5. Summary

Summarising, we argued in this section that the first stage of the petroleum boom in Mexico coincided with a generalised production boom in
which all major sectors of the economy participated. This production
boom ended in 1982, with the onset of the debt crisis, well before the
petroleum boom had itself ended. The production boom during 1977–81
was accompanied by an immense investment boom; we estimate that
nearly 90% of the windfall was invested domestically in those years. The
investment boom was concentrated in the business sector; whereas business fixed investment more than doubled during these four years, residential investment actually declined considerably as a fraction of GDP.
Savings were also high during the 1977–81 boom. We estimate that 33% of
the windfall during these years was saved. This left, however, a substantial fraction of the domestic investment to be financed with expedient
foreign borrowing. We estimate that the windfall-induced investment
was roughly 930 billion 1980 pesos; of this 580 billion 1980 pesos—roughly
two-thirds—was financed by foreign borrowing.

The end of the production boom in 1982 had little to do with developments in petroleum markets, and much more to do with an inability to
service the external debts that had accumulated during the previous four
years. This external crisis was associated with very rapid capital flight in
1981 and 1982, which suggests that the private sector desired and was able
to increase its holdings of foreign assets. After 1982 production, employment, and investment declined as consistently as they had previously
risen; the depression, like the boom before it, was not confined to any
specific sectors.

Relative prices move in ways that can be understood in light of the
investment boom, which was associated with an increase in the relative
price of construction, and changes in competitiveness associated with
variations in the real exchange rate. However, changes in broad price
indexes—and specifically the real exchange rate—are associated much
more with changes in the monetary and macroeconomic environment
than with developments in the petroleum sector.

These developments raise at least two important questions. First, what
explains the huge increase in investment during the 1977–81 period? This
question is of very general interest, because the external deficits that
triggered the debt crisis in 1982 were clearly associated with high investment, rather than low rates of national saving. This brings us to the second
puzzle: given the fact that Mexican external deficits were associated with
an investment boom, rather than low rates of national savings, why did
they lead to payments difficulties at all? Put differently, why was the
apparent return on the 1977–81 investment so low? We suggest below that
misguided government policy responses to the petroleum boom explain

both puzzles. To see this we must now look more carefully at the private and public responses to the petroleum boom.

18.5. Private and Public Responses

18.5.1. Savings, Investment and Foreign Borrowing

We now investigate the private and public responses to the aggregate boom developed above. We begin by estimating private and public savings and investment behaviour. Unfortunately, the Mexican national income accounts do not provide exactly the disaggegation that we need, so the following analysis utilises a combination of budgetary and national income data. We use the national income accounts for national savings and investment and the budgetary accounts to obtain an estimate of the public sector's savings and investment. Private sector outcomes are then estimated as the difference between national and public sector quantities.

In order to make meaningful comparisons an important adjustment must be made to the budgetary data. Those data treat all interest payments as a transfer of income to the private sector. In an inflationary environment, however, a substantial portion of interest payments is not real private sector income, but merely compensates holders of peso-denominated debt obligations for inflation-induced erosion in the real value of that debt. Except where noted below, we subtract this component of interest payments from domestic government expenditure.[16] If this adjustment was not made, private sector savings and public sector dissavings would be grossly overestimated, especially in 1982, when the Mexican price level increased approximately 100%.

Table 18.10 gives our estimates of private and public sector savings and investment. Notice first that public sector savings increased somewhat from their rather low 1977 level. This increase was not large, and it vanished in 1981 and 1982. During those two years public sector savings, at 3.3% of GDP, are actually less than in 1977; this despite the massive oil windfall that was received by the government in those years.

Public sector investment meanwhile surged from 7.6% of GDP in 1977 to nearly 13% of GDP in 1981. This surge in investment, unaccompanied as it was by any significant increase in public saving, led to an increase in the overall deficit from less than 4% of GDP in 1977 to nearly 10% of GDP in 1981.[17]

Movements in the private sector's savings and investment were less dramatic. Savings remained relatively high until 1982, whereas investment increased from 15% of GDP in 1977–78 to 17.6% in 1980. There was some decline in domestic investment during 1981, which was also the period of rapid capital flight, so that the excess of private savings over

Table 18.10. Savings and investment by sector (*percentage of GDP*)

	Public sector			Private sector			Total		
	S	I	Net	S	I	Net	S	I	CAS
1977	3.6	7.6	−3.9	17.2	15.2	1.9	20.8	18.9	−2.0
1978	4.4	8.7	−4.3	16.6	14.9	1.7	21.0	19.3	−2.7
1979	5.2	9.8	−4.5	17.1	16.2	0.9	22.3	21.4	−3.6
1980	5.6	9.6	−4.0	16.6	17.6	−1.0	22.2	23.2	−5.0
1981	2.9	12.9	−9.9	18.5	14.5	4.0	21.4	17.4	−6.0
1982	3.7	10.2	−6.5	18.7	12.7	6.0	22.4	16.4	−0.5
1983	9.9	7.5	2.4	14.8	13.3	1.5	24.7	23.2	3.9
1984	8.3	6.7	1.6	14.2	13.1	1.0	22.5	21.4	2.6
1985	7.6	6.1	1.5	14.9	15.1	−0.2	22.5	22.7	1.3

Note: Public sector savings and investment are from budgetary figures, while national data are from the national income accounts. The private sector's savings are computed as the difference between national savings and public sector savings. An adjustment for inflation is made to the figures for private and public savings, as described in the text

investment rose to 4% of GDP. But this increase was not enough to prevent a major increase in Mexico's current account deficit, which rose from 2% of GDP in 1977 to 6% in 1981.

Explaining the current account deficits that emerged during the petroleum boom clearly requires a better understanding of government income and spending, so we turn now to a more detailed examination of the fiscal accounts.

18.5.2. Fiscal Policy

The question we need to address is: how did the government dispose of the windfall oil revenue? How is it that this massive increase in government resources during the 1980–82 period led to huge fiscal deficits? Some insights are provided in Table 18.11, which presents basic budgetary data.[18]

Comparing the 1981 with the 1977 budget, we identify the following key influences on the budget. During this period petroleum sector revenue rose by much less than our estimate of the oil windfall. During 1980 and 1981 petroleum sector revenue is only 3.5 percentage points of GDP above the 1977 level, considerably less than our estimate of the oil windfall in those years. There is a sharp drop in non-oil parastatal revenue, from roughly 9.5% of GDP in 1977–78 to less than 8% of GDP in 1981. Non-interest transfers increase from 7.2% of GDP in 1977 to 9.7% of GDP in 1981. Current expenditure does *not* rise dramatically but, as was discussed above, capital spending surges from 7.6% of GDP in 1977 to nearly 13% of GDP in 1981.

Table 18.11. Finances of the public sector (*percentage of GDP*)

	1977	1978	1979	1980	1981	1982	1983	1984	1985
Revenue									
Non-oil federal revenue	10.9	11.3	11.5	11.2	11.0	9.7	9.4	9.0	9.3
Petroleum sector	4.3	5.0	6.1	7.8	7.7	11.1	16.1	15.1	13.3
Other parastatal	9.4	9.6	9.1	8.0	7.9	8.1	7.4	8.1	8.6
Total revenue	24.6	25.9	26.7	26.9	26.7	28.9	32.9	32.2	31.2
Expenditure									
Wages and purchases	12.1	12.0	11.4	10.6	11.7	11.8	11.3	11.3	11.8
Capital spending	7.6	8.7	9.8	9.6	12.9	10.2	7.5	6.7	6.1
Interest	3.0	3.2	3.4	3.5	5.0	8.3	12.4	11.9	11.5
Other transfers	7.2	7.6	8.2	9.2	9.7	13.4	9.4	8.9	9.3
Current expenditure	22.4	22.7	22.9	23.3	26.4	33.4	33.0	32.1	32.6
Total expenditure	30.0	31.4	32.7	32.9	39.2	43.6	40.5	38.8	38.6
Saving	2.2	3.3	3.8	3.6	0.3	−4.5	−0.1	0.1	−1.4
Overall Surplus	−5.3	−5.4	−6.0	−6.0	−12.6	−14.6	−7.6	−6.6	−7.4

Source: *La Economía Mexicana en Cifras* (1988)

The first and quantitatively most important task is to explain why petroleum sector revenues were so much smaller than our estimate of the public sectors' windfall income from the oil boom. In Table 18.3 above, we calculated that the oil windfall should have augmented the public sector's income by some 7.5% of GDP in 1980 and 1981, rising to over 10% of GDP in 1982. Yet we see that *gross* petroleum sector revenue (which includes all Pemex receipts plus the proceeds of a gasoline tax) was only 3.5% of GDP higher in 1980–81 than in 1977, and was only 6.8% of GDP higher in 1982. Net proceeds presumably increased less, and the question we address now is why.

The answer lies in the policy of selling petroleum-based products at very steep discounts in the domestic market. These pricing policies brought domestic Mexican energy prices very far out of line with world prices. To illustrate: in 1980–81 the domestic relative consumer price of petroleum products was only 8% higher than it had been in 1970, despite the fact that the relative world price had risen nearly eightfold in that period. Indeed, Buffie and Krause (1989) estimate that the domestic price of all energy products was in 1980 only one-quarter of the world price. In addition to distorting consumption and production decisions, these price subsidies had very major fiscal implications. Here we focus on petroleum price subsidies, though it should be remembered that electricity, public transport, and some food products were also very heavily subsidised.[19]

In order to estimate the magnitude of domestic petroleum subsidies,

Table 18.12 lists the revenue obtained per barrel of oil sold on the domestic market and compares it with the revenue obtained per barrel of oil sold for export. Nearly all export sales are of crude, whereas all domestic sales are of refined products, so we would expect the revenue per barrel of domestic sales to be substantially higher, and so it was during the 1960s (not shown).

During the 1960s domestic sales yielded about ten 1988 dollars per barrel more than foreign sales, or roughly 25 cents per gallon. In the early 1970s this relationship changed dramatically, as prices charged by Pemex in domestic markets failed to keep pace with world prices. By 1975 domestic sales were earning Pemex *less* per barrel than were foreign sales, despite the fact that foreign sales were (largely) crude and domestic sales were entirely refined product. For purposes of rough quantification, we take the 1975 price differential as a baseline and measure changes in subsidies relative to that baseline. Remember, however, that the baseline already incorporates a substantial subsidy element, so that the figures in Table 18.12 should not be interpreted as measures of the total cost of petroleum subsidies, but rather the change from 1975 levels.

Column (1) of Table 18.12 lists actual Pemex revenue per barrel of oil exported. As is to be expected, this tracks the world price very closely. Column (2) lists the revenue earned by Pemex per barrel of domestic sales, and column (3) gives the volume of domestic sales in thousands of barrels.

Table 18.12. Domestic oil subsidy

	US$ revenue per barrel		Domestic sales ('000 bbl)	Revenue cost of subsidy		
	Export	Domestic		US$	1988 US$	Percentage of GDP
1975	11.45	10.92	242.8	0.00	0.00	0.00
1976	12.74	9.60	260.3	0.68	1.21	0.78
1977	13.75	8.28	282.3	1.40	2.33	1.75
1978	13.69	8.35	310.5	1.49	2.31	1.49
1979	20.29	9.86	332.1	3.29	4.58	2.51
1980	32.49	10.96	378.4	7.95	9.75	4.21
1981	34.34	11.22	412.5	9.32	10.46	3.87
1982	29.63	7.74	409.8	8.76	9.45	5.35
1983	27.32	11.51	398.7	6.09	6.48	4.55
1984	27.49	14.05	421.9	5.45	5.67	3.29
1985	25.50	13.94	438.4	4.84	4.99	2.75
1986	11.98	10.90	473.8	0.26	0.27	0.21
1987	16.12	12.07	429.3	1.51	1.55	1.13

Note: The benchmark is 1975 pricing behaviour, not world prices. The subsidies listed in this table should therefore be understood to be in addition to the subsidies implicit in 1975 pricing policies

In column (4) we estimate the increase in revenue that would have been generated if the domestic price had borne the same relation to the world price that it bore in 1975: that is, if the domestic revenue per barrel had been 53 cents below the world price instead of the figure given in column (2). Column (5) translates this into 1988 dollars, deflating as before with the US producer price index, and the final column gives the change in subsidies relative to GDP.

The lesson that emerges from Table 18.12 is that the price subsidy was of very major importance. In 1980 and 1981 this subsidy alone increased by 4% of GNP, compared with pre-boom years, which is more than half as large as the public sector's windfall income from the oil boom.[20] Thus, domestic petroleum subsidies were the dominant mechanism through which oil boom revenue was recycled to the private sector. The increase in petroleum subsidies was, by the same token, the most important single adverse influence on the fiscal situation in the early 1980s.

Table 18.13 draws out the implications of these estimates by computing the public sector and the private sector changes in income after accounting for these petroleum price subsidies.[21] In the absence of an increase in petroleum price (or other) subsidies the private sector would have been made worse off by the petroleum price movements that occurred, because the public sector would earn the oil revenue and the private sector would pay more for petroleum products. The changes in petroleum subsidies that in fact occurred are large enough to make the private sector

Table 18.13. The petroleum windfall by sector: before and after price subsidies (*bn. 1988 US$*)

	Before subsidies		After subsidies	
	Public	Private	Public	Private
1975	0.00	0.00	0.00	0.00
1976	0.47	−0.16	−0.74	1.05
1977	1.70	−0.38	−0.63	1.95
1978	2.14	0.24	−0.17	2.55
1979	8.18	−2.53	3.60	2.05
1980	17.76	−6.38	8.01	3.37
1981	21.25	−6.31	10.79	4.15
1982	19.26	−3.77	9.81	5.68
1983	14.87	−2.42	8.39	4.06
1984	16.18	−2.86	10.51	2.81
1985	13.60	−2.37	8.61	2.62
1986	−1.01	4.44	−1.28	4.71
1987	3.09	2.3	1.54	3.90

Source: Author's estimates, as described in text

substantially better off in every year. In the years when the windfall was large, the subsidies amount to roughly half the public sector's windfall.

Table 18.14 ties this discussion together by summarising various important influences on the fiscal accounts during 1978–82. The first row gives the change in public sector windfall income between 1977 and the year of interest. Thus, in 1981 the public sector's petroleum windfall income was 6.3 percentage points higher than in 1977. The last column of this table summarises the outcomes by adding up the yearly figures. Thus, roughly speaking, during the five-year period 1978–82 the petroleum windfall augmented the Mexican public sector's income by about 25% of a year's GNP.

Subsequent rows of Table 18.14 give the various means by which the public sector disposed of this windfall. The second row of Table 18.14 gives the revenue forgone by domestic petroleum price subsidies. During 1978–82 this sums to 17.5% of a year's GNP, just over 71% of the oil windfall. The third row gives the impact on the budget of higher explicit (non-interest) transfers. These transfers cover a wide range of items; it has been estimated, for example, that in 1980 food subsidies comprised nearly 3% of the Mexican GDP (El Mallakh *et al.* 1984: 50). Transfers like this were, during the period as a whole, the second most important means by which the oil revenue was channelled to the private sector. Indeed, by 1982 these subsidies were more significant than even the oil price subsidies. Over the 1978–82 period as a whole they cumulate to 12% of a year's GNP, about half the magnitude of the petroleum windfall income. The third significant item is the reduction in income earned by non-oil parastatal corporations. This largely represents price subsidies on publicly provided goods such as electricity, transportation, and so on. The

Table 18.14. Influences on the budget, 1977–82 (*percentage of GDP*)

	1978	1979	1980	1981	1982	Sum
Petroleum windfall	0.1	3.1	6.2	6.3	9.0	24.7
Domestic oil subsidy	−1.5	−2.5	−4.2	−3.9	−5.4	−17.5
Budgetary transfers	−0.4	−1.0	−2.0	−2.5	−6.2	−12.1
Parastatal income	0.2	−0.3	−1.4	−1.5	−1.3	−4.3
Inflation tax	−0.3	0.3	0.6	0.6	5.5	6.7
Other factors	2.6	1.3	1.2	−1.7	−0.9	2.5
Public saving (adj.)	0.7	0.9	0.4	−2.7	0.8	0.1
Investment spending	−1.1	−2.2	−2.0	−5.3	−2.6	−13.2
Overall surplus	−0.4	−1.3	−1.6	−8.0	−1.8	−13.1

Note: This table gives changes in the budgetary accounts compared with 1977, not absolute levels

Source: Author's estimates, as described in text

only form of revenue that increased significantly during these five years was the inflation tax on nominal debt; this was offset, however, by increased nominal interest payments, and real interest payments remained high in all years except 1982, when the inflation rate suddenly and unexpectedly jumped upwards.

In short, the Mexican government responded to the petroleum windfall by increasing domestic subsidies. The most significant of these subsidies seems to have been the subsidy on domestic sales of petroleum products. Thus, the oil windfall was used largely to shelter the private sector from the painful petroleum price increases that the rest of the world was experiencing. But other transfers were increased significantly as well.

18.5.3. Summary

We sought to address two related questions here. First, we uncovered the sectoral patterns that underlay the national savings and investment trends discussed in the previous section. We found that, whereas private sector savings remained reasonably high, the public sector moved increasingly into deficit—and dramatically so in 1981 and 1982. We then identified the mechanisms by which the government transferred the oil windfall—and more—to the public sector. We found that petroleum and other subsidies increased during the 1977–82 period by even more than the increase in windfall income, with the result that over the 1978–82 period government savings declined slightly. This meant that the surge in government investment that took place during these same years translated directly into the public sector's fiscal deficit.

18.6. Summary and Assessment

The oil boom of 1977–85 was an immense windfall for Mexico; our estimate of windfall income peaks at about 8% of 1982 GDP. The *ex post* windfall amounted to an increase in Mexico's permanent income of roughly 4% of 1977 GDP. The oil boom was in fact temporary, and government authorities perceived it as such, though they thought that it would last longer than it did.

The eight-year oil boom divides into two clearly delineated phases; an immense boom from 1977 until the first half of 1982, and an equally impressive bust after the onset of the debt crisis in August 1982. The most notable aspect of the first phase was a breathtaking boom in non-residential investment, which more than doubled between 1976 and 1981. We estimate that 90% of the boom in income during the 1977–81 period was invested domestically. Construction, not surprisingly, boomed during this period, but so did the rest of the economy. There is in particular no evidence that the expansion of the construction or oil sectors crowded out other sectors of the economy.

A substantial fraction, though not the preponderance of the windfall, was saved; we estimate that 33% of the 1977–81 windfall was saved. This left a substantial fraction of the investment boom to be financed by borrowing from abroad; of the 930 billion 1980 pesos-worth of windfall investment, 345 billion financed with windfall saving, and 585 billion was financed by borrowing from abroad. This borrowing amounted to roughly 13% of Mexico's annual GDP in that period.

In the first instance, the windfall accrued entirely to the government. It returned the windfall to the private sector in the form of petroleum subsidies, subsidies on products provided by parastatals other than Pemex, and explicit budgetary transfers. In fact, the government returned the windfall income so effectively that the increased transfers soon amounted to more than the government's windfall income. The boom ended in the resulting fiscal and external payments crisis of August 1982. It bears repeating that the end of the production boom in mid-1982 had very little to do with developments in petroleum markets.

The Mexican experience raises at least two intriguing questions. First, what explains the investment boom of 1977–81? Changes in investment were at the heart of the external payments deficits that triggered the debt crisis in Mexico—a fact that contrasts sharply with the Brazilian, the Argentine, and to a lesser extent the Chilean experiences in these years (Dornbusch 1985).

We note first that the 1977–81 investment boom was economy-wide and not confined to one or a few sectors. Though investment increased most dramatically in the petroleum sector, most of the investment was in fact in the non-petroleum sector and, until 1981, the private sector responded as aggressively as did the public sector. Theories that focus on the impact of high savings in an environment of limited capital mobility cannot explain the Mexican experience. First, investment in Mexico rose significantly more than did savings; indeed, our estimate of windfall investment was more than twice as large as the estimate of windfall savings. Far from high domestic savings rates pushing domestic investment upward, the Mexican experience was one in which high domestic investment pulled in foreign savings. A second ground for ruling out 'savings-push' explanations is the absence of binding restrictions on capital outflows, as evidenced by the very high rates of capital flight experienced during 1981 and 1982. These suggest that domestic residents were in fact able to place their savings abroad relatively easily when they so desired.

We suggest that the response of private investment had much more to do with other aspects of the control regime in place during the boom, and in particular with the implicit and explicit production subsidies instituted by the government. Because the final goods sector was at least partially protected from foreign competition, the price of import-competing goods rose during the income and expenditure boom of 1977–81. Meanwhile, the price of inputs was held artificially low by, most importantly, domestic energy price subsidies, which held the cost of energy as low as one-quarter world prices. These explicit subsidies were augmented by the effects of a major real exchange rate overvaluation during 1977–81, which dramatically reduced the price of imported intermediate goods and capital goods. There is evidence that producers were induced to switch towards production techniques that are intensive in such intermediate inputs for, even after the production boom ended, imports of raw materials and intermediate goods were very substantially higher than they were before the boom began. In short, private investors seem to have been taking advantage of the fact that the government was, implicitly, offering to pay for a significant fraction of their products' true production cost. This explains their willingness to expand production so dramatically and to invest in new capacity during 1977–81.

This brings us to the second question posed by the Mexican experience. We established that Mexican external deficits were very clearly associated with an investment boom rather than low rates of national savings. Why, then, did they lead to payments difficulties at all? Here again government price subsidies enter the picture, and in two ways. On the one hand, they were the chief cause of the fiscal difficulties that emerged in 1980 and became unsustainable in 1981. In the absence of the fiscal haemorrhaging caused by these subsidies the monetary disorders, overvaluation, and consequent capital flight that characterised 1980, 1981, and 1982 might not have emerged and would certainly have been less severe. Second, the subsidies must have induced producers to invest in production techniques that were heavily reliant upon energy and imported intermediate goods, and the protection of domestic markets made it privately profitable to produce for satisfaction of domestic demand rather than export sales. Though privately profitable, these investments certainly had very low, and conceivably negative, value-added at world prices. Thus, the social return on much of the investment undertaken during the 1977–81 boom may have been quite low, so that when world interest rates became positive in the early 1980s, the massive investments undertaken during 1977–81 were of little help in servicing the external debt.

The Mexican experience yields lessons of general significance. First, it underscores the fact that not only trade policy, but also macroeconomic policy more generally can respond endogenously to resource booms, and it illustrates the unfortunate consequences that emerge when the policy response is perverse. It also highlights important interactions between macroeconomic and microeconomic policy responses. In particular, the energy price policies that were financed by the oil boom had both macroeconomic and microeconomic dimensions. They were the chief cause of the public sector fiscal crisis that, in turn, underlay the monetary disorders of the period. They may also have been a key cause of the investment boom, which explains the external deficits that emerged in the early 1980s. And they help explain why that investment boom did not, in the end, generate income sufficient to service the external debt that had financed much of the investment. In the end it was the macroeconomic dislocations implied by energy subsidies and other extravagant fiscal policies that were decisive in turning the oil boom into nightmare.

NOTES

1. Petroleum sector wages were, however, much higher than average, reflecting the high skills required and physically demanding nature of much petroleum sector work. In addition, the petroleum workers' union was considered the strongest in Mexico, and it seems likely that the high wages in this sector reflect that power to some degree. Thus, although the petroleum sector in 1973 employed only 0.6% of the workforce, its wage bill was roughly 2% of aggregate wage payments.
2. During the ten years up to and including 1973, petroleum sector investment was about 6.3% of aggregate investment, and its share of the capital stock was probably somewhat higher.
3. Here, and throughout this chapter, we deflate dollar values with the United States producer price index, which we take to be a good proxy for the world price of Mexican imports. (Imports from the United States comprise roughly 60% to 70% of Mexico's total imports.) Thus, the numeraire is the price of imported goods.
4. The following discussion follows Randall (1989), El Mallakh *et al.* (1984), and especially Teichman (1988). Teichman contains a particularly useful discussion of bureaucratic and political aspects of Mexican oil policy.
5. United States government estimates of Mexican oil reserves exceeded official Mexican estimates by a factor of two in this period (see Gentleman 1984).
6. The following analysis is not particularly sensitive to the estimate of extraction costs, because during the boom period world prices were so much higher than plausible estimates of cost. That the estimated cost is reasonable, and in particular not too low, can be seen from the fact that the Mexican petroleum industry was in reasonably good shape during the 1960s and early 1970s, when the world price was approximately US$5.00 per barrel (again, in 1988 prices) and domestic sales were at subsidised prices. The analysis that underlies the estimated extraction cost is contained in a technical appendix that is available from the author upon request.

7. In fact the government did increase energy-price subsidies, by enough to be of major budgetary and macroeconomic significance. We discuss these subsidies below.

8. Teichman (1988: 64), quoting from *Proceso*, 286 (26 April 1979).

9. Gentleman (1984: 85), citing Díaz Serrano, 'Economic and Social Conditions in Mexico', *Comercio Exterior*, Dec. 1977.

10. As a fraction of total investment, however, investment in the petroleum sector increased substantially, rising from about 5% of the total to average about 12% during the boom, and reaching a peak of nearly 15% of total investment in 1981. After 1981 investment in the petroleum sector declined much more rapidly than total investment, until by 1985 the share of the petroleum sector in total investment had declined to about 6%, in line with previous historical experience.

11. See the summary in Buffie and Krause (1989: 152).

12. The second reason, which we shall take up below, is that the private sector had a substantially higher savings rate than did the public sector during this episode.

13. This is a bilateral real exchange rate *vis-à-vis* the United States dollar, computed using Mexican and US consumer price indices. An increase in the index represents a depreciation of the Mexican real exchange rate.

14. The price of domestic manufactures rises considerably if compared with the price of imported goods. Manufactures must, therefore, have received some protection from the commercial policy regime that was then in place. That this protection was not absolute is illustrated by the large increase in manufactured imports that took place during the 1977–81 boom.

15. These price indexes, referring as they do to domestic value-added, are for domestic production in these sectors. The sharp appreciation of the real exchange rate that occurred during the 1977–81 boom ensures that the relative prices of imported investment goods would have declined sharply during that period. The subsequent depreciation of the real exchange rate means that the prices of imported investment goods would have risen sharply after the 1982 crisis. Thus, the relative prices of imported investment goods and of domestic value-added in the construction sector move in opposite directions in both phases of the petroleum boom.

16. Computation of the inflation adjustment is straightforward. The peso-denominated debt at the beginning of a year is multiplied by price inflation between the beginning and the end of the year. The reader can easily see that this is the payment to debt-holders that would suffice to maintain the real value of the outstanding debt.

17. The conventionally estimated deficit, that is, without the inflation adjustment described above, increases to roughly 13% of GDP in this year.

18. These data do *not* make the inflation adjustment described above, but are otherwise consistent with the figures for savings and investment given in Table 18.10.

19. These subsidies manifest themselves in the decline of non-oil parastatal income documented in Table 18.11.

20. See Table 18.3, where we estimate that the public sector's windfall income from the oil boom amounted to 7.5% of GDP in 1980 and 1980.

21. These figures should be compared with those in Table 18.3, above.

REFERENCES

Baker, G. (1984) *Mexico's Petroleum Sector: Performance and Prospects*, Tulsa, Okla.: PenWell Publishing.

Buffie, Edward and M. Krause (1989) 'Mexico 1958–86' in J. Sachs (ed.) *Developing Country Debt and the World Economy*, Chicago, Ill.: University of Chicago Press.

Carrada-Bravo, F. (1982) *Oil, Money, and the Mexican Economy*, Boulder, Colo.: Westview Press.

Dornbusch, R. (1985) 'Overborrowing: Three Case Studies', in G. Smith and J. Cuddington (eds) *International Debt and the Developing Countries*, Washington, DC: World Bank.

El Mallakh, Ø. Noreng and B.W. Poulson (1984) *Petroleum and Economic Development: The Cases of Mexico and Norway*, Lexington, Mass.: Lexington Books.

Fisher, B., E. Gerken and U. Hiemenz (1981) *Growth, Employment, and Trade in an Industrializing Economy: A Quantitative Analysis of Mexican Development Policies*, Tübingen: J.C.B. Mohr (Paul Siebeck).

Gentleman, J. (1984) *Mexican Oil and Dependent Development*, New York: Peter Lang.

Hampson, F. (1986) *Forming Economic Policy: The Case of Energy in Canada and Mexico*, London: Frances Pinter.

Looney, R.E. (1978) *Mexico's Economy: A Policy Analysis with Forecasts to 1990*, Boulder, Colo.: Westview Press.

Nacional Financeria de Mexico (1978, 1986, 1988) *La Economia Mexicana en Cifras*.

Randall, L. (1989) *The Political Economy of Mexican Oil*, New York: Praeger.

Scherr, S.J. (1985) *The Oil Syndrome and Agricultural Development: Lessons from Tabasco, Mexico*, New York: Praeger.

Teichman, J.A. (1988) *Policymaking in Mexico: From Boom to Crisis*, Boston, Mass.: Allen and Unwin.

United Nations ECLA (1987) *Statistical Yearbook for Latin America and the Carribean*, New York: United Nations Publications.

Velasco, J.-A. (1982) *Impacts of Mexican Oil Policy on Economic and Political Development*, Lexington, Mass.: Lexington Books.

19

Thailand: Trade Shocks and Domestic Responses

PETER G. WARR AND SOONTHORN CHAIYINDEEPUM

19.1. Introduction

Like most developing countries, Thailand has experienced its share of internally and externally induced economic and political shocks. The internal shocks have included domestic political turmoil through-out most of the past sixty years. Authoritarian military govern-ments alternated with brief periods of democracy or semi-democracy, all combined with repeated *coups*, attempted *coups*, threatened *coups*, and general political unrest. The paradox is the stability of Thailand's economic policies and performance despite its apparent political instability.

External shocks affecting Thailand have also been impressive. They have included: a perceived military threat from Vietnam in the 1960s; the side-effects of the Vietnam war, including a flood of American aid and military spending during the war, followed by its abrupt cessation; the boom in international primary commodity prices of 1972–73; the two massive petroleum price increases of 1973–74 and 1979–80; the high interest rates of the early 1980s; the world recession of the first half of the 1980s; and finally a foreign investment boom in the late 1980s. Moreover, Thailand has experienced a long-term secular decline in its terms of trade—from an index of 100 in 1970 to around 60 in 1990. But whereas many developing countries, including some of Thailand's Southeast Asian neighbours, were badly destabilised by these and similar shocks, the Thai economy showed surprising resilience.

Thailand's macroeconomic performance is summarised in Table 19.1. Over the period 1965–90 the average annual growth rate of real GNP per capita in Thailand was 4.2%, compared with an average of 2.5% for low- and middle-income countries. More remarkable than this was the stability of Thailand's growth. Almost uniquely among oil-importing countries, Thailand has not experienced a single year of negative per capita growth since 1958. Quite recently, over the four years to 1990, the Thai economy

Table 19.1. Macroeconomic summary, 1970–91

Variable	1970	1971	1972	1973	1974	1975	1976	1977	1978	1979	1980
GNP, real (% growth rate)	7.4	4.6	5.4	9.1	4.1	5.0	8.9	9.8	9.3	5.9	6.2
Exports (% growth rate)	0.3	10.7	26.6	33.2	44.9	-7.8	24.9	14.9	21.7	29.4	27.0
Imports (% growth rate)	4.0	1.2	13.8	36.1	49.2	3.8	12.2	30.3	15.9	38.4	23.2
Terms of trade (export unit value/import unit value)	100	101	111	155	130	116	107	101	102	105	100
Inflation (% growth rate)	0.8	0.4	4.8	15.6	24.3	5.3	4.2	7.1	8.4	9.9	19.7
Current account balance/GDP (%)	-3.8	-2.5	-0.6	-0.5	-0.7	-4.1	-2.7	-5.7	-1.5	-7.7	-6.2
Money supply (M_1) real (% growth rate)	9.7	11.0	17.7	17.9	13.0	11.0	12.4	9.0	17.1	17.0	13.8
Total debt/GDP (%)	16.6	17.2	16.8	14.3	13.2	15.5	13.1	14.8	18.5	20.2	25.7
Total debt service/exports (%)	17.1	18.9	17.4	15.3	14.8	15.1	12.8	16.7	17.4	19.1	14.5
Exchange rate (Baht/US$)	20.80	20.80	20.80	20.40	20.00	20.00	20.00	20.00	20.34	20.42	20.48

Variable	1981	1982	1983	1984	1985	1986	1987	1988	1989	1990	1991
GNP, real (% growth rate)	5.2	4.8	7.1	6.3	3.0	4.6	9.7	13.3	12.4	10.3[a]	7.4[b]
Exports (% growth rate)	14.1	6.0	-4.6	14.1	10.5	20.7	28.8	33.9	27.7	14.4	23.6[a]
Imports (% growth rate)	14.3	-9.6	20.1	3.8	4.6	-3.0	39.0	46.1	29.8	28.5	16.6[a]
Terms of trade (export unit value/import unit value)	87	79	85	83	80	89	89	86	83	81	80[a]
Inflation (% growth rate)	12.7	5.2	3.8	0.9	2.4	1.9	2.5	3.8	5.4	6.0	5.7
Current account balance/GDP (%)	-7.1	-2.7	-7.3	-5.1	-4.1	0.6	-0.7	-2.7	-3.6	-4.9	-4.9[b]
Money supply (M_1 real) (% growth rate)	6.5	12.0	10.3	5.4	8.4	18.2	24.9	8.0	11.7	8.5	n.a.
Total debt/GDP (%)	31.0	34.2	35.0	36.4	46.9	44.6	35.9	30.1	28.2	31.3	31.6[b]
Total debt service/exports (%)	14.4	16.0	19.1	21.5	25.3	25.4	17.1	13.7	12.4	9.8	15.2[b]
Exchange rate (Baht/US$)	21.82	23.00	23.00	23.64	27.13	26.30	25.70	25.30	25.80	25.60	25.60

[a] Preliminary, from Bank of Thailand, *Quarterly Bulletin*, Dec. 1991

[b] Forecast, from Asian Development Bank, *Asian Development Outlook*, 1991; the 1991 real GNP growth rate estimate relates to GDP

n.a. = not available

Sources: Bank of Thailand, *Quarterly Bulletin*, various issues; World Bank, *World Development Report*, various issues; Asian Development Bank, *Asian Development Outlook*, 1991

was the fastest growing in the world. While income distribution has apparently become more unequal over the last two decades, the incidence of absolute poverty has declined significantly. The rate of inflation has been low, averaging only 3.8% from 1965 to 1990, compared with an average rate of 32% for all low- and middle-income developing countries, and its exchange rate has been remarkably stable (Nidhiprabha 1993). All this was achieved with only moderate growth of external debt and with stable international reserves. Considering the degree to which other economies were destabilised by internal and external shocks seemingly no more severe than those listed above, the Thai experience of stable growth is remarkable.[1]

This chapter attempts to chart the sources of the resilience of the Thai economy in the face of adverse external shocks and in the course of this to apply to Thailand the methodology for the study of adjustment to temporary trade shocks developed by Bevan *et al.* (1990 and Chapter 2 in this book). The period of study is from 1970 to 1991. An earlier starting-point might have been chosen except for data considerations. The coverage of the revised national accounts data series recently published by the Thai government begins with 1970.[2] We end with 1991 because at the time of completion of our study that was the latest year for which full statistical coverage was available.

The chapter is organised into six sections. The next section outlines the major external shocks impinging upon Thailand during the last two decades. These shocks include those affecting the trade account as well as the services account. Section 19.3 concentrates on the effects of the trade shocks. It attempts to estimate the magnitude of the terms of trade shocks, measured in terms of income loss to the national economy. In Section 19.4, the response of the economy to terms of trade changes is investigated by focusing on the response of Thailand's savings and investment behaviour. Section 19.5 studies the response of the government sector via its fiscal policies. The last section concludes.

19.2. The Nature of the Shocks

Generally, the word 'shock' implies that something has happened that is, first, unexpected, and second, serious enough to require a response. The shock can be positive (e.g. a sudden rise in the price of exportable goods or foreign aid received) or negative (e.g. a sudden rise in the price of importable goods or a fall in foreign aid). In an open economy, the shock is reflected by a sudden change in the current or capital account of the balance of payments. In the last two decades, Thailand was affected by eight major external shocks that can be characterised in chronological order as follows:

19.2.1. The Commodity Boom, 1973–74

There were unprecedented rises in the prices of the primary commodities of which Thailand was major exporter. For example, the world price of Thai rice rose from US$149.92 per metric ton in 1972 to US$541.50 per metric ton in 1974, and the price of Thai rubber rose from US¢12.78 per pound in 1972 to US¢30.92 per pound in 1974 (IMF 1989). This commodity boom resulted in a rise in the unit value of exports by 53% while the volume of exports fell by 7% (IMF 1989).

19.2.2. The First Oil Price Rise, 1974

The Arab–Israel conflict resulted in a sharp rise in the price of oil. The price of Saudi Arabian oil (Ras Tanura) increased from an average of US$2.70 per barrel in 1973 to US$9.76 per barrel in 1974 (IMF 1989). The cost of oil imports to Thailand went up from US$226 million in 1973 to US$617 million in 1974. The oil price rise also caused the inflation rate to soar from an average of 2% over the three years 1970–72 to 16% in 1973 and 24% in 1974.

19.2.3. The Fall in US Government Expenditure, 1975

During the 1950s and 1960s, US government expenditure was a major source of foreign exchange receipts. However, following the Communist victories in Indochina, US involvement in the region gradually declined. In 1975 the US government completely withdrew its military bases from Thailand. This led to a fall in US government expenditure within Thailand from 0.4% of Thai GNP at the beginning of the 1970s to less than 0.05% from 1976 onwards.

19.2.4. The Second Oil Price Rise, 1979–82

In 1979, the oil-producing countries in the Middle East broke away from their long-term commitment to supply oil to the major oil companies and began to sell it on the spot market. At the same time, there was a cut back in oil production in Iran after the Islamic revolution. This led to another period of rising oil prices. The Iraq–Iran war in 1980 induced a further increase in oil prices. The price of Saudi Arabian oil went up from US$12.70 per barrel in 1978 to US$28.67 per barrel in 1980, and to a peak of US$33.47 per barrel in 1982 (IMF 1989). The import cost of oil in Thailand jumped from US$1.12 billion in 1978 to US$2.87 billion in 1980. As with the first oil price shock, it caused inflation to rise, from 8.4% in 1978 to 19.7% in 1980.

19.2.5. World Recession and High International Interest Rates, 1980–82

Adjustments in the industrial countries in response to the second oil price rise led to a second-round shock that affected developing countries. These were the tightening fiscal and monetary policies in the industrialised countries, which led to a slowdown of growth in the industrial countries and a decline in demand for exports from developing countries. The international interest rate also rose sharply as a result of tight monetary policies in the OECD countries.

In Thailand, the average annual growth rate of real GDP fell to 5.1%, compared with 7.0% during 1970–79. The value of exports did not fall but grew only marginally, from US$6.45 billion in 1980 to US$6.83 billion in 1982. The current account deficit as a percentage of GDP rose from 4.80% in 1978 to 7.37% in 1981.

19.2.6. The Fall in Oil Prices, 1983–89

An attempt by oil-importing countries to reduce their dependency on imported petroleum and the collapse of the OPEC monopoly led to an excess supply of oil in the world market by 1983. The price of Saudi Arabian oil softened from a peak of US$34 per barrel in 1982 to US$29.30 per barrel in 1983. In 1986 the price of oil dropped to US$13.80 per barrel (IMF 1989). The import cost of oil in Thailand declined from US$2.87 billion in 1980 to US$1.23 billion in 1986. The fall in oil prices also contributed to an improvement of the trade balance in Thailand.

19.2.7. The Rise in Services Income, 1980–91

Although Thailand's trade balance continued to worsen in the 1980s, there was also a surplus on the services account. This came from an increase in workers' remittances and income from tourism. The increase in workers' remittances came largely from contracted workers in the Middle East, and income from tourism rose because of increasing tourism in the region. In 1991 the receipts of workers' remittances and income from tourism in Thailand amounted to US$1.02 billion and US$4.5 billion, respectively.

It should be noted that the increase in services income in this period cannot entirely be described as an external shock. It was also in part the result of Thai government policies intended to improve the current account balance. However, the increase in services income might not have been sustainable if there had not been a favourable external environment that complemented such policy initiatives. An important example is the increased affluence of the Middle East countries, which led to more

demand for personal services from Thailand as well as other countries in
South and Southeast Asia.

19.2.8. The Investment Boom, 1988–91

The restructuring of the Newly Industrialised Economies (NIEs), as they
entered the next stage of development in the mid-1980s, led to a relocation
of labour-intensive industries into Southeast Asia. A stronger Japanese
yen resulting from Japan's chronic balance of payments surplus also encouraged Japanese investment in the region to avoid rising production
costs. This led to an unusual foreign investment boom in Southeast Asia.
Thailand benefited most from this investment influx, with net direct foreign investment amounting to US$2.39 billion in 1990. It is notable, how-
ever, that similar foreign investment booms also occurred at this time in
Malaysia, Indonesia, and southeastern China.

Figure 19.1 summarises these shocks in so far as they involved Thailand's
terms of trade, separating the overall terms of trade into an 'overall terms
of trade' and a 'petroleum terms of trade' component. Figure 19.2 shows

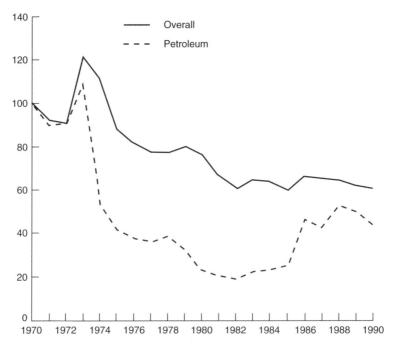

Figure 19.1. Overall terms of trade index and petroleum terms of trade index,
1970–90 (*1970 = 100*)

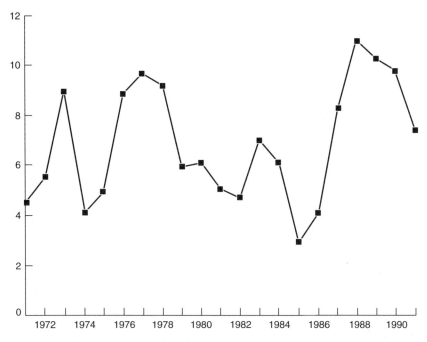

Figure 19.2. Real GNP growth rate, 1971–91 (%)

that the external shocks had visible effects on Thailand's growth perform-ance. The periods to focus upon are 1974–75 and 1979–80—the two oil price shocks—and the period of high interest rates in the early 1980s.

The effects that these external shocks had on Thailand's balance of payments can be seen in Tables 19.2 and 19.3. Table 19.3 provides the same information as in Table 19.2, but expressed as a percentage of Thai-land's GNP. Table 19.3 reveals two interesting points. First, the value of non-fuel primary commodity exports as a percentage of GNP in Thailand was more or less maintained until 1990, with a remarkable surge in 1974 caused by the commodity boom. Second, the adverse effect of the 'trade' shocks was greater in the 1970s, but in the 1980s the positive effect of the 'non-trade' shocks started to play a compensating role. For example, it can be seen that from 1986 onwards income from tourism alone could easily offset the total cost of petroleum imports.

19.3. Estimation of the Terms of Trade Loss

The previous section identified eight major external shocks affecting the Thai economy in the 1970s and 1980s. In this chapter, we concentrate on

Table 19.2. The magnitude of external shocks affecting the balance of payments (*m. US$*)

	Total exports	Exports of non-fuel primary products	Total imports	Imports of petroleum products	Workers' remittances	Income from tourism	US government expenditure	Net direct investment
1970	686.0	629.2	1,269.6	112.0	0.0	104.3	29.5	42.8
1971	802.5	705.7	1,288.8	131.0	0.0	106.2	25.0	38.9
1972	1,045.7	864.3	1,472.8	150.0	0.0	130.7	20.1	68.6
1973	1,515.6	1,201.8	2,039.5	226.0	0.0	164.6	17.3	77.8
1974	2,405.6	2,006.1	3,104.7	617.0	0.0	186.8	11.2	188.3
1975	2,176.9	1,785.4	3,166.1	699.0	18.4	219.9	8.2	85.6
1976	2,958.9	2,399.4	3,502.3	818.0	23.8	195.6	5.2	79.1
1977	3,454.1	2,804.3	4,706.1	1,024.0	44.7	225.8	2.6	106.1
1978	4,043.8	3,041.6	5,405.9	1,124.0	103.8	437.3	5.3	49.7
1979	5,234.1	3,883.0	7,515.4	1,599.0	187.0	550.0	4.6	51.3
1980	6,447.3	4,578.0	9,278.6	2,868.0	376.1	867.4	4.5	186.3
1981	6,884.4	4,981.1	9,899.2	2,984.0	477.9	983.3	8.1	291.6
1982	6,834.9	4,914.6	8,405.2	2,642.0	618.3	1,038.2	10.1	188.6
1983	6,307.7	4,284.2	10,186.0	2,481.0	846.0	1,089.1	18.4	356.2
1984	7,340.1	4,779.8	10,248.9	2,426.0	893.3	1,155.5	22.1	407.1
1985	7,058.3	4,221.7	9,327.5	2,088.0	876.1	1,169.7	10.9	161.2
1986	8,801.6	4,821.2	9,341.8	1,230.0	794.7	1,419.0	9.5	261.6
1987	11,590.2	5,449.2	13,284.5	1,717.0	839.7	1,944.9	8.2	183.2
1988	15,783.6	7,597.0	19,740.6	1,536.0	926.7	3,118.2	13.5	1,081.4
1989	19,856.9	8,625.0	25,226.0	2,329.0	943.9	3,753.3	19.2	1,729.5
1990	22,808.2	7,821.0	32,561.8	3,064.0	974.1	4,324.3	21.6	2,390.2
1991	28,267.7	n.a.	37,811.0	3,439.0	1,020.7	4,539.0	27.2	1,848.2

Sources: Bank of Thailand; data on exports of non-fuel primary products are derived from World Bank, *World Tables 1991* and World Bank, *World Development Report, 1991–1992*

Table 19.3. The magnitude of external shocks affecting the balance of payments (*percentage of GNP*)

	Total exports	Exports of non-fuel primary products	Total imports	Imports of petroleum products	Workers' remittances	Income from tourism	US government expenditure	Net direct investment
1970	9.67	8.87	17.89	1.58	0.00	1.47	0.42	0.60
1971	10.89	9.58	17.49	1.78	0.00	1.44	0.34	0.53
1972	12.83	10.61	18.08	1.84	0.00	1.60	0.25	0.84
1973	14.13	11.20	19.01	2.11	0.00	1.53	0.16	0.73
1974	17.56	14.64	22.66	4.50	0.00	1.36	0.08	1.37
1975	14.63	12.00	21.27	4.70	0.12	1.48	0.05	0.58
1976	17.46	14.16	20.67	4.83	0.14	1.15	0.03	0.47
1977	17.52	14.22	23.87	5.19	0.23	1.15	0.01	0.54
1978	16.97	12.77	22.69	4.72	0.44	1.84	0.02	0.21
1979	19.34	14.35	27.77	5.91	0.69	2.03	0.02	0.19
1980	20.09	14.27	28.92	8.94	1.17	2.70	0.01	0.58
1981	20.07	14.52	28.86	8.70	1.39	2.87	0.02	0.85
1982	18.97	13.64	23.33	7.33	1.72	2.88	0.03	0.52
1983	15.87	10.78	25.62	6.24	2.13	2.74	0.05	0.90
1984	17.77	11.57	24.81	5.87	2.16	2.80	0.05	0.99
1985	18.45	11.04	24.38	5.46	2.29	3.06	0.03	0.42
1986	20.84	11.41	22.12	2.91	1.88	3.36	0.02	0.62
1987	23.33	10.97	26.75	3.46	1.69	3.92	0.02	0.37
1988	26.00	12.52	32.52	2.53	1.53	5.14	0.02	1.78
1989	27.82	12.08	35.34	3.26	1.32	5.26	0.03	2.42
1990	27.06	9.28	38.64	3.64	1.16	5.13	0.03	2.84
1991	29.16	n.a.	39.01	3.55	1.05	4.68	0.03	1.91

Source: Calculated from Table 19.2

the effects of the terms of trade changes. In this section, we estimate the terms of trade loss, measured in terms of its effect on national income, by comparing the actual cost of imports to the country with the counterfactual cost of these imports—what the cost would have been if the terms of trade had remained unchanged from their value in a specified base period. The calculation is done in US dollars at constant 1970 prices.

The above data reveal that Thailand has experienced two major trade shocks: a moderate decline in the non-oil terms of trade; and a proportionately much larger decline in the oil terms of trade. Thus, the following section attempts to calculate the extent to which the decline in the non-oil and oil terms of trade produced costs to the Thai economy, measured in terms of loss of income. Since we are most interested in the analysis of the trade shocks occurring since 1970, the calculation will start from 1970 and extend to 1991.

Table 19.4 calculates the extent to which the non-oil terms of trade shock caused a loss of income. This is called the 'non-oil terms of trade loss' and is calculated for any year t as:

$$L_t^N = Q_t^{NM}(P_t^{NM}/P_t^X) - Q_t^{NM}(P_0^{NM}/P_0^X) = Q_t^{NM}(P_t^{NM}/P_t^X) - Q_t^{NM}$$

where

Q_t^{NM} = actual real value of non-oil imports in year t (valued at 1970 prices);

P_t^{NM} = non-oil imports price index for year t (1970 = 100);

P_t^X = exports price index for year t (1970 = 100);

P_0^{NM}, P_0^X = non-oil imports and exports price indices at the base year of 1970. We normalise such that $P_0^{NM} = P_0^X = 1$.

The actual real value of non-oil imports is calculated by deflating the current value of non-oil imports with the non-oil import price index. Thus, the term $Q_t^{NM}(P_t^{NM}/P_t^X)$ is the equivalent value of exportable goods that has to be sacrificed to obtain the current value of non-oil import in year t. The term $Q_t^{NM}(P_0^{NM}/P_0^X) = Q_t^{NM}$ is the counterfactual value of non-oil imports, and is equivalent to the value of exportable goods that would have been sacrificed to obtain the observed quantity of imports if the non-oil terms of trade had remained at its base year level.

Similarly, Table 19.5 calculates the extent to which the oil terms of trade shock caused a loss of income. This is called the 'oil terms of trade loss' and is calculated as:

$$L_t^P = Q_t^{PM}(P_t^{PM}/P_t^X) - Q_t^{PM}(P_0^{PM}/P_0^X) = Q_t^{PM}(P_t^{PM}/P_t^X) - Q_t^{PM}$$

where

Q_t^{PM} = actual real value of oil imports in year t (valued at 1970 prices);

P_t^{PM} = oil imports price index for year t (1970 = 100);

P_0^{PM}, P_0^X = oil imports and exports price indices at the base year of 1970. Again we normalise such that $P_0^{PM} = P_0^X = 1$.

Table 19.4. Magnitude of the non-oil terms of trade shocks

	Export price index (1970 = 100)	Non-oil import price index (1970 = 100)	Non-oil terms of trade (1970 = 100)	Actual non-oil imports (m. US$, at 1970 prices)	Counterfactual non-oil imports (m. US$, at 1970 prices)	Non-oil terms of trade gain (m. US$, at 1970 prices)
	(1)	(2)	(3)	(5)	(6)	(7)
1970	100.00	100.00	100.00	1,157.55	1,157.55	0.00
1971	89.86	118.45	75.86	977.41	741.43	−235.97
1972	98.70	118.08	83.59	1,120.28	936.45	−183.83
1973	151.35	129.07	117.27	1,405.10	1,647.71	242.61
1974	208.92	188.32	110.94	1,321.02	1,465.54	144.52
1975	197.11	196.85	100.13	1,253.28	1,254.93	1.65
1976	191.71	205.92	93.10	1,303.55	1,213.57	−89.97
1977	195.85	221.49	88.42	1,662.41	1,469.97	−192.44
1978	211.74	244.05	86.76	1,754.50	1,522.17	−232.33
1979	253.02	267.73	94.50	2,209.79	2,088.33	−121.46
1980	299.07	293.17	102.01	2,186.62	2,230.63	44.01
1981	308.07	341.49	90.21	2,024.98	1,826.80	−198.19
1982	286.23	354.08	80.84	1,627.65	1,315.75	−311.91
1983	331.25	340.11	97.40	2,265.47	2,206.46	−59.01
1984	287.71	351.68	81.81	2,224.43	1,819.80	−404.63
1985	295.52	380.21	77.72	1,904.05	1,479.92	−424.13
1986	303.78	396.00	76.71	2,048.44	1,571.39	−477.06
1987	325.21	426.56	76.24	2,711.80	2,067.50	−644.30
1988	352.35	487.84	72.23	3,731.67	2,695.27	−1,036.41
1989	362.64	518.24	69.98	4,418.21	3,091.69	−1,326.53
1990	370.23	533.33	69.42	5,530.83	3,839.43	−1,691.40
1991	382.49	558.56	68.48	6,153.67	4,213.88	−1,939.79

Notes:
Col. 3: Col. 1/Col. 2
Col. 6: Col. 4 × Col. 5
Col. 7: Col. 6 − Col. 5
Source: Bank of Thailand, with the base year readjusted to 1970

Table 19.5. Magnitude of the oil terms of trade shocks

	Export price index (1970 = 100) (1)	Oil import price index (1970 = 100) (2)	Oil terms of trade (1970 = 100) (3)	Actual oil imports (m. US$, at 1970 prices) (5)	Counterfactual oil imports (m. US$, at 1970 prices) (6)	Oil terms of trade gain (m. US$, at 1970 prices) (7)
1970	100.00	100.00	100.00	112.00	112.00	0.00
1971	89.86	112.74	79.70	116.20	92.61	−23.59
1972	98.70	110.60	89.25	135.63	121.04	−14.58
1973	151.35	134.16	112.81	168.46	190.04	21.59
1974	208.92	436.30	47.88	141.42	67.72	−73.70
1975	197.11	479.48	41.11	145.78	59.93	−85.85
1976	191.71	520.18	36.85	157.25	57.95	−99.30
1977	195.85	559.53	35.00	183.01	64.06	−118.95
1978	211.74	553.55	38.25	203.05	77.67	−125.38
1979	253.02	772.27	32.76	207.05	67.84	−139.22
1980	299.07	1,306.31	22.89	219.55	50.26	−169.28
1981	308.07	1,589.85	19.38	187.69	36.37	−151.32
1982	286.23	1,655.24	17.29	159.61	27.60	−132.01
1983	331.25	1,448.82	22.86	171.24	39.15	−132.09
1984	287.71	1,400.45	20.54	173.23	35.59	−137.64
1985	295.52	1,553.33	19.02	134.42	25.57	−108.85
1986	303.78	851.07	35.69	144.52	51.59	−92.94
1987	325.21	947.35	34.33	201.75	69.26	−132.49
1988	352.35	810.48	43.47	162.14	70.49	−91.65
1989	362.64	923.45	39.27	287.36	112.85	−174.51
1990	370.23	1,127.40	32.84	331.80	108.96	−222.84
1991	382.49	1,143.97	33.44	305.04	101.99	−203.05

Notes: as for table 19.4
Source: Bank of Thailand, with the base year readjusted to 1970

The actual real value of oil imports is the current value of oil imports deflated by the oil imports price index. The term $Q_t^{PM}(P_t^{PM}/P_t^X)$ is the equivalent value of exportable goods that has to be sacrificed to obtain the current value of oil imports in year t. The term $Q_t^{PM}(P_0^{PM}/P_0^X) = Q_t^{PM}$ is the counterfactual value of oil imports, and is equivalent to the value of exportable goods that would have to be sacrificed if the oil terms of trade remained at the base year.

Table 19.6 summarises our estimates of the total income loss resulting from both the non-oil and oil terms of trade changes. It is estimated that from 1971 to 1991 there was a loss of Thai national income of about US$12 billion as a result of the total terms of trade loss. About 20% of this loss was

Table 19.6. Total terms of trade loss

	Non-oil terms of trade gain (m. US$, at 1970 prices) (1)	Oil terms of trade gain (m. US$, at 1970 prices) (2)	Total terms of trade gain (m. US$, at 1970 prices) (3)
1970	0.00	0.00	0.00
1971	−235.97	−23.59	−259.56
1972	−183.83	−14.58	−198.41
1973	242.61	21.59	264.19
1974	144.52	−73.70	70.82
1975	1.65	−85.85	−84.20
1976	−89.97	−99.30	−189.27
1977	−192.44	−118.95	−311.39
1978	−232.33	−125.38	−357.71
1979	−121.46	−139.22	−260.68
1980	44.01	−169.28	−125.27
1981	−198.19	−151.32	−349.51
1982	−311.91	−132.01	−443.92
1983	−59.01	−132.09	−191.10
1984	−404.63	−137.64	−542.27
1985	−424.13	−108.85	−532.98
1986	−477.06	−92.94	−570.00
1987	−644.30	−132.49	−776.79
1988	−1,036.41	−91.65	−1,128.06
1989	−1,326.53	−174.51	−1,501.04
1990	−1,691.40	−222.84	−1,914.23
1991	−1,939.79	−203.05	−2,142.84
1971–73	−177.19	−16.58	−193.78
1974–78	−368.57	−503.19	−871.76
1979–85	−1,475.32	−970.42	−2,445.73
1986–91	−7,115.48	−917.47	−8,032.95
1971–91	−9,136.56	−2,407.66	−11,544.22

Note:
Col. 3: Col. 1 + Col. 2

directly attributable to the oil terms of trade shock. This is a significant result. Discussion of the terms of trade decline experienced by Thailand since the early 1970s have focused primarily upon the effects of the two OPEC-induced oil price rises of 1973–74 and 1979–80. Our calculations show that from 1970 to 1991 oil price changes in themselves accounted for less than one-quarter of Thailand's overall loss from terms of trade changes.

19.4. Macroeconomic Responses

This section investigates the manner in which Thai savings and invest-ment levels adjusted in response to the changes in income caused by the above terms of trade shocks. First we examine the data on Thailand's aggregate savings and investment responses and second we attempt to quantify these responses. The latter is done by estimating the correspond-ing changes in domestic investment and foreign assets as the country experienced the change in income resulting from the terms of trade shocks, as estimated above.

19.4.1. Adjustment of Aggregate Savings and Investment

We now turn to the data on Thailand's aggregate levels of savings and investment, shown in Figure 19.3 as proportions of GDP. Shock I, the 1973–74 commodity price boom, was too short-lived to be open to analysis within this framework, but the response to the Shock II (1974–76) round of oil price

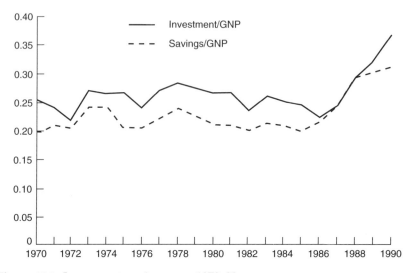

Figure 19.3. Investment–savings gap, 1970–90

increases is clearer. Investment was maintained; savings fell. The shock was treated as if it were temporary. Consumption and investment were maintained on the implicit assumption that the shock would not last. As income growth recovered, through the late 1970s, both the investment/ GDP and savings/GDP ratios increased, but in parallel. The contribution of foreign savings to the financing of total investment remained steady.

The response to the Shock III (1979–80) round of petroleum price increases was initially similar. The shock was again treated as being temporary. From 1979 to 1985 investment rates were again maintained, with the brief exception of 1982, and savings rates fell slightly. But by 1985 the external imbalance implied by this was becoming a serious policy issue. From 1986 onwards, adjustment took two forms. First, savings rates rose and investment rates fell. Thereafter, the adjustment story is complicated by Shock IV, the export- and investment-led boom of the late 1980s. The GDP growth rate rose sharply and both savings and investment rates responded. The response of savings was larger, however, virtually eliminating the investment–savings gap over the interval 1986 to 1989. From 1990 a widening current account deficit was again becoming evident.

Figures 19.4 and 19.5 are helpful in decomposing these data further. From Figure 19.3 above it is clear that in the late 1970s the main reason for the rising savings–investment gap was rapidly growing aggregate investment as a proportion of GDP with stagnant aggregate savings. Figure 19.4 shows that public fixed investment was responsible for this expansion in investment. From 1980 onwards, the story changed. The main explanation for the continuation of a high investment–savings gap from 1980 to 1986

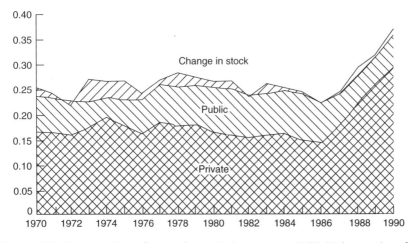

Figure 19.4. Composition of gross domestic investment, 1970–90 (*proportion of GNP*)

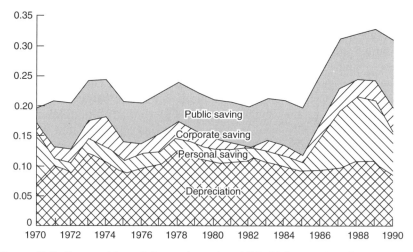

Figure 19.5. Composition of domestic saving, 1970–90 (*proportion of GNP*)

was a dramatic decline in gross national savings. The decline from 1980 to 1985 was from 20.7% of GDP to 17.1%. As a share of GDP, gross national savings had fallen by more than one-sixth.

The role of public sector savings during the first half of the 1980s received a great deal of discussion in Thailand and on the part of foreign observers. The growing external debt was widely attributed to the behaviour of the public sector deficit. A significant decline in public sector savings did indeed occur, but by far the major part of the explanation lay in the behaviour of *household* savings. The drop from 13.7% of GDP to 9.0% was a drop of more than one-third.

The decline in household savings as a share of GDP accounted for well over half of the total savings–investment gap. Two hypotheses have been advanced for this drop in household savings.[3] One is that the slowdown in income growth was not matched by a slowdown in consumption growth, perhaps since it was perceived as being only temporary. A second, and more speculative hypothesis rests on a distributional argument. It is that the contraction of rural incomes resulting from low commodity prices squeezed household savings because rural Thais have a higher marginal propensity to save than urban dwellers. Although the second hypothesis is interesting, it seems unlikely that its quantitative significance could be large enough to explain the decline in savings that actually occurred.

Figure 19.5 reveals another significant point. The response of savings to GDP growth in the late 1980s was influenced partly by public savings, but the response of personal savings was by far the main element of the story. A simple conclusion can be drawn from this and the experience of the first half of the 1980s. Public sector savings behaviour, operating through fiscal policy, may have had a stabilising role—indeed, our discussion later in this chapter will confirm that it does. But a more important stabilising role was played by the *household* sector, through its savings behaviour. Personal savings are highly responsive to changes in growth—more sensitive than total investment or public sector savings—and this point must surely be central to an understanding of the long-term macroeconomic stability of the Thai economy.

19.4.2. Quantification of Aggregate Responses

In order to quantify Thailand's aggregate responses to external shocks the key requirement is to estimate the counterfactual levels of savings and investment—the levels that would hypothetically have been observed in the absence of the shocks. The results of our attempt to do this are presented in Tables 19.7 and 19.8, respectively. In Table 19.7, the first column is the actual real income, which is constructed by subtracting from observed GDP at pre-shock constant prices the estimates of the total terms of trade loss, also at pre-shock prices, in Table 19.6. Observed GDP at pre-shock constant prices represents real GDP netted out of the effect of the domestic price changes. By subtracting the terms of trade loss this becomes actual income including the effect of the terms of trade changes. Column (2) is the propensity to acquire domestic assets in the form of gross fixed capital formation (GFKF). It is determined as a ratio of GFKF to GDP at current prices. Column (3) is actual gross fixed capital formation calculated by multiplying actual real income by the propensity to acquire GFKF.

The counterfactual real income and investment in columns (4) and (5) are calculated as:

$$Y_t^* = Y_t^0 - r\left(\sum_{t=t_0}^{t-1}(d(\text{GFKF})_t + \text{NDI}_t)\right),$$

where

Y_t^*	= counterfactual real income in year t;
Y_t^0	= GDP at constant pre-shock prices;
r	= real rate of return on investment, assumed equal to 10%;
$d(\text{GFKF})_t$	= actual GFKF − counterfactual GFKF (windfall GFKF) in year t;
NDI_t	= net direct investment from abroad in year t;
$(\sum_{t=t_0}^{t-1}(d(\text{GFKF})_t + \text{NDI}_t))$	= cumulative GFKF windfall plus net direct investment from abroad, lagged one year; and
t_0	= the base year.

Table 19.7. Counterfactual income and capital formation (*m. US$*)

	Actual			Counterfactual			GFKF windfall			
	Real income (GDP at 1970 prices adjusted by TOT gain)	GFKF/GDP (at current prices)	GFKF	Real income (GDP at 1970 prices corrected for returns on TOT gain)	GFKF/GDP (at current prices)	GFKF	Annual windfall	Net direct investment	Cumulative	Return at 10%
1970	7,085.82	0.2560	1,813.97	7,085.82	0.2560	1,813.97	0.00			
1971	5,996.82	0.2421	1,451.83	6,256.38	0.2410	1,507.79	−55.96	38.9	−17.06	−1.71
1972	6,770.49	0.2168	1,467.84	6,970.61	0.2410	1,679.92	−212.07	68.6	−160.53	−16.05
1973	8,574.73	0.2699	2,314.32	8,326.59	0.2410	2,006.71	307.61	77.8	224.88	22.49
1974	6,518.21	0.2663	1,735.80	6,424.90	0.2410	1,548.40	187.40	188.3	600.58	60.06
1975	6,515.91	0.2675	1,743.01	6,540.05	0.2410	1,576.15	166.85	85.6	853.03	85.30
1976	6,954.32	0.2398	1,667.65	7,058.29	0.2410	1,701.05	−33.40	79.1	898.73	89.87
1977	7,423.48	0.2688	1,995.43	7,645.00	0.2410	1,842.45	152.99	106.1	1,157.82	115.78
1978	8,345.09	0.2816	2,349.98	8,587.02	0.2410	2,069.47	280.51	49.7	1,488.02	148.80
1979	8,321.68	0.2721	2,264.33	8,433.56	0.2410	2,032.49	231.84	51.3	1,771.17	177.12
1980	8,043.15	0.2777	2,233.58	7,991.30	0.2410	1,925.90	307.68	186.3	2,265.15	226.51
1981	7,094.12	0.2799	1,985.64	7,217.12	0.2410	1,739.33	246.32	291.6	2,803.06	280.31
1982	7,180.17	0.2694	1,934.34	7,343.79	0.2410	1,769.85	164.49	188.6	3,156.15	315.61
1983	8,643.70	0.2846	2,460.00	8,519.19	0.2410	2,053.12	406.87	356.2	3,919.22	391.92
1984	8,548.12	0.2860	2,444.76	8,698.47	0.2410	2,096.33	348.43	407.1	4,674.75	467.47
1985	7,249.73	0.2716	1,969.03	7,315.23	0.2410	1,762.97	206.06	161.2	5,042.01	504.20
1986	8,718.41	0.2578	2,247.61	8,784.20	0.2410	2,116.99	130.61	261.6	5,434.22	543.42
1987	9,291.23	0.2764	2,568.09	9,524.60	0.2410	2,295.43	272.67	183.2	5,890.08	589.01
1988	10,006.38	0.3068	3,069.96	10,545.42	0.2410	2,541.45	528.51	1,081.4	7,499.99	750.00
1989	10,688.33	0.3463	3,701.37	11,439.37	0.2410	2,756.89	944.48	1,729.5	10,173.98	1,017.40
1990	11,774.03	0.4016	4,728.45	12,670.86	0.2410	3,053.68	1,674.77	2,390.2	14,238.95	1,423.89
1991	12,979.72	0.4178	5,422.93	13,698.66	0.2410	3,301.38	2,121.55	1,848.2	18,208.70	1,820.87

Table 19.8. Actual and counterfactual foreign assets (FA) (*m. US$*)

	Stock of FA (at 1970 prices)	Actual FA propensity	Counterfactual FA propensity	Counterfactual stock of FA	Change in net FA
1970	156.45	0.0221	0.0221	156.45	0.00
1971	70.93	0.0113	0.0724	452.96	−382.04
1972	119.30	0.0171	0.0724	504.67	−385.37
1973	289.26	0.0348	0.0724	602.85	−313.59
1974	320.85	0.0498	0.0724	465.16	−144.32
1975	184.27	0.0279	0.0724	473.50	−289.23
1976	116.68	0.0163	0.0724	511.02	−394.34
1977	−45.41	−0.0059	0.0724	553.50	−598.91
1978	−58.62	−0.0067	0.0724	621.70	−680.32
1979	−259.51	−0.0302	0.0724	610.59	−870.10
1980	−676.25	−0.0828	0.0724	578.57	−1,254.82
1981	−950.42	−0.1277	0.0724	522.52	−1,472.94
1982	−1,180.61	−0.1549	0.0724	531.69	−1,712.30
1983	−1,538.51	−0.1741	0.0724	616.79	−2,155.30
1984	−1,763.49	−0.1940	0.0724	629.77	−2,393.26
1985	−1,955.16	−0.2512	0.0724	529.62	−2,484.78
1986	−2,218.92	−0.2389	0.0724	635.98	−2,854.89
1987	−2,098.82	−0.2085	0.0724	689.58	−2,788.40
1988	−1,492.45	−0.1340	0.0724	763.49	−2,255.94
1989	−976.42	−0.0801	0.0724	828.21	−1,804.63
1990	−693.04	−0.0506	0.0724	917.37	−1,610.41
1991	−572.26	−0.0378	0.0724	991.78	−1,564.04

The counterfactual propensity to acquire GFKF is assumed to be equal to the simple average of the GFKF/GDP ratio at current prices during the pre-shock period 1965–70. Thus, in 1970 counterfactual real income is observed GDP in that year, and the share of GFKF/GDP is the propensity to acquire GFKF. Hence, there is no change in GFKF windfall. In 1971 counterfactual real income is again observed real GDP in that year. Counterfactual GFKF is then counterfactual real income multiplied by the counterfactual propensity to acquire GFKF. This reflects the level of GFKF that would have been observed if the economy had maintained its average propensity to acquire GFKF as if there were no shock.

The difference between actual and counterfactual GFKF is the GFKF windfall. This GFKF windfall is then added to the value of net direct investment from abroad in that year to arrive at the total GFKF windfall. This is then the basis for calculating the return to investment in that year. In subsequent years counterfactual real income is observed real GDP minus the assumed 10% return on the cumulative GFKF windfall of previous years. The result of these calculations is an attempt to estimate the counterfactual level of real income in the absence of the shock and when all possible sources of income growth from actual GFKF were excluded. The calculation of the GFKF windfall is then repeated with a similar procedure.

In Table 19.8 we focus on the acquisition of net foreign assets (FA). The first column is the stock of foreign assets, defined as the difference between total foreign exchange reserves and total foreign debt, and deflated by the import price index. The actual propensity to acquire FA is measured by the observed ratio of the stock of foreign assets to GDP at current prices.[4] The counterfactual FA propensity is the simple average of the observed ratio of net foreign assets to GDP during the pre-shock period 1965–70. The counterfactual stock of foreign assets is then calculated by multiplying counterfactual real income in Table 19.7 by the counterfactual FA propensity. This reflects the level of the net stock of FA that would have been observed if the economy had maintained its average propensity to acquire FA as if there were no shock. The last column is the estimated change in the stock of foreign assets owing to the effect of the terms of trade changes. It is obtained by subtracting the counterfactual stock of FA from the observed stock of FA.

Table 19.9 summarises the results. The overall period of analysis is separated into four sub-periods, corresponding to the major terms of trade changes observed in Figure 19.1. Shock I (1971–73) represents the period of the commodity boom. Shock II (1974–78) is the adjustment period after the first oil price rise. Shock III (1979–85) represents the adjustment period after the second oil price rise. Shock IV (1986–91) is the most recent period, one of economic boom in Thailand, when the oil terms of trade improved, exports boomed and foreign investment increased

Table 19.9. Summary of aggregate terms of trade loss, investment and foreign assets (*counterfactual A*)

	Shock I (1971–73)	Shock II (1974–78)	Shock III (1979–85)	Shock IV (1986–91)	Single shock (1971–91)
1. Total terms of trade loss	335	556	228	686	5,272
Non-oil	309	−100	−45	786	2,642
Oil	26	656	273	−100	2,630
2. GFKF windfall	−28	334	242	453	1,052
3. Accumulation of foreign assets	−902	−82	−2,480	953	−8,144
4. Total acquisition of assets	−930	251	−2,238	1,406	−7,092
5. Dissavings ratio	−2.78	0.45	−9.81	2.05	−1.35

Note: Base periods for counterfactuals are: Shock I, 1968–70; Shock II, 1971–73; Shock III, 1976–78; Shock IV, 1983–85; Single shock, 1968–70. Units for rows 1–4: net present value in US$m., discounted at 10% to base year of 1970. Row 4: row 2 + row 3; row 5: row 4/row 1

dramatically. To analyse these shocks individually, we have taken an average of the three years immediately prior to each shock as the base period for the construction of the relevant counterfactual. For example, the base period for the construction of the counterfactual for Shock I (1971–73) is an average of the years 1968 to 1970; the base period for Shock II (1974–78) is an average of the years 1971 to 1973, etc. The last column shows the aggregate effect as if the whole period 1971–91 was considered as a single shock with the base period the same as for Shock I. For reasons that will be apparent below, this set of results is called 'Counterfactual A'.

In the Shock I period, and despite the commodity boom, the present value of the total terms of trade loss was US$335 million at 1970 prices. In this period, the response to the fall in income was a reduced acquisition of domestic assets (negative GFKF) and increasing foreign indebtedness (negative accumulation of FA) by US$902 million at 1970 prices. In effect, Thailand responded to the temporary commodity boom by dissaving about 2.7 times the loss of income owing to the terms of trade change. In the Shock II and Shock III periods, the terms of trade deterioration resulted in net losses of US$556 million and US$228 million, respectively. Unlike the Shock I period, the response to the adverse shocks was increased acquisition of domestic assets. That is, there were GFKF windfalls of US$334 million (Shock II) and US$242 million (Shock III). At the same time, the stock of foreign debt increased by US$82 million and US$2,480 million, respectively. In total, there were savings of US$251 million in the Shock II period and dissavings of US$2,238 million in the Shock III period. Overall, Thailand responded to the oil price rises by dissaving between 1 and 1.5 times the loss of income.

It would not be sensible to aim for great precision in the above calculations because the results are highly sensitive to the choices involved in the construction of counterfactuals, including the choice of the base periods used. For example, the difference in aggregate response during the first and second oil price shocks (Shocks II and III above) vanishes if the base period before Shock I is used in constructing the counterfactuals. This is revealed by Table 19.10, which uses results called 'Counterfactual B' to distinguish them from the results summarised in Table 19.9. In this table, the base period 1968–70 is used to construct the counterfactuals for all shocks. This choice of base period would be strange, perhaps even indefensible, for the latter periods, Shocks III and IV, but the significant point is that the estimated response to Shock II would be very different under this counterfactual than under the counterfactuals underlying Table 19.9. The results are sensitive to the choice of base period. The response to Shock II would then resemble, in qualitative terms, the responses to the other three shocks—dissaving in response to negative external shocks and accumulation of external debt.

The pattern of response to Shock IV shown in Table 19.9 also requires

Table 19.10. Summary of aggregate terms of trade loss, investment and foreign assets (*counterfactual B*)

	Shock I (1971–73)	Shock II (1974–78)	Shock III (1979–85)	Shock IV (1986–91)	Single shock (1971–91)
1. Total terms of trade loss	335	915	1,979	2,042	5,272
Non-oil	309	201	516	1,616	2,642
Oil	26	714	1,463	427	2,630
2. GFKF windfall	−28	288	234	556	1,052
3. Accumulation of foreign assets	−902	−1,128	−3,775	−2,339	−8,144
4. Total acquisition of assets	−930	−840	−3,540	−1,783	−7,092
5. Dissavings ratio	−2.78	−0.92	−1.79	−0.87	−1.35

Note: Base period for counterfactuals is 1968–70 for all shocks. Units for rows 1–4: net present value in US$m., discounted at 10% to base year of 1970. Row 4: row 2 + row 3; row 5: row 4/row 1

qualification. As indicated in Table 19.9, the estimated gain in the terms of trade owing to a decline in petroleum prices was outweighed by the loss arising from changes in the non-oil terms of trade. But the late 1980s were a period of massive economic boom in Thailand and this boom arose from factors that were largely unrelated to the terms of trade and that had effects that dominated the terms of trade changes that occurred. It follows that the positive accumulation of GFKF, foreign assets and (thus) total savings indicated in Table 19.9 should not be related in a causal way to the small changes in the terms of trade that occurred in this period.

Viewed as a single shock, with 1968–70 as the base period, the terms of trade loss from 1971 to 1991 was US$5,272 million. The estimated response to this fall in income was an increase in domestic assets, or the acquisition of GFKF, of US$1,052 million, and foreign finance of US$8,144 million. Thus, Thailand dissaved by US$7,092 million, or about 1.35 times the total income loss.

The results of the above calculations were dependent upon our assumptions about the counterfactual scenario. This is inevitable, since the difference between the actual and the counterfactual outcomes determines the estimated response. The construction of counterfactual estimates such as real income and GFKF propensity also depends upon the real rate of return being used, although this is presumably less important than the choice of base period for the construction of the counterfactual. Although this question is discussed in Bevan *et al.* (1990 and Chapter 2 of this book), there does not appear to be a truly satisfactory method to estimate the rate of return that would have obtained in the hypothetical situation in which the observed shock did not occur. Thus, the calculation could be performed with varying rates to see how sensitive the estimates are to the rate of return we use. In any case, in a country like Thailand, where the changes in major macroeconomic indicators (e.g. the GFKF propensity) are less dramatic, the estimates may be more robust than in countries experiencing less macroeconomic stability.

19.5. Fiscal Responses

The previous section discussed the response of the Thai economy in aggregate terms. However, the private and government sector may have different objective functions and/or different perceptions of the nature of the shock and its likely duration. Accordingly, they may respond to the same shock differently. Thus, it is appropriate to investigate the response of the government sector separately. Having studied the government response, an induction regarding the private sector response could be derived residually from the aggregate response.

19.5.1. Adjustment of Public Sector Accounts

Over the decade prior to the first oil crisis Thailand's public sector deficit was relatively small. The steady expansion of the economy resulted in a similar expansion in revenue. The emphasis of fiscal policy was to modify the indirect tax system with a view to promoting exports and supporting import-substitution industrialisation. Public expenditure, which was concentrated mostly on infrastructure, expanded moderately.

The first oil shock, together with the subsequent world commodity boom, raised revenues. The high prices of commodity exports and high domestic inflation caused tax revenue to increase substantially (28% in 1973 and 48% in 1974). Domestic inflation in the wake of the first oil price shock also halted the planned expansion in public expenditure, to the tune of 7% and 11% in 1973 and 1974, respectively. These changes resulted in a public sector surplus in fiscal year 1973–1974 (FY1973–FY1974) and substantially improved the financial position of the public sector. The government took this opportunity to reduce indirect tax rates, to lessen the inflationary effects on production costs and income.

After 1975, substantial increases in public sector expenditure occurred, most associated with increases in expenditure on defence and administration and the capital expenditures of the state enterprises. Defence expenditure increased by 31% and 26% in 1976 and 1977, respectively, and public expenditure on administration increased by 11% and 14% for the same period. Simultaneously, capital expenditure by the state enterprises jumped dramatically, from 21% in FY1975 to 35% in FY1976, 61% in FY1977, and 59% in FY1978. This increase in public expenditure was facilitated by a new foreign borrowing decree that increased the defence loan allocation and authorised the Ministry of Finance to give financial guarantees to state enterprises to borrow from abroad. In aggregate, public expenditure rose at an average growth rate of 24.3%, while revenue rose 18.8%. In FY1978, the public sector's cash deficit was equivalent to 3.3% of GDP. The foreign indebtedness of the public sector increased from US$87 million in 1976 to US$200 million in 1978.

The second oil shock had a more serious effect on Thailand's public finances because it was followed by a slump in primary commodity prices, occurring in 1981–82. The slump in world commodity prices, which subsequently led to a recession, caused a large drop in tax revenue. The oil price shock caused domestic inflation to increase dramatically and it peaked at 25% during one quarter of 1980. The average rate for the year was 20%. By the standards of Thailand's conservative economic managers, these were unacceptably high rates of inflation.

The Ministry of Finance responded to the second oil shock (1979–80) by heavily subsidising public enterprise prices and public utility charges. This resulted in increased transfers from the central government to the state enterprises. Over the period between FY1979 and FY1982, the expenditure of the state enterprises continued to expand at a rate slightly higher than the overall growth rate of public expenditure—over the same period, 20.6% for state enterprises and 19.3% for the public sector. The growth of public revenue, which averaged 16.3%, lagged behind the growth of public expenditure and caused the public sector deficit to widen—to the equivalent in 1982 of 7.9% of GDP.

The enlarged public sector deficit was reflected in a serious balance of payments problem. It was apparent that there was an urgent need to reduce the public sector deficit. The period between 1980 and 1986 was marked by a cut in expenditure and a string of tax reforms to boost revenue, but this did little to close the deficit gap. The slowdown in GDP growth was the main factor making revenue mobilisation difficult. As a result, public expenditure continued to grow faster than revenue and the deficit, which reached 61 billion baht in FY1985, widened. The growth in public expenditure continued to be dominated by debt repayments, the capital expenditure of state enterprises, defence and administration.

19.5.2. *The Role of Public Capital Formation*

The flexibility of Thai fiscal policy is demonstrated by the ability of the government to manipulate the level of its expenditure and revenues. However, on the expenditure side, capital spending has been relatively more flexible than consumption expenditure. When fiscal tightness was desired it was easier to postpone large public investment projects than to delay increases in civil servants' salaries during periods of inflation. Although the government was able to freeze the wages of public employees from time to time, the controllability of public consumption spending was subject to political influences and inflationary expectations.

The ratios of public and private investment to GDP exhibited a strikingly inverse relationship (Figure 19.6), suggesting that public investment may stabilise the Thai economy by maintaining a high and stable proportion of total capital formation relative to income. When a private investment boom occurred in 1974, public investment declined. Whereas private investment remained sluggish from 1979 to 1985 after the second oil price shock, public investment expanded to offset the decline in private investment. Similarly, during the investment boom of the late 1980s, the public investment/GDP ratio declined. It might be argued that the inverse relationship was the result of a crowding-out effect of public investment, which raised the level of the interest rate and discouraged private investment, but borrowing from the non-bank private sector constituted a small portion of deficit financing. A large part of the deficit was money-financed, thereby creating favourable conditions for private investors since there was no upward pressure on the interest rate. Crowding-out was not the cause.

The inverse relationship illustrated in Figure 19.6 resulted from the combined effects of monetary and fiscal policy. The domestic rate of interest increased relative to the foreign interest rate as monetary growth was reduced. When fiscal policy was expansionary, as indicated by rising public investment, monetary policy could be tightened, causing a decline in the private investment/income ratio. On the other hand, when fiscal policy was contractionary, as indicated by a slowdown in public investment, monetary policy brought about the increase in private expenditure through easing the control of monetary growth.

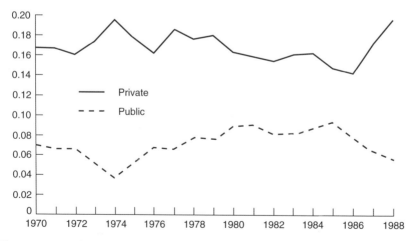

Figure 19.6. Public and private capital accumulation 1970–88 (*ratio to GDP*)

19.5.3. Structure of Expenditure and Taxation

A law introduced in 1959, known as the budgetary law, stipulated that the excess of planned spending over planned revenue was not permitted to exceed 20% of the level of planned spending. In 1973, the limit on spending was relaxed by the amendment of the budgetary law: the deficit must not exceed 20% of the planned expenditure plus 8% of the principal repayments of the public debt.

The effectiveness of the budgetary law in restraining the growth of public expenditure can be seen in Figure 19.7. The maximum amount of public spending (G_m) is calculated by multiplying the level of planned revenue by 1.25 and adding 8% of the level of expenditures allocated to principal repayments of public debt. The ratios of planned expenditure (G_e) and actual expenditure (G_a) to the maximum expenditure permitted by the budgetary law are shown in the figure. Since the actual level of spending was always below the planned level, G_e/G_m was less than G_a/G_m. Except during 1972–74, the actual level of expenditures was well below the permitted level.

The role of the central government in providing infrastructure diminished substantially in the 1980s. The share of capital expenditure in total expenditures declined from 26.3% during 1971–74 to only 14.2% during 1986–89. It seems that it is more expedient to cut capital expenditure than current expenditure. If classified by function, except for unallocable and economic services expenditures, the share of social services, defence, and administration remained relatively stable. The budget allocated to de-

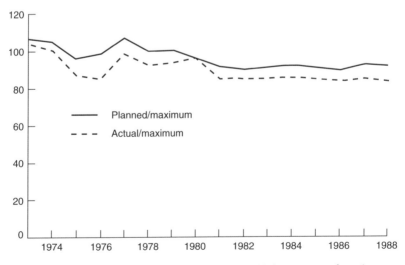

Figure 19.7. Effectiveness of budgetary law, 1970–80 (*percentage of maximum expenditure*)

fence amounted to 19%. Nevertheless, the rate of change in defence expenditure fluctuated widely. During the expansionary years, it expanded by 22%, whereas it was cut to only 2.7% during the tight fiscal years of 1986 to 1989.

The top priority of the budget is social services—hospitals, schools, police, etc. Although the share of administration gradually declined over time, the importance of economic services expenditure fell more significantly, from 24% in the early 1970s to only 14.6% in the late 1980s. The slowdown in public expenditure on infrastructure was the result of the attempt to restrain the rise in public spending. Its effect was to reduce the size of public capital stock relative to aggregate output.

To determine the responsiveness of government expenditure and revenue to changes in income and the price level, Warr and Nidhiprabha (1995: esp. ch. 7) employed a log-linear regression analysis utilising data from 1970 to 1988. All variables were expressed in real terms. The previous period's revenue rather than current revenue was used as a basis for calculating the expenditure elasticities to reflect the realities of Thailand's budgetary process.

The findings suggest that government expenditures are inelastic with respect to changes in revenue. The current expenditure elasticity was 0.82, whereas the capital expenditure elasticity was lower, at 0.36, and was not statistically significant. However, capital expenditures were responsive to changes in the price level, as indicated by the high (negative) value of their elasticity with respect to the price level. Thus, public investment projects can be delayed in real terms if the nominal cost of capital is rising. Capital expenditures are not fixed in real terms. Actual expenditure will be lower than the planned level, even in nominal terms, if the allocated budget cannot cover the rising cost of capital. If the budgeted funds are insufficient to purchase the particular expenditure item, they will not be spent at all. Thus quantity adjustment does occur in the public investment sector.

Public investment expenditure is very sensitive to inflation. This is confirmed by Warr and Nidhiprabha's estimate of the nominal expenditure elasticity with respect to the GDP deflator (-2.53). Its large negative value implies that increased inflation causes *nominal*, and not merely real, expenditure on capital goods to decline when inflation rises. Nevertheless, the current expenditure elasticity was not significantly different from zero, as indicated by the low value of the t-statistic. The estimated value of the elasticity of total public expenditure with respect to total (previous-period) revenue was 0.75, implying that when income is increasing total expenditure will not rise as fast as total revenue. Similarly, the effect of price-level changes on total expenditure in real terms is small and not highly significant.

Inflation seems to have no effect on public revenues in real terms, but it has an important *negative* impact on public expenditures, as indicated by the significance of the GDP deflator. The negative responsiveness of real expenditure with respect to the price level seems to have increased in absolute value over time. This finding indicates that fiscal policy also contributes to price stability, since the government did not insist on acquiring the intended level of expenditures, in real terms. As a result, aggregate demand would be more elastic than the case when public expenditures are fixed in real terms. During an economic boom that pushes the price level higher, there would be less inflationary pressure from the public sector. During an economic slump caused by an energy price shock, there would also be less inflationary pressure, since the public sector does not want to maintain the same quantity of purchasing.

The analysis summarised above suggests that the Thai fiscal system has a stabilising function. First, inflation reduces real capital expenditures; at the same time it increases tax revenue from corporations. Second, although expenditures are relatively insensitive to collected revenues, the latter tend to be sensitive with respect to economic activity. Thus, during boom years when the price level starts rising, there is a propensity for a budgetary surplus.

19.5.4. Quantification of Fiscal Responses

This section constructs counterfactual estimates of how fiscal outcomes would have developed in the absence of the trade shocks. The estimation follows a similar method to the previous section and the results are presented in Table 19.11. The first three columns are the actual revenues, current consumption, and capital expenditure in constant 1970 prices. They are constructed by multiplying the actual real income in Table 19.7 by the observed ratios of revenues, current consumption, and capital expenditure to GDP in each year. Similarly, the counterfactual fiscal outcomes are calculated by multiplying the counterfactual income, also in Table 19.7, by the counterfactual ratios of revenues, current consumption, and capital expenditure to GDP in each year. These counterfactual ratios are similarly determined as the simple average of the observed ratios during the pre-shock period 1965–70. The estimated fiscal gain is the difference between the actual and counterfactual components. The last column of Table 19.11 is the primary deficit, which is the difference between total government revenues and expenditure.

A summary of the fiscal responses to the terms of trade shocks is presented in Table 19.12, which classifies the period of analysis into four subperiods similar to those in Tables 19.9 and 19.10. In the Shock I period, there was a fall in revenues by US$236 million. The response of the government to the fall in income was a reduction in capital expenditure of US$65 million but a rise in current consumption of US$93 million. This leaves an estimated primary deficit of US$264 million. In the Shock II

Table 19.11. Actual and counterfactual fiscal outcomes (*m. US$; 1970 prices*)

	Actual			Counterfactual			Fiscal gain			Primary deficit
	Revenues (1)	Current consumption (2)	Capital expenditure (3)	Revenues (4)	Current consumption (5)	Capital expenditure (6)	Revenues (7)	Current consumption (8)	Capital expenditure (9)	(10)
1970	903.51	827.12	381.30	959.42	787.94	335.87	−55.91	39.17	45.43	−140.51
1971	756.56	736.82	327.44	847.11	695.71	296.55	−90.56	41.11	30.89	−162.56
1972	857.28	830.33	309.87	943.82	775.13	330.41	−86.54	55.20	−20.54	−121.20
1973	1,040.43	961.71	301.78	1,127.42	925.92	394.68	−86.99	35.79	−92.90	−29.89
1974	909.49	674.57	148.10	869.93	714.45	304.54	39.56	−39.88	−156.44	235.88
1975	850.00	752.86	217.66	885.52	727.25	310.00	−35.52	25.61	−92.34	31.21
1976	875.06	847.85	309.27	955.69	784.88	334.56	−80.63	62.96	−25.30	−118.30
1977	994.58	903.43	312.76	1,035.13	850.12	362.37	−40.55	53.31	−49.62	−44.24
1978	1,114.58	1,000.23	324.61	1,162.68	954.88	407.02	−48.10	45.35	−82.42	−11.04
1979	1,171.51	1,044.80	287.24	1,141.90	937.81	399.75	29.60	106.99	−112.51	35.12
1980	1,167.15	1,152.65	324.93	1,082.02	888.63	378.79	85.13	264.02	−53.85	−125.04
1981	1,043.72	982.27	263.02	977.20	802.54	342.09	66.52	179.73	−79.07	−34.14
1982	1,015.55	1,102.45	272.43	994.35	816.63	348.10	21.21	285.82	−75.66	−188.96
1983	1,362.36	1,304.60	282.40	1,153.50	947.33	403.81	208.86	357.26	−121.41	−27.00
1984	1,301.80	1,356.59	243.66	1,177.77	967.27	412.31	124.03	389.32	−168.64	−96.65
1985	1,148.15	1,193.07	236.50	990.48	813.45	346.74	157.67	379.62	−110.25	−111.70
1986	1,352.49	1,381.40	244.53	1,189.38	976.80	416.37	163.11	404.60	−171.84	−69.64
1987	1,497.85	1,339.55	232.19	1,289.63	1,059.14	451.47	208.22	280.42	−219.27	147.07
1988	1,714.25	1,285.13	196.19	1,427.85	1,172.65	499.85	286.40	112.47	−303.66	477.59
1989	1,975.49	1,361.21	226.40	1,548.89	1,272.06	542.23	426.60	89.15	−315.82	653.27
1990	2,221.67	1,344.67	298.18	1,715.63	1,409.00	600.60	506.04	−64.33	−302.41	872.78
1991	2,392.44	1,487.39	386.25	1,854.80	1,523.29	649.32	537.64	−35.90	−263.07	836.61

Notes:
Col 7: Col. 1 – Col. 4
Col 8: Col. 2 – Col. 5
Col 9: Col. 3 – Col. 6
Col 10: Col. 7 – Col. 8 – Col. 9

Table 19.12. Summary of fiscal responses to the terms of trade shocks (*m. US$, 1970 prices*)

	Shock I (1971–73)	Shock II (1974–78)	Shock III (1979–85)	Shock IV (1986–91)	Single shock (1971–91)
1. Change in total revenues	−236.46	108.92	303.99	123.30	−198.39
2. Change in current consumption	93.35	−114.06	440.53	−383.02	553.28
3. Change in capital formation	−65.33	−205.69	−125.46	−89.34	−900.20
4. Primary surplus	−264.48	428.67	−11.08	595.66	148.54

Note: Base periods for counterfactuals are: Shock I, 1968–70; Shock II, 1971–73: Shock III, 1976–78; Shock IV, 1983–85; Single shock, 1968–70. Units for rows 1–4: net present value in US$ m., discounted at 10% to base year of 1970. Row 4: Row 1 − row 2 − row 3

period, the negative oil price shock caused total revenues to rise by US$109 million. The government responded to the inflation caused by the shock by substantially reducing current consumption and capital expenditure. As a result, there was a primary surplus of US$429 million in this period. The inferred pattern of these events is again sensitive to the choice of base period. When the pre-Shock I period is used to construct the counterfactual for Shock II the estimated change in revenues has the opposite sign from that described above—a reduction in revenues (US$151 million) but a contraction in capital expenditure is again evident (US$262 million), as is an increase in the resulting primary surplus (US$98 million).

In the Shock III period, total revenues rose by US$304 million. There was still an increase in current consumption, of US$441 million, but a continued reduction in capital expenditure by US$125 million. The primary deficit reversed to US$11 million. In the Shock IV period, total revenues continued to increase, by US$123 million and current consumption and capital expenditure both declined. This resulted in a primary surplus in the Shock IV period of US$596 million.

When the entire period is viewed as a single shock, there was an increase in government total revenues of US$198 million during the 1971–91 period. The response of the government was to increase current consumption at the expense of capital expenditure. Subsequently, there was a primary surplus of US$149 million. The central picture of heavy reductions in capital expenditures in response to the shocks—we have seen above that inflation is the principal trigger in these responses—comes through in all these counterfactual calculations.

With the information about fiscal responses as estimated above, it is possible to estimate the private sector's response as a residual from the aggregate response. That is, in the Shock I period, both private and government sector responded to the fall in income by dissaving. Consumption was maintained and foreign borrowing increased. In the Shock II period, the government responded to the oil price shock by reducing capital consumption and became a net saver, whereas the private sector continued to maintain consumption and acquire domestic assets. After the Shock II period, an accumulation of domestic assets took place in the private sector and the government continued to reduce capital consumption. Thus, it seems that the government actively responded to the shocks by adjusting its saving to enable the private sector to maintain its absorption (consumption plus accumulation of GFKF).

19.6. Conclusions

This paper has applied to the case of Thailand the methodology for the investigation of temporary trade shocks developed by Bevan *et al.* (1990 and Chapter 2 of this book). It first identified eight major external shocks affecting the country during the period from 1970 to 1991. Of these external shocks, the 'trade' shocks, namely the commodity boom and the oil price rises, were dominant in the 1970s, and the 'non-trade' shocks, such as a rise in services income and a surge in net direct investment, played an offsetting role in the 1980s.

The response of the Thai economy to these shocks was studied first by focusing on Thailand's aggregate savings and investment behaviour. We then considered the response of the government sector in terms of its fiscal reaction. Over the 1971–91 period, the loss in income as a result of the terms of trade deterioration in Thailand was estimated to be US$5,272 million at 1970 prices. The economy responded to this fall in income by building up net foreign debt of US$8,144 million at 1970 prices. At the same time it also accumulated domestic assets by gross fixed capital formation of US$1,052 million. The building-up of the stock of foreign debt was primarily to finance the acquisition of GFKF and to maintain consumption in the private sector.

Two features of Thailand's fiscal system have promoted a stabilising response to external shocks. First, the institutional mechanisms determining public investment expenditure in Thailand have a built-in anti-inflationary feature. When rapid inflation occurs in the prices of capital goods required for public sector capital formation, public sector purchases of these materials contract markedly in real terms. Construction materials are a prime example. The result is a significant negative correlation between private sector investment and public sector investment spending.

Second, legal limits on planned public expenditures, which date to laws introduced during the late 1950s and early 1960s, have contributed to fiscal discipline by limiting tightly the overall magnitude of planned fiscal deficits. In effect, these laws have constrained the capacity of fiscal policy to be *destabilising*, both in the short term and the long term.

NOTES

1. A detailed review of Thailand's macroeconomic performance over this period is available in Warr (1993) and in Warr and Nidhiprabha (1995).
2. This revised data series, released in 1987, differs so much from previously available data that it is difficult to compare Thai economic data immediately before and after 1970. Data for years before 1970 involve classifications and definitions substantially different from the revised, post-1970 data and if it is possible to avoid using the pre-1970 data it is desirable to do so. Hence our starting-point.
3. See the references in Warr and Nidhiprabha (1995).
4. An alternative procedure would have been to compute the propensity as the change in the *flow* of foreign assets (change in the stock) relative to GDP, rather than the level of the *stock* of foreign assets relative to GDP, as above.

REFERENCES

Bevan, D., P. Collier and J.W. Gunning (1990) *Controlled Open Economies*, Oxford: Clarendon Press.

Chaiyindeepum, S. (1993) 'External Shocks and Macroeconomic Adjustments in the Philippines and Thailand: A Comparative Study', unpublished Ph.D. dissertation, Australian National University.

IMF (1988) *World Economic Outlook*, Washington, DC: International Monetary Fund (October).

——(1989) *International Financial Statistics: Yearbook 1989*, Washington, DC: International Monetary Fund.

Nidhiprabha, B. (1993) 'Monetary Policy', in P.G. Warr (ed.) *The Thai Economy in Transition*, Cambridge: Cambridge University Press.

Warr, P.G. (1993) 'The Thai Economy' in P.G. Warr (ed.) *The Thai Economy in Transition*, Cambridge: Cambridge University Press.

Warr, P.G. and B. Nidhiprabha (1995) *Thailand's Macroeconomic Miracle: Stable Adjustment and Sustained Growth*, Washington, DC: World Bank.

20

Temporary Shocks, Consumption Smoothing and Economic Adjustment: Sri Lanka, 1973–76

SISIRA JAYASURIYA

20.1. Introduction

The large trade shocks experienced by both developed and developing countries during the 1970s and early 1980s associated with oil (and other commodity) price shocks and the discovery of new resource stocks led to the development of the now familiar Dutch Disease literature.[1] This provided a framework for the analysis of the general equilibrium effects of a shock by decomposing its effects into a relative price effect ('the resource-movement effect') and an income effect ('spending effect'). An increase in the price of an exportable, for example, alters its relative price and thereby its relative profitability; this 'booming sector' then attracts resources from other sectors and expands. Further, the resulting increase in national income leads to higher expenditures on both tradable and non-tradable goods. In a small open economy which faces exogenously given tradables prices, this higher demand for tradables is met by higher imports without any price change, but the higher demand for non-tradables—whose prices are determined by domestic supply and demand—leads to increases in their prices (and their relative profitability). This spending effect therefore tends to raise the relative price of non-tradables to tradables, that is, it appreciates the real exchange rate. Depending on the relative magnitudes of the resource-movement and spending effects, and the factor intensities, the non-tradables sector may expand or contract. However, the diminished relative profitability of the tradables sectors unaffected by the export price increase unambiguously leads to their contraction (the so-called 'de-industrialisation' effect of resource booms). This basic framework has been extended in various ways to cover many real world complexities.

Typically, most trade shocks are temporary. Hence even quite large shocks have only relatively minor permanent income effects. This insight has led to the development of a new strand of literature in the analysis of temporary trade shocks, which is becoming known as the 'theory of construction booms'.[2] If agents have access to well-functioning capital markets and correctly anticipate that the shocks are temporary, then the permanent income hypothesis would predict that such shocks lead primarily to changes in savings rather than in expenditures. In other words, the 'spending effect' of the Dutch Disease literature would be relatively minor. On the other hand there would be significant effects in asset markets: increased savings can be held in many forms, depending on the range and characteristics of available assets. Thus factors such as the nature of the domestic financial system and the capital market, the exchange rate regime, the nature of controls on foreign asset acquisition and the related degree of integration of the domestic and world capital markets become important. The aggregate outcomes are of course the result of the interaction of the responses of both private agents and the government; it is possible that the shocks and private agents' responses may even lead to changes in the policy regime.

In many developing countries private agents are constrained in their capacity to acquire foreign assets, and domestic financial markets are insulated, to varying degrees, from world markets. In such circumstances, higher savings resulting from a positive trade shock, perceived as being temporary, would be directed towards acquisition of domestic assets, including non-tradable capital goods such as buildings. Note the contrast with the Dutch Disease literature, where increased spending leads to higher prices of non-tradable consumer goods and services. Here, the higher demand for assets leads to increases in prices of non-tradable assets, such as buildings, and generates a 'construction boom'. To the extent that part of the savings is deposited in the domestic financial sector, there will be downward pressure on domestic interest rates; if there is financial repression, such deposits will facilitate the easing of liquidity constraints. In either case, investment is encouraged. Thus export price booms are likely to lead to higher investment levels, and not just to a change in its composition.

This chapter presents an analysis of the shocks experienced by Sri Lanka during 1973–75, and is a contribution to an ongoing research project analysing the experiences of a series of temporary shocks in twenty-five developing countries. The focus of the study is to test the validity of some of the key propositions of the theory of construction booms.

During the first half of 1970s Sri Lanka experienced a severe decline in the terms of trade, a number of domestic supply shocks, stringent trade and exchange restrictions, and an insurgency which dislocated economic activity. The second half of the decade saw a sharp upturn in the terms of trade, a change in government which implemented a major policy liberalisation, and a period of historically unprecedented growth. These contrasting domestic developments were closely linked; the political and policy changes during the latter half of the decade were rooted in the experiences of the earlier period.[3]

In this chapter the key propositions of the theory of construction booms[4] are tested through a detailed analysis of the adjustment experiences of the first half of the 1970s, with the emphasis on developments during 1973–76. To provide a broader and longer-term perspective on developments during this period we also examine the response of the economy to terms of trade fluctuations over the 1955–90 period. In purely economic terms, the 1973–76 period is still considered by Sri Lankans to be the most traumatic since the 1930s, and the impact of that experience continues to exert a potent political influence. None of the political parties which were associated with the government during that time was pushed into a prolonged period in the political wilderness by the electorate in 1977. A decisive shift away from control regimes towards liberal economic policies took place.[5]

20.2. Background

The nature of the economy and the behaviour of private economic agents and the government during the early 1970s can be understood only when seen in the concrete economic and political setting. When it gained independence from Britain in 1948, Sri Lanka inherited 'a classic dualistic export economy' (Snodgrass 1966) which was highly trade-dependent, exporting plantation crops (tea, rubber and coconut), and importing rice, wheat and sugar, as well as manufactured consumer goods.[6] It also inherited an extensive welfare system involving large public expenditures on food, health and education; this welfare system was further extended during the export price boom of the Korean War period. After the collapse of the boom the government attempted to prune back these expenditures, but was thwarted by political opposition, which took the country to the verge of revolution in 1953.

Sri Lanka's economic fortunes began a steady decline from the mid-1950s. A long secular fall in its terms of trade (Table 20.1) generated payments problems, to which governments responded by imposing ever more stringent import controls. This shift away from free trade was accompanied and reinforced by a shift in government political ideologies towards greater state intervention and import-substitution industrialisation policies, reinforced by export pessimism. Meanwhile welfare payments expanded as the population grew and took an ever increasing share of public expenditures. Finance Ministers and governments which attempted to cut welfare expenditures were forced out of power.

Government responses to terms of trade declines were conditioned by both economic and political circumstances. Given the downward rigidity of current expenditures imposed by the above political constraints, and

Table 20.1. Terms of trade, 1950–90 (*1980 = 100*)

	Terms of trade		Terms of trade
1950	327	1971	152
1951	293	1972	143
1952	223	1973	126
1953	280	1974	112
1954	329	1975	90
1955	308	1976	117
1956	267	1977	154
1957	294	1978	151
1958	286	1979	109
1959	286	1980	100
1960	268	1981	95
1961	268	1982	87
1962	239	1983	109
1963	200	1984	133
1964	220	1985	109
1965	220	1986	105
1966	207	1987	107
1967	193	1988	101
1968	183	1989	94
1969	172	1990	85
1970	161		

Source: Central Bank of Ceylon, *Review of the Economy*
(various issues)

because export taxes were the dominant source of government revenues, TOT declines resulting from falling export prices tended to produce public sector dissaving; on the other hand, entrenched anti-inflationary attitudes, availability of foreign assistance and the electoral political cycles were also major influences on expenditures.

During the latter half of the 1960s a centre-right government attempted to reduce welfare payments, and initiated a rather half-hearted policy liberalisation in 1968. Imports surged in 1969 in response to the relaxation of import controls by the previous government, precipitating a payments crisis; private agents justifiably interpreted that to be temporary, particularly in view of the likely defeat of the government in the impending election the next year. External conditions worsened in 1970 as the terms of trade decline continued. The government suffered a crushing electoral defeat and a centre-left government, which included two major leftist parties, came into power. The new government's decision to restore welfare expenditures in line with its election pledges worsened the payments situation. The debt service ratio passed the 20% mark, and sources of external financing almost completely disappeared. In late 1970 the government imposed stringent import and exchange controls.

The next two years witnessed major economic and political difficulties. In 1971 there was an armed uprising of radical rural youth, which sent shockwaves through the government and the wider Sri Lankan community. Real GDP growth was negative and per capita GDP fell by 3.1%. The emergence of a radical challenge moved the government to protect its political base among the poor and, in 1972, a land reform was proclaimed. Although this was confined initially to domestically owned land, the takeover of the foreign-owned plantations was foreshadowed.[7] The immediate impact was a decline in the standards of management and investment, and a decline in output (Fernando 1980). Rice production, and the agricultural sector in general, was affected by bad weather. The terms of trade decline continued, and indeed accelerated. This, combined with a marginal decline in export volumes, reduced the import purchasing power of exports in 1972 to 84% of the 1970 level and increased pressure on the balance of payments.

Sri Lanka's domestic capital market was almost completely insulated from the world capital market until very recently; not only private agents but, during this period, even the government had poor access to the world capital market. IMF drawings, which had been an important source of funds, were not available after 1968, since they had been fully utilised; World Bank funds were ruled out because they imposed politically unacceptable conditions. Short-term suppliers' credits and commercial bank credits, which had higher interest charges, had been increasingly used but were drying up as the debt situation deteriorated. Private agents were legally barred from acquiring foreign assets and the foreign exchange controls were fairly effective in controlling capital flight.[8] The stringent import controls had also eliminated all 'non-essential' imports; as a consequence, domestic industry was very vulnerable to any further cuts in imported capital goods and raw materials. Thus, when the oil price shock and associated commodity price shocks came in 1973, there was little room for economic or political flexibility.

20.3. The Shocks of 1973–76[9]

As indicated earlier, Sri Lanka had been experiencing a significant terms of trade deterioration since the mid-1950s. This had been interrupted by relatively short-lived and minor fluctuations during the 1960s, but the long-term trend was never in doubt. The falls were particularly sharp in the early 1960s and again in the early 1970s (Table 20.1).[10]

For many non-oil primary commodity exporting countries, the adverse TOT shocks associated with the first oil price increase were, at least initially, moderated (and at times even dominated) by the commodity price boom of 1973–74. Unfortunately for Sri Lanka, the overall effect of the commodity price boom was to exacerbate the impact of the oil price shock. Its export prices did improve; the world price of natural rubber began to rise in 1973, partly owing to rising costs of petroleum-based feed-stocks in the synthetic rubber industry, and tea prices benefited in 1974 from a global shortage of tea as a result of bad weather in the other main producing countries. Coconut products' prices were also more favourable. However, these could not offset the sharp increases in the prices of rice, wheat and sugar. By 1974 effective import prices of rice and sugar had risen by more than four times above 1972 prices, and wheat prices had almost tripled; overall the terms of trade slumped by 23% during this period. By 1975, the combined impact of these price changes was such that the terms of trade index was 39% below its 1972 level.[11] Recovery started in 1976, when the terms of trade started to improve, helped by a tea price increase; this went on to become a major price boom in 1977, and in its wake raised overall terms of trade by over 30% in 1977. (A summary of the main economic variables during the 1970s is presented in Table 20.2.)

This period was also characterised by a number of domestic supply shocks. Rice production fell in 1973, rose sharply in 1974 but fell drastically again the following year.[12] Aggregate export volumes were affected by a sharp decline in tea output in 1974 and fluctuations in rubber production, which was significantly higher in 1973 and 1975 but was sharply lower in 1974 (Table 20.2).[13] Coconut production was badly affected by a pest attack in 1972, with continuing consequences in both 1973 and 1974; in 1973, domestic shortages and higher prices resulted in a two-year ban on exports of coconut oil and copra. The overall result of the output changes and the terms of trade decline was that the import purchasing power of exports declined by nearly 35% between 1973 and 1975 (Table 20.2). Even when prices began to recover in 1976, tea output fell again, nullifying some of the beneficial effects.

20.4. Magnitude of the Shock

The first step in our analysis is the quantification of the loss in national income attributable to the terms of trade shock and the supply shocks. This depends crucially on the assumptions made about the counterfactual movements of the key price and output variables. One approach is to take the long-term trend of the relevant variables as the counterfactual on the basis that agents would have expected the trend to continue. But this would be an oversimplification owing to the many factors which can affect expectation formations, particularly in a volatile domestic and international environment. On the other hand, given that there was a sharp fall in the terms of trade during the late 1960s, a recovery or at least some stability could have been expected.

Table 20.2. Movement of major economic variables, 1960–78

	Annual average 1960–69	Annual average 1970–72	1973	1974	1975	1976	1977	1978
Economic growth (annual %)								
Real GDP	3.9	1.7	4.1	3.3	2.3	2.9	4.6	8.2
Per capita GDP	1.4	−0.4	2.1	1.4	0.4	1.3	3.0	6.4
Employment growth (annual %)	2.6	3.5	−1.7	5.5	2.7	9.4	1.5	3.5
Consumption, savings and investment								
Real per capita consumption (1970 = 100)	90	97	89	93	94	84	96	103
Real investment (1970 = 100)	80	89	77	64	70	77	64	116
Private (1970 = 100)	75	94	88	69	73	56	60	82
Savings/GDP ratio (%)	12.2	15.4	12.5	8.3	8.1	13.9	18.1	15.2
Private savings (%)	12.1	16.8	11.8	7.2	8.6	14.2	17.8	16.5
Investment/GDP ratio (%)	15.4	15.6	13.5	12.5	13.9	15.4	13.8	19.9
Private investment (%)	8.5	8.9	7.7	8.2	7.9	8.7	7.2	8.9
Incremental capital/output ratio (%)	3.5	4.4	4.9	3.4	3.3	3.5	4.2	2.0
Prices and wages								
General price level (% change)								
CPI	2.6	6.7	20.5	25.3	3.7	5.6	9.2	9.7
GDP deflator	3.5	3.5	15.6	22.9	8.1	6.3	20.2	7.6
Real Wage index (1978 = 100)								
Private sector	93	84.1	68.4	64.1	71.0	69	77	100
Public sector	157	62.2	65.5	73.7	81.5	105	97	100
Exchange rates								
Nominal exchange rate (Rupees/US$)								
Official rate	5.2	6.3	6.5	6.6	7.2	8.4	8.9	15.6
Official rate with FEEC premium	5.9	9.4	10.6	10.9	11.6	14.5	14.81	—
Curb-market rate	12.6	16.0	11.25	12.1	14.8	13.8	17.8	21.3
Trade and balance of payments (SDR millions)								
Trade balance	−47	−46	−39	−158	−168	−73	29	−144
Current account balance	−48	−41	−21	−113	−91	5	117	−75
Basic balance	−30	4.7	36	−44	−43	−56	149	−57
Foreign reserves in import-month equivalent	2.2	2.7	3.6	2.2	1.9	3.1	10.6	5.9
Debt-service ratio (%)	7.5	21.8	22.9	17.8	22.8	20.6	15.9	5.5
Trade indices (1978 = 100)								
Export volume	81	104	103	89	107	102	94	100
Import volume	112	71	60	42	53	52	73	100
Terms of trade	144	100	82	72	58	80	96	100
Import purchasing power of export earnings	170	103	84	64	62	78	102	100

Source: Based on Athukorala and Jayasuriya (1994)

Random changes in climatic factors, which are intrinsically difficult to predict, and, in the case of coconut, a completely unanticipated pest attack affected output. Perhaps output declines owing to managerial inefficiency ought to have been reasonably anticipated; but at the time in Sri Lanka there were euphoric expectations that land reform, if anything, was going to increase, rather than decrease, output; once the tillers got the land, the incentives to increase output would be larger.[14]

In the following computations, the counterfactual—except where explicitly stated otherwise—has been assumed to be the average value of the variable during 1970–72, rather than the long-term trend. On this basis the difference between actual and counterfactual values of export revenues (in dollars) was calculated using the terms of trade index (1970 = 100), and this was attributed to the impact of the shock. This procedure was applied separately to aggregate exports and to domestic rice production (which was valued at the c.i.f. price of imported rice). These 'losses' owing to the shocks were then added together and deflated by the import price index to provide an estimate of their real value at 1970 prices. These were converted to Rupees using the base exchange rate.[15]

The estimates of losses owing to the terms of trade ('export loss') and those owing to rice output fluctuations ('rice loss'), and the total losses are presented in Table 20.3. Although the total loss, converted at both the standard (or base) official rate and the higher ('FEEC') rate, is shown in this table, only the estimate using the base rate was used in subsequent analyses.[16] Note that the bumper harvest of rice in 1974 tended to mitigate the impact of the overall negative effects flowing from the declines in the terms of trade and aggregate export volume, but in the following year its output fall significantly exacerbated the losses.

The present value of the cumulative annual losses owing to the shocks during 1973–76 (at 1970 prices) was 1,982 million Rupees, which was

Table 20.3. Total losses owing to terms of trade and supply shocks

	Export loss (US$ m.)	Rice loss (US$ m.)	Total loss (US$ m.)	Total loss 1 (Rp m.)	Total loss 2 (Rp m.)	Total loss 1 at 1970 prices (Rp m.)	Total loss 2 at 1970 prices (Rp m.)
1967	−73.8						
1968	−60.3						
1969	−27.4						
1970	−30.4	13.4	−16.9	−100.8	−156.4	−100.8	−156.4
1971	4.4	−2.9	1.6	9.3	14.5	8.7	13.5
1972	25.5	−7.7	17.7	205.9	176.7	93.8	156.5
1973	80.0	−12.8	67.1	429.6	708.8	287.8	474.8
1974	305.3	40.0	345.3	2,296.4	3,788.2	868.9	1,433.4
1975	373.9	−60.4	313.5	2,197.8	3,630.7	710.6	1,173.9
1976	164.0	−26.7	137.3	1,154.8	2,000.7	422.1	731.3

Notes: Total loss 1 is valued at the official (base) exchange rate; Total Loss 2 is valued at the higher FEEC rate. All subsequent computations are based on Total Loss 1

equal to 11% of GDP at a discount rate of 10%.[17] This would have reduced permanent income by only a little over 1% per year of 1973 GDP. In a world of perfect capital markets and rational agents whose expenditure decisions are based on permanent income, if this shock was perceived to be a temporary one, it should have had only a very minor impact on expenditure levels. Dissaving/borrowing would have smoothed consumption.

20.5. Expectations

As noted, the 1973–76 period was characterised by considerable output fluctuations. Sri Lankan farmers have had long experience with these crops and their output fluctuations. Some events, such as the pest attack on coconuts, were genuinely unexpected but, given their nature, expected to be temporary. Purely climate-related output shocks are unexpected only in terms of their precise timing and intensity, and again are expected to be temporary. The managerial dislocation caused by land reform too was expected to be a temporary state of affairs. Generally it seems reasonable to assume that both government and private agents would have anticipated that the output-related fluctuations would be temporary; in other words, using the terms coined by Bevan *et al.* (1991a), expectations were 'inclusive' with regard to output shocks.

The situation was more complex in relation to the terms of trade. Their long secular decline had been driven mostly by price falls of tea, rubber and coconut products, rather than by any dramatic increases in import prices, at least until the late 1960s (see Table 20.1). There was a general pessimism current about the future price prospects for these 'traditional' exports (see, for example, the Five-Year Plan issued by the Ministry of Planning and Employment in 1972). But there were no compelling reasons to expect that import prices would rise sharply. All the evidence suggests that the dramatic increases of food import prices, as well as the oil price shock, caught both government and private agents by surprise. The mainly anecdotal evidence which is available suggests that the general community expectation was that the terms of trade would continue to languish at the historically low levels reached by 1971–72, rather than decline further; certainly, there is no evidence to suggest that a sharp decline was expected. However, once the price shocks actually occurred, expectations may have been revised. As elsewhere in the world, there was a widespread view that oil prices would not fall again.[18] There was also considerable concern in Asia that food prices might be headed up, though it was recognised that the price peaks of the 1973–75 period were the product of special and transient circumstances, and unlikely to be sustained.

Within the government, the left leaders in particular were seriously concerned that a major world depression was on the cards, with all the attendant consequences for the terms of trade of a primary commodity exporter like Sri Lanka. At this time these leaders wielded a large political influence within the government.[19] Certainly public pronouncements by the government at the time stressed that the international economic situation was likely to worsen, and that the country faced a very difficult external situation. But such statements, of course, cannot be taken at face value. The emphasis on continuing adversity was a useful political tool to soften up the electorate for unpopular measures, such as reductions in the food subsidy. However, it is likely that the government was convinced that at least part of the terms of trade decline might be of a longer-term nature, and in the terms of Bevan *et al.*, represented a case of 'exclusive, partial revision' of expectations.

To the extent that at least a part of a shock is considered permanent, it will result in a larger change in current expenditures and savings compared to the situation in which the entire shock is expected to be transient. The evidence on aggregate savings behaviour is examined to see the extent to which it actually changed.

20.6. Changes in Aggregate Savings and Assets

At the aggregate level, savings can lead to acquisition of domestic assets in the form of gross fixed capital formation (GFKF), inventory accumulation and foreign assets. Inventory accumulation is of relatively minor significance in Sri Lanka, and there are serious data problems.[20] Therefore we focus on the other two components in this analysis.

To compare actual and counterfactual scenarios, it is necessary to estimate a shock-adjusted actual real income series and values of GFKF, as well as counterfactual incomes and values of GFKF and changes in foreign assets. The actual shock-adjusted real income series is developed by subtracting the estimated losses owing to the shocks from a pre-shock constant price (1970) GDP series.[21] By multiplying this by the actual proportion of GFKF in GDP we obtain the real value of GFKF at 1970 prices (i.e. before any relative price changes had occurred). The counterfactual real income series is constructed by assuming that the income losses owing to the shock are reflected in lower domestic investments with a one-year lag. Thus in 1973 counterfactual income was assumed to be the same as actual income at 1970 prices, while in each subsequent year the 'forgone' returns from the previous years' investments were added to the 1970 constant price GDP series. The counterfactual propensity to acquire domestic assets in the form of GFKF out of income was set at 14% of GDP.[22] By assuming that a rate of return of 10% would obtain from the investments, the income lost owing to forgone investment was computed (Table 20.4).[23] In all years, except 1976, actual GFKF was below counter-factual GFKF.[24] In 1976 there was a noticeable change in the business environment owing to the departure from the government of the major left-wing party and its leaders (including the Minister for Finance) and a general climate of optimism as terms of trade started to improve. This was reflected in the significantly higher rate of actual investment. The present value of forgone acquisitions of DFKF in 1973 (at 1970 prices) was 687 million Rupees.

A similar analysis for the propensity to accumulate foreign assets was conducted, again using the estimated real income series, and the results are presented in Table 20.5. Note that the table presents data on use of foreign assets rather than acquisition of such assets. The results show that

Table 20.4. Counterfactual growth and capital formation (*Rp m.*)

	Actual			Counterfactual			Negative impact		
	GFKF/Y (%)	Real income (1970 prices)	Value of GFKF	Real income (1970 prices)	GFKF/Y (%)	Value of GFKF	Annual	Cumulative	Return at 10%
	(1)	(2)	(3)	(4)	(5)	(6)	(7)	(8)	(9)
1973	13.5	13,790	1,862	14,078	14.5	2,041	179	179	17.9
1974	12.5	13,667	1,708	14,565	14.5	2,112	403	582	58.2
1975	13.9	14,162	1,969	14,960	14.5	2,169	201	783	78.3
1976	15.2	14,890	2,263	15,383	14.5	2,231	−32	751	75.1

Notes: The counterfactual GFKF ratio was set at 14.5%, rather than at the mean value of the 1970–72 period, in view of the steady downward trend since 1970 attributable to political factors. Computations follow the procedures in Table 2 of Bevan *et al.* (1991)

Table 20.5. Use of foreign savings

	Value of foreign savings (1970. Rp m.)	Foreign savings propensity	Counterfactual foreign savings propensity	Counterfactual value of foreign savings (1970 Rp m.)	Increase in use of foreign savings owing to shocks (Rp m.)
1973	−107.8	−0.8	−1.5	−206.9	−99.0
1974	−343.2	−2.4	−1.5	−205.0	138.2
1975	−249.6	−1.7	−1.5	−212.4	37.2
1976	−18.3	−0.1	−1.5	−223.3	205.1

Notes: The counterfactual savings propensity was set below the mean value of 1970–72 (−1.8%) because (a) 1970 was a year of payments crisis with a high current account deficit and (b) the deficits had been trending downwards, partly as a result of foreign credit constraints. The counterfactual value of foreign savings was obtained by multiplying this factor (1.5%) by the estimated real income (adjusted for the impact of the shocks)

there was an increase in the use of foreign savings by domestic residents; in other words, the country acquired foreign liabilities as it dissaved in response to the impact of the shocks to the value of 221 million Rupees in 1973 at 1970 prices.

The total dissaving attributable to the impact of the shocks is the sum of these two minus the dissaving which would have occurred as a result of the cut in permanent income owing to reduced investment. This amounts to 865 million Rupees in 1973 at 1970 prices. According to our calculations in Table 20.3, the present value in 1973 of the total income loss owing to the shocks is 1,982 million Rupees. Thus dissavings amounted to 44% of the loss in income owing to the shock. This accords with the hypothesis that agents responded to the negative shocks at least partly by dissaving and attempting to smooth consumption. This is consistent with the expected response of 'rational' agents to income losses which are, at least partly, considered to be temporary.[25] Later we will show that, as this aggregate picture is examined more closely, important differences appear between the behaviour of private agents and the government.

20.7. Impact on Goods Markets

The moderation of the reduction of current expenditures in response to the negative shock by dissaving would imply a smaller change in goods markets compared to the case where the entire shock was considered permanent. The reduction in demand for both non-tradable capital goods and non-tradable consumer goods would be expected to lead to a lowering of their prices relative to those of tradables.

Annual price movements in manufacturing, construction and non-tradable consumption goods are presented in Table 20.6. Price movements

Table 20.6. Annual price movements (*percentage per year*)

	Non-tradable consumption goods	Manufacturing	Construction	Banking, insurance and real estate	GDP
1971	4.1	13.6	6.1	0.0	3.5
1972	6.2	−2.3	3.0	9.1	7.2
1973	0.4	20.0	10.4	10.8	15.6
1974	4.9	35.3	17.7	17.3	23.0
1975	7.6	25.3	10.5	−14.1	8.0
1976	6.2	−3.9	8.3	39.9	6.3

Sources: Deflators computed from data in Savundranayagam (1983); Central Bank of Ceylon, *Review of the Economy* (various issues)

for tradables are proxied by the implicit deflator for manufacturing, that for non-tradable capital goods by the implicit deflator for the construction sector and, that for non-tradable consumer goods by the index of the miscellaneous group in the consumer price index.[26] Final output price data for manufacturing and non-tradable capital goods were not available. It is clear that the relative prices of non-tradable capital goods and non-tradable consumer goods declined during this period, with non-tradable consumer goods prices declining faster. This would suggest that both Dutch Disease and construction boom effects were operating, a finding consistent with the view that the shocks were perceived as having both temporary and transient components, with the former being marginally stronger.

20.8. Impact on Factor Markets

Unfortunately the data base for examining the sectoral changes in investment and employment is quite weak. Reliable annual estimates of the sectoral composition of employment do not exist,[27] and the composition of investment is classified into categories which do not readily lend themselves to the type of sectoral breakdown which is desirable for our analysis. However, the data given in Table 20.7 can give some feel for the nature of the sectoral changes in investment during the study period, particularly in relation to the construction sector.

It is clear that investment in the construction sector fell significantly during this period; in fact it fell both relatively and absolutely. To the extent that the construction sector represents the non-tradable capital goods sector, this is consistent with the construction boom hypothesis.[28] It is not possible to disaggregate further to examine changes in investment in other sectors.

The real wage data available for this period need to be treated with a

Table 20.7. Composition of gross domestic capital formation at constant 1963 prices (*percentage*)

	1973	1974	1975	1976
(1) *Private sector and public corporations*				
Planting and replanting	7	7	7	6
Building and construction	48	44	36	33
Machinery	19	17	23	23
Transport equipment	7	12	10	11
(2) *Public sector*	17	20	23	27

Source: *Statistical Abstract of Sri Lanka 1977*

great deal of caution. Unfortunately, there are no data at all available for this period on the wage rates of workers in the non-tradables sectors, the bulk of whom would have been in the unorganised sector and hence not covered by government wage awards. Given that real wages appear to have declined even in the organised sectors (see Table 20.2), it is probable that wages in the non-tradables sectors would have fallen at least to the same extent, if not more.[29] Again, this is consistent with both Dutch Disease and construction boom theories, since both non-tradable capital goods and non-tradable consumer goods were probably relatively labour intensive.

20.9. Incidence and Transmission of Shocks

The aggregate response to the shocks does not distinguish between the public and private sectors. It is important, however, that the responses of the private agents and the government be examined separately so as to draw useful policy lessons from the experience of the shocks. We begin by examining the initial incidence of the shocks and the patterns of transmission of them between the private and public sectors.

The initial impact of the domestic supply shocks would have been directly felt by both the private agents and the government. In the case of the plantation crops, tea, rubber and coconut, the impact on the government would have taken place through the export tax regime: reduced volumes of exports directly reduced government trade taxes.[30] There was a secondary effect through direct taxes, and through import duties, to the extent that income changes of private agents would have been translated into changes in the volume of imports. In the case of rice, the transmission mechanism was different. The government purchased rice from farmers at a guaranteed price, and used this to provide a subsidised ration to consumers, any shortfall being met by imports. Changes in domestic output normally led to changes in the quantity which farmers sold to the government, and affected its import bill; if the domestic open market rice price increased significantly, the government was forced to offer a higher purchase price or import more.

In the case of external price shocks, too, there was an analogous situation. The export taxes were levied on a sliding scale, so that the impact of price increases had a muted impact on producer revenues whereas government revenues increased more than proportionately. By 1973, practically all imports were subject to some form of quantitative restriction. The government directly imported a range of consumer essentials, including rice, sugar and wheat flour; it also had a monopoly on petroleum imports. These were distributed to consumers at regulated prices. Import price increases thus directly increased the government's import bill. In such cases private agents were affected only to the extent that the government passed on international price increases to the consumers. Since many of the imports were 'essentials', full transmission of external price increases to domestic prices was a politically sensitive and difficult affair.[31] Thus the foreign trade regime largely insulated domestic prices from international price movements, though the government was periodically compelled during the study period to attempt to reduce its import expenditure bill by reducing the gap between domestic and international prices. Higher world prices were reflected in increases in the administered domestic prices and shortages.

20.10. The Policy Response

The fiscal response to the shocks went through two stages, with the two phases being associated with a split within the government and the replacement of the Minister of Finance in 1975. In our analysis of the fiscal policies adopted, we begin by comparing the actual response with a counterfactual scenario based on the assumption that the pre-shock fiscal stance had remained unaltered.

The basic structure of the actual fiscal pattern, showing government revenue, current and capital expenditures and the primary deficit as a percentage of GDP during 1970 to 1976, is presented in Table 20.8. It is clear that government revenues declined during the period of the shock; in fact they declined both as a share of GDP and in real terms. This decline was primarily due to the reduced volume of trade, which reduced trade tax revenues. Current expenditures, too, fell—the fall being particularly sharp in 1974, when capital expenditures also fell. In both 1973 and 1974,

Table 20.8. Actual fiscal pattern 1970–76 (*as a percentage of GDP*)

	Government revenue	Current expenditure	Capital expenditure	Total expenditure	Primary deficit
1970	21.1	19.9	6.1	26.0	4.9
1971	23.9	21.7	5.9	27.6	3.7
1972[a]	21.8	22.6	5.8	28.4	6.6
1973	22.4	21.4	6.2	27.5	5.2
1974	20.9	19.7	5.6	25.2	4.3
1975	20.1	20.4	7.7	28.1	8.0
1976	20.7	20.0	10.1	30.1	9.4

[a] The figures for 1972 were originally for fifteen months owing to a change in fiscal year from that year; this has been adjusted for a twelve-month period

Source: Central Bank of Ceylon, *Review of the Economy* (various issues)

Table 20.9. Fiscal responses to the shock (*Rp m.*)

	Reductions in				Difference between reductions in revenue and expenditure
	Revenue	Current expenditure	Capital expenditure	Total expenditure	
1973	−14.0	−5.4	−31.8	−377.2	23.2
1974	319.6	356.2	83.0	439.2	−119.6
1975	417.7	244.5	−228.6	15.9	401.8
1976	269.8	230.2	−604.8	−374.6	644.4

current revenues exceeded current expenditures; thus public savings were positive in the first two years of this period. In 1975 the reins on expenditure appear to have loosened. Current expenditure, and in particular capital expenditure, increased. The following year saw a surge in capital expenditure.

To what extent were these fiscal outcomes the result of the shock-induced income changes, rather than of a deliberate shift in the policy stance? This is examined by means of the counterfactual scenario, which assumed that the GDP shares of the various budget components were held at the 1970–72 mean values, applying these to the estimated counterfactual real income (Table 20.9). In 1973 there appears to have been no shift in fiscal policy, but a tightening is seen in 1974; expenditure cuts were larger than needed just to compensate for the revenue losses. This is reversed in 1975, and even more sharply in 1976. These results suggest that a policy shift occurred in 1975; the change in savings behaviour observed earlier was not merely due to exogenous changes in national income. Of course, 1975 was the year in which the political split occurred within the government, leading to the change in the Minister of Finance.

At this point it is instructive to look at the differences between private and public savings behaviour. As seen in Table 20.10, there was a steep decline in private savings from 1973 to 1975, and it started to recover again in 1976. Government savings moved in the opposite direction in 1973 and 1974. Even in 1975 and 1976, government dissaving was below average; as seen in Table 20.8, higher government expenditures were a result of increased capital expenditures. Overall, the Sri Lankan response to the 1973–76 negative shocks was to increase saving (or reduce dissaving).

What motivated this response? As mentioned earlier, there was a significant and influential group within the government (including the Minister of Finance) which felt that the terms of trade shock was at least in part a permanent shock; indeed it was even seen as foreshadowing worse to come. If the government was convinced that such a pessimistic outlook

Table 20.10. Private, public and gross domestic savings (*as a percentage of GDP at current prices*)

	Private savings	Government savings	Gross domestic savings
1970	16.5	−0.9	15.6
1971	17.0	−1.9	15.1
1972	17.0	−1.3	15.7
1973	11.9	0.6	12.5
1974	7.2	1.0	8.2
1975	8.6	−0.5	8.1
1976	14.3	−0.4	13.9

Source: Central Bank of Ceylon, *Annual Report* and *Review of the Economy* (various issues)

was justified, then it made sense to attempt to counteract the 'short-sighted' private sector response of dissaving.

On the other hand, there were severe constraints on the adoption of a 'financing' (dissaving) strategy even if the shocks were felt to be temporary. Not only was Sri Lanka's external asset position weak, it was almost impossible to obtain large-scale external financing to sustain a financing strategy. The constraints in this case were primarily political: neither the Western governments nor donor agencies were prepared to provide such assistance without major changes in domestic policies, and perhaps in foreign policies as well. These conditions could not be accommodated by the coalition government of the day; the leading leftist party was already under pressure from its radical critics for selling out socialism. In this situation, irrespective of the perceptions regarding the duration of the shock, liquidity constraints would have imposed an 'adjustment' rather than a 'financing' strategy.[32] Such a strategy, involving the implementation of the tight budgetary policy, required reductions in subsidies and other transfers. Significant cuts were made to food subsidies in particular, despite their political unpopularity.

The government's monetary policy stance reinforced the fiscal stance. For the first time since the early 1950s, inflationary pressures, partly imported, built up in the economy. The government considered inflation to be a major danger to economic stability and adopted tight monetary policies as well.[33] The reduction of the budget deficit was accompanied by steps to obtain non-inflationary domestic financing to meet the remaining deficit; money financing of budget deficits was typically a key source of inflationary pressures. A major source of non-inflationary financing to meet budget deficits was the Employees' Provident Fund—a repository of enforced savings—which was a captive source, being directly under government control. Use of these funds, which were paid negative real

Table 20.11. Basic indicators of import compression before and during the
1973–75 crisis episode (*1978 = 100*)

	1960–69	1970–72	1973	1974	1975
Import volume indices					
Total	82	71	60	42	52
Consumer goods	130	122	114	77	83
Food	126	133	125	75	87
Intermediate goods	134	116	64	62	76
Investment goods	63	48	39	23	45
Import composition (%)	100	100	100	100	100
Consumer goods	56	55	53	47	51
Food	43	46	46	43	48
Intermediate goods	24	24	30	42	36
Oil	7	2	11	20	17
Investment goods	20	21	17	11	13
Import/GDP ratio (%)[a]	25.2	15.2	13.2	12.4	13.3

[a] Estimated using constant (1970) price data

Source: Athukorala and Jayasuriya (1994)

interest rates during this entire period, provided a mechanism for a resource transfer from private agents to the public sector. On the other
hand, increases in nominal interest rates were insufficient to counteract
the impact of inflation on real interest rates; real interest rates turned
negative and reinforced private sector dissaving, though liquidity constraints probably made this of minor significance.

Given the dissavings of the private sector, it was inevitable that pressure would mount on the balance of payments. The response was a
further tightening of import controls, primarily by means of even more
stringent quantitative restrictions. The impact of this policy can be seen in
Table 20.11. The consequences for economic activity, particularly in the
industrial sector, were severe. One unintended consequence was that the
government was forced to make large budgetary transfers to loss-making
public enterprises, which in turn constrained the reduction of fiscal
deficits.

20.11. The Political Response and the Aftermath

The political stresses generated within the government by widespread
shortages and general dissatisfaction with the tight fiscal and monetary
policy stance came to a head in 1975. Partly as a result of halving fertiliser
imports, domestic rice production slumped, rice prices increased and
government procurement levels slumped. The government banned free

movement of rice within the country in response. This became the occasion for the internal conflicts to develop into an open split in the government, and the leading leftist party and its leaders, including the Minister of Finance, were forced to leave the government. The government changed its policy stance, relationships with Western governments and donor agencies warmed somewhat, and external assistance picked up. In 1976, these developments, together with improving terms of trade saw the economy moving out into recovery mode.

In late 1976 tea prices started to climb rapidly, and with the gradual decline of import prices, terms of trade improved dramatically in 1977 (Table 20.1). The current account deficit was practically eliminated in 1976, and it registered a healthy surplus in 1977. The government eased its deflationary policy stance in 1976, but the economy was slow to respond, since import controls inhibited a rapid recovery of imports and economic activity. General elections were held in 1977 and the electorate delivered a stunning blow to the government and the leftist parties which had been associated with it. The opposition United National Party was returned to power in a landslide on a economic liberalisation programme which openly proclaimed a fundamental break with past economic policies. The policies of shock management pursued by the previous regime had paved the way for a fundamental change in economic policies. It had also delivered to the new government an economy which, by design or by force of circumstances, was ready for a major liberalisation episode, with healthy external reserves and without a debt overhang.

20.12. Savings and Trade Shocks during 1955–90

How well do the experiences of the 1973–76 period fit in with the longer-term patterns of adjustments to temporary trade shocks?[34] This issue was examined by using time-series data for the 1951–90 period to analyse savings responses to TOT fluctuations, testing the hypothesis that private savings would be significantly affected by temporary TOT fluctuations and would exhibit consumption-smoothing behaviour.[35]

In the literature, it is hypothesised that real savings may be related to real GDP, TOT and the real interest rate. (Real GDP—which excludes price effects—together with the terms of trade provides an estimate of real income.) Other variables, such as foreign capital inflows, the population growth rate (which changes the age structure of the population) and changes in the policy environment (such as those resulting from the 1978 policy reforms) could also impact on private savings directly as well as by altering the degree of interest rate sensitivity. Given our interest in the long run as well as the dynamics of short-run adjustment, we drew on recent econometric approaches to the estimation of dynamic models.

Table 20.12. Integration tests for data series

Variable	Test for I(0)	
	ADF test $H_0:I(1)$ *versus* $H_1:I(0)$	KPSS $H_0:I(0)$ *versus* $H_1:I(1)$
Real private savings (in logs)	−5.31 (1)	0.06
Real GDP (in logs)	−3.41* (2)	0.42*
Terms of trade (in logs)	−3.90 (1)	0.23*
Real interest rate	−3.51* (2)	0.13*
Real capital inflow	−0.19* (1)	0.39*

  * Acceptance (or non-rejection) as I(1)

Notes: The test statistic reported in the ADF test is the t-ratio on a_1 in the following auxiliary regression:

$$\Delta y_t = a_0 + a_1 y_{t-1} + \sum_{j=1}^{P_t} a_2 \Delta y_{t-j} + a_3 T + \varepsilon_t$$

where y is the variable under consideration, T is a time trend, and ε_t, is the statistic error term. The lag length (p) was chosen to ensure residual whiteness of the estimated equation. T was included since, for most economic time-series, the main alternative to the presence of a unit root is a deterministic linear trend. The critical value at 5% for the ADF tests was approximately 3.53 in all cases, that for KPSS tests was 0.116. The real interest rate was computed as the average interest rate on one-year bank deposits minus the inflation rate of the previous year

These typically involve testing for the order of integration of time-series, and the order of integration of each variable was tested by the Dickey–Fuller and KPSS tests.[36]

The results indicated that the key variables of interest did not have the same order of integration; in particular, the real private savings series was stationary in level form, I(0), whereas real GDP was not (Table 20.12). We therefore opted to use an error-correction model using the 'general-to-specific' methodology to minimise the possibility of estimating spurious relationships while retaining long-run information.[37] Many of the postulated explanatory variables, such as the real interest rate, dummy variables for different policy regimes, and capital inflows had statistically insignificant coefficients consistently in experimental runs and were dropped in the final equation. The constant term too was omitted because it was correlated with some of the lagged variables. The final parsimonious estimated equation, which passes all the standard tests, is presented in Table 20.13.[38]

From the point of view of terms of trade dynamics, the positive sign of the DTOT variable confirms the hypothesis that short-run TOT changes have a very significant positive impact on private savings, and it supports the proposition of consumption-smoothing behaviour by private agents in response to temporary terms of trade shocks. Given the undeveloped

Table 20.13. Estimated private savings model, 1952–90[a]

$$DPS_t = 0.52DTOT_t - 0.32TOT_{t-1} - 0.54D74 + 0.16GDP_{t-1} - 0.36PS_{t-1}$$
$$(2.51)^{**} \quad (-3.69)^{***} \quad (-3.19)^{***} \quad (3.92)^{***} \quad (-3.65)^{***}$$

$\bar{R}^2 = 0.50$, SEE $= 0.16$, D.W. $= 1.75$, LM[b]$(1,34) = 0.40$

RESET[c]$(1,34) = 0.62$, NORM[d]$(2) = 0.67$, HT[e]$(1,42) = 0.75$

where PS = real private savings, $DPS_t = PS_t - PS_{t-1}$, TOT = terms of trade (1980 = 100), $DTOT_t = TOT_t - TOT_{t-1}$, GDP = real gross domestic product at 1980 prices. (All level variables are in logarithmic form.)

[a] Figures in parenthesis are *t*-ratios; **denotes significant at 5%; ***denotes significant at 1%
[b] LM = Lagrange multiplier test of residual serial correlation, F-version
[c] Ramsey's RESET test for functional form misspecification, F-version
[d] NORM = Jarque–Bera test for the normality of residuals
[e] HT = Engle's autoregressive conditional heteroscedasticity test of residuals, F-version

capital market, full-scale consumption smoothing behaviour cannot, of course, be expected. The relationship between long-run (permanent) changes in terms of trade and private savings is ambiguous in theory.[39] The long-run response elasticity of private savings to terms of trade changes[40] (-0.9) indicates a strong negative relationship in Sri Lanka, suggesting that private agents increase savings when faced with lower future real incomes as a result of a long-run terms of trade deterioration.

Not surprisingly, no sensible equations for public saving could be estimated. As indicated in the background discussion, public savings were affected by complex political factors as well as by exogenous factors such as availability of external aid, and any systematic relationship to terms of trade changes could not be discovered.

20.13. Conclusions

In this study we examined the experience of Sri Lanka during the 1973–76 period, when it was subjected to a combination of domestic supply shocks and terms of trade shocks, to verify whether the predictions of the construction boom theory find support. Our research suggested that the perceptions of the shocks at the time were such that it was considered partly temporary and partly permanent. In particular, influential policymakers considered that there was a significant permanent component. In this context, and given the relatively underdeveloped capital market, we expected to observe both Dutch Disease and construction boom effects.

Results of our analysis, subject to the various data constraints, confirm these prior expectations. Private agents responded to the negative shocks with significant dissaving and attempted to smooth consumption, in line with anticipated behaviour of rational agents to a temporary shock. Nevertheless such dissaving did not fully counteract the income and expenditure cuts flowing from the shocks, and hence (negative) Dutch Disease effects did appear, but in a more moderate form.[41] On the other hand, despite much political unpopularity, the government attempted to increase savings to counteract the expenditure effects of private agents dissaving. These attempts relied on ever greater controls on trade and markets.

It is not clear to what extent this policy was dictated by the perception that the shocks had an important permanent component, and to what extent it was a result of the political constraints on access to external funds. However, it did have the effect that a major inflationary or balance of payments crisis was avoided, and there was no build-up of a large external debt. But the economic hardships which were imposed on the community by this course of action paved the way for a fundamental change in the Sri Lankan political and economic policy environment.

The econometric analysis of dynamic savings behaviour since the early 1950s confirmed the view that private agents act to smooth consumption in response to temporary terms of trade changes, whereas they increase savings in response to permanent terms of trade changes. This demonstrates that the observed pattern of private agents' responses to the shocks of 1973–76 was not an aberration and provides firm support for the main foundation of the theory of construction booms: temporary shocks which have little impact on permanent income will only have minor expenditure effects.

NOTES

1. See Corden and Neary (1982) and Corden (1984) for an exposition of the key elements of this literature.
2. See Bevan *et al.* (1987, 1991a and b), Collier (1993) and van Wincoop (1993).
3. See Athukorala and Jayasuriya (1994).
4. For a survey of the theoretical and empirical literature see Collier (1993) and references therein.
5. A further consideration was that relatively fewer negative shocks appear to have been analysed to verify the 'construction boom' theory. Initially it was hoped that a more recent negative shock, that associated with the Gulf War crisis, could also be analysed, but this was not done for two main reasons. First, it had a relatively minor impact on Sri Lanka's economy. Second, the period covered was exceptional in many ways in that the economy was beginning a strong recovery after restoration of political stability in much of the country after massive dislocation in the previous three years.

6. In 1950 the ratio of imports and exports to GDP was over 70%.

7. Foreign-owned plantations were taken over by the government in 1975 and compensation was paid to the plantation owners.

8. There is evidence that exchange controls were flouted by individuals as well as firms but the extent of such activity appears not to have been very extensive.

9. The period 1973–76 was chosen for detailed analysis, though 1972 was also a year of significant shocks; 1972 was dominated by the recovery from the political crisis of the previous year. The terms of trade decline in 1972 was mainly due to rising food prices in world markets; this was understood to be due to weather-related harvest shortfalls in producer countries and was expected to be short-lived. Despite some reductions in the food subsidies, private agents were largely insulated from their impact; the government controlled imports and domestic retail prices of major food items, including rice and sugar, and passthrough of external price changes was relatively muted.

10. These are based on unit values and suffer from the well-known problems of trade indices based on unit values. In particular, note that the composition of exports and imports since the 1970s has changed greatly, with a decline in the importance of traditional tree crops in total exports, and of food in imports. For a discussion of these problems, see Athukorala and Jayasuriya (1994).

11. These figures are based on the terms of trade index with 1967 as the base year.

12. Rice output fell 9% below what would have been predicted on the basis of the growth trend estimated over the past five years in 1973; it was above that by 13% in 1974 and below that by 19% in 1975. (The deviations were measured using the same predicted value since no positive trend was apparent for many years after 1972.)

13. Note that the bulk of tea and rubber production was exported and, therefore, the export volume changes closely correspond to domestic production changes.

14. The then-accepted view of the inefficiency of share-tenancy arrangements, and the popularly accepted view that the rich landlords did not fully exploit the potential of the land supported such an expectation.

15. During this period there was a dual, fixed exchange rate system in operation. The standard official rate applied to the bulk of exports (including tea, rubber and coconut) and imports; a higher rate (which during this period was 65% higher), known as the Foreign Exchange Entitlement Certificate (FEEC) rate, applied to 'non-essential' imports and to 'non-traditional' exports. In addition there was a black-market rate, which was generally close to the FEEC rate.

16. There are clearly issues related to the appropriate exchange rate to be used for conversions of this type in an economy where taxes and quantitative controls on both domestic and foreign trade are pervasive; we ignore them here.

17. Real values were computed at 1970 prices throughout.

18. The oil price increase was not considered an unmitigated disaster. For example, until the negative effects of the recession on demand for motor cars and hence on tyres was recognised, there was much optimism about prospects for natural rubber.

19. The Minister of Finance, Dr N. M. Perera, was the leader of the ex-Trotskyist Lanka Sama Samaja Party, and enjoyed a reputation for his economics knowledge and analytic capabilities. His views on economic issues influenced the community across the political spectrum, and certainly commanded respect within government ranks during the early years of this period. (This was to change later.) Public statements and private conversations both attest to his strong concerns about the likelihood of a world depression. The author is personally aware of a number of private conversations where this concern was strongly expressed.
20. Aggregate savings data, particularly private savings data, have several weaknesses (see Athukorala and Jayasuriya 1994).
21. For a detailed discussion of this approach, see Bevan *et al.* (1991b). In the Sri Lanka case, note that factor incomes from abroad, such as migrant worker remittances, were negligible until the late 1970s.
22. This was lower than the average for the 1970–72 period, since there was a significant downward trend. This trend could be attributed to the general worsening of the investment environment for private agents owing to various regulatory measures of the government and the perceived increase in the probability of nationalisation of private businesses. (In 1971, the government had passed a Business Undertakings Acquisition Act that empowered the Minister of Finance to acquire any business firm if it was considered to be in the national interest.)
23. This may well be an underestimate; the capital–output ratio was sharply lower during 1974–76 and was in the range 3.3 to 3.5.
24. There is relatively small but significant drop in 1973, the assumed first year of the shocks. This arises from using a GFKF ratio higher than that actually observed in 1973. This is probably not unreasonable in view of the earlier discussion of the sharpness of the shocks in 1972.
25. Of course it may also be due to sluggish adjustment of consumption to current income by Keynesian-type agents.
26. The construction of a domestic tradables price index in Sri Lanka for this period is extremely difficult owing to the pervasiveness of quantitative restrictions (rather than tariffs) on imports, the many adjustments that were made to these during the study period itself, the existence of price controls on most imported goods, and the generally imperfectly competitive nature of the domestic goods markets.
27. The figures for the sectoral distribution of employment are available for 1971 and 1981, but these are of little relevance for an analysis of the 1973–76 period. The 1981 figures reflect the massive changes in the economy that took place after changes in government, policy regime and an investment boom.
28. The construction sector is rather broadly defined so that even buildings that may be intended for production of consumer non-tradables and import substitutes can be included within it.
29. Estimates of unemployment during this period indicate a significant increase; in such a situation informal wages are more likely to have moved down.
30. Taxes on international trade in some form or another contributed nearly half of government revenues during this period, having fallen somewhat from even higher levels in the past.

31. Government industrial enterprises made up a large part of industrial firms in the country; price increases for investment goods and raw materials increased their operating expenses and ended up by drawing larger government transfers.

32. The attitudes and views of the Minister of Finance and other influential figures involved in economic policymaking are discussed by Hewavitharana (1975), an academic economist closely associated with the Minister of Finance.

33. For a discussion of the political and historical roots of the anti-inflationary bias in Sri Lankan economic policies, see Athukorala and Jayasuriya (1994).

34. There are several studies of savings patterns in Sri Lanka but none of them has attempted to isolate the impact of TOT changes on savings (see Athukorala and Jayasuriya (1994) and Wickramanayake 1993). Fry (1986) included Sri Lanka in a pooled sample of fourteen countries in a study of TOT dynamics in Asia and concluded that savings rates were positively correlated with TOT movements, but there was no attempt to isolate the impact of temporary TOT changes from permanent changes.

35. The influences on investment behaviour were subject to many complex factors owing to the periodic changes in governments with widely differing attitudes to the private sector—both domestic and foreign—and access to foreign savings. A detailed analysis of investment was deemed to be beyond the scope of this study.

36. A series is integrated of order d, or $I(d)$, if it needs to be differenced d times to yield a stationary series, and unit root tests are employed to test for stationarity. We used the Kwiatkowski–Phillips–Schmidt–Shin (KPSS) test (Kwiatkowski *et al.* 1992) to supplement the widely used Augmented Dickey–Fuller (ADF) test; the latter tests the null of a unit root against the alternative of stationarity whereas the former tests the null of stationarity against the alternative of a unit root. For a survey of recent developments in econometric analysis of time-series, see Muscatelli and Hurn (1992).

37. Note that it is possible for a combination of two $I(1)$ variables to be $I(0)$. Hence, on the basis of the KPSS results the theoretical possibility of a consumption-smoothing long-run relationship between private savings and real GDP and TOT cannot be rejected. Since the variables appeared to be relatively close to being $I(0)$ at a slightly lower level of statistical significance, a two-stage Engle–Granger model was also estimated for comparison—with the first-stage static equation being estimated by the Phillip–Hansen 'fully modified' procedure to avoid the weaknesses of OLS estimation. The results on the terms of trade dynamics were found to be remarkably similar to those obtained with the 'general-to-specific' approach reported here. Results are available from the author on request.

38. For details of the general procedure, see Section 8.5 in Harvey (1990).

39. See Frenkel and Razin (1987) and Svensson and Razin (1983).

40. This elasticity is obtained by dividing the coefficient of the lagged TOT variable (TOT_{t-1}), by the coefficient of lagged savings variable (PS_{t-1}), with the sign reversed.

41. This is consistent with the fact that available measures of the real exchange rate showed little change during this period (Athukorala and Jayasuriya 1994).

REFERENCES

Athukorala, P. and S. Jayasuriya (1994) *Crises, Adjustment and Growth: Macroeconomic Policies in Post-Independence Sri Lanka*, World Bank, Washington, DC.

Bevan, D.L., P. Collier and J.W. Gunning (1987) 'Consequences of a Commodity Boom in a Controlled Economy: Accumulation and Redistribution in Kenya 1975–83', *The World Bank Economic Review*, 1(3): 489–513.

——(1991a) 'Macroeconomics of External Shocks' in V.N. Balasubramanyam and S. Lall (eds), Current Issues in Development Economics, London: MacMillan (pp. 91–117)

——(1991b) 'The Kenyan Coffee Boom of 1976–79', Centre for the Study of African Economies, University of Oxford.

Central Bank of Ceylon (various years) *Review of the Economy*, Central Bank of Ceylon, Colombo.

——(various years) *Annual Report*, Central Bank of Ceylon, Colombo.

Collier, P. (1993) 'Trade Shocks: Consequences and Policy Responses: Theory and Evidence from Africa, Asia and Latin America', Centre for the Study of African Economies, University of Oxford.

Corden, W.M. (1984) 'Booming Sector and Dutch Disease Economics: Summary and Consolidation', *Oxford Economic Papers*, 36: 359–80.

Corden, W.M. and J.P. Neary (1982) 'Booming Sector and De-industrialisation in a Small Open Economy', *Eoonomic Journal*, 92: 825–48.

Department of Census and Statistics (1977) *Statistical Abstract of the Democratic Socialist Republic of Sri Lanka*, Government Printing Press, Colombo.

Fernando, W.N. (1980) 'Continuity and Change in Plantation Agriculture: An Analysis of the Case of Sri Lanka with Special Reference to Tea Plantations', unpublished Ph.D. dissertation, University of Wisconsin, Madison.

Frenkel, J.A., and A. Razin (1987) *Fiscal Policies and the World Economy*, MIT Press, Cambridge.

Fry, M.J. (1986) 'Terms of Trade Dynamics in Asia: An Analysis of National Saving and Domestic Investment Responses to Terms of Trade Changes in 14 Asian LDCs', *Journal of International Money and Finance*, 5: 57–73.

Harvey, A. (1990) *The Econometric Analysis of Time Series*, Second Edition, Philip Allan, London.

Hewavitharana, B. (1975) 'Recent Trends in the Management of External and Internal Finance in Sri Lanka', *Marga Quarterly Journal*, 2(4): 1–37.

Kwiatkowski, D., P.C.B. Phillips, P. Schmidt and Y. Shin (1992) 'Testing the Null Hypothesis of Stationarity Against the Alternative of a Unit Root: How Sure Are We that Economic Time Series Have a Unit Root?', *Journal of Econometrics*, 54(1): 159–79.

Muscatelli, V.A. and S. Hurn (1992) 'Cointegration and Dynamic Time Series Models', *Journal of Economic Surveys*, 6(1): 1–43.

Savundranayagam, T. (1983) 'Estimates of Sri Lanka's Gross National Product from 1950 to 1981', *Staff Studies*, 13(1&2): 170–202.

Snodgrass, D.R. (1966) *Ceylon: An Export Economy in Transition*, Richard Irvin, Homewood.

Svensson, L.E.O and A. Razin (1983) 'The Terms of Trade and the Current Account: The Harberger/Laursen/Metzler Effect', *Journal of Political Economy*, 91: 91–125.

Van Wincoop, E. (1993) 'Structural Adjustment and the construction Sector', *European Economic Review*, 37: 177–201.

Wickramanayake, J. (1993) 'Financial Policy and Economic Development in Developing Countries: The Case of Sri Lanka', unpublished Ph.D thesis, La Trobe University, Australia.

21

The Impact of Temporary Trade Shocks on an Economy in Disequilibrium: The Philippines, 1986–89

RAUL FABELLA AND SISIRA JAYASURIYA

21.1. Introduction

The 1980s were a period of tremendous political and economic turbulence in the Philippines. The combination of the second OPEC oil price increases—the Philippines is a net oil importer—and the collapse of commodity prices (sugar, coconut and copper) led to a terms of trade deterioration of 30% between 1979 and 1985. Its effects were aggravated by the rise in world interest rates and drying-up of capital flows to heavily indebted developed countries during the early 1980s. Since the mid-1970s the Philippines—both the public sector, under the authoritarian control of President Ferdinand Marcos, and the politically favoured private enterprises whose borrowings were underwritten by the government—had accumulated a large foreign debt; the sharp fall in its terms of trade in the mid-1970s had been countered by higher public expenditures, and recorded economic growth was quite respectable during this period. With the change in the external circumstances in the early 1980s, the Philippines found itself in a common Latin American predicament.[1]

The combined effects of the terms of trade decline and the inability to access new borrowings to pay interest on existing borrowings led to an economic crisis. This was compounded by a political crisis precipitated by the murder of Marcos's main political rival, Benigno Aquino, in 1983. The economy nosedived and massive capital flight took place as political uncertainty gripped the nation; in 1985, GNP fell by 4.4% and investment fell by nearly 22%. The overthrow of Marcos in 1986 and the accession to power of Mrs Cory Aquino, the widow of the murdered leader, started a process of slow recovery of stability and confidence. This process was facilitated by a change in the external economic circumstances soon after the change in the political regime.

Starting in 1986 the world oil price collapsed and, aided by the recovery in the world economy in the second half of the 1980s, this brought a rapid improvement in the terms of trade; by 1988 the terms of trade index stood

Table 21.1. Import prices, export prices and terms of
trade, 1970–91 (*1985 = 100*)

	Import prices	Export prices	Terms of trade
1970	8.0	17.0	212.5
1971	9.0	18.0	200.0
1972	10.0	18.0	180.0
1973	13.0	26.0	200.0
1974	21.0	43.0	204.8
1975	24.0	37.0	154.2
1976	24.0	33.0	137.5
1977	26.0	34.0	130.8
1978	27.0	37.0	137.0
1979	32.0	46.0	143.8
1980	40.0	49.0	122.5
1981	47.0	50.0	106.4
1982	43.0	45.0	104.7
1983	56.0	62.0	110.7
1984	95.0	102.0	107.4
1985	100.0	100.0	100.0
1986	90.0	97.0	107.8
1987	91.0	108.0	118.7
1988	93.0	122.0	131.2
1989	98.0	123.0	125.5
1990	123.0	134.0	108.9
1991	133.0	155.0	116.5

Source: IMF, *International Financial Statistics* (various issues)

31% higher than in 1985 (Table 21.1). Given the circumstances of 1985, this positive terms of trade movement represented perhaps a windfall of even greater significance than indicated by its numerical magnitude. The extent to which the patterns of private and public sector responses to this favourable shock conformed to the predictions of the theory of construction booms is the focus of this study.[2]

21.2. Macroeconomic Environment

During the period 1986–89, the Philippines witnessed a confluence of circumstances that at the outset would seem to have warranted a heterodox response. In summary these were: (1) the economy was coming out of the worst recession in recent history with a cumulative decline in real GDP of about 10% during the previous two years (see Table 21.2). (2) It faced a huge debt problem which did not end but rather worsened with the resumption of growth and which had several subfeatures: a continuing heavy negative net resource transfer (Table 21.2, row 11); foreign

Table 21.2. Some macroeconomic indicators, 1985–90

Indicator	1985	1986	1987	1988	1989	1990
1. GNP growth (%)	−4.4	1.5	4.6	6.4	5.6	3.1
2. Consumption growth (%)	−0.1	−0.8	5.9	6.2	6.2	4.8
3. Investment growth (%)	−21.7	−9.1	34.2	17.3	14.8	6.8
4. Trade balance (US$m.)	(482)	(202)	(1,017)	(1,085)	(2,598)	(4,020)
5. Current account deficit (US$m.)	(103)	954	(444)	(390)	(1,465)	(2,645)
6. Inflation (%)	23.1	0.8	3.8	10	10.6	14
7. T-bill rates (%)	27	16	13	15.7	19.7	30
8. Devaluation (%)	11.4	9.6	0.9	2.6	3	24
9. Exchange rate (Peso/US$)	18.6	20.4	20.6	21.1	21.7	28
10. Public sector deficit (as % of GNP)	6.1	4.8	2.2	3.1	4.1	5
11. Net resource transfers (US$m.)		(1,352)	(2,102)	(2,785)	(1,929)	(2,179)
12. Direct foreign investment (US$m.)	17	140	326	986	854	480
13. Savings rate (GDS/GDP)	12.2	11.7	12.3	12.7	10.4	9.2
14. Government expenditures (% of GDP)						
a. Nat. gov. exp.	16.2	18.9	22.7	20.9	18.7	21.3
b. Personnel	3.9	4.4	4.6	5.4	5.6	6.0
c. Operations and maintenance	2.2	2.2	2.8	2.4	2.5	3.2
d. Interest	2.6	3.5	5.5	5.7	4.3	6.6
e. Investment	2.5	2.0	0.7	0.7	0.6	0.5
f. Capital	5.2	4.3	3.0	2.3	3.0	6.6

Sources:
1. Diokno (1990)
2. Department of Finance (1990)
3. World Bank reports No. 8933-PH and No. 11061-PH
4. Tan (1993)

borrowing from non-official sources was precluded; and the government had committed itself to honour its debt obligations regardless of cost. (3) Its capacity to tap official and multilateral loan sources and to clinch debt-restructuring agreements was conditioned on trade and market liberalisation. (4) A price stablisation scheme known as the 'Oil Price Stabilisation Fund' (OPSF) operated in the market. (5) Euphoria, confusion and political stability had followed the collapse of the Marcos regime after twenty years in power and the new government's hold on power was quite tenuous. These factors influenced the way the terms of trade shock was transmitted into the economy and conditioned the responses of economic agents.

The construction boom theory predicts, among other things, a non-tradable sector construction boom as a consequence of temporary positive trade shocks. The phenomenon in focus here is primarily the impact of the collapse of the price of a principal import (oil). Was this considered temporary? The gradual collapse of OPEC control of the world oil price was due to many well-known and perhaps lasting causes, but the depth of the oil price drop in 1986 was largely attributed to the continuing Iran–Iraq war. Few people believed that the fall of the petroleum price to such low levels was permanent, and it would have been surprising if the government was unaware of this. But this was a government on a very short leash, and the fact is that when the oil price plummeted, the authorities initially responded as if the change was permanent: (1) in October 1987, the tariff on oil imports was reduced from 20% to 10%, which allowed a rollback of the petrol pump (retail) price, and (2) when the world oil price fell even lower, to US$9 per barrel, the Energy Regulatory Board, which managed the OPSF, reduced the reference price[3] from US$16 to US$11.28 per barrel, which again allowed the pump price to go down further in October 1988.

There are several other reasons why the predictions of the theory of construction booms may fail to find distinct expression in this positive shock in the Philippines in 1986–89. One reason is foreign investment, which by all anecdotal accounts was considerable but not fully captured by official statistics. By the latter count alone, DFI moved from US$140 million in 1986 to US$986 million in 1988 (Table 21.2, row 12). By itself, this could have had a significant impact in the economy. But 1986–89 was also the time when Taiwan was waking up to foreign investments in view of its huge reserves and responded to the excitement generated in the Philippines by a home-grown real estate bubble. A good deal of the acquisitions and new real estate projects were supposed to be financed by 'Taiwan money', which, however, passed through the unofficial but efficient network of the clannish Chinese community. Taiwan money and speculative fever went hand in hand. The second reason is that 1986–89 was, as observed, a recovery period characterised by large excess capacity overhang. Rapid output growth in one sector does not necessarily draw away factors from another sector until the factor markets become tight. The third reason was the huge debt service obligation, which, if nothing else, should have created a 'reverse Dutch Disease' atmosphere and constrained the government's set of options on the disposal of any windfall.

This last factor is crucial for understanding subsequent developments. The government assumed most of the country's foreign debt obligations.

To service the debt, it borrowed heavily from the private sector in order to purchase foreign currencies (primarily US dollars) in the hands of private agents, especially 'OCW' remittances.[4] To do this, the government had to offer very attractive rates (see Table 21.2, row 7). This was a windfall to holders of liquid assets, such as the commercial banks and other deposit-takers. Indeed, the commercial banks became very profitable during this period.[5] With inflation rates in low single figures between 1986 and 1988, real returns to investment in government securities (both direct and indirect via time deposits) were very high. The other aspect of the government's constrained choice set was that the size of the fiscal deficit was governed by successive IMF stabilisation programmes. Thus, the deficit had to be kept within strict bounds (see Table 21.2, row 10). Caught between the large interest payment obligations, which increasingly translated into domestic borrowing (see Table 21.2, row 14d), and a tight fiscal deficit ceiling, the government had to reduce other spending. These cuts fell on capital and infrastructure spending (Table 21.2, rows 14c, e).

The high real and nominal interest rates crowded out new capital investments. Growth in the tradable sector output was achieved by soaking up excess capacity. The recovery was widely characterised as consumption-led (Table 21.2, row 2), being precipitated by upward wage-and-salary adjustments plus the impact of the terms of trade windfall in 1986–88. In short, the Philippines in 1986–88 was clearly an economy in disequilibrium.

21.3. Oil Price Stabilisation Fund (OPSF)

The shock we are concerned with here (largely owing to the oil price drop) is especially interesting because of the oil price stabilisation programme governing domestic price movement, which mediated the transmission of international price changes to the domestic economy. Similar to other price stabilisation programmes, the OPSF was a fund which decumulated when the world oil price was above the reference price (the price which, in combination with the exchange rate, was the basis of the domestic pump price) and accumulated when the price was below the reference rate. By law, the OPSF fund was extra-budgetary and not available to fund fiscal spending. A drastic drop in oil price would therefore only bloat the OPSF and would not directly impact on domestic decisions. Government had no immediate access to the windfall;[6] nor was the private sector affected, except indirectly through a resulting exchange rate appreciation.

Thus, without any adjustment in the reference rate or in the tariff on oil, the only impact of the shock would have been an improvement in the reserve position of the economy. The actual reserve position deteriorated in 1987 and 1988 but this was mainly due to the drain from debt service;

the dip in the reserve position would have been more severe in the absence of the windfall.

In fact, part of the oil price fall was transmitted to the private sector. It was politically embarrassing to carry the fund at a very high (20 billion peso) level, and the reference rate was moved down drastically from mid-twenties a barrel to US$16 and finally to US$11.28 a barrel in October 1988. This allowed a rollback of the pump price of petrol and passed on some of the windfall to the general public. Likewise, the 50% tariff reduction cited earlier allowed further pass-on to the private sector, but this time at the expense of government revenue.

21.4. Counterfactual Analysis

The practical problems in doing counterfactual analysis of a trade shock, namely the dependence on the *ceteris paribus* assumption, are demonstrated very clearly when attempting an analysis of the Philippines during this period. Ideally, the economy should be on a steady-state growth path when the shock occurs, which would then account for subsequent changes. Of course this happens very rarely in any case. In the case of the Philippines, there was hardly any period during the past two decades when such a scenario could plausibly have been assumed, and the period 1986–89 was one when the economy was coming out of a particularly turbulent tailspin. On the other hand, this is not necessarily a drawback: it is interesting to examine which features, if any, of the construction boom theory found observable expression in this disequilibrium milieu.

21.5. Magnitude and Duration of the Windfall

Table 21.3 gives the counterfactual estimate of the windfall owing to the terms of trade improvement, based on the 1980–86 average.[7] By 1990, the windfall was over, witness to the shock's (*ex post*) transitoriness. The accumulated windfall gain over the 1987–89 was P57.8 billion at 1986 prices. This, at a 10% discount rate, implies an addition to permanent income of only 1% of average GNP. In other words, the windfall represented a rather small addition to permanent income. Could this have been enough to alter current expenditure levels and patterns significantly?

Although small in relation to the potential contribution to permanent income, the windfalls of US$1,250 million and US$1,091 million in 1988 and 1989 were not small by the standard of other incremental flows (flows other than customary and programmable—i.e. exports, OCW remittances and standard foreign savings). For example, recorded foreign direct investment reached a peak of US$986 million in 1988. Inflows from official

Table 21.3. Estimate of windfall gains, 1987–89

	Actual value of exports (US$m.) (1)	Counterfactual value of exports (US$m.) (2)	Estimated windfall (US$m.) (3)	Estimated windfall (peso bn.) (4)	Real value of windfall at 1986 prices (5)
1986	4,842.0	4,852.0			
1987	5,720.0	5,205.2	514.8	10.6	10.5
1988	7,074.0	5,823.9	1,250.1	26.4	25.5
1989	7,821.0	6,729.9	1,091.1	23.7	21.8
1990	8,186.0	8,115.1	−70.9	−1.7	−1.3

Notes: Windfall estimates based on 1980–86 average value of Terms of Trade (1985 = 100) = 108; col. (5) = col. (4) deflated by import prices (1986 = 100); export volumes at actual levels

Sources: *International Financial Statistics*, various issues; Philippine Statistical Yearbook, various issues

and multilateral agencies were sucked in by debt service, resulting in negative net resource transfers. In this financial desert, the oil price windfall attracted more attention than perhaps its absolute value warranted.[8]

However, the pass-through of this favourable external price movement to private agents was muted. Table 21.4 shows the trajectories of different price indices throughout the 1980s (1986 = 100). Note that the export price index (PEX86) rose faster than the import price index (PIM86). The domestic price index for export commodities (DFEX86) rose faster than that for imports (DFIM86). But the external terms of trade (EXTTOT) improvements outpaced those in the internal terms of trade (INTTOT) for the period. Thus, domestic prices did not reflect fully the improvement in the TOT; the former improved by 12.7% between 1986 and 1988, compared with a 21.7% improvement in the external price index. This was not surprising. In addition to government regulations, such as those in the oil sector, many commodity markets were characterised by non-competitive structures which impeded full pass-through of external prices to domestic producers and consumers (de Dios 1984).

21.6. Savings

21.6.1. Aggregate Savings

Did this windfall express itself in savings behaviour?[9] Table 21.5 gives data on aggregate savings between 1980 and 1991. Note the drastic fall in the national savings rate from 1983 to 1986, the crisis years. The savings

Table 21.4. Transmission of foreign prices to domestic prices of tradables (*1986 = 100*)

	PIM86	PEX86	DFEX86	DFIM86	EXTTOT	INTTOT
1980	44.4	50.5	37.2	39.2	113.7	94.9
1981	52.2	51.5	40.8	43.5	98.7	93.7
1982	47.8	46.4	42.7	46.0	97.1	92.7
1983	62.2	63.9	50.5	59.4	102.7	85.1
1984	105.6	105.2	77.2	91.3	99.6	84.6
1985	11.1	103.1	100.8	101.3	92.8	98.9
1986	100.0	100.0	100.0	100.0	100.0	100.0
1987	101.0	111.3	106.8	102.2	110.1	104.5
1988	103.3	125.8	115.7	102.7	121.7	112.7
1989	108.9	126.8	121.8	116.5	116.5	105.0
1990	136.7	138.1	136.4	135.0	101.1	101.1
1991	147.8	159.8	163.0	149.9	108.1	108.8

PIM86 = Import price index
PEX86 = Export price index
DFEX86 = Domestic price index (deflator) of export commodities
DFIM86 = Domestic price index (deflator) of import commodities
EXTTOT = Terms of trade (PEX86/PIM86)
INTTOT = DFEX86/DFIM86

Source: *Philippine Statistical Yearbook*, 1992

Table 21.5. Savings behaviour (*current prices in millions of pesos*)

	GNP	GDS	GDS/GNP (%)
1980	243,300	49,206.0	20.2
1981	280,500	56,543.0	20.1
1982	313,500	55,532.0	17.7
1983	363,300	69,073.0	19.0
1984	508,500	62,684.0	12.3
1985	555,900	37,271.0	6.7
1986	596,600	44,167.0	7.4
1987	673,900	75,708.0	11.2
1988	795,700	103,447.0	13.0
1989	913,800	116,082.0	12.7
1990	1,076,800	125,892.0	11.7
1991	1,261,700	126,863.0	10.1

Source: *Philippine Statistical Yearbook*, 1992

rate recovered starting in 1987, but by 1988 it was still below its level in the early 1980s. However, aggregate savings behaviour from the mid-1980s shows features which are consistent with consumption-smoothing behaviour.

Table 21.6. Household savings rate (*percentage*)

1980	1981	1982	1983	1984	1985	1986	1987	1988	1989	1990	1991
16.6	19.1	18.9	20.3	13.4	12.2	11.7	12.3	12.7	10.4	9.2	5.1

Source: Tan (1993)

The unprecedented collapse of GDP during the crisis years 1984–86 was clearly not expected to be permanent, and the sharp drop in the savings rate suggests that, in aggregate, agents dipped into savings to maintain consumption. The removal of Marcos in 1986 was a major step towards political stability, and an economic recovery was on the cards even in the absence of any terms of trade improvement. As it was, the TOT windfall came at the same time. Both factors helped raise the aggregate savings rate, but the savings rate began to decline again as the windfall waned. This behaviour of aggregate savings of course reflected the net impact of private and public savings behaviour, and we now turn to examine each component separately.

21.6.2. Private Savings

The household savings rate, which was on a steep decline during the first half of the 1980s, experienced a mild recovery in 1987 and 1988 (12.3% and 12.7%). But the decline resumed in 1989 (Table 21.6). There is some weak indication, however, that the windfall may have had a positive impact on household savings. Total private savings obtained from National Accounts data suggest a broadly similar picture, though the savings rate is considerably higher.

21.6.3. Government Savings and Fiscal Patterns

Table 21.2 and Table 21.7 show the evolution of the fiscal picture in the 1980s. Total government revenue, as a percentage of GDP, recovered from 1985 on (but note that real GDP actually fell in 1985). Government investment fluctuated but was very low overall in the second half of the 1980s. Thanks in large measure to this reduction in investment expenditures, the government realised an increasing primary surplus. 'Other expenses' and 'transfers' also fell from 1986 but interest payments rose rapidly and led to a continuing overall deficit. With access to foreign borrowing greatly curtailed, debt-service payments were financed mainly through increased domestic borrowings.

Table 21.7. Fiscal patterns (as percentages of GDP)

	Total revenue	Government consumption	Gross fixed capital formation	Total exhaustive expenditure	Primary surplus	Other expenses/ transfers	Total interest	Total transfers	Overall deficit	Net domestic borrowing	Net foreign borrowing
1980	14.1	9.0	1.4	10.4	3.8	4.2	0.9	5.1	1.4	0.5	0.9
1981	12.7	8.4	2.1	10.5	2.2	5.6	0.9	6.5	4.3	2.2	2.1
1982	12.0	8.6	1.4	10.0	2.0	5.4	1.1	6.5	4.5	3.1	1.5
1983	12.4	8.0	1.3	9.3	3.0	3.7	1.4	5.0	2.0	0.6	1.5
1984	10.8	6.2	0.9	7.1	3.7	3.6	2.0	5.6	1.9	1.5	0.3
1985	12.1	7.1	0.6	7.7	4.4	3.8	2.6	6.4	2.0	1.8	0.0
1986	13.0	8.2	0.8	8.9	4.1	5.7	3.4	9.1	5.0	4.4	0.6
1987	15.0	8.5	0.9	9.5	5.6	2.6	5.4	8.0	2.4	1.5	1.0
1988	14.1	8.3	0.2	8.5	5.6	2.8	5.7	8.5	2.9	2.4	0.5
1989	16.5	9.5	0.5	10.0	6.5	2.7	5.9	8.6	2.1	1.2	0.9
1990	16.8	9.9	0.9	10.8	6.0	2.8	6.6	9.5	3.5	3.0	0.4
1991	17.8	9.8	1.2	11.0	6.8	2.9	6.1	8.9	2.1	1.6	0.6

Sources: International Financial Statistics, various issues; Philippine Statistical Yearbook, various issues

21.7. Investment

We saw earlier that aggregate investment did indeed rise in 1987 and 1988 (Table 21.2). Here we attempt a counterfactual estimate of the additional gross fixed capital formation (GFKF) which may be attributed to the windfall. Table 21.8 shows (column 7) our estimated addition to GFKF owing to the windfall.

In estimating this, we were faced with the problem mentioned at the start of this section: what would be the appropriate counterfactual figure? If we use a relatively long-run average GFKF/GNP ratio, such as the average for 1975–85 (25%), counterfactual GFKF exceeds actual (Table 21.9), an implausible outcome. Since 1983, investment had been in steep decline. With large excess capacity in the economy—GDP had fallen in 1984–85—no improvement in economic circumstances would have produced a leap back to such high levels. We used the GFKF/GNP

Table 21.8. Actual and counterfactual gross fixed capital formation

	Actual			Counterfactual			
	GFKF/GNP (current prices)	Real income: GDP (at 1986 prices) with windfall	GFKF at 1986 prices	Real income	GFKF/GNP	GFKF	Windfall GFKF
	(1)	(2)	(3)	(4)	(5)	(6)	(7)
1980	27.3						
1981	27.8						
1982	27.8						
1983	30.3						
1984	25.3						
1985	18.0						
1986	17.2	623.0	106.9	623.2	17.2	107.2	−0.3
1987	17.3	664.5	114.8	654.0	17.2	112.5	2.3
1988	18.0	720.0	129.6	694.4	17.2	119.4	10.1
1989	21.0	755.1	159.6	733.3	17.2	126.1	33.5
1990	21.7	758.6	165.0	757.3	17.2	130.3	34.7
1991	19.7	766.3	150.9	754.3	17.2	129.7	21.7

Notes: GFKF/GNP (%) used in counterfactuals is the one for 1986 (17.2%). Real income in column (2) is the sum of real GDP, real value of migrant workers' remittances (deflated by import price index (1986 = 100)) and real value of windfall

Sources: *International Financial Statistics*, various issues; *Philippine Statistical Yearbook*, various issues

Table 21.9. Actual and counterfactual gross fixed capital formation

	Actual			Counterfactual			
	GFKF/ GNP (current prices)	Real income: GDP (at 1986 prices) with windfall	GFKF at 1986 prices	Real income	GFKF/GNP	GFKF	Windfall GFKF
	(1)	(2)	(3)	(4)	(5)	(6)	
1980	27.3						
1981	27.8						
1982	27.8						
1983	30.3						
1984	25.3						
1985	18.0						
1986	17.2	623.0	106.9	623.2	25	155.8	−48.9
1987	17.3	664.5	114.8	654.0	25	163.5	−48.7
1988	18.0	720.0	129.6	694.4	25	173.6	−44.0
1989	21.0	755.1	159.6	733.3	25	183.3	−23.7
1990	21.7	758.6	165.0	757.3	25	189.3	−24.3
1991	19.7	766.3	150.9	754.3	25	188.6	−37.7

Notes: GFKG/GNP (%) used in counterfactuals is the actual for the period 1975–85. Real income in column (2) is the sum of real GDP, real value of migrant workers' remittances (deflated by import price index (1986 = 100)) and real value of windfall

Sources: *International Financial Statistics*, various issues; *Philippine Statistical Yearbook*, various issues

ratio for 1986 (17.2%) as our counterfactual level on the grounds that political stability was still tenuous and the most that could be expected was an end to the decline in investment rather than any significant increase.[10]

But the crucial point is that the heavy debt service and the enforced negative net resource transfer were now a political constraint which was not there between 1975 and 1985. This emasculated the capacity of the government to undertake even urgently needed investments. In turn, this constrained private investment on two counts: (1) poor infrastructure[11] and (2) high interest rates, which crowded out private investment. Hence, the depressed level of investment in 1986 was probably a far more appropriate estimate of the counterfactual than appears at first glance.

As shown in Table 21.8, windfall GFKF, as high as 21% of actual GFKF in 1987 and 1988, made quite a significant contribution to total investment.

21.8. The Pattern of Investments

Unfortunately a sectoral break down of investments is not available to determine where these increased investments took place. But some observations can be made.

Construction itself began to recover its share in GDP rather slowly (Table 21.10), although its value-added rose the fastest among the various major sectors except 'Finance and housing', which also grew very rapidly (Table 21.11). Thus, although there is evidence that the construction sector

Table 21.10. Industrial origin of gross domestic product at current prices (*percentage distribution*)

	1984	1985	1986	1987	1988
Agriculture, fishery and forestry	26.5	26.5	25.0	24.2	23.1
Industry	35.0	32.8	32.4	32.6	32.9
Mining and quarrying	1.8	1.9	1.6	1.5	1.6
Manufacturing	26.0	24.6	24.8	24.6	24.5
Construction	5.9	4.5	3.6	4.0	4.3
Electricity, gas, water	1.3	1.8	2.4	2.5	2.5
Services	38.5	40.7	42.6	43.2	44.1
Transport, communication and storage	6.4	6.2	6.3	6.0	5.6
Trade	16.9	19.3	19.4	19.5	19.9
Finance and housing	5.9	5.3	6.1	6.9	6.8
Other services	9.3	9.9	10.8	10.9	11.9
GDP at market prices	100.0	100.0	100.0	100.0	100.0

Source: World Bank Report No. 8933-PH

Table 21.11. Industrial origin of gross domestic product at 1972 constant prices: growth rates (*percentage*)

	1984	1985	1986	1987	1988
Agriculture, fishery and forestry	2.3	3.3	3.7	−1	3.4
Industry	−10.2	−10.2	−2.1	7.7	8.9
Mining and quarrying	−10.7	0.7	−11.9	−2.4	3.4
Manufacturing	−7.1	−7.6	0.8	6.7	8.7
Construction	−23.7	−27.4	−20.6	17.2	12.8
Electricity, gas, water	12.5	6.8	20.2	10.7	5.3
Services	−7.4	−4.4	3	6.6	7.1
Transport, communication and storage	−4.4	−1.6	3.1	2.9	6.2
Trade	1	0	1.9	5.7	4.9
Finance and housing	−32.3	−16.5	12.7	20.7	7.9
Other services	−2.8	−5.4	0.5	3.5	9.8

Source: World Bank Report No. 8933-PH

was recovering, a stronger boom may have been aborted by the real estate speculative bubble, which may have sucked resources away from physical construction.

Although investment rebounded in 1987 and 1988, arguably the quality of investment deteriorated, as indicated by the shares in new investment registered by the Securities and Exchange Commission (see Table 21.12). According to this, manufacturing's share in new investments in 1988 was 22%, way below its share in 1978 (29%). Construction's share was 9.5% in 1978 and, instead of increasing, it was a low 2.4% in 1988. Finally the 'financing, insurance, real estate and business services' share rose from 28% in 1978 to 53% in 1988. Incidentally, these areas (financing etc.) were the biggest money-makers during the 'recovery' period (financing and insurance because of access to high returns; government securities and real estate because of rapidly rising real estate values; anecdotal evidence has it that real estate prices rose in three years in excess of 500%). Only real estate investments (the acquisition and sale of existing stock) could compete with high treasury bill rates.

Yet another development involved the direction taken by investment and capital per worker. The share of investments classified by the Bureau of Investment (BOI) as export-oriented fell from 72% of total investment in 1986 to 55% in 1989. Capital per worker, according to available data, rose from P12,000 to P46,000 for BOI-approved projects (Table 21.13). A potential outcome of a temporary boom which then increases investment is that investments may be extended to less productive projects. There is certainly some evidence that a substantial proportion of new investments went into low-productivity sectors. The overall productivity of industry, manufacturing, construction and trade sectors declined between 1986 and 1988. However, this could probably more justifiably be blamed on the

Table 21.12. Shares in initial paid-up investment of newly incorporated domestic stock: corporations and partnerships by major industry group, 1978–88 (*percentage*)

	1978	1988
Agriculture, fishery and forestry	4.72	3.89
Mining and quarrying	2.08	1.52
Manufacturing	28.62	21.95
Electricity, gas, water	0.09	0.04
Construction	9.46	2.40
Wholesale and retail trade	13.57	10.11
Transport storage and communication	7.73	3.40
Financing, insurance, real estate and business services	28.36	52.36
Community, social and personal services	5.38	4.13

Source: Basic data from the Securities and Exchange Commission

Table 21.13. Selected investment and productivity data

	1986	1987	1988	1989	1990
Export-oriented investments to total investment (%)	72.0	62.0	50.0	55.0	—
Capital per worker ('000 pesos, 1983 prices)	12.0	15.0	26.0	46.0	—
Productivity (real)					
Agriculture	14.2	15.1	15.7	16.2	15.8
Industry	74.7	71.0	69.4	73.0	75.6
Manufacturing	76.9	75.1	74.9	77.6	83.2
Construction	45.4	41.8	38.7	45.4	43.8
Service	31.8	32.4	32.9	33.5	33.3
Trade	39.3	37.1	36.1	35.5	36.3

Note: Investments refer to new and expansion-project approvals by BOI
Source: World Bank Report No. 11061-PH; BOI

general economic and political environment at the time rather than attributed to the exhaustion of productive investment opportunities.

21.9. Foreign Savings

Did the TOT shock precipitate a change in the use of foreign savings? Foreign savings use is proxied here by the recorded current account balance. Using the average foreign savings propensity for 1975–85 (4.9%), the counterfactual use of foreign savings was well below actual use. Cumulated through 1989, the difference amounted to P103m (Table 21.14). This is consistent with experience elsewhere (e.g. the 1970s Kenyan coffee boom), but this entire amount should not be attributed to the effects of the TOT windfall. First, the depressed state of the economy—GDP growth in 1986 was only 1.5% (well below the historical average of 3.5%)—had its dampening effect on investment. Overall, it seems clear that it was the sharp decline of investment from its previous high levels, despite the small positive impact of the windfall-inspired increase, which was primarily responsible for the lower utilisation of foreign savings. However, as we saw, private domestic savings improved, and the higher level of investment attributable to the windfall was smaller than the addition to savings. When the economy grew at 4.6% and 6.4% in 1987 and 1988, respectively, both rates beyond the historical norm (3.5%), the positive contribution of the windfall helped reduce greater reliance on foreign savings.

Table 21.14. Actual and counterfactual utilisation of foreign savings

	Foreign savings propensity		Foreign savings (at 1986 prices)		
	Actual	Counterfactual	Actual	Counterfactual	Windfall
1986	−3.2	4.9	−19.4	30.5	−50.0
1987	1.4	4.9	9.0	32.0	−23.0
1988	1.2	4.9	8.0	34.0	−26.1
1989	4.0	4.9	29.1	35.9	−6.9
1990	6.5	4.9	47.9	37.1	10.8

Note: Counterfactual foreign savings propensity (col. 2) is the average figure for 1975–85
Sources: *International Financial Statistics*, various issues; *Philippine Statistical Yearbook*, various issues

Official restrictions on private capital movements did not allow private agents legally to acquire foreign assets with their savings. In the case of the Philippines, such restrictions have not been very effective; unofficial private capital outflows have been a regular occurrence.[12] But there is no evidence that private agents, on any significant scale, attempted to buy foreign assets with their windfall-related savings during this period. In fact, the data on exchange rate movements show that the gap between official and black-market rates actually narrowed during the windfall period, suggesting a decline in net demand for foreign currencies (Table 21.15).[13]

Although private agents may not have invested their savings in foreign assets, the government's debt-service payments were rising (see Table 21.2, rows 11 and 14d). The boom enabled the government to resist to some degree the political pressures to run an expansionary fiscal policy to push the economy out of deep recession. While a limited fiscal expansion did take place, the improvement in the terms of trade permitted a smaller budget deficit than would have been the case otherwise. Thus, the windfall facilitated reserve accumulation for debt service and, in effect, the government indirectly utilised part of the windfall gains to reduce foreign debt, increasing the country's net foreign assets. Further, reduced pressure on the balance of payments front allowed the government to undertake trade policy reforms, which had the immediate effect of improving international investor confidence in the Philippines.[14]

This policy of debt reduction created heated political debate. Would the social rate of return have been higher if the windfall savings had been used for infrastructure investment? The economic costs of not investing in infrastructure have been all too obvious in the past few years. On the other hand, it can be argued that, had the government declared a debt

Table 21.15. Exchange rates, 1980–91

	1980	1981	1982	1983	1984	1985	1986	1987	1988	1989	1990	1991
Nominal official exchange rate[a]	7.51	7.90	8.54	11.11	16.70	18.61	20.39	20.57	21.09	21.74	24.31	27.48
Nominal official exchange rate[b]	7.60	8.20	9.17	14.00	19.76	19.03	20.53	20.80	21.34	22.44	28.00	26.65
Nominal black-market exchange rate	8.04	8.13	9.08	13.73	20.80	20.80	20.41	20.95	21.55	21.93	25.40	—
Nominal effective exchange rate	202.75	202.05	201.35	160.80	110.59	110.59	78.78	71.51	65.93	65.79	58.84	50.89
Real effective exchange rate[c] (1985 = 100)	02.38	105.66	109.68	92.26	91.39	91.39	78.03	71.80	69.84	74.94	72.90	71.99

[a] Period average
[b] End of period
[c] International Monetary Fund

Sources: International Financial Statistics, various issues; black-market rate from *Pick's Currency Yearbook,* various editions

moratorium, in addition to the costs of drastically reduced access to world capital markets which would have followed such a policy, the windfall gains would have been frittered away in low- or even negative-value-added investments.[15] Whatever would have been the theoretically optimal policy in this respect, the responses of both private agents and the government had this common feature: a substantial part of the gains from the TOT boom was saved rather than consumed.

21.10. Prices

Table 21.16 gives the movements of prices of traded capital (PDE) and those of construction (non-traded capital) (PCON). Construction prices rose faster than traded capital prices, as predicted by both the construction boom and Dutch Disease theories.

Table 21.17 compares price movements of construction and non-traded consumer goods. Note that (non-traded) services prices lagged significantly behind construction prices.[16] Again, the direction and patterns of price changes are consistent with the theory of construction booms: if consumption expenditure effects had been very large, services prices would have been expected to rise more.[17]

Thus, overall, the movements in domestic prices are consistent with the predictions of the construction boom theory, though only a part of the price changes can be attributed to the TOT boom and its effects.

Table 21.16. Price movements of construction and durable equipment (*1986 = 100*)

	PDE	PCON
1980	38.8	45.2
1981	38.9	48.8
1982	41.1	52.5
1983	51.2	58.3
1984	81.4	88.7
1985	96.8	96.8
1986	100.0	100.0
1987	101.6	110.4
1988	111.0	119.5
1989	116.3	137.2
1990	128.2	160.9
1991	152.8	191.7

PDE = (Implicit) price index of durable equipment
PCON = (Implicit) price index of construction
Source: *Philippine Statistical Yearbook*, various issues

Table 21.17. Price movements of construction and consumer non-tradables: food and services (*1986 = 100*)

	Agriculture	Services	Construction (PCON)
1980	42.6	38.1	45.2
1981	47.1	43.1	48.8
1982	49.4	47.8	52.5
1983	57.0	53.5	58.3
1984	90.5	79.1	88.7
1985	99.0	95.0	96.8
1986	100.0	100.0	100.0
1987	107.9	105.9	110.4
1988	118.0	117.5	119.5
1989	131.2	128.6	137.2
1990	146.6	147.2	160.9
1991	161.6	175.8	191.7

Sources: Philippine Statistical Yearbook, 1991; World Bank, Report No. 11001–PH

21.11. Summary, 1986–89

The Philippine economy in the second half of the 1980s exhibited features that made it less than an ideal laboratory for testing trade shock theories. There was considerable direct foreign investment adding to demand pressure on domestic factors; on the other hand, the economy was just pulling out of the worst recession in many decades, with many sectors saddled with excess capacity, and serious political uncertainties, which followed the demise of an authoritarian regime, continued to cast a shadow over the behaviour of economic agents. Further, there were external sector constraints which influenced policymaking: the huge debt overhang and servicing burden and the agreements with the IMF which limited the set of fiscal and monetary policy options.

None the less, certain predictions of the construction boom theory still found expression in the tangle of outcomes. There was a boom in investments in real estate, although a real estate speculative bubble appeared to nip the physical construction boom in the bud.[18] The prices of non-tradable capital (construction), as expected, raced ahead of all other prices (non-traded services and traded capital goods). Despite the fact that there was ample noise to blur indications that the TOT shock primarily affected private and government *savings* (rather than expenditures), some evidence supportive of such an outcome was seen. Both private agents and the government acted to increase savings—behaviour in line with a rational response to a transient boom.

However, the results of this analysis remain open to the criticism that observed responses may have been primarily conditioned by the rather unique economic and political circumstances of the 1986–89 period. Further, some of the responses, though supportive of the construction boom theory, may have been generated by changes unrelated to the TOT boom. Hence it is pertinent to examine the longer-term experience of the Philippines in relation to economic adjustments to temporary trade shocks and place the 1986–89 developments in a longer-term context. This we do in the next section by an econometric analysis of savings behaviour during the 1951–90 period, with particular attention to the short-run dynamics of adjustment to terms of trade fluctuations.

21.12. Savings and Terms of Trade, 1951–90

The core hypotheses which is being tested in this analysis is that temporary terms of trade shocks would lead to significant changes in savings in line with consumption-smoothing behaviour. The basic approach followed in the specification and testing of a dynamic model is similar to that adopted in Chapter 20. The explanatory variables hypothesised to affect real savings were real GDP, TOT, real interest rate, foreign capital inflows and changes in the policy and institutional environment. (Note that real GDP—which excludes price effects—and TOT together give an estimate of real national income.)

Tests for order of integration for the variables were conducted using both Dickey–Fuller tests and KPSS tests.[19] The two tests gave conflicting results on the order of integration of certain key variables and indicated that some of the variables may not be integrated of the same order.[20] In the circumstances, we opted to use an error-correction model using the 'general-to-specific' methodology; this was considered to minimise the possibility of estimating spurious relationships, while retaining long-run information.[21]

The estimated equations for real per capita private savings and real per capita gross domestic (aggregate) savings are presented in Tables 21.18 and 21.19, respectively.[22] Many of the hypothesised variables proved to be statistically insignificant and were deleted; these included the real interest rate, net foreign capital inflows, as well as several dummy variables designed to capture significant political changes (such as the period of the Marcos administration and the crisis years of 1982–86). Several features of the estimated equations should be noted.

First, in both equations, the DTOT variable—the first difference of the terms of trade—has a positive and statistically significant coefficient, implying an impact elasticity of 0.41 in the case of private savings and 0.38 in the case of aggregate savings in response to short-run TOT changes.

Table 21.18. Estimated private savings model, 1951–90[a]

$$DPS_t = -2.21 + 0.41DTOT_t + 0.13TOT_{t-1} + 1.11GDP_t - 0.53PS_{t-1}$$
$$\quad\ (-2.41)^{**} \quad (1.80)^* \qquad (0.85) \qquad (2.63) \qquad (3.08)^{***}$$

$\bar{R}^2 = 0.24$, SEE $= 0.13$, D.W. $= 2.19$
$LM^b (1,34) = 0.94$, RESET$^c (1,34) = 6.64$
$NORM^d = 1.45$, $HT^e(1,38) = 0.03$

where PS = real private saving, $DPS_t = PS_t - PS_{t-1}$, TOT = terms of trade (1985 = 100), DTOT = $TOT_t - TOT_{t-1}$, GDP = real gross domestic product at 1985 prices.

---

[a] Figures in parenthesis are t-ratios; ***, **, * denote significant at 1%, 5% and 10% respectively
[b] LM = Lagrange multiplier test of residual serial correlation, F-version
[c] Ramsey's RESET test for functional form misspecification, F-version
[d] NORM = Jarque–Bera test for normality of residuals
[e] HT = Engle's autoregressive conditional heteroscedasticity test of residuals, F-version
All level variables are in logarithmic form

Table 21.19. Estimated gross domestic savings model, 1951–90[a]

$$DGDS_t = -2.21 + 0.38DTOT_t + 1.11DGDP_t + 0.23TOT_t + 1.05GDP_t - 0.45GDS_{t-1}$$
$$\qquad\ (-2.65)^{**} \quad (2.03)^{**} \qquad (2.10)^{**} \qquad (1.91)^* \qquad (2.78)^{***} \quad (-2.74)^{***}$$

$\bar{R}^2 = 0.27$, SEE $= 0.11$, D.W. $= 2.12$
$LM^b (1,33) = 0.91$, RESET$^c (1,33) = 7.45$
$NORM^d = 1.31$, $HT^e(1,38) = 0.002$

where GDS = real gross domestic saving, $DGDS_t = GDS_t - GDS_{t-1}$, TOT = terms of trade (1985 = 100), DTOT = $TOT_t - TOT_{t-1}$, GDP = real gross domestic product at 1985 prices.

---

[a] Figures in parenthesis are t-ratios. ***, **, * denotes significant at 1%, 5% and 10% respectively
[b] LM = Lagrange multiplier test of residual serial correlation, F-version
[c] Ramsey's RESET test for functional form misspecification, F-version
[d] NORM = Jarque–Bera test for normality of residuals
[e] HT = Engle's autoregressive conditional heteroscedasticity test of residuals, F-version
All level variables are in logarithmic form

Second, the lagged TOT variable is not statistically significant in the private savings equation but is positive and significant in the aggregate savings equation, with an implied long-run response elasticity of savings to terms of trade changes of 0.51. The relationship between private savings and long-run terms of trade changes is ambiguous in theory (Frenkel and Razin 1987; Svensson and Razin 1983). The behaviour of public savings, which drives the result for aggregate savings, suggests that Philippines' governments, in contrast to private agents, have tended to reduce savings in response to long-term terms of trade deteriorations.[23]

Third, structural-stability and predictive-failure tests were carried out to determine if the estimated relationships were robust over the study period. In particular, it was tested whether there was evidence of a structural break between the pre-1982 and post-1982 periods. The relevant F-tests rejected the hypothesis of such a break. This provides support for the view that the results of our detailed analysis of the 1986–89 period, which indicated behaviour consistent with the predictions of the construction boom theory, should not be attributed solely to the unique circumstances of that period.

21.13. Conclusions

In this study we examined the experience of the Philippines during the 1987–89 period, when it experienced a temporary terms of trade upswing. The 1982–86 period was one of acute political crisis and sharp economic recession. Thus the terms of trade boom, which was widely perceived as being temporary, coincided with the recovery of political stability and business confidence. Thus this was clearly not a 'normal' period, even by Philippine standards of political and economic volatility.

Such periods of economic disequilibrium are not uncommon in many developing countries, and the examination of economic responses by private agents and the government to a temporary trade shock in such conditions is of value and can have lessons of relevance to many developing-country situations. But the analysis itself is hampered by the fact that observed changes in the economic variables cannot necessarily be attributed solely to the trade shocks.

In the case of the Philippines we combined the detailed study of this period with an econometric analysis of a longer period (1951–90). This enabled us to verify that the relationships observed during the study period were consistent with longer-term patterns. The study revealed that the central hypothesis of the construction boom theory was supported: savings respond significantly to temporary shocks, in a manner consistent with some degree of inter-temporal consumption smoothing. In the study period, this was true of both private agents and the government. The government's response was to reduce foreign debt; note, however, that this was probably forced on it, since the government had little freedom to do otherwise.

NOTES

1. See Montes *et al.* (1989) for background information on the Philippine economy.

2. The theory of construction booms is an extension of the Dutch Disease theory to the case of temporary booms in developing economies; it argues that a temporary boom in a tradables sector would have only minor expenditure effects but large savings effects owing to consumption-smoothing behaviour by economic agents. A surge in savings tends to reduce interest rates and/or relax liquidity constraints and stimulate investment even in a small country when the domestic capital market is insulated from the world capital market. For a more comprehensive discussion, see Chapter 20.

3. This was the price on which the pump retail price was based and, in theory, was its subjective estimate of the long-term price for oil; in practice, political considerations were known to be factored.

4. Remittances by workers employed overseas.

5. An added attraction was the 20% final tax on interest income against the 35% ceiling on corporate and income taxes.

6. It can be argued that, in practice, these funds could have been available to the government at some subsequent time, which would have enabled it to raise expenditures without enhancing the fiscal deficit. If that had been done, the familiar Dutch Disease consequences would have followed.

7. The choice of the 1980–86 average as the benchmark to assess TOT movements for the 1986–89 period was made on the grounds that the terms of trade appear to have suffered a permanent decline during the 1970s (see Table 21.1).

8. Indeed, the temporary drop in the price of 'galunggong', a cheap dried-fish staple popular with poor households was well commented on.

9. The main data sources, except where otherwise specified, are IMF, *International Financial Statistics* (various issues) and *Philippines Statistical Yearbook* (various issues).

10. Note that investment was maintained at almost the same level in 1987 (17.3%) before the full impact of the windfall had been felt.

11. One example is the major shortage of power, which has persisted until this year. The government was unable to afford required investments to maintain adequate power supplies, and periodic blackouts became a regular feature of Philippine life.

12. See Boyce and Zarsky (1988) for supporting evidence.

13. This was partly due to unofficial private capital inflows, which were attracted by the greater political stability as well as the opportunities for speculative gains in the real estate boom.

14. See Fabella (1989) for a discussion of trade policy reforms in this period.

15. Furthermore, arguably, capital expenditures on infrastructure could have been financed while meeting debt repayments if the government had the will to reduce 'personnel spending', which, instead, experienced a rapid growth (Table 21.2, row 14b). For a discussion of some of the debates on the debt repayment strategy, see Tan (1988).

16. Food prices also lagged but the gap was smaller.

17. The recession in the economy and high unemployment would have probably made services supplies quite elastic and dampened their price increases. But note that the construction sector, too, had access to a large pool of unemployed labour.

18. Because of the confluence of disparate forces working in the economy in the

second half of the 1980s, the nascent construction boom seems to have been quickly transformed into a real estate/speculative boom. Indeed there should be room for such speculative bubbles in an expanded construction boom theory. If a speculative bubble occurs, both the tradable and non-tradable sectors may yield to the emerging storm. If so, there would be a need to consider a different interventionist role for government in economies in disequilibrium experiencing a terms of trade shock.

19. For more details on these tests, see Chapter 20.
20. The detailed test results are not reported here but are available from the authors on request.
21. Two-stage Engle–Granger models were also estimated for comparison, since the Dickey–Fuller tests tended to indicate that all key variables were first difference-stationary (I(1)). The first-stage static equation was estimated using the 'fully modified' Phillip–Hansen procedure. The results were broadly similar to those obtained with the 'general-to-specific' procedure. Results are available from the authors on request.
22. As the reported statistics show, these pass all standard tests, except that for functional form.
23. This broad pattern of response is consistent with policy responses through the Marcos period. For example, the government's response to the collapse of the terms of trade in the mid-1970s was to undertake a large programme of foreign borrowing. As it turned out, the terms of trade decline was permanent, and the borrowing strategy became one of the root causes of the 1980s economic difficulties (Jayasuriya, 1987).

REFERENCES

Boyce, J.K. and L. Zarsky (1988) 'Capital Flight from the Philippines, 1962–86', Working Paper 1988–11, Department of Economics, University of Massachusetts, Amherst.

de Dios, E. *et al.* (1984) *An Analysis of the Philippine Economic Crisis*, University of the Philippines Press, Manila.

Department of Finance (1990) 'The Philippine Agenda for Sustained Growth and Development: A Progress Report,' Department of Finance, Republic of Philippines, Manila.

Diokno, B. (1991) 'Fiscal Performance in the 1980s: A Policy Perspective,' *The Phillipine Economic Journal*, 30: 1–43.

Fabella, R. (1989) 'Trade and Industry Reforms in the Philippines 1980–87: Performance, Process and the Role of Policy', in M.F. Montes *et al.* (eds.) *Philippine Macroeconomic Perspective: Development and Policies*, Institute of Developing Economies, Tokyo.

Frenkel, J.A. and A. Razin (1987) *Fiscal Policies and the World Economy*, MIT Press Cambridge.

International Monetary Fund (Various issues) *International Financial Statistics*, IMF, Washington, DC.

Jayasuriya, S.K. (1987) 'The Politics of Economic Policy in the Philippines during the Marcos Era', in R. Robison, K. Hewison and R. Higgot (eds.) *Southeast Asia in the 1980s: The Politics of Economic Crisis*, Allen and Unwin, Sydney.

Montes, M.F. *et al.* (eds.) (1989) *Philippine Macroeconomic Perspective: Development and Policies*, Institute of Developing Economies, Tokyo.

National Statistical Coordination Board, *Philippine Statistical Yearbook*, Manila.

Svensson, L.E.O. and A. Razin (1983) 'The Terms of Trade and the Current Account: The Harberger/Laursen/Metzler Effect', *Journal of Political Economy*, 91: 91–125.

Tan, E.A. (1988) 'The Philippine Economy: Recovery and Prospects for High Sustained Growth', in *Southeast Asian Affairs, 1988*, Institute for Southeast Asian Studies, Singapore.

——(1993) 'Saving and Saving Mobilization Policy and Experience in the Philippines,' paper prepared for the 'Economic Dialogue amongst the Governments of Cambodia, Lao PDR, Thailand and Vietnam', Asia and Pacific Development Centre.

22

The Remittance Boom in Bangladesh, 1978–86

JEAN-PAUL AZAM AND QUAZI SHAHABUDDIN

22.1. Introduction

Bangladesh is widely regarded as a symbol of poverty and natural disaster: floods, droughts, cyclones, etc. have stricken this overpopulated economy recurrently, leaving millions in destitution (Sen 1981; Ravallion 1987). With about 110 million inhabitants for only 144 thousand square kilometres, it is one of the most densely populated countries in the world. Its population density is about eight times that of France, and nearly twice that of the Netherlands. In 1983, it was second poorest, after Ethiopia, in the ranking of countries by per capita GNP, according to the *World Development Report 1985* (World Bank 1985). Although it enjoys a steady growth rate of per capita income well above that of most African countries (1.9% per annum on average in 1980–91), but lower than that of the neighbouring countries, it remains nowadays among the poorest countries in the world: in 1991 per capita GNP was US$220 (World Bank 1993a).

Before independence from Britain in 1947, East Bengal (now Bangladesh) was a fairly poor hinterland of Calcutta, the regional capital city. Then it became Eastern Pakistan, under the quasi-colonial rule of the then Western Pakistan. It gained independence in 1971, after a brutal war of liberation, with some help from India. While Bangladesh was still in the process of stabilising its political system after independence, it was hit by the 1974 flood and the resulting famine (Sen 1981; Ravallion 1987).[1]

Because of its geographical position, the country is very exposed to natural disasters. It is almost entirely a flood plain, located in a delta where three giant rivers merge before reaching the Indian Ocean: the Ganges (*Padma*), the Brahmaputra (*Jamuna*) and the Meghna. The Padma river drains all the southern part of the Himalayas, and the Jamuna river drains the whole northern part, before turning south towards Bangladesh. The Meghna river has its source south of the Himalayas, in an area where the monsoon season brings among the world's heaviest rains. Hence, river overflow can be disastrous in summer, as it was recently in 1974, 1987 and

1988. Moreover, this country is very close to sea-level, and very flat, so that some of the tidal waves coming from the gulf of Bengal can inundate areas far inland, with lethal consequences for many people, as occurred in 1990. Lastly, the country is often affected by cyclonic storms, with similar results (e.g. 1991). But, quite paradoxically, it is not immune from drought during the dry season, since the soil has poor water-retention capacity. The development of small-scale irrigation is thus an important input into the process of agricultural development in Bangladesh, increasing the potential for dry-season agriculture.

But the people of Bangladesh are very resilient, and they have fought against unfavourable natural conditions for centuries. A striking illustration of this fact is provided by food production, which generally increases, so as to compensate for the losses owing to natural calamities, by above normal production in the post-calamity season (Sen 1981; Hossain 1990). However, a new phenomenon started in the late 1970s: a large outflow of workers going abroad, in particular to work in the Middle East oil-producing countries. Although the number of people migrating each year is well known (Stahl and Habib 1989; World Bank 1993b), it is much harder to find an estimate of the stock of Bangladeshi workers already abroad. Stahl and Habib (1989) quote the figure of 200,000 workers in 1982, without putting too much faith in the precision of this number. Mahmud (1989) puts this figure at 155,000 in 1982 and 252,100 in 1986. These numbers are small compared with the total population of the country. Even if the actual number was in fact twice this estimate, this would still have a negligible impact on the labour market. But the economic significance of this movement results from the inflow of remittances which is entailed in these migrations. Such a phenomenon has given rise recently to some interesting theoretical and empirical analyses (Stark 1991). In the case of Bangladesh, the remittance flow is negligible before 1975, and becomes significant in 1977/78. It then grows quite swiftly, and reaches a steady level in 1983, being worth about 4.5% to 5% of GNP from then on. It has become a major source of foreign currency for the country, since it was worth 93.9% of exports in 1983, and more than 85% in 1986 and 1987. Bakht and Mahmood (1989) and Mahmud (1989) provide a lot of background information on migration and remittances.

Hence, we observe in this case what seems to be a permanent shock, which provides a non-negligible easing of the foreign currency constraint felt by the country. The aim of this chapter is to analyse the macroeconomic consequences of this positive shock. This case study is especially interesting because the government reacted to the increase in the remittance flow by creating the Workers Earnings Scheme (WES), which is analysed in detail below (Lewis 1990). This in effect amounted to the adoption of a dual exchange rate system, with a flexible rate at the second window. The flow of currency so attracted was used to subsidise non-traditional exports, following a mechanism spelt out below. Interestingly enough, this same period of time witnessed the extremely fast development of the ready-made garments sector, which became a major earner of foreign currency for Bangladesh, overtaking the jute manufactures sector in 1984/85 (Brajard 1991). The following analysis suggests some links between these two trends.

We stop the analysis in 1986 in order to avoid the years 1987 and 1988, which have witnessed two so-called centenary floods in a row. These exceptional floods put about two-thirds of the country under water, entailing a massive disruption of economic activity. They have a very low probability of occurring, according to specialists. They were of the same order of magnitude as the 1974 one, which was followed by a terrible famine (Sen 1981; Ravallion 1987). This outcome was avoided during the 1987–88 floods thanks both to international aid and to the improved food policy pursued in Bangladesh. Hossain (1989) presents a brief history of food policy in the country.

The next section identifies the external shock entailed by the remittance flow up to 1986, and provides a counterfactual path of GNP, in order to estimate the contribution of this shock to GNP. Section 22.3 describes the government response to this shock, with special emphasis on the working of the Workers Earnings Scheme. Then, Section 22.4 describes public finance and Section 22.5 analyses the reaction of the private sector. Section 22.6 concludes.

22.2. Identification of the Shock

We restrict the analysis here to the flow of official remittances. Many reasons suggest that the actual flow might differ from the official one, but the latter might as plausibly provide an underestimate as an overestimate of the true figure. For example, returning migrants are freely entitled to import durable goods, and the value of these imports could be added to the remittance flow. Moreover, migrants are liable to remit the money by illegal channels, using the services of a *hundi* (Bakht and Mahmood 1989). These middlemen deliver the taka value of the remittances in Bangladesh, while keeping the foreign currency in a bank account abroad. This enables them to intermediate capital outflows from Bangladesh, by providing to Bangladeshis seeking to evade exchange controls the foreign currency which they want to get abroad, against takas in the country. These two examples suggest that the official figures might tend to underestimate the actual flow. However, because of the premium earned through the WES scheme (see below), the official flows might also lead to an overestimate: some importing or exporting agents might be induced to misinvoice their foreign transactions in order to repatriate some foreign currency with the help of migrant workers and to collect the premium. Hence, some of the official remittance figures might in fact correspond to leakages from the trade balance.

Therefore, there are arguments going in both directions, so that it seems reasonable to use the official figures, on the basis of the Principle of Insufficient Reason.

22.2.1. The Migrants

In Table 22.1, the first two columns represent the number of Bangladeshi workers migrating each year, according to two slightly different series. The one on the left is from the ILO (from Stahl and Habib 1989). These numbers differ somewhat from the World Bank data (World Bank 1993b), which cover only the years since 1980, and which are reproduced in the second column. In both cases, the growth of the numbers involved can be readily observed.

One may divide the overseas migrants into two different groups. There

Table 22.1. Outflow of Bangladeshi migrant workers and remittances (*1975–90*)

	Outflow of migrant workers (thousands)		Real value of remittances (US$ m.)	Share of GDP (%)
	(1)	(2)		
1975	n.a.		48.08	0.24
1976	6,092		43.57	0.39
1977	16,225		86.00	0.85
1978	22,809		149.01	1.33
1979	24,465		162.02	1.65
1980	33,275	30,573	204.18	2.02
1981	55,787	55,787	376.74	3.33
1982	62,805	57,575	439.83	3.64
1983	59,216	59,200	657.59	5.26
1984	56,754	56,753	674.70	4.85
1985	77,694	77,694	517.70	3.38
1986	68,658	68,663	620.80	3.94
1987	68,750	74,017	696.00	4.27
1988	68,121	68,621	689.43	4.06
1989	n.a.	101,718	638.25	3.85
1990	n.a.	103,784	565.38	3.41

Note: In this chapter, year *t* refers to the fiscal year *t* − 1/*t*. In Bangladesh, the fiscal year begins in July each year

Source: Stahl and Habib (1989), World Bank (1993b)

has been for a long time an outflow of Bangladeshi migrants to the Western world, and in particular to the UK (mainly), the USA, Canada and Germany (Bakht and Mahmood 1989). This concerns semi-permanent migration of highly skilled people. On the other hand, the more recent phenomenon of migration to the Middle East concerns short-term migrants of a lower skill level on average. The balance between the two types of migrants has changed during the period under study. Over the period 1977–86, unskilled workers made up 50.98% of the gross outflow of migrants, whereas professionals only amounted to 6.52%. The remainder was made up of skilled (34.68%) or semi-skilled (7.82%) workers. In the earlier part of the period (1977–80), when the outflow to the Middle East was relatively less important, the professionals provided 14.31% of the migrants (Mahmud 1989). Table 22.2 illustrates this point by dividing the flow of official remittances by geographical origin. It shows that the remittances from the Middle East have become dominant since 1980. In the period 1983–86, they account for about 80% of the total. The relative weights were nearly the exact inverse in 1977.

The government played some part in starting this process, through the Bureau of Manpower, Employment and Training (BMET). On average over the period 1977–80, 27.64% of the migrants were in fact recruited by the BMET, whereas private recruiting agents claimed only 13.43% of the migrants (Mahmud 1989). The remainder left on their own initiative. But this government involvement may be seen as a simple 'pump-priming' role, since the corresponding figures for 1985–86 are 45.7% for recruitment by private agents and 2.36% for the BMET (Mahmud 1989).

This increase in the flow of remittances had an important impact on the economy of Bangladesh, as we now show.

Table 22.2. Geographical origin of remittances (*percentage*)

	Middle East	Western countries	All others
1977	19.68	76.44	3.70
1978	37.35	55.12	7.53
1979	45.48	49.80	4.75
1980	50.95	48.77	0.27
1981	62.20	37.29	0.50
1982	72.79	23.29	3.92
1983	77.98	19.13	2.89
1984	77.61	18.81	3.58
1985	75.74	22.99	1.27
1986 (up to April)	81.92	17.66	0.42

Source: Exchange Control Dept., Bangladesh Bank (quoted in Bakht and Mahmood 1989)

22.2.2. The Remittance Boom

The value of the remittance flow over the period 1975–90, in terms of imported goods, is represented in the third column of Table 22.1. The nominal flow of remittances, in US dollars (World Bank 1993b), has been deflated by the import price index (World Bank 1993c), taking the base value 1 in 1987. The final column of this table shows the ratio of the remittance flow to GDP. It shows that remittances formed a significant share of GDP after 1982. The series starts from 48.1 million 1987 US dollars in 1975, which is about 0.24% of GDP, and reaches a high level in 1983, at 657.6 million 1987 US dollars, worth 5.26% of GDP that year. It seems to have plateaud from then on, in terms of its share of GDP. In this chapter, we interpret this path as showing a permanent positive shock. The flood years 1987–88 did not significantly change this share, which carried on at about the same order of magnitude even afterwards.

Hence, this table suggests a decomposition of the series into four subperiods. From 1975 to 1977, the flow of remittances is negligible, and these years may be called the 'pre-boom' years. After 1983, we find a new steady-state level of remittances, as a share of GNP; 1987 and 1988 should be left aside as the flood years. The years 1978–82 may be called the 'traverse' period, during which the share of remittances in GDP grows from the pre-boom low level to the new steady-state level. Therefore, the analysis in this chapter will focus on the 1978–86 period, comprising two sub-periods: the traverse, up to 1982, and the new steady state, in 1983–86.

Table 22.3 illustrates the importance of the remittance flow for the balance of payments of Bangladesh. It shows the real value of imports, exports and remittances, all deflated by the import price index. Hence, we

Table 22.3. Imports, exports and remittances (*in terms of 1972–73 imports*)

	Imports	Exports	Remittances
1977	491	227	34
1978	800	290	67
1979	745	292	69
1980	1,010	308	90
1981	960	270	144
1982	990	241	163
1983	972	289	264
1984	1,022	357	240
1985	1,214	424	217
1986	1,082	373	266

Source: Mahmud (1989)

can see that remittances cover on average 23.3% of imports during the steady-state period 1983–86, whereas they only covered 6.92% of them in 1977. Moreover, if we compare these data to petroleum imports, we get on average over 1983–86 a ratio of 145.95%. However, this figure should not be interpreted as a sort of partial balance of payments with the oil-exporting countries of the Middle East, since not all the remittances come from that area, and some goods other than oil are also imported from these countries.

Bakht and Mahmood (1989) report on a survey of 306 returning migrants from the Middle East, providing some information on the use of the remittance money. They show a fairly homogenous behaviour, with twelve items accounting for 72.64% of the total money. Among the main items, some are related to physical investment, such as the construction and development of a house (accounting for 19% of the sums), or the purchase of land (15.25%) or a vehicle (3.01%). Others are concerned with building up financial assets, such as saving the money in a fixed bank deposit (9.11%) or the repayment of loans (4.39%). Finally, some uses of the money have a more social value, such as covering the expenses of a wedding (8.86%) or donating money to relatives (2.07%). Hence, in all these cases, we see that returning migrants tend to invest the remittance money in durable assets. It is plausible that an increase in their permanent income follows. Moreover, this survey shows that the use of the money may be slightly different according to the skill category of the migrants. The purchase of land is in any case a major item, claiming 28.23% of the remittance money of the professionals, 32.74% of that of the skilled workers, and 25.26% of that of the unskilled ones. Whereas the professionals and the skilled workers use the largest share of their money to invest in a business (32.08% and 30.25%, respectively), unskilled workers use the largest share of the money for building or developing a house (27.73%). Nevertheless, even unskilled workers may use a large share of their remittances to invest in a business (25.71%).

We now proceed to a counterfactual analysis, in order to estimate the contribution to GNP made by this remittance boom.

22.2.3. Counterfactual Analysis

The aim of the counterfactual analysis is to estimate the contribution of the shock to GNP, by providing a counterfactual path which simulates the series which would have prevailed had the shock not taken place. We apply here the method used in the Kenya template (Chapter 2 in this book), based on a very simple dynamic simulation model which gives a reasonable picture of the contribution of the shock to GNP.

More precisely, we generate recursively the counterfactual paths of GNP and investment with the following two-equation dynamic model:

$$Y_t = Y_t^c + R_t + rS(I_{t-1} - I_{t-1}^c),\tag{22.1}$$

$$I_t^c = vY_t^c.\tag{22.2}$$

In this model, Y_t stands for GNP, I_t stands for investment and the superscript c stands for 'counterfactual'. The remittance flow is denoted R_t, r is the rate of return on investment (net of depreciation) and v is the propensity to invest. The aim of this exercise is to correct the observed GNP figures not only for the value of the external shock (here R_t), but also for the additional investment which this extra income has generated. In this application, we have assumed for the sake of simplicity that $r = 10\%$, and we have taken for v the average value over the 1975–77 period, namely 10.14%. (Note that the investment share of GNP is very low in this country.) The computation with this model starts by assuming that $Y_{t=}Y_t^c$ in 1977. Then the figures reproduced in Table 22.4 are computed recursively using equations (22.1) and (22.2).

The percentage windfall is computed as the ratio of the additional income resulting from the shock, or windfall income, to the level of counterfactual GNP. It thus measures the increase in income owing to the remittance boom. We see in this table that the contribution of the shock builds up progressively during the traverse period, going from 0% in 1977 to 8.62% in 1983. This contribution amounts on average to 7.93% of counterfactual GNP in the steady-state period 1983–86.

This counterfactual analysis leads to the view that the remittance boom in Bangladesh resulted in a permanent increase in income of about 8% from 1983 onwards, with a transitional path lasting five years, when the economy moved from a low-level steady state to a higher-level one. We analyse in what follows the macroeconomic impact of this shock. An

Table 22.4. Actual and counterfactual GNP and investment (*bn. 1987 takas*)

	GNP			Investment	
	Actual	Counterfactual	Windfall (%)	Actual	Counterfactual
Average 1975–77	327.34	327.34	0	33.06	33.06
1977	334.42	334.42	0	37.71	33.73
1978	358.94	353.79	1.46	47.92	35.87
1979	380.15	372.29	2.11	50.02	37.75
1980	385.48	374.88	2.83	70.01	38.01
1981	421.82	401.54	5.05	72.17	40.72
1982	437.48	412.18	6.14	70.65	41.80
1983	457.70	421.36	8.62	56.66	42.73
1984	478.55	441.69	8.35	59.33	44.79
1985	493.37	461.58	6.89	66.92	46.80
1986	513.81	476.45	7.84	61.46	48.31

Source: Computed from World Bank (1993c)

essential element in the determination of this impact is the introduction by the government of the Workers Earnings Scheme, whereby remittances were attracted to the official foreign exchange market by offering a premium over most other sales of currency.

22.3. The Workers Earnings Scheme

The government reacted very fast to the emergence of the remittance flow by creating a sort of second window on the foreign exchange market, in order to attract remittances, at the beginning of 1978. We now describe this system, before discussing its impact on the macroeconomy.

22.3.1. *A* de facto *Dual Exchange Rate System*

Under the WES, migrant workers sending remittances of foreign exchange from abroad received, first, in exchange for their foreign currency, the equivalent amount of takas at the official exchange rate and, second, an entitlement to import selected items of equivalent value (Khan and Hossain 1989). These entitlements were freely transferable, at a price called the premium. This price was determined by a committee consisting of representatives of eight nationalised, private and foreign banks, with the Bangladesh Bank acting only as an observer (IMF 1989). In the absence of intervention by the latter, the premium may thus be regarded as equating supply and demand in this segment of the foreign exchange market (Lewis 1990). At the beginning of the operation of this scheme, in 1977/78, this premium was as high as 31%. The WES exchange rate is thus equal to the official one, augmented by the premium. Table 22.5 presents the official (or 'Principal') exchange rate, the WES (or 'Secondary') exchange

Table 22.5. Official and secondary exchange rates (*takas/US$, annual average*)

	Official	Secondary	Premium	Premium/official (%)
1978	15.12	17.42	2.30	15.21
1979	15.22	20.04	4.82	31.67
1980	15.48	19.30	3.82	24.68
1981	16.34	20.58	4.24	25.95
1982	20.04	22.38	2.34	11.68
1983	23.76	24.57	0.81	3.41
1984	24.95	27.28	2.33	9.34
1985	26.06	28.86	2.80	10.74
1986	29.92	33.11	3.19	10.66

Source: Computed from World Bank (1993b)

rate and the premium. The final column presents the latter as a percentage of the official exchange rate. It can be seen that it is very sizeable, especially during the traverse period. It is only in 1983 that the premium falls significantly below 10% of the official rate.

This scheme was rather successful in attracting remittances; the amount of foreign exchange available under this system became nearly as important as that obtained in return for exports as seen above. Moreover, this scheme provided some flexibility in the import-licensing system, since firms were able to purchase these import entitlements. The share of imports under the WES scheme went from 3% at the beginning up to 20% in the mid-1980s (Khan and Hossain 1989). The government of Bangladesh expanded over time the list of goods covered by the import entitlements.

The importance of this *de facto* dual exchange rate system for the Bangladeshi economy was reinforced by the creation of the Export Performance Licensing system, which became the Export Performance Benefit (XPB) system after 1985. The XPB system is related to the WES system, in that firms exporting non-traditional exports were given, in addition to the taka value of the foreign exchange surrendered, similar import entitlements to those allocated under the WES system, for a fraction of their export value (ranging generally between 40% and 100%). These import entitlements were similarly freely transferable, commanding the same premium as the ones allocated under the WES.

Therefore, the secondary exchange rate may be regarded as a budgetarily neutral way of subsidising exporters of non-traditional exports, as well as protecting the sectors producing the goods substitutable for those covered by the import entitlements. The non-traditional exporters get a subsidy equal to the WES premium rate times the fraction of retained foreign currency from their exports. The latter changed quite often (Lewis 1990; Khan and Hossain 1989), since the government sometimes tried to compensate exporters for some reduction of the premium by increasing this fraction. Moreover, the list of sectors covered by the XPB system was expanded over time, and at the end of the 1980s only primary commodities such as raw jute, raw leather and tea were governed by the official exchange rate. The marginal importers of the goods covered by the import entitlements, who purchase them on the secondary market, are taxed at a rate equal to the premium rate, and this provides some quasi-tariff protection to the producers of substitutable goods. This system is automatically neutral for the budget, and not detrimental for the balance of payments, since the import entitlements are generated by the inflow of remittances and a fraction of the proceeds of non-traditional exports. Therefore, this system offers some automatic support to the prices of certain tradable goods, as a response to the inflow of foreign currency.

22.3.2. An Anti-Dutch Disease Device

It is interesting to analyse the working of this system in the light of the Dutch Disease theory (Corden and Neary 1982). As emphasised by Bevan *et al.* (1991), the theory is better suited to the case of a permanent external shock (such as the remittance boom in Bangladesh) than to the case of a temporary shock. In the Corden and Neary (1982) terminology, a remittance boom of the type experienced by Bangladesh may have a sizeable spending effect, with a negligible resource-movement effect. Therefore, the theoretical prediction in this case is that the shock will be followed by an appreciation of the real exchange rate: given the prices of tradable goods, the prices of non-tradable goods will rise in order to accommodate the increased demand. As a result, the output of the tradables sector will shrink. If there is no externality, this real exchange rate appreciation is optimal, and no policy reaction is required. However, as shown by van Wijnbergen (1984), if a significant level of learning-by-doing occurs in the tradables sector, the latter may require an increased subsidy in the face of a positive external shock.

In the case of Bangladesh, the sectors which have been granted some protection under the dual exchange rate system are precisely those sectors where one would expect quite a lot of learning-by-doing to occur: non-traditional exports, importable manufactured final goods, etc. Primary commodities, where very little learning-by-doing can be expected to be generated, have been left out of the system. The selectivity of this dual exchange rate system thus removes one of the drawbacks of exchange rate protection, as analysed by Corden (1981). Corden shows how the use of a nominal devaluation to prevent the real appreciation of the exchange rate which may result from a resource boom is quite inefficient, since it requires a very strong cut in aggregate demand to be consistent with equilibrium of the non-traded goods market. On the contrary, the use of a tax-cum-subsidy combination might provide the required protection of the tradables sector, with a lower cost in terms of aggregate demand. Hence, the introduction of the dual exchange rate in 1978 may be regarded as a mixture of a nominal devaluation on the one hand, since the new marginal rate, premium included, is higher than the fixed official rate, and a tax-cum-subsidy on the other hand, since the *de facto* rate of devaluation is different for the various sectors. It is a move that concentrates the negative effect of the Dutch Disease on the traditional tradables sectors, while protecting the non-traditional export sectors and the import-substituting ones.

Table 22.6 illustrates roughly this impact, by showing the evolution of the sectoral GDP deflators as ratios of the economy-wide GDP deflator. It shows that the industrial sector was somewhat protected from a Dutch Disease effect, at least until 1984. However, if we consider that technical

Table 22.6. Relative sectoral GDP deflators
($1978 = 100$)

	Agriculture	Industry	Services
1978	100.0	100.0	100.0
1979	102.5	94.4	99.2
1980	98.6	99.4	103.1
1981	93.0	104.3	109.3
1982	91.3	104.1	111.9
1983	92.7	103.6	110.2
1984	97.7	93.7	107.1
1985	103.5	89.6	101.2
1986	98.1	92.1	107.5

Source: Computed from World Bank (1993b)

progress is usually faster in industry than in the other sectors (Balassa 1964; Azam 1980), then the decline in its GDP deflator after 1984 may not be evidence of a real appreciation. This table also shows that the agricultural sector faced negative protection over most of the period, except in 1985, as predicted from the discussion above. The third column shows that the increase in the relative price of non-tradables, here represented by the relative GDP deflator of services, was not completely avoided. But, this Dutch Syndrome (Neary 1984) was kept within moderate limits. The maximum real appreciation was below 12% in 1982, neglecting the effect of differential technical progress alluded to above.

Moreover, since the quantity of import entitlements is determined endogenously by the inflow of foreign exchange, this system gives rise to what Bevan *et al.* (1990) call an 'endogenous trade liberalisation'. At the beginning of the boom, in the mid-1970s, imports were subject to extensive quantitative restrictions. There was a positive list of authorised imports. Later, a major step in the process of import liberalisation in the mid-1980s was the switch to a negative list of restricted imports. Therefore, a lot of goods which are intrinsically tradable were in fact turned into non-tradable goods, at least at the margin, by trade restrictions. As the flow of remittances and of eligible export proceeds expanded during the boom, the government expanded the list of the goods covered by the import entitlements. Therefore, many sectors switched from being non-tradable at the margin to being tradables, although they remained protected by the WES premium. Eventually, the gap between the two rates narrowed over time, and became negligible at the beginning of the 1990s. The system was scrapped in 1992, when the foreign exchange market was unified.

In other words, this dual exchange rate system only offered temporary protection to some sectors, which were supposed to promote a lot of learning-by-doing. The rapid expansion of the ready-made garment sector, alluded to above, is probably one of the results of this policy. It might be interpreted as an unusual application of the infant-industry argument: while the inflow of remittances was providing the additional capital required for investment, the WES system offered the temporary protection required for the learning-by-doing process. Moreover, by providing some temporary protection to some importable sectors, when their non-tariff protective barriers were being dismantled, this scheme helped to liberalise imports in a gradual way.

Besides this exchange rate policy, the government reacted to the shock by changing its fiscal policy. This is what we analyse next.

22.4. Public Finance

Faced with such a permanent positive shock, the government has a strong incentive to increase its level of consumption, according to the standard permanent income theory. Similarly, the households who have sent some of their members abroad for a while get a positive shock to their permanent income, insofar as they invest the remittances productively, and should be observed as increasing their consumption level. Similarly, the households who have not yet sent a member abroad, and who are planning to do so, enjoy an increase in their permanent income. The question arises of the borrowing constraint which they might face, preventing them from bringing forward the benefit of the future migration.

In Bangladesh, as in most developing countries, there exists an informal credit market alongside the formal one, which makes the credit constraint story unconvincing (Maloney and Ahmed 1988). However, the study by Bakht and Mahmood (1989) shows that a very small share of the remittance money is in fact lent out in the informal market (less than 5%). Migrants use the remittance money as a substitute for borrowing, and very few of them are prepared to lend it. In other words, although the opening of new opportunities for migrating creates an incentive to consume more now, it does not increase the supply of loanable funds. We can thus expect that the marginal interest rate on the informal market goes up as a response to the shock, making it more costly for households to increase their consumption level. The government is then in a position to help them by cutting taxes. This is, roughly speaking, what we observe during the period under study.

22.4.1. Government Revenues

Table 22.7 presents the series of current government revenues, grants included, from the *World Tables 1992* (World Bank 1993c). The first column

Table 22.7. Current government revenues (*bn. 1987 takas*)

	Actual	Percentage of GNP	Counterfactual	Windfall
1977	48.22	14.42	48.22	0
1978	52.35	14.58	51.02	1.33
1979	52.39	13.78	53.68	−1.29
1980	53.67	13.92	54.06	−0.39
1981	53.90	12.78	57.90	−4.00
1982	68.95	15.76	59.44	9.51
1983	68.72	15.01	60.76	7.96
1984	60.10	12.56	63.69	−3.59
1985	58.69	11.90	66.56	−7.87
1986	66.18	12.88	68.70	−2.52

Source: Computed from World Bank (1993c)

presents the actual data in terms of billions of 1987 takas. The second column shows the share of government revenues in GNP. It shows a slight decline of the tax pressure over time, with an average figure of 14.16% during the traverse period and an average rate of 13.09% in the steady-state period 1983–86. The third column represents the counterfactual value of these current government revenues. It is produced by multiplying counterfactual GNP, presented above, by the average tax rate for 1977, namely 14.42%. The final column presents windfall government revenue, defined as the difference between actual and counterfactual government revenues.

This table shows that the tax effort did not keep pace with the boom, since we observe an increasingly negative level of windfall as time unfolds. Some of the potential increase in government revenues was actually handed over to the private sector as a reduction in the tax pressure. In fact, government consumption increased faster than income, as shown below.

22.4.2. Government Expenditures and Saving

Table 22.8 shows government consumption. The first column represents the actual series, in billions of 1987 takas. The second one shows its share of GNP, and it is readily observable that it increased over time, going from nearly 5% in 1978 to more than 8% in 1986. The third column reproduces the counterfactual level of government consumption. It is computed by multiplying counterfactual GNP, presented above, by the share of government consumption in GNP in 1977, namely 5.07%. In other words, this column shows what the level of government consumption would have been had the boom not occurred and had the share of government consumption in GNP remained constant after 1977. The final column presents

Table 22.8. Government consumption (*bn. 1987 takas*)

	Actual	Percentage of GNP	Counterfactual	Windfall
1977	16.94	5.07	16.94	0
1978	17.39	4.84	17.94	−0.55
1979	23.78	6.26	18.88	4.90
1980	24.25	6.29	19.01	5.24
1981	28.03	6.65	20.36	7.67
1982	31.04	7.10	20.90	10.14
1983	25.98	5.68	21.36	4.62
1984	31.30	6.54	22.39	8.91
1985	36.33	7.36	23.40	12.93
1986	42.31	8.23	24.16	18.15

Source: Computed from World Bank (1993c)

Table 22.9. Government saving behaviour (*bn. 1987 takas*)

	Actual	Percentage of government revenue	Counterfactual	Windfall
1977	31.28	64.87	31.28	0
1978	34.96	66.78	33.08	1.88
1979	28.60	54.60	34.81	−6.21
1980	29.42	54.83	35.05	−5.63
1981	25.88	48.00	37.54	−11.66
1982	37.91	54.99	38.54	−0.63
1983	42.74	62.20	39.40	3.34
1984	28.80	47.92	41.30	−12.50
1985	22.36	38.10	43.16	−20.80
1986	23.87	36.07	44.55	−22.68

Source: Computed from World Bank (1993c)

the series of windfall government consumption, defined as the difference between actual and counterfactual government consumption. Hence, according to these calculations, the government responded to the permanent increase in GNP entailed by the remittance boom by increasing significantly its level of current consumption.

Since the level of government current revenue did not keep pace with income, while the level of current government consumption grew faster than GNP, government savings decreased over this period. This is confirmed by Table 22.9.

The first column measures the actual level of government saving, computed as the difference between current government revenue and current government consumption. The second column shows this series as a ratio to the level of government revenue. The fall in the government saving effort shows up quite clearly from this series. Roughly speaking, between 1978 and 1986, the government goes from saving two-thirds of its revenue to saving only one-third. The next column shows counterfactual government saving, computed as above by assuming that it is a constant fraction of counterfactual GNP (9.35%). The final column of this table shows windfall government saving, defined as the difference between actual and counterfactual government saving. It can be seen that it is negative over most of the period, and increasingly so over time.

This gradual fall in government saving as a response to the remittance boom raises a problem of interpretation. If one applies to government behaviour a simple version of the Friedmanite permanent income theory, as suggested above, then one would expect no permanent change in the saving propensity as a response to a potential permanent increase in revenue. Hence, government saving should go down during the traverse period, as consumption responds to the increased permanent income before observed income increases, but should eventually return to a constant fraction of revenues in the new steady state. We observe just the contrary, with the government reducing its effort both at collecting taxes and at saving revenues. A potential explanation along neoclassical lines would observe that workers' outmigration is a less capital-intensive method of producing income than goods production, so that less investment is required in the long run, relative to GNP. However, such an explanation does not square easily with the observed increase in global investment which occurred during the boom, shown in Table 22.2.

Another potential explanation has to do with the supply of loanable funds to the government of Bangladesh: as the inflow of foreign currency increases, the financially constrained government is offered more external financing, since it is perceived as offering better collateral. This type of behaviour, where the government amplifies the boom by increasing its borrowing abroad, largely supply-determined, is fairly frequent in the cases of external shocks. In the case of Bangladesh, the problem is compounded by aid, which finances most of the current account deficit. Hence, public expenditures are to some extent aid-driven, and the observed increase in government consumption might result from an increase in aid.

22.4.3. The Aid Flow

Table 22.10 shows that this is indeed the case, during the period under study. The first column shows the current account deficit, deflated by the import price index (1987 = 100). The second column shows the amount of aid disbursement, measured in the same units. We may notice that it is

Table 22.10. Current account deficit and aid disbursement (*in terms of 1987 imports*)

	Current account deficit	Aid disbursement	Share of loans in aid (%)
1977	614.3	747.4	52.3
1978	978.6	1,048.9	52.9
1979	863.6	1,070.7	51.3
1980	1,267.1	1,079.5	46.8
1981	1,240.0	995.2	48.2
1982	1,474.1	1,147.8	47.3
1983	1,040.8	1,115.9	50.1
1984	901.2	1,206.9	42.1
1985	1,322.3	1,274.6	44.7
1986	1,169.5	1,408.4	26.3

Sources: World Bank (1993b,c)

often larger than the deficit itself. The final column shows the share of loans in aid disbursement. We see that it is roughly constant, showing maybe a slight decline over time. If we regard the latter as significant, it suggests that aid became more and more concessionary over time, as if the government was in fact less and less willing to accept loans. This would reveal that government consumption behaviour was more and more driven by the supply of grants. Hence, the puzzling government consumption behaviour spotted above might be the result of some 'aid-pushing' by donors. But the evidence in support of this interpretation is not very strong.

To sum up, the government of Bangladesh reduced fiscal pressure over the period 1977–86, while increasing government consumption and reducing government saving. This has been supported by increased aid; the flow of aid disbursement has nearly doubled in real terms over this decade.

It is interesting to recall some elements of Bangladesh political history, in order to shed some light on these moves. At independence in 1971, the Awami League was ruling the country, under the leadership of Sheikh Mujibur Rahman. It had definite socialist leanings, and a lot of firms were nationalised at independence. This was partly due to the fact that a lot of firms had been left by fleeing Pakistani owners (Mallon and Stern 1991), but it squared very well with government ideology. The government developed further the plethora of controls inherited from Pakistani rule. For example, in 1973 it set a limit of Tk. 2.5 million on private sector investment, in effect limiting it to the small- and cottage-industry sector. By 1974, 62% of manufacturing sector output was in the hands of the government (Mallon and Stern 1991). President Mujibur Rahman was assassinated in 1975, after he had declared illegal all political parties other than the Awami League. Martial law was then declared.

After a series of coups, Major-General Zia ur-Rahman was called to the presidency in 1977, and won the elections the year after. His party, the Bangladesh Nationalist Party (BNP), won the general elections in 1979. (The BNP is a moderate, pro-market party which returned to power after the 1991 democratic elections. President Zia's widow, Begum Khaleda Zia, then became Prime Minister.) Under President Zia, the government switched to a more favourable policy towards the private sector and the industrial sector. Private investment was supported, and many firms were privatized.

President Zia ur-Rahman was assassinated in 1981, and Lt.-Gen. Ershad took over in 1982, after a short Presidency by Addus Sattar, a member of the BNP. His moderate Jatiyo Party, founded in 1983, won the 1986 general elections, boycotted by the BNP. President Ershad launched a stabilisation programme in 1983, based on demand management, with a cut in public investment, and an active exchange rate policy. However, Table 22.10 shows that this did not trigger a massive change in the trend in aid disbursement. Many jute mills and cotton mills were then returned to the private sector, showing the pro-market leaning of the government.

Hence, during most of our period of analysis, Bangladesh was ruled under martial law, by pro-market presidents who gradually dismantled the control regime of the earlier period. This may explain why the tax pressure was cut gradually. But government consumption went up, probably driven by foreign aid. It is not possible to ascertain whether the upward trend of foreign aid was the result of the policy reforms. But one can observe that on average the level of aid disbursement was higher in 1978–83 (under Zia) than in 1977, and higher in 1983–86 (under Ershad) than in 1978–83. In real terms, the average figures are 1,068.42 for 1978–82, and 1,251.45 for 1983–86 (17.1% up). These figures do not contradict the view that the aid-driven growth of government consumption was partly the result of the government's visible pro-market ideology.

22.5. Private Sector Response

In this section we analyse private saving behaviour as a residual, as the difference between aggregate saving and government saving.

22.5.1. Private Saving

Table 22.11 is built along the same principles as the preceding ones. It shows that the aggregate saving behaviour of the Bangladeshi economy was like that of its government, namely a reduction in the saving effort as

Table 22.11. Private savings behaviour (*bn. 1987 takas*)

	Actual	Percentage of GNP	Counterfactual	Windfall	Private windfall
1977	21.90	6.55	21.90	0	0
1978	8.72	2.43	23.17	−14.45	−16.33
1979	9.85	2.59	24.38	−14.53	−8.32
1980	14.72	3.82	24.55	−9.83	−4.20
1981	26.00	6.16	26.30	−0.30	11.36
1982	17.04	3.90	27.00	−9.96	−9.33
1983	25.42	5.56	27.60	−2.18	−5.52
1984	27.17	5.68	28.93	−1.76	10.74
1985	23.61	4.79	30.23	−6.62	14.18
1986	27.96	5.44	31.21	−3.25	19.43

Sources: Computed from World Bank (1993)

a response to the boom. This is shown by the negative windfall saving figures. However, the last column of the table shows that private saving recovered at the end of this period: windfall private saving became positive during the steady-state period.

22.5.2. Private Consumption Smoothing

In order correctly to interpret these changes, in behavioural terms, it is useful to compute windfall private consumption. From the GNP data presented in Table 22.4 and the government revenue data presented in Table 22.7, we can compute an actual and a counterfactual series of disposable income. Then, a figure for windfall disposable income can be computed as the difference between the two, and is presented as the first column of Table 22.12. The increase in disposable income is due both to the remittance boom and to the tax cuts, as seen above. Then, windfall private consumption can be computed as the difference between windfall disposable income and windfall private saving, presented in Table 22.11. This yields the second column of Table 22.12. The final column is the ratio of the two, showing the propensity to consume windfall disposable income.

Examination of this table suggests that on average the results are in agreement with the usual type of permanent income theory. During the traverse period, the representative private consumer brings forward the expected increase in income, for consumption-smoothing reasons. He then has a windfall consumption level above his windfall income, with an average propensity to consume windfall income of 200% over the period 1978–82. When the new steady state is reached, permanent income

Table 22.12. Private consumption behaviour

	Windfall disposable income	Windfall private consumption	Propensity to consume
1978	3.82	20.15	5.27
1979	9.15	17.47	1.91
1980	10.99	15.19	0.72
1981	24.28	12.92	0.53
1982	15.79	25.12	1.59
1983	28.38	33.90	1.19
1984	40.45	29.71	0.73
1985	39.66	25.48	0.64
1986	39.68	20.25	0.51

Sources: Computed from Tables 22.4, 22.6 and 22.10

Table 22.13. Money and inflation

	M_1/GNP (%)	Inflation rate (CPI) (%)
1978	3.76	5.25
1979	4.50	14.68
1980	4.87	13.53
1981	5.15	16.17
1982	5.28	12.45
1983	6.92	9.45
1984	8.85	10.55
1985	9.30	10.63
1986	9.65	11.07

Source: Computed from World Bank, *World Tables 1991*

becomes closer to observed income, and the propensity to consume returns to a normal level. The propensity to consume windfall income then becomes on average 76% for the period 1983–86. We thus find here a clear example of forward-looking consumption-smoothing behaviour, as predicted by most modern theories of consumer behaviour.

22.5.3. *Demand for Money*

The demand for money increased considerably in Bangladesh over this period, despite some positive inflation. This can be seen from Table 12.13. This is probably the result of the increase in permanent income, as well as the effect of some diversification of the economy.

The monetary policy pursued over this period by the government of Bangladesh has been criticised by the World Bank (World Bank 1988).

Basically, the Bangladeshi financial sector was then typical of the financial repression going on in most LDCs. The level and structure of interest rates were regulated by the government, and some credit rationing was required to clear the market. The rationing scheme was based on priority allocation to some favoured sectors, within an overall industrial policy. But the stance of monetary policy was somewhat expansionary overall (World Bank 1988). As a share of GDP, credit outstanding to the private sector went from 8.7% in 1978 to 16.7% in 1987. This is probably the reason for the above-10% rate of inflation seen in Table 22.13. However, this is pretty low by modern standards for an LDC.

22.6. Conclusion

Bangladesh benefited at the end of the 1970s from a remittance boom. This was a permanent positive shock, giving rise to a permanent increase in income of about 8%. The government played a part in initiating the boom, by temporarily using its Manpower Bureau as a recruiting agent. It also had an institutional reaction to the boom which played a part in implementing a transition between the heavily controlled economy of the early days of independence and the more liberal economy which developed from the mid-1980s on. It is a rare example of a government which have used an external shock as a stepping-stone in a reform programme. In the African context, examples abound of governments which have used a boom to expand the government grip over the economy, as illustrated by the case of Sénégal (Chapter 7 in this book).

The government created the Workers Earnings Scheme (WES) and the Export Performance Benefit (XPB), which formed a *de facto* dual exchange rate system, in order to attract the inflow of remittances to the official foreign exchange market, and to use the proceeds for helping to modernise its economy. Exporters of non-traditional exports and producers of import-substitutable goods were given some implicit subsidy or were granted some protection. Moreover, this scheme was budgetarily neutral by construction. As a result, it seems that there was an accelerated development of the manufacturing sector, and in particular of the garments industry, which became a major exporter within five years, starting from scratch. This was accompanied by a private investment boom.

However, saving behaviour did not follow the same pattern. The government did not increase its revenues in line with GNP, although it increased its consumption even faster than GNP. As a result, there was in fact a fall in saving. This illustrates that in an open economy, the saving and investment process can be split, with the latter responding mainly to profit opportunities, such as those opened by the dual exchange rate system, and the former often being dominated by financial constraints, such as increased collateral leading to increased borrowing. Moreover, in Bangladesh, the increase in government consumption was partly fuelled by foreign aid. It is plausible that the doubling of aid disbursement over the decade analysed here resulted from the government's move towards a more liberal economy. This led paradoxically to an expansion of the size of the government in terms of current expenditures.

NOTE

1. This dramatic episode played a large part in shaping the new ideas about poverty and famines which evolved in the 1980s. It helped economists abandon the 'Food Availability Decline' (FAD) approach to famines, in favour of the 'Entitlement Approach' (Sen 1981), since this famine occurred while the rice crop reached record levels.

REFERENCES

Azam, J.-P. (1980) 'The Slow Economic Growth of the UK Since the Second World War: A Comparison with France', Ph. D. thesis, London School of Economics: London (unpublished).

Bakht, F. and R.A. Mahmood (1989) *Overseas Remittances and Informal Financing in Bangladesh*, Research Report No.101, Bangladesh Institute of Development Studies: Dhaka.

Balassa, B. (1964) 'The Purchasing Power Parity Doctrine: A Reappraisal', *Journal of Political Economy*, 72, 584–96.

Bevan, D., P. Collier and J.W. Gunning (1990) *Controlled Open Economies: A Neo-Classical Approach to Structuralism*, Clarendon Press: Oxford.

Bevan, D., P. Collier and J.W. Gunning (1991) 'The Macroeconomics of External Shocks', in V.N. Balasubramaniam and S. Lall (eds) *Current Issues in Development Economics*, 91–117, Macmillan: Basingstoke.

Brajard, N. (1991) 'A Study of Garments Industry in Bangladesh: Its Role as a factor of Economic Development', report to the Indosuez Bank (Dhaka), CERDI: Clermont-Ferrand.

Corden, W.M. (1981) 'Exchange Rate Protection', in R.N. Cooper (ed) *The International Monetary System Under Flexible Exchange Rates: Global, Regional, and National*, Ballinger: Cambridge.

Corden, W.M. and J.P. Neary (1982) 'Booming Sector and De-Industrialisation in a Small Open Economy', *Economic Journal*, 92, 825–48.

Edwards, S. (1988) 'Terms of Trade, Tariffs, and Labor Market Adjustment in Developing Countries', *World Bank Economic Review*, 2, 165–85.

Hossain, M. (1989) 'Food Aid, Development and Food Security', in Bangladesh Planning Commission, *Food Strategies in Bangladesh*, 159–75, University Press Limited: Dhaka.

——(1990) 'Natural Calamities, Instability in Production, and Food Policy in Bangladesh', *Bangladesh Development Studies*, 28, 33–52.

IMF (1989) 'Bangladesh: Recent Economic Developments', IMF: Washington, DC (unpublished).

Khan, A.R. and M. Hossain (1989) *The Strategy of Development in Bangladesh*, Macmillan: Basingstoke.

Lewis, J.D. (1990) 'The Macroeconomics of Policy Reform: Experiments with a CGE Model of Bangladesh', *Bangladesh Development Studies*, 18, 1–35.

Mahmud, W. (1989) 'The Impact of Overseas Labour Migration on the Bangladesh Economy: A Macro-Economic Perspective', in R. Amjad (ed.) *To the Gulf and Back: Studies on the Economic Impact of Asian Labour Migration*, 55–93, ILO-ARTEP: New Dehli.

Mallon, R.D. and J.J. Stern (1991) 'The Political Economy of Trade and Industrial Economy Reform in Bangladesh', in D. Perkins and M. Roemer (eds.) *Reforming Economic Systems in Developing Countries*, 189–218, HIID: Cambridge, Mass.

Maloney, C. and A.B. Sharfuddin Ahmed (1988) *Rural Savings and Credit in Bangladesh*, University Press Limited: Dhaka.

Neary, J.P. (1984) 'Real and Monetary Aspects of the "Dutch Disease"', in D.C. Hague and K. Jugenfeld (eds) *Structural Adjustment in Developed Open Economies*, London: Macmillan.

Ravallion, M. (1987) *Markets and Famines*, Clarendon Press: Oxford.

Sen, A. (1981) *Poverty and Famines*, Clarendon Press: Oxford.

Stahl, C.W. and A. Habib (1989) 'The Impact of Overseas Workers' Remittances on Indigenous Industries: Evidence from Bangladesh', *Developing Economies*, 27, 269–85.

Stark, O. (1991) *The Migration of Labour*, Basil Blackwell: Oxford.

van Wijnbergen, S. (1984) 'The "Dutch Disease": A Disease after all?', *Economic Journal*, 94, 41–56.

World Bank (1985) *World Development Report 1985*, World Bank: Washington, DC.

——(1988) 'Bangladesh: Adjustment in the Eighties and Short-Term Prospects', Report No. 7105-BD, World Bank: Washington, DC.

——(1993a) World Development Report 1993, World Bank: Washington, DC.

——(1993b) 'Bangladesh Implementing Structural Reform', Report No. 11569-BD, World Bank: Washington, DC.

——(1993c) World Tables 1992, World Bank: Washington, DC.

23

An Evaluation of the 1979–85
Petroleum Boom in Malaysia

DAVID GREENAWAY AND SUBRAMANIAM S. PILLAY

23.1. Introduction

Malaysia is a rapidly developing nation in Southeast Asia that is poised to join the ranks of the Newly Industrialising Countries (NICs) of Asia. It comprises the eleven states of Peninsular Malaysia and the two Borneo states of Sabah and Sarawak. Peninsular Malaysia, which is separated from the Borneo states by the South China Sea over a distance of about 800 km, has a land area of 131,598 km², which is close to 40% of the total land area of 329,758 km². Sabah and Sarawak have an area of 73,711 km² (22%) and 124,449 km² (38%) respectively. The population is more heavily concentrated in Peninsular Malaysia, with more than 82% of the 1990 population of 17.8 million living there.

The country has in general enjoyed steady economic growth with low inflation since it gained its independence from the United Kingdom in 1957. Table 23.1 shows the basic macroeconomic indicators for the period 1970–90. At the time of independence, its export-oriented economy depended very much on the production and export of two primary commodities, tin and rubber. By 1980 it had successfully diversified its exports, so that although its economy was still dependent on primary commodities, the dependence was more evenly spread among petroleum, palm oil, timber, rubber and tin. In addition, the manufacturing sector has been playing an increasingly important role in terms of its share in both GDP and in total exports. Owing to major structural changes in the economy, especially during the latter half of the 1980s, the manufacturing sector's role in the Malaysian economy has now become more dominant. Manufacturing exports constituted about 60% of total exports in 1991 compared to only 12% and 21% in 1970 and 1980, respectively.

Petroleum exports became significant only after 1975, following the first oil shock. Given the diversified nature of the Malaysian economy, at no time did petroleum exports exceed 29% of total gross exports, as can be seen from Figure 23.1. Yet they played a crucial role in the balance of payments and public finances of Malaysia, especially between 1975 and

Table 23.1. Selected economic indicators

	Real GDP growth	Total GDP (RM m.)	Proportion of GDP %					
			Construction	Mining	Manufacturing	Agriculture	Government	Others
1970		10,708	4.5	5.7	12.2	32.1	7.4	38.1
1971	8.2	11,589	4.7	5.7	12.4	31.2	7.5	38.6
1972	9.4	14,238	4.0	6.2	14.4	29.1	12.1	34.2
1973	11.7	15,904	4.1	5.4	15.8	29.1	11.4	34.3
1974	8.3	17,227	4.2	4.6	16.1	28.8	12.0	34.4
1975	0.8	17,365	3.8	4.6	16.4	27.7	12.7	34.9
1976	11.6	19,373	3.7	4.9	17.4	27.8	12.5	33.6
1977	7.8	20,875	3.8	4.6	17.9	26.4	13.0	34.2
1978	6.6	37,886	4.1	10.3	19.0	25.1	10.8	30.6
1979	9.3	41,428	4.3	11.1	19.3	24.3	10.6	30.5
1980	7.4	44,512	4.6	10.1	19.6	22.9	10.3	32.5
1981	6.9	47,602	5.0	9.0	19.2	22.4	11.9	32.5
1982	5.9	50,430	5.2	9.2	19.2	22.6	12.0	32.0
1983	6.3	53,582	5.4	10.0	19.5	21.1	11.8	32.3
1984	7.8	57,741	5.2	10.5	20.3	20.1	11.8	32.1
1985	−1.1	57,093	4.8	10.5	19.7	20.8	12.2	32.0
1986	1.2	57,751	4.1	11.0	21.0	21.4	12.6	30.0
1987	5.4	60,863	3.4	10.5	22.6	21.7	12.4	29.4
1988	8.9	66,303	3.2	10.3	24.4	21.0	11.8	29.4
1989	9.2	72,405	3.3	10.2	25.5	20.4	11.3	29.3
1990	9.7	79,430	3.6	9.7	26.9	18.6	10.8	30.4

Source: Treasury Economic Reports, various years

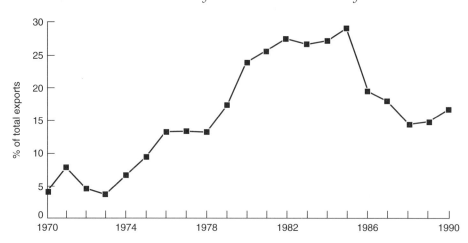

Figure 23.1. Petroleum exports from Malaysia, 1970–90

1985. The world oil market has been subject to three marked price shocks over the post-war period: 1973–74, 1979–80 and 1991. This chapter examines the economic impact of the 1979–80 petroleum price shock on the Malaysian economy. The study is organised as follows. In the next section we examine the nature of the trade shocks caused by petroleum price changes. In Section 23.3, we will examine how the savings and investment behaviour of the public and private sectors was affected by these shocks. Section 23.4 focuses on the impact on the shock on the relative price of tradables and non-tradables and Section 23.5 assesses the changes in the policy environment. Finally, Section 23.6 concludes.

23.2. The Nature of the 1979–80 Petroleum Shock

Petroleum-related trade shocks in Malaysia during the 1970s and 1980s were caused by sharp changes in prices as well as in the quantity of output. Figure 23.2, which is based on Table 23.2, shows the price, production and export revenues of petroleum for the period 1970–90. Two distinct price shocks occurred; the first occurred in 1973/74, when the export unit value index (EUVI) for petroleum quadrupled from 100.0 in 1972 to 408.3 in 1974. This increased price was maintained until 1978. As can be seen more clearly in Figure 23.3, beginning in 1979, there was another round of price hikes induced by the disruption to the petroleum market associated with the Iranian revolution. This led to the EUVI reaching a peak of 1,302 in 1981, that is, 13 times higher than the price in 1972! In 1986 global excess supply meant that prices dropped to half the level of 1985. At 544, the price index in 1986 came almost back to the 1978/79 price level.

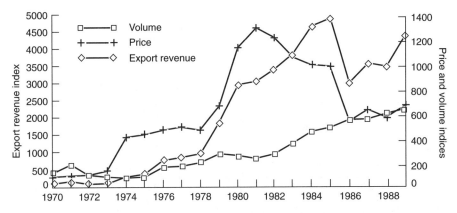

Figure 23.2. Petroleum price volume, and export revenue trends for Malaysia, 1970–89 (*1972 = 100*)

Table 23.2. Petroleum exports, 1970–89

	Total exports (RM m.)	Oil and gas exports Gross (000 t)	(RM/t)	(RM m.)	(%)	Export volume index	Export price index	Export revised index
1970	5,163.1	4,696.2	43.1	202.6	3.9	110.4	82.3	90.9
1971	5,016.8	7,926.7	49.2	389.9	7.8	186.3	93.9	174.8
1972	4,854.0	4,255.3	52.4	223.0	4.6	100.0	100.0	100.0
1973	7,372.1	3,826.9	70.3	269.2	3.7	89.9	134.2	120.7
1974	10,194.7	3,168.0	214.0	677.8	6.6	74.4	408.3	303.9
1975	9,230.9	3,794.5	226.9	861.0	9.3	89.2	433.0	386.1
1976	13,442.0	7,217.6	244.6	1,765.1	13.1	169.6	466.7	791.5
1977	14,959.2	7,722.7	258.8	1,998.6	13.4	181.5	493.9	896.2
1978	17,073.9	9,152.9	245.5	2,247.0	13.2	215.1	468.5	1,007.6
1979	24,222.0	12,034.5	350.1	4,213.5	17.4	282.8	668.2	1,889.5
1980	28,171.6	11,226.9	597.3	6,706.1	23.8	263.8	1,139.9	3,007.2
1981	27,109.4	10,143.2	682.4	6,921.4	25.5	238.4	1,302.2	3,103.8
1982	28,108.2	11,973.9	642.6	7,694.2	27.4	281.4	1,226.3	3,450.3
1983	32,771.2	15,575.0	558.7	8,702.0	26.6	366.0	1,066.3	3,902.2
1984	38,646.9	19,955.4	526.8	10,512.4	27.2	469.0	1,005.3	4,714.1
1985	38,016.7	21,090.3	521.5	10,997.9	28.9	495.6	995.2	4,931.8
1986	35,318.6	23,988.0	285.4	6,846.9	19.4	563.7	544.7	3,070.4
1987	45,224.9	24,013.0	338.1	8,117.9	18.0	564.3	645.2	3,640.3
1988	55,260.0	26,017.0	305.6	7,952.0	14.4	611.4	583.3	3,565.9
1989	67,824.5	27,801.0	358.2	9,958.0	14.7	653.3	683.6	4,465.5

Source: Treasury Report, various years

The changes in export revenues shown in Figure 23.4 are even more striking. At its peak in 1985, the export revenue from petroleum products was almost 50 times that in 1972. This was largely due to the interaction of the price increases discussed above and a more permanent increase in the

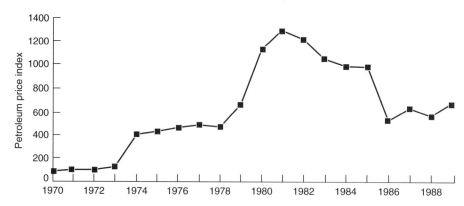

Figure 23.3. Petroleum price trend for Malaysia, 1970–89 (*1972 = 100*)

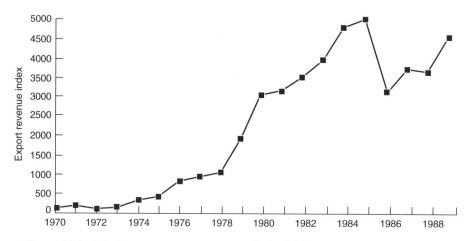

Figure 23.4. Petroleum export revenue trends for Malaysia, 1970–89 (*1972 = 100*)

quantity of petroleum that was produced and exported. As can be seen in Figure 23.5, the volume of exports increased steadily, from about 4 million tonnes in the early 1970s to 30 million tonnes in 1991. This was largely due to new discoveries, particularly in Peninsular Malaysia, and the subsequent development of oil and gas deposits from 1975.

When the first oil shock took place, Malaysia's oil exports were just marginally higher than its imports. Hence the net impact of the price increase was not very significant. All of Malaysia's crude oil was produced in the Borneo state of Sarawak. The increase in the price of petroleum gave a big boost to exploration, particularly in the off-shore areas of Sarawak and Sabah as well as the east coast of peninsular Malaysia. New discoveries and development meant that, by the time the second oil shock

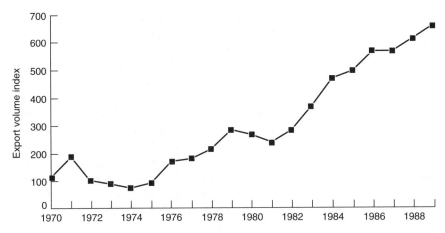

Figure 23.5. Petroleum export volume trend for Malaysia, 1970–89 *(1972 = 100)*

took place, petroleum production and exports had become significant in the Malaysian economy. In 1974, the export of petroleum amounted to 3.17 million tonnes, which constituted 6.6% of total exports; in 1978, the corresponding figures were 9.2 million tonnes and 13.2%, respectively. With the second oil shock petroleum had become the most important export commodity, overtaking the more traditional export rubber. The second oil shock began in mid-1979 and lasted until 1985. As Figure 23.3 shows, the prices after the shock were almost back to the pre-shock 1978 price. We focus only on the second oil shock: at the time of the first, oil was relatively unimportant; by the time of the second it was sufficiently important to be expected to exert a significant impact on economic activity.

The studies reviewed by Bevan *et al.* (1993) show some diversity of private and public sector responses, depending upon the destination of the windfall gains and perception with respect to whether the shock was temporary or permanent. As we shall see the oil industry is largely in public ownership. Thus we need to evaluate its impact primarily by reference to the effects on government revenue and expenditure. The evolution of expenditure gives a fairly clear indication of government perceptions as to the nature of the shock. However, we also have some interesting explicit price expectations. The Malaysian government produces a regular five-year plan which contains price forecasts for the principal primary exports. The Third Malaysia Plan, published in 1975, assumes no change in petroleum prices for the period 1976–80, indicating that the 1973–75 shock was seen as a once-and-for-all upward adjustment (Malaysia 1976: 133). Of course, oil prices subsequently showed a real increase, albeit a modest one, between 1975 and 1980. The shock which is the focus of this paper dates from 1979. One year after the beginning of the shock the Fourth Malaysia Plan appeared. This assumes a continued real increase in oil prices until 1985, implying a belief that the boom was seen as permanent. To quote the plan, 'The export volume of crude oil is projected to increase by 3.0% per annum. With an increase in the export price of 16.0% per annum, the export receipts are expected to increase by 19.5% per annum' (Malaysia 1981: 314). This projection was vastly overoptimistic. In reality, the export volume increased by 8.3% per annum, export price decreased by 2.5% per annum and export receipts increased by only 5.5% per annum (Malaysia 1986: 47). When the Fifth Malaysia Plan was published in 1985, a combination of supply expansion and demand contraction had led to a sharp fall in petroleum prices. This translated into an assumed continued fall through until 1990. 'With the decline in the average price of crude oil, the price of liquid natural gas is expected to decline at a rate of 8.7% per annum' (Malaysia 1986: 421).

Two things stand out. First, the implicit mechanism which is evidently being followed by the government is a fairly naïve expectations process—one which extrapolates the most recent experience/shock. Second, because the second shock came behind a real increase in prices, it was assumed that this was in effect a change in slope rather than an intercept and, therefore, that the boom was permanent rather than temporary. This being so, what was the order of magnitude of the windfall and how was it used?

23.3. Responses to the Windfall

Table 23.3 shows the computation of the counterfactuals and the windfall in export revenues. In constructing the counterfactual price, we have extrapolated linearly between the actual price in the pre-shock year (1978) and the post shock year (1986). We have also assumed that the volume of petroleum exports would have been the same in both cases since short-run supply elasticities are low for capital-intensive extractive industries like the petroleum industry. Decisions to develop the oil wells would have been made before 1979. The windfall amounts to RM 28.4 billion at current prices and RM 20.7 billion in 1978 real prices. The latter is equivalent to 121% of 1978 total exports and 54% of 1978 GDP.

If this windfall had been converted into permanent income, using a 10% discount rate, the present value of the boom in 1979 would have been RM 13,745 million. Again using 10% rate of return, this implies a permanent income increase of RM 1,375 million, which is equivalent to 3.6% of 1978 GDP.

Like most oil boom cases, almost all the windfall accrued to the public sector, since all property rights to oil and gas fields have been assigned to the national petroleum company (Petronas) by an act of parliament.

Table 23.3. Actual and counterfactual petroleum exports, 1979–85

	Total exports (RM m.)	Oil and gas exports				Counterfactual		Windfall (RM m.)	Windfall (as % of total expenditure)	Windfall (as % of GDP)	Windfall (in 1978 Prices)
		Gross (000 t)	(RM/t)	(RM m.)	(%)	Price (RM/t)	Exports (RM m.)				
1978	17,073.9	9,152.9	245.5	2,247.0	13.2	245.5	2,247.0	0.0			
1979	24,222.0	12,034.5	350.1	4,213.5	17.4	250.5	3,014.5	1,199.0	5.0	2.6	1,109.2
1980	28,171.6	11,226.9	597.3	6,706.1	23.8	255.5	2,868.2	3,837.9	13.6	7.2	2,989.0
1981	27,109.4	10,143.2	682.4	6,921.4	25.5	260.5	2,641.9	4,279.5	15.8	7.4	2,905.3
1982	28,108.2	11,973.9	642.6	7,694.2	27.4	265.5	3,178.5	4,515.7	16.1	7.2	3,065.7
1983	32,771.2	15,575.0	558.7	8,702.0	26.6	270.4	4,212.1	4,489.9	13.7	6.4	3,195.7
1984	38,646.9	19,955.4	526.8	10,512.4	27.2	275.4	5,496.2	5,016.2	13.0	6.3	3,674.9
1985	38,016.7	21,090.3	521.5	10,997.9	28.9	280.4	5,914.0	5,083.9	13.4	6.6	3,763.1
1986	35,318.6	23,988.0	285.4	6,846.9	19.4	285.4	6,846.2	0.7			
Sum								28,422.2			20,702.8
NPV											13,745.0

Petronas in turn has entered into production-sharing agreements with oil multinationals such as Shell and Exxon to explore and develop new oil fields.

The government captured the windfall through direct taxes (company tax, petroleum income tax and petroleum royalty) and indirect taxes (export duty on crude petroleum and excise duties on petroleum products). In addition, dividends from fully owned Petronas have become the single largest source of non-tax revenue. According to the central bank of Malaysia, during the 1980s petroleum-based revenues rose to about one-third of federal government revenues, from about one-tenth in the early 1970s. A 'US$1 increase in oil price is estimated to yield an additional RM 100 million in revenue from petroleum income tax, export duty and royalties in the first year and another RM 400 million in the following year' (Bank Negara 1990: 206).

In Table 23.4 we have attempted to compute the share of government revenue directly attributable to petroleum. Since we were unable to get the amounts for income tax and excise duty which originate from petroleum, the total petroleum revenue figure is clearly an underestimate of the actual contribution of petroleum to government revenue. In addition,

Table 23.4. Actual and counterfactual petroleum and government revenue, 1970–88

	Total revenue (RM m.)	Petroleum income taxes (RM m.)	Petroleum royalty (RM m.)	Petroleum export taxes (RM m.)	Total petroleum revenue (RM m.)
1970	2,400	0	0	0	0
1971	2,418	4	0	0	4
1972	2,920	0	23	0	23
1973	3,402	27	25	0	52
1974	4,788	144	46	0	190
1975	5,117	322	78	0	400
1976	6,157	322	84	0	406
1977	7,760	776	111	0	887
1978	8,841	771	116	0	887
1979	10,505	829	160	0	989
1980	13,926	1,736	345	677	2,758
1981	15,806	1,978	417	1,241	3,636
1982	16,690	2,075	425	1,354	3,854
1983	18,608	1,998	491	1,477	3,966
1984	20,805	2,570	581	1,629	4,780
1985	21,114	3,130	619	1,639	5,388
1986	19,518	3,072	246	1,076	4,394
1987	18,143	1,533	0	1,170	2,703
1988	21,967	2,208	0	1,149	3,357

dividends paid by Petronas to the federal government have also been excluded since detailed data were not available. Nevertheless, it is clear that the 1979–85 oil boom has a non-trivial impact on federal revenue. During the three years prior to 1980, the share of petroleum-based revenue was only about 10.3%. In 1980, it doubled to almost 20%. The proportion was maintained above the 20% mark until 1986. With the fall in price in 1986, the revenue, which has a lag of six to twelve months, dropped substantially, from RM 5.4 billion in 1985 to RM 2.7 billion in 1987. The share dropped from 25.5% to 14.9% over the same period.

We have computed the counterfactual petroleum revenue by assuming that its share in the total revenue during the 1980–86 period would have remained at 10.3%, which is the average for 1977 to 1979. Windfall petroleum revenues range from RM 1.48 billion in 1980 to a high of RM 3.58 billion in 1985. The windfall as a percentage of the total revenue ranged from 10.6% to 17.0% of the federal revenue. We have to keep in mind that these estimates understate the true extent of the windfall for the reasons elaborated above.

It is interesting to examine what the government did with this windfall. As we saw in Section 23.2, the government implicitly assumed a

share total revenue	Counterfactual		Windfall government revenue (RM m.)	Windfall (as % of original revenue)	Windfall (as % of GDP)
	Total revenue (RM m.)	Petroleum revenue (RM m.)			
.0					
.2					
.8					
.5					
.0					
.8					
.6					
.4					
.0					
.4					
.8	12,449	1,281	1,477	10.6	2.8
.0	13,566	1,396	2,240	14.2	3.9
.1	14,308	1,472	2,382	14.3	3.8
.3	16,321	1,679	2,287	12.3	3.3
.0	17,863	1,838	2,942	14.1	3.7
.5	17,530	1,804	3,584	17.0	4.6
.5	16,859	1,735	2,659	13.6	3.7
.9					
.3					

Table 23.5. Federal government finances, 1970–90

	Current revenue	Current expenditure	Current Surplus	Development expenditure	Overall surplus	Net external borrowing	Net domestic borrowin
1970	2,400	2,163	237	712	−475	−2	306
1971	2,418	2,398	20	1,070	−1,050	372	677
1972	2,920	3,068	−148	1,223	−1,371	354	836
1973	3,399	3,342	57	1,106	−1,049	69	876
1974	4,791	4,318	473	1,854	−1,381	223	828
1975	5,117	4,900	217	2,118	−1,901	912	1,209
1976	6,157	5,828	329	2,334	−2,005	638	1,636
1977	7,760	7,398	362	3,138	−2,776	269	1,884
1978	8,841	8,041	800	3,699	−2,899	541	1,164
1979	10,505	10,040	465	4,150	−3,685	679	2,508
1980	13,926	13,692	234	7,338	−7,104	310	2,311
1981	15,806	15,686	120	11,135	−11,015	3,419	4,072
1982	16,690	16,672	18	11,189	−11,171	4,894	6,047
1983	18,608	18,374	234	9,417	−9,183	4,569	4,503
1984	20,805	19,806	999	8,074	−7,075	3,093	3,156
1985	21,115	20,066	1,049	6,756	−5,707	965	3,591
1986	19,518	20,075	−557	6,949	−7,506	1,348	4,930
1987	18,143	20,185	−2,042	4,111	−6,153	−2,438	8,693
1988	21,967	21,812	155	4,045	−3,890	−3,095	7,854
1989	25,273	24,832	441	5,701	−5,260	−1,038	2,459
1990	29,521	27,105	2,416	7,932	−5,516	−787	3,816

Source: Treasury Report, various issues

continued increase in oil prices in its planning horizon of 1981 to 1985, as envisaged in the Fourth Malaysia Plan, which was prepared in 1980. What eventually turned out to be a temporary shock was assumed to be a permanent one *ex ante*. So if we examine public sector expenditure over the period, as shown in Figure 23.6 and Table 23.5, the development budget rose sharply with the oil boom in the early 1980s, leading to a large increase in the overall budget deficit. Whereas the overall budget deficit was less that 9% of GDP prior to 1980, in 1980 it rose to 13.3%. In the next year, when oil prices were at their peak, the budget deficit reached a peak of 19.1% of GDP. Obviously, the federal government was not following a counter-cyclical policy.

To finance the budget deficits, the government resorted to external borrowing. As can be seen from Table 23.5, net foreign borrowing increased by more than 11 times in 1981, to RM 3,419 million from RM 310 million the year before.

In looking for the reasons for this behaviour, we have to examine the expectations of government planners. The general policy has been to have a more-or-less balanced current budget, which is quite evident from Figure 23.6. Therefore, the overall budget deficit is determined largely by

The 1979–85 Petroleum Boom in Malaysia   319

Special receipts	Change in assets	Surplus (as % of GDP)	Revenue (as % of GDP)	Total expenditure (as % of GDP)	Current expenditure (as % of GDP)	Development expenditure (as % of GDP)
17	154	−3.9	19.7	23.7	17.8	5.9
40	−39	−8.4	19.3	27.7	19.2	8.6
66	115	−10.1	21.4	31.5	22.5	9.0
13	91	−5.6	18.2	23.8	17.8	5.9
8	322	−6.0	21.0	27.0	18.9	8.1
7	−227	−8.5	22.9	31.4	21.9	9.5
8	−227	−7.1	21.9	29.1	20.8	8.3
10	613	−8.6	24.0	32.6	22.9	9.7
3	1,191	−7.7	23.3	31.0	21.2	9.8
2	496	−7.9	22.6	30.6	21.6	8.9
1	4,482	−13.3	26.1	39.4	25.7	13.8
36	3,288	−19.1	27.4	46.6	27.2	19.3
1	229	−17.9	26.7	44.5	26.6	17.9
4	107	−13.1	26.6	39.7	26.3	13.5
46	780	−8.9	26.2	35.0	24.9	10.1
12	1,148	−7.4	27.3	34.6	25.9	8.7
11	1,117	−10.5	27.3	37.7	28.0	9.7
0	−102	−7.7	22.8	30.5	25.4	5.2
91	−1,160	−4.3	24.2	28.5	24.0	4.5
38	3,601	−5.1	24.6	29.8	24.2	5.6
52	2,435	−4.8	25.5	30.3	23.5	6.9

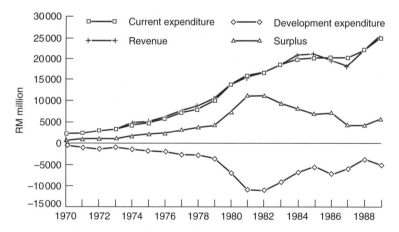

Figure 23.6. Federal government public finance, 1970–89

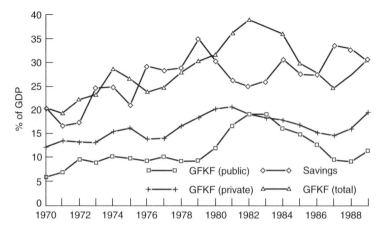

Figure 23.7. Investments and savings in Malaysia, 1970–89

development expenditures. This again is shown clearly in Figure 23.6, where the development expenditure curve is almost a mirror image of the budget deficit curve. If the windfall revenues in the oil boom years of the early 1980s had been perceived as temporary, the government would have more likely saved the windfall. But it perceived the price shocks to be permanent; in fact, it assumed (as is evident in the Fourth Malaysia Plan) that the price would keep increasing. In addition to that, there was easy availability of credit from foreign banks because Malaysia had and still has a very good credit rating. Thus, government spending was increased with expectations that the loans incurred could all be repaid with ever increasing revenues from petroleum and natural gas.

When the oil boom ended in 1985, there was a sharp reversal in policy. Now the expectations were that oil prices would keep falling. Development spending was pruned, so that in 1987 it was only RM 4.1 billion, which is just a third of the 1982 figure. The overall deficit was still very high because of the drop in federal revenues. In fact, 1986 and 1987 were the first years since the formation of Malaysia in 1963 when federal government revenue was lower than in the previous year. This was clearly due to the sharp decline in petroleum prices.

23.4. Changes in the Relative Prices of Tradables and Non-tradables

Construction booms appear to be a common feature of trade shocks in developing countries, especially in the least developed. The mechanism at work is generally one which is triggered by constrained investment

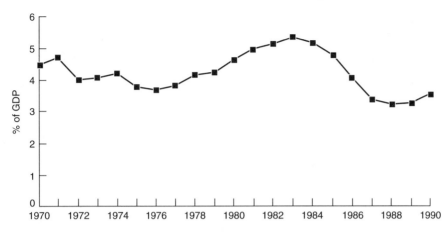

Figure 23.8. Construction sector in Malaysia, 1970–90

options. The presence of pervasive exchange controls pushes private sector agents into the property/land market. This may be reinforced by increased government expenditure.

Two features of the Malaysian case differ from the typical case. First, at least in terms of its primary effects (which is what we are concerned with), the boom was essentially a public sector boom. Petroleum extraction and refining is partly state-owned and extensively regulated. Thus the windfall accrued to the public sector. Second, insofar as the windfall did spill over to the private sector, the absence of exchange controls, together with a rapidly growing manufacturing sector, offered a wide menu of investment opportunities. Nevertheless, if we look at Figure 23.8 we still find evidence of a construction boom. Unfortunately, data are only available for the aggregate output of the construction sector, but they are available on a time-series basis for the period 1970–90. In the year before the petroleum shock, construction accounted for just over 4% of GDP. This increased to almost 5.5% of GDP in 1983, subsequently declining to 4% in 1986. Figure 23.9 reports data on an index of the relative price of non-tradables to tradables constructed from CPI subseries. Between 1975 and 1980 this is stable at around 0.85. In 1981 it increases sharply to 1.00, peaking at 1.15 in 1986, before declining to 1.00 in 1990.

These are classic trade shocks by-products. Given the points made earlier regarding the sectoral impact of the shock, what is driving the increase in construction activity and the associated change in the relative price on non-tradables? Refer again to Figure 23.6. The impact of the petroleum shock on the government budget is very transparent: the increased government revenues feed though the so-called developed budget, which essentially funds public sector capital projects. Over this

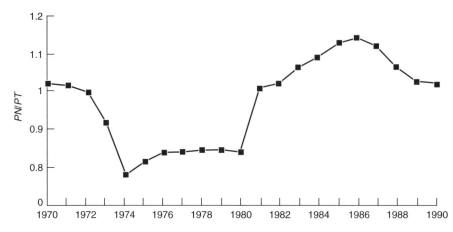

Figure 23.9. Price of non-tradables vs tradables, 1970–90

period the windfall from the petroleum shock was invested in infra-structural improvements. The government followed a balanced budget policy where recurrent expenditures were concerned, as it always has done, but increased expenditure through the capital budget. As it became apparent that the boom was not permanent, development expenditure, much of which was finding its way into the construction sector, also declined.

23.5. Changes in the Policy Environment

We have seen in Section 23.4 that the pattern of fiscal adjustment in Malaysia in response to the shock was distinctive by comparison with the aftermath in many other countries. Fiscal expansion followed by a period of fiscal rectitude meant that the legacy of the shock, in public finance terms, was not a 'negative dowry'. What of trade policy? One of the striking features of trade shocks in developing countries, especially Sub-Saharan Africa, has been an endogenous trade policy. Pre-shock policy is often characterised by a control regime and all of the accoutrements this brings. Adjustment to the shock brings in its wake a trade liberalisation. Against the background of an unsustainable fiscal position, the liberal trade regime turns out to be unsustainable and ultimately the liberalisa-tion is reversed. Was this the case in Malaysia?

    If one looks at Malaysian trade policy post-independence, one can identify three overlapping but ultimately distinct phases. At the time of independence, government intervention was clearly geared to the promo-tion of primary-product exports. This was transformed in the 1960s into a

recognisable programme of import substitution. This in turn was transformed in the 1970s into a policy of export promotion. According to Ariff
(1991) this was actually taking place as early as 1968: 'A radical shift from
an inward looking, defensive industrialisation strategy of import substitution, to an outward looking, aggressive strategy of export promotion took
place after 1968, when it became obvious that import substitution could
no longer provide a viable basis for sustained industrial expansion, given
the small domestic market' (Ariff 1991: 10). Other evaluations date the
transformation less precisely than this. What is clear, however, is that
several important legislative measures were enacted around this time,
with the objective of providing export incentive. The Investment Incentives Act of 1968 offered depreciation allowances and export allowances
as well as a range of fiscal incentives to export-oriented firms. This was
followed in 1971 by the Free Trade Zone Act, which provided a wide
range of investment and fiscal incentives to both indigenous and foreign-
owned firms setting up production facilities targeted at the export market.
This commitment to development of an export base for manufactures was
further reinforced in both the Second and Third Malaysia Plans (1971–75
and 1976–80, respectively).

It is, however, important to note that the provision of export incentives
occurred against the background of an import tariff structure which was
becoming more, rather than less, protectionist. Thus, whereas average
nominal tariffs on import substitutes were 13% in 1965, by 1978 they were
22%. Average effective tariffs, which were 25% in 1965, rose to over 50%
in 1978. However, over the same period, the proportion of manufacturing
industries with negative effective tariffs declined from almost 40% to 13%.
In other words, in the 1970s, the Malaysian trade regime underwent
changes which can be characterised as moving it towards a neutral trade
regime in the sense that relative prices of the output of the two tradables
sectors tends towards unity. This is a regime of the type which characterises for example Korea, rather than a non-interventionist/liberal regime of
the type which characterises Hong Kong. Export promotion has been
dirigiste rather than *laissez faire*.

The petroleum shock did not directly affect trade policy. Indirectly it
did so through the sharp appreciation of the real exchange rate between
1980 and 1984, which put pressure on exporters in general and exports
manufactures in particular. There was, however, no endogenous trade
liberalisation of the sort which has been observed so often elsewhere. The
reason for this is straightforward: Malaysia in the early 1980s did not
exhibit characteristics of a controlled regime. Thus, foreign exchange restrictions were virtually absent and a wide portfolio of assets was available for investment of the windfall (see GATT 1993). Moreover, as we
have seen, one of the defining characteristics of this shock is that, at least
in terms of its initial impact, it was concentrated in the public sector.

Private sector windfalls did contribute to the fuelling of a construction boom. Although there was such a boom, it was driven by public sector expenditure and was neither as marked nor as protracted as many observed elsewhere.

Although, as we noted earlier, we can associate the shift form import substitution to export promotion with particular legislation, that export promotion was of the 'neutrality' variety rather than the free trade variety. Notwithstanding this, it is important to see the evolution of trade policy as a gradual process in the 1980s, but it should also be seen as part of a longer-term evolution, rather than as a response to the petroleum shock. Import tariffs gradually fell from an unweighted average of 22% in 1978 to 14% in 1993, although, as GATT (1993) implies, this latter figure overstates the extent of import liberalisation since, if one takes composite and alternative duties into account, the average tariff is in fact 22%. However, throughout the 1980s, the policy of vigorously promoting exports through the Free Trade Zone policy continued, with much of this being driven by inward investment. As a result, Malaysian exports grew at 13% per annum in real terms between 1983 and 1993.

In summary, then, the trade policy environment was unaffected by the petroleum boom. The policy of export promotion against the background of selective import protection which was initiated in the late 1960s and developed in the 1970s was sustained in the 1980s. The absence of a significant impact on trade policy can be attributed to a number of factors. First, the economy was relatively diversified at the time of the shock; second, at least in terms of primary effect, the shock impacted on the public sector; third, the economy had few of the attributes of a controlled regime, with a side menu of alternative investment options available.

23.6. Conclusions

We have in this chapter evaluated the impact of a petroleum boom in Malaysia, that which followed the Iranian-revolution-induced hike in world oil prices. This was manifestly an externally induced shock and one which was clearly externally generated. Although the Malaysian economy is well diversified, it affected a sector which accounts for over 20% of Malaysian exports. The shock had a very substantial effect on real incomes in Malaysia. The windfall from increased revenues was equivalent to 121% of 1978 exports, and 54% of 1978 GDP. Converted into a permanent income stream, the boom was equivalent to 3.5% of 1978 GDP.

One important characteristic of this very substantial windfall was that it was concentrated, at least initially, in the public sector, owing to the fact that the oil industry is state-owned. Although the government clearly perceived the boom to be permanent in 1978/80, not revising its expectations on this until 1982/83, and although it increased its expenditure, interestingly this went through the development budget rather than the current budget. There was a limited construction boom. This was essentially due to expenditure on infrastructure. This 'boom-stretching' was initiated through public sector investment. As a result, the legacy of the petroleum boom was not the millstone of an unsustainable fiscal deficit as in so many other episodes but rather the bounty of enhanced social capital. In contrast to many other cases the windfall was capitalised in (social) investment goods rather than consumption goods.

REFERENCES

Ariff, M. (1991) *The Malaysian Economy*, Oxford, Oxford University Press.
Bank Negara (1990) *Annual Report*, Kuala Lumpur, Bank Negara.
Bevan, D., Collier, P. and Gunning, J. (1987) 'Consequences of a Commodity Boom in a Controlled Economy', *World Bank Economic Review*, 1: 489–513.
——(1993) 'Trade Shocks in Developing Countries', *European Economic Review*, 37: 557–65.
Corden, W.M. (1984) 'Booming Sector and Dutch Disease Economics: Survey and Consolidation', *Oxford Economic Papers*, 36: 359–80.
GATT (1993) *Malaysia: Trade Policy Review*, Geneva, GATT.
Malaysia (1976) *Third Malaysia Plan 1976–80*, Kuala Lumpur.
——(1981) *Fourth Malaysia Plan 1981–85*, Kuala Lumpur.
——(1986) *Fifth Malaysia Plan 1986–90*, Kuala Lumpur.

24

Indonesia: Trade Shocks and Construction Booms

PETER G. WARR

24.1. Introduction

Indonesia is the world's third largest developing country, after China and India, and by far the most populous member of the Organisation of Petroleum Exporting Countries (OPEC). Like all petroleum exporting countries, Indonesia was greatly affected by the volatility of international petroleum prices during the 1970s and 1980s. This chapter deals with the way in which Indonesia adjusted to that external environment.

Indonesia gained independence from the Netherlands in 1949, but the Dutch left an impoverished, poorly educated and disunited population spread over the world's largest archipelago. The first decade-and-a-half of nationhood was chaotic, but impressive economic achievements followed from the late 1960s onwards. After economic and political chaos in the early and mid-1960s, Indonesian real GNP per capita has subsequently grown at an average annual rate of 4.6%.

Much, but definitely not all of Indonesia's economic success has been due to petroleum. By the mid 1980s the country's oil and gas sector accounted for around three-quarters of total export earnings and two-thirds of total government revenue. When the price of oil moves, the economic implications for Indonesia are profound. Clearly, the country was a prime candidate for a 'Dutch Disease' during the 1970s and studying its economic manifestation in Indonesia became a small industry in itself. Indonesians point out, only partly in jest, that this was the country's second 'Dutch Disease'. The first was the legacy of Dutch colonisation.

Indonesia is not a typical OPEC country. Despite its external dependence on petroleum, Indonesia's oil and gas output accounts for only a few per cent of OPEC output and for only 12% of Indonesian GDP. More than half of the Indonesian workforce remains in agriculture and around 30% produce services. Industry accounts for a further 15% of the workforce, but the petroleum sector employs only a tiny proportion. Indonesia's petroleum sector is a classic enclave industry.

This chapter focuses on the economic effects which externally induced trade shocks have had within Indonesia. These effects include the now-familiar Dutch Disease phenomena associated with rising petroleum revenues. They include reduced profitability in the non-oil traded goods sectors of the economy and sluggish economic performance in those sectors. The study also attempts to determine whether the theory of construction booms applies well to the Indonesian experience.

Section 24.2 summarises the important trade shocks for Indonesia and presents an overview of Indonesian macroeconomic performance since 1970. Section 24.3 summarises the economic predictions of the Dutch Disease and construction boom theories. Sections 24.4 to 24.6 analyse Indonesia's actual adjustment to the oil shocks experienced since 1970, focusing on the degree to which that experience confirms the predictions of economic theory. Sections 24.4 and 24.5 concentrate on Indonesia's short-run adjustment by means of time-series statistical analysis of the effects of the fluctuating magnitude of petroleum revenues on relative prices within Indonesia (Section 24.4) and on the sectoral composition of Indonesian GDP (Section 24.5). Section 24.6 applies to Indonesia the methodology for the macroeconomic analysis of temporary trade shocks developed by Bevan *et al.* in Chapter 2. The method estimates the macroeconomic consequences of Indonesia's petroleum price booms by means of 'counterfactual' analyses of income, asset accumulation, savings rates, and consumption.

24.2. Indonesia's Trade Shocks and Macroeconomic Performance

24.2.1. The Shocks

Figure 24.1 summarises the movement of Indonesia's external terms of trade. Naturally, the series is dominated by movements in international petroleum prices. Three periods can be distinguished:

1. the 1973–74 oil price *increase* (OPEC I);
2. the 1978–79 oil price *increase* (OPEC II); and
3. the petroleum price *declines* and high international interest rates of the early and mid-1980s.

Figure 24.2 shows the fluctuations of petroleum export revenues and tax revenues resulting from these price movements. In Figure 24.3 these fluctuations are shown as proportions of GDP. It would seem that none of these three events can strictly be described as 'temporary'. OPEC I seemingly changed Indonesia's terms of trade permanently. OPEC II was only semi-permanent. It remains to be seen whether the oil price decline since 1985 will prove to be temporary.

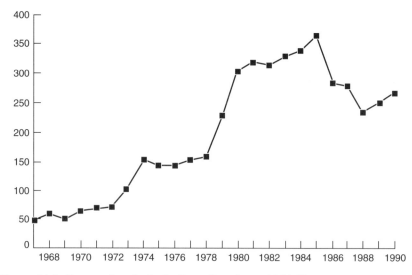

Figure 24.1. Terms of trade, including oil and gas, 1967–88

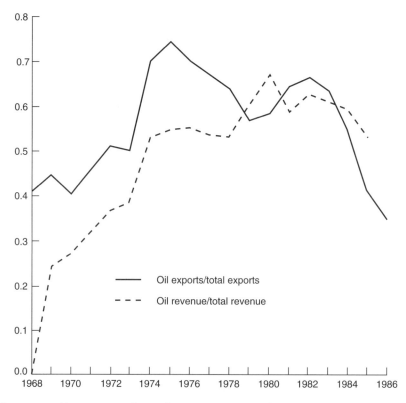

Figure 24.2. Importance of petroleum in exports and government revenue, 1968–86

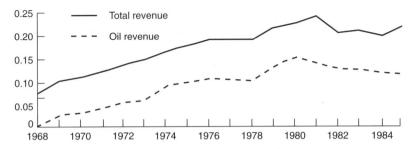

Figure 24.3. Total revenue/GDP and oil revenue/GDP, 1968–85

To understand the events that followed OPEC I and II, three features of Indonesia's experience must be remembered. First, as with most other petroleum exporters, the fluctuating revenues were received directly by the government. How these revenues were absorbed into the domestic economy, and the timing of their absorption, depended on government policy. Second, the economic implications of the windfalls resulting from the oil price shocks were seen within Indonesia as being temporary. This was not because future price movements were predicted; Indonesians were no more prescient in that respect than anyone else, including economists. The petroleum reserves themselves were regarded as temporary. It was thought that even if the prices remained high the reserves would be largely depleted within two to three decades. Even during the euphoria of the oil price booms of the 1970s Indonesian policymakers were thinking about the country's future without petroleum exports.

Third, the Soeharto government, which still rules Indonesia, came to power in 1965 in the midst of a hyperinflation caused by massive government deficits financed by money creation. The new government was determined to prevent a recurrence. The fiscal and monetary measures put in place to achieve this end reduced inflation to single-digit levels within three years—a remarkable achievement. But, paradoxically, these same measures later proved to have perverse effects in the context of an export boom.

24.2.2. Macroeconomic Performance

Indonesia's macroeconomic adjustment to the shocks described above is summarised in Table 24.1. There was no year of significant negative growth over the period covered and the uncontrolled inflations seen in Nigeria and Mexico did not occur.[1] Indonesia experienced serious adjustment problems in the mid-1980s and the term 'crisis' has been used by some observers to describe this period (Table 24.2). However, these problems did not lead Indonesia to abandon its free foreign exchange system,

Table 24.1. Macroeconomic summary, 1968–90

	1968	1969	1970	1971	1972	1973	1974	1975	1976	1977	1978	1979
GDP real growth rate (%)	10.9	6.8	7.6	6.7	9.4	11.3	7.6	5.0	6.9	8.8	6.9	5.8
Inflation (CPI growth rate) (%)	84.8	17.4	12.3	4.4	6.4	31.0	40.6	19.1	4.8	11.0	8.1	20.6
Export unit value (US$, 1980 = 100)	5.3	6.1	10.2	10.1	12.2	17.7	38.7	40.9	43.0	48.1	48.7	68.4
Terms of trade (Index, 1980 = 100)	14.3	16.5	27.6	25.3	29.0	36.1	56.1	56.0	58.1	63.3	62.4	82.4
Exchange rate (Rp/US$)	326	326	378	415	415	415	415	415	415	415	634	632
Total government revenue/GDP (%)	7.2	10.0	10.8	12.0	13.7	14.7	16.7	18.0	19.1	19.1	19.1	21.9
Oil tax revenue/GDP (%)	0	2.4	3.0	3.8	5.1	5.7	8.9	9.9	10.6	10.3	10.2	13.3
Total debt outstanding (US$ bn.)	2.7	3.0	2.9	4.3	5.1	6.7	9.2	11.8	14.6	16.2	19.0	21.2
Total debt service (US$ bn.)	0.05	0.06	0.08	0.09	0.13	0.2	0.3	0.6	0.8	1.3	2.1	2.1
International reserves (US$ bn.)	0.1	0.1	0.2	0.2	0.6	0.8	1.5	0.6	1.5	2.5	2.6	4.1
Exports–total (US$ bn.)	0.7	0.9	1.1	1.2	1.8	3.2	7.4	7.1	8.5	10.9	11.6	15.6
Exports–oil (US$ bn.)	0.3	0.4	0.4	0.6	0.9	1.6	5.2	5.3	6.0	7.3	7.4	8.9
Imports (US$ bn.)	0.7	0.8	1.0	1.1	1.6	2.7	3.8	4.8	5.7	6.2	6.7	7.2

	1980	1981	1982	1983	1984	1985	1986	1987	1988	1989	1990
GDP real growth rate (%)	8.5	7.2	0	0.3	6.7	2.5	5.9	4.8	5.7	7.4	7.0
Inflation (CPI growth rate) (%)	18.5	12.2	9.5	11.8	10.5	4.7	9.1	9.3	8.0	6.5	7.4
Export unit value (US$, 1980 = 100)	100	100.1	97.8	86.7	85.7	100	56.7	65.4	74.9	80.3	84.5
Terms of trade (Index, 1980 = 100)	100	105.7	101.9	96.4	97.4	93.9	69.7	70.0	69.9	74.9	78.9
Exchange rate (Rp/US$)	627	644	692	994	1,074	1,125	1,641	1,650	1,686	1,770	1,900
Total government revenue/GDP (%)	22.9	24.4	20.8	21.1	20.0	21.6	20.2	21.3	20.2	15.9	16.1
Oil tax revenue/GDP (%)	15.4	14.2	13.1	12.9	12.0	11.3	6.6	9.1	7.4	8.1	9.0
Total debt outstanding (US$ bn.)	22.5	27.2	32.2	35.6	36.6	42.5	49.8	59.8	58.0	60.5	74.8
Total debt service (US$ bn.)	1.8	2.0	2.2	2.5	3.2	4.0	4.4	5.4	7.3	7.7	9.5
International reserves (US$ bn.)	5.6	5.0	3.1	3.7	4.8	5.0	4.1	5.6	5.0	5.3	4.4
Exports–total (US$ bn.)	21.9	22.3	22.3	21.2	21.9	18.6	16.1	17.1	19.2	22.1	25.7
Exports–oil (US$ bn.)	12.9	14.4	14.9	13.5	12.1	7.7	5.2	5.9	7.7	8.7	11.1
Imports (US$ bn.)	10.8	13.3	16.9	16.4	13.9	10.3	10.7	12.9	13.2	16.4	21.9

Table 24.2. Impact of oil price decline in the 1980s

	1978	1979	1980	1981	1982	1983	1984	1985	1986
Dollar price of oil	44.1	59.6	100.0	114.7	115.0	100.2	95.5	90.8	58.7
Non-gold reserves in months	19.5	24.3	25.3	23.2	12.6	9.6	16.4	25.5	23.3
Current account balance as a percentage GDP	−2.7	1.9	4.0	−0.6	−5.6	−7.8	−2.2	−2.3	−5.2
GDP growth rate	7.7	6.2	7.9	7.4	0.0	3.3	6.0	2.4	3.1
M_1 growth rate	17.8	33.7	42.5	33.0	23.5	5.5	8.7	15.6	14.9
Inflation CPI	8.1	20.6	18.5	12.2	9.5	11.8	10.5	4.7	5.9

Table 24.3. Value of non-petroleum exports, 1969–80 (*1974 = 100*)

	1969	1970	1971	1972	1973	1974	1975	1976	1977	1978	1979	1980
Volume at constant prices	n.a.	n.a.	73.9	83.4	96.3	100.0	99.6	111.9	121.0	118.0	160.0	144.5
Value in US$	28.6	33.6	36.6	40.0	73.2	100.0	82.6	115.2	159.7	166.4	253.7	276.4
Value in import purchasing power	52.2	58.5	59.4	60.2	91.1	100.0	74.2	103.8	133.0	123.0	162.4	155.9
Value in domestic purchasing power	51.6	60.1	66.9	73.7	103.2	100.0	69.5	80.8	100.9	103.6	184.6	170.8

to increase the use of price controls or to attempt to restrict imports through increased protectionism. Indeed, the opposite occurred. Protectionism through quantitative restrictions was a feature of the booming 1970s. But in spite of some temporary reversals, the experience of the 1980s was predominantly one of liberalisation of trade policy.

Three significant devaluations against the US dollar occurred in the post-OPEC period:

1. November 1978—50%;
2. March 1983—28%; and
3. September 1986—45%.

The November 1978 devaluation was undertaken explicitly for 'exchange rate protection' reasons. It was designed to counteract the declining profitability of the non-oil traded goods sectors—especially agriculture—which had resulted from the Dutch Disease effects of OPEC I. This decline is evident from the value of non-petroleum exports in the mid-1970s, shown in Table 24.3, and will be clearer from production data to be presented in Section 24.5. The devaluation was clearly not motivated primarily by balance of payments concerns, although its precise timing apparently involved external balance considerations (Warr 1984). The other two devaluations did reflect balance of payments problems.

In 1975 a serious financial crisis resulted from the swashbuckling financial practices of the state petroleum company, Pertamina. This produced the decline in central bank assets shown in Table 24.4. Although the event was costly, observers have speculated that in some ways it was fortuitous. It led subsequently to much more cautious financial practices within the state enterprises—the source of the much larger financial problems experienced later by some other oil-exporting countries.

The Soeharto government had been anxious to avoid the public deficit financing of the pre-1965 Sukarno period. For this purpose a 'balanced budget' rule had been adopted which limited government spending to revenue plus foreign funds. But after 1973 foreign funds were plentiful. The 'balanced budget' rule made it difficult to control public spending, and monetary management was hampered by reliance on bank credit ceilings as the main instruments of monetary control. Inflation in Indonesia consequently exceeded that of its trading partners in the post-OPEC period, thus necessitating periodic recourse to devaluations.

The underlying causes of Indonesia's inflation problem were important, but it is also notable that the government was prepared to use the instrument of devaluation when required. Indonesia thus largely avoided the chronic exchange rate overvaluation that can so easily decimate an oil-exporting country's non-oil traded goods sectors.

24.3. Theoretical Predictions

Dutch Disease theory and construction boom theory are described in Chapter 1 of this book. If the construction boom theory is valid for Indonesia, and if our assumption that expectations are partially revised is also correct, we should find most of the usual Dutch Disease phenomena, but also:

1. changes in savings and investment to be positively correlated, given international interest rates;
2. changes in investment to be related to the absolute magnitude of trade shocks, rather than their sign;
3. prices of non-tradable capital goods such as 'construction' to rise relative to tradable capital goods such as machinery, and relative to non-tradable consumer goods such as housing and services; and
4. the prices of non-tradable inputs into construction and the wages of labour specific to construction to respond similarly.

Table 24.4. Petroleum revenues, monetary growth and inflation, 1969–1986

	1969	1970	1971	1972	1973	1974	1975	1976	1977
Oil and gas tax (bn. Rp)	65.8	99.2	104.7	230.5	382.2	957.2	1,248.0	1,635.3	1,948.7
Central Bank									
Foreign assets as total assets (%)	18.3	21.3	17.7	38.9	41.7	49.0	12.0	22.7	31.2
Change in reserve money (bn. Rp)	60.0	47.0	60.0	122.0	153.0	308.0	282.0	248.0	340.0
Change in M_1 (bn. Rp)	67.0	67.0	69.0	155.0	197.0	271.0	332.0	327.0	405.0
Rate of growth of reserve money (%)	60.0	29.0	29.0	45.7	39.3	56.8	33.2	21.9	24.6
Rate of growth of reserve M_1 (%)	57.8	36.6	27.6	48.6	41.6	40.4	35.2	25.7	25.3
Inflation (CPI) (%)	17.4	12.3	4.4	6.4	31.0	40.6	19.1	19.8	11.0

	1978	1979	1980	1981	1982	1983	1984	1985	1986
Oil and gas tax (bn. Rp)	2,308.7	4,259.6	7,019.6	8,627.8	8,170.4	9,520.2	10,429.9	11,144.4	9,738.2
Central Bank									
Foreign assets as total assets (%)	32.3	39.3	46.1	39.6	28.4	34.5	39.0	39.8	32.1
Change in reserve money (bn. Rp)	165.0	593.0	897.0	545.0	187.0	1,031.0	563.0	1,020.0	1,449.0
Change in M_1 (bn. Rp)	482.0	828.0	1,695.0	1,463.0	646.0	456.0	1,005.0	1,543.0	1,507.0
Rate of growth of reserve money (%)	9.6	31.5	36.2	16.1	4.8	25.1	11.0	17.9	21.6
Rate of growth of reserve M_1 (%)	24.0	33.3	51.1	29.2	10.0	6.4	13.3	18.0	14.9
Inflation (CPI) (%)	8.7	20.6	18.5	12.2	9.5	11.8	10.5	4.7	5.8

24.4. Trade Shocks and Relative Prices

24.4.1. 'Real' Exchange Rates

Two measures of 'real' exchange rates are shown in Figure 24.4, which updates a similar diagram for the years 1971 to 1982 presented and discussed in detail in Warr (1986). For the reasons discussed there, the relative price series—a direct calculation of tradables and non-tradables relative prices—is considered a more useful measure for discussions of the Dutch Disease. Readers are referred to the earlier paper for an account of the construction of the two series.

The data show the combined effects of two phenomena. There are significant Dutch Disease declines in the prices of tradables relative to non-tradables, interrupted by surges in tradables prices caused by the

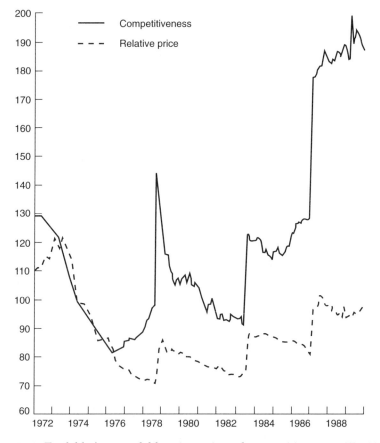

Figure 24.4. Tradable/non-tradable price ratio and competitiveness, 1974–89 (*quarterly, 1974 = 100*)

three devaluations of 1978, 1983 and 1986. The Dutch Disease effect is particularly strong in the post-OPEC I period. There is no evidence of a Dutch Disease following the 1986 devaluation—but no such effect would be expected. This was a period of low oil revenues and low inflation.

It is important to realise that there is no automatic link between a positive trade shock and a Dutch Disease. Declines in the tradables/non-tradables price ratio can happen without trade shocks. Increased nominal domestic demand causes non-tradables prices to rise. If the exchange rate is fixed, tradables prices will not rise. When this happens without a trade shock, a current account deficit results. What a trade shock does is to make an expansion of domestic demand consistent with balance of payments equilibrium. Furthermore, a trade shock such as an oil boom need not cause a Dutch Disease at all. Relative prices change only as a result of the domestic absorption of the foreign exchange generated by the shock. But the revenues could have been accumulated abroad had that been the chosen response to the shock. This point is especially important when the revenues from the shock accrue to the government.

24.4.2. Nominal Prices

The operation of the exchange rate—affecting the nominal prices of tradables—and nominal domestic demand (especially monetary policy)—affecting the nominal prices of non-tradables—is demonstrated by examining nominal price data. Warr (1984) shows that the nominal wholesale prices of imported commodities respond mainly to exchange rate changes and the steady increases in nominal international prices which were also occurring in the background. It is difficult to discern effects of trade shocks from inspection of these data or from their relative price counterparts, and econometric analysis is helpful.

24.4.3. Econometric Results

Data on petroleum's contribution to GDP will be used as a measure of trade shocks. The price of petroleum is exogenous for Indonesia and we shall treat petroleum output as being exogenous also. Because of our interest in the construction sector, in this chapter we focus on the price of construction materials relative to tradables (imported commodities) and non-tradable consumer goods (housing).[2] The estimated OLS regression equations using annual data from 1971 to 1988 were

$$\log(P_c/P_T)_t = 12.27 + 0.19\log R_t^* + 0.082E_t,$$
$$(0.069) \quad (0.0058)$$
$$2\% \qquad 20\% \qquad\qquad (24.1)$$

$$\overline{R}^2 = 0.297, \quad \text{D.W.} = 1.216, \text{ autocorrelation test: inconclusive}$$

and

$$\log(P_c/P_H)_t = -2.245 + 0.148 \log R_t^*,$$
$$(0.04)$$
$$1\% \tag{24.2}$$

$$\overline{R}^2 = 0.423, \quad \text{D.W.} = 1.176, \text{ autocorrelation test: inconclusive,}$$

first-order correlation coefficient = 0.405, where P_C denotes the wholesale price index of construction materials, P_T denotes the wholesale price index of imported commodities, P_H denotes the housing component of the CPI, R_t^* denotes petroleum revenues as a proportion of GDP, E_t denotes the rate of change of the exchange rate relative to year, and t denotes time. Numbers in parentheses are standard errors and percentages below them are significance levels.

The overall goodness of fit of these equations is not high but the estimated coefficients are significant. Adding the variables 'percentage change of exchange rate' and 'real effective exchange rate' to the right-hand side did not improve the regressions and these variables were not significant. The first equation indicates that positive trade shocks cause construction materials prices to rise relative to traded goods prices. This result is consistent with the construction boom theory.[3] The second equation is a more direct test of construction boom theory and the theory also passes this test. Construction materials prices relative to housing prices responded to trade shocks, and in the predicted direction.

24.4.4. Wages in the Construction Sector

Wage data for Indonesia are poor, as they are for most developing countries. A series of construction sector wages exists, and the real wages implied by it are shown in Figure 24.5. The two series shown use different

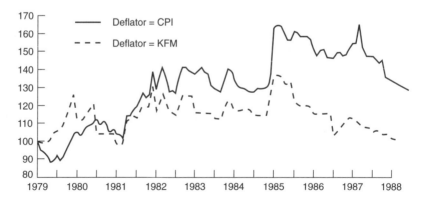

Figure 24.5. Real wages in the construction sector, 1979–88 (*monthly, 1983 = 100*)

deflators—the CPI compiled by the Central Bureau of Statistics and an independent cost-of-living series (KFM). The CPI is probably the more reliable. Comparison of Figure 24.5 with Figures 24.1 and 24.3 appears to show that wages in construction rise following positive wage shocks, but with a lag—e.g. 1979–80—and fall after negative shocks—e.g. following 1985. However, the period of observation would seem to be too short for econometric testing to be reasonable.

24.5. Changes in the Composition of National Income

24.5.1. Savings and Investment

Indonesia's aggregate savings and investment performance are displayed in Figure 24.6. These data (from 1981 onwards) are disaggregated into public and private sector components in Table 24.5. From examination of these data, and in particular from comparison of Figure 24.6 with Figures 24.1 and 24.3, it appears that aggregate saving responds positively to trade shocks. The effect on investment is less obvious. We shall present some econometric evidence on the relationships involved, using annual data from 1968 to 1988.

Changes in savings and investment are not significantly correlated. The simple (Pearson) correlation coefficient between first differences in the ratios of these variables to GDP was 0.179, but this value was not significantly different from zero at the 10% level of significance. Lagging saving by one period did not improve this relationship. We shall now look separately at the determinants of savings and investment.

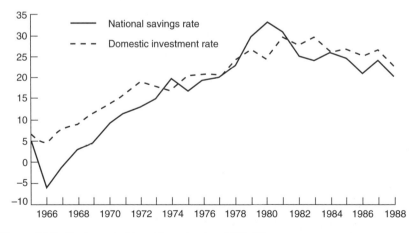

Figure 24.6. Savings and investment rates, 1965–88

Table 24.5. Public and private sector saving–investment balances 1981–88
(*as a percentage of GDP*)

	1981	1982	1983	1984	1985	1986	1987	1988
Public sector								
Investment	10.7	12.7	12.6	10.3	10.9	9.7	9.3	9.1
Saving	9.2	8.2	9.4	10.2	8.3	4.9	5.7	6.0
Saving–investment gap	−1.5	−4.5	−3.2	−0.1	−2.6	−4.8	−3.6	−3.1
Private sector								
Investment	18.9	14.8	16.8	15.2	15.6	14.9	17.0	13.1
Saving	21.2	16.6	14.4	15.5	16.0	15.6	18.1	13.8
Saving–investment gap	2.2	1.7	−2.4	0.3	0.4	0.7	1.1	0.7

Savings function We expect savings to be responsive to income and the domestic interest rate. In the case of the income variable, the distinction between income derived from petroleum and non-petroleum sources is potentially important. The theory of construction booms predicts that in the case of partially revised expectations, the propensity to save out of the partially transitory income derived from trade shocks will exceed that out of more stable income components.

First, we ran the regression

$$S_t^* = 2.97 + 108.4R_t^* + 0.094r_t,$$
$$\qquad\qquad (12.8) \qquad (0.0045)$$
$$\qquad\qquad 1\% \qquad\quad 10\%$$

(24.3)

$$\overline{R}^2 = 0.779, \quad \text{D.W.} = 0.732, \text{ autocorrelation test: autocorrelation present,}$$

where S_t^* is total saving as a proportion of GDP, R_t^* is defined as before and r_t is the real rate of interest on bank deposits.

Savings were positively and significantly affected by trade shocks. The interest rate variable also had the expected positive sign, but was significant only at the 10% level. When the lagged value was included the regression was not improved and the lagged variable was non-significant. Autocorrelation was present in this regression, with a first-order correlation coefficient of 0.61.

The hypothesis that propensities to save out of trade shock and non-trade shock incomes are different was tested in the following regression.

$$S_t = -546377 + 18.2G_t^N + 92.1R_t + 729r_t,$$
$$\qquad\qquad\quad (2.74) \quad (2.74) \quad (2034)$$
$$\qquad\qquad\quad 1\% \qquad 1\% \qquad \text{n.s.}$$

(24.4)

$$\overline{R}^2 = 0.959, \quad \text{D.W.} = 1.07, \text{ autocorrelation test: inconclusive,}$$

where S_t denotes total savings deflated by the GDP deflator, G_t^N denotes non-oil GDP, deflated as above, R_t denotes the total petroleum and gas contribution to GDP, deflated as above,[4] and r_t is defined as above. The coefficients on G_t^N and R_t were each highly significant. Moreover, the coefficient on R_t was much higher than that on G_t^N, as predicted by construction boom theory, and the difference was significant at the 1% level. The Durbin–Watson test for autocorrelation was inconclusive (first-order correlation coefficient 0.433). It should be noted that the interest rate variable was not significant.

Investment function We expect investment to respond positively to changes in the profitability of investment and negatively to changes in its price, as reflected in domestic interest rates. Obtaining appropriate data on interest rates is a major problem in Indonesia, as in most developing countries. We shall estimate an investment function based on the following theory.[5] Net investment is given by

$$I_t^N = K_t - K_{t-1} = a(K_t^D - K_{t-1}),\qquad(24.5)$$

where K_t denotes the capital stock at time t, K_t^D is the desired capital stock and a is a partial adjustment coefficient. Gross investment, I_t, is net investment plus depreciation.

$$I_t = I_t^N + dK_{t-1},\qquad(24.6)$$

where d is the rate of depreciation. Now the desired capital stock depends on permanent income, Y^P, and the interest rate:

$$K_t = bY^P + cr_t.\qquad(24.7)$$

By rearranging terms,

$$I_t = abY_p + (d-a)K_{t-1} + acr_t,\qquad(24.8)$$

the question now arises of how trade shocks affect Y^P and hence I_t. We substitute current petroleum revenues for Y^P in the above equation and estimate the regression

$$I_t^* = 6.16 + 58.5R_t^* + 6.66K_{t-1}^* + 0.065r_t,$$
$$(7.7)\qquad(1.24)\qquad(0.028)$$
$$1\%\qquad\ \ 1\%\qquad\ \ 5\%\qquad\qquad(24.9)$$
$$\overline{R}^2 = 0.859,\quad D = 2.003,\ \text{autocorrelation test: absent.}$$

As before, asterisks on quantity variables denote that they have been expressed as a proportion of GDP. The results again mostly confirm the qualitative predictions of construction boom theory. The positive coefficient on the interest rate variable is surprising and presumably reflects the poor quality of the interest data used. The data relate to the rate of return on domestic bank deposits. This is not the relevant interest rate and a more suitable one may be found. Autocorrelation was not present in the regression.

Savings–investment gap Combining the savings and investment results we find that petroleum revenues positively affect savings and investment, but the effect on savings was approximately twice as large. Positive trade shocks reduce the savings–investment gap; negative trade shocks widen it. Clearly, Indonesia kept a substantial part of the revenues from the boom abroad, rather than absorbing them immediately.

These results confirm the partial revision of expectations hypothesis outlined above. If changes in petroleum revenues had no effect on expectations, there should be no effect on investment. If these changes caused full revision of expectations there should be no effect on savings. The evidence suggests an intermediate case, but one closer to the no revision than the full revision extreme.

The results do not suggest that interest rates play a role in determining savings decisions. The result for investment was perverse, but this result is probably spurious. It seems worthwhile to test the construction boom hypothesis about domestic interest rate determination more directly. The theory says that the margin between domestic real interest rates and foreign real interest rates is reduced when domestic savings rises, such as in response to a positive trade shock.

The exogenous variables in this story are the foreign real interest rate and the petroleum revenues. We therefore ran the regression

$$r_t = 23.5 + 149.5R_t^* + 0.128i_t,$$
$$(44.9) \quad (0.087)$$
$$1\% \quad\;\; 20\% \tag{24.10}$$

$$\overline{R}^2 = 0.43, \quad D = 1.309, \text{ autocorrelation test: inconclusive,}$$

where r_t is the real domestic interest rate on bank deposits and i_t is the real Eurodollar interest rate—the nominal rate minus the rate of change of the export unit value index for industrialised countries. This result is consistent with the construction boom theory. The overall goodness of fit is low but this is expected because domestic interest rates in Indonesia are partially controlled and are affected by domestic expectations of exchange rate changes.

The results suggest that although positive trade shocks do seem to reduce the gap between foreign and domestic real interest rates (though not necessarily because of their effects on savings), the resulting decline in the domestic real interest rate does not have a significant effect on domestic savings.

24.5.2. *Sectoral Composition of GDP*

The changing composition of Indonesian output is shown in Figure 24.7, drawn from Indonesia's newly revised national income series. We shall look in detail at the construction sector in the next subsection but in this

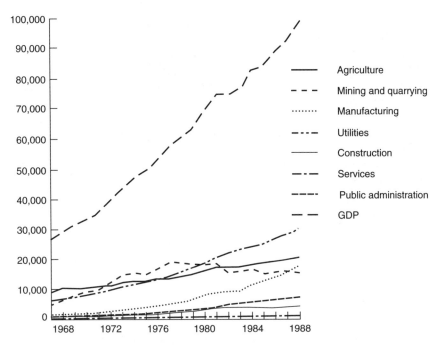

Figure 24.7. Gross domestic product by industrial origin at constant 1983 prices, 1967–88 (*bn. Rp*)

subsection we focus on the Dutch Disease. Do increases in petroleum revenues cause the composition of *non-oil* GDP to shift in favour of non-tradables?

We attempted to test the Dutch Disease hypothesis first for agriculture's share of non-oil GDP, second for industry's share, and then for their combined share. We ran the following regressions

$$S_t^A = 0.048 - 0.084R_t^* + 0.872S_{t-1}^A,$$
$$\quad\quad (0.037) \quad\quad (0.034)$$
$$\quad\quad 5\% \quad\quad\quad 1\%$$

(24.11)

$$\overline{R}^2 = 0.983, \quad D = 2.98, \text{ autocorrelation test: negative autocorrelation,}$$

$$S_t^I = 0.028 + 0.0063R_t^* + 0.862S_{t-1}^I,$$
$$\quad\quad (0.049) \quad\quad (0.126)$$
$$\quad\quad \text{n.s.} \quad\quad\quad 1\%$$

(24.12)

$$\overline{R}^2 = 0.767, \quad D = 2.15, \text{ autocorrelation test: absent, and}$$

$$S_t^T = 0.117 - 0.125R_t^* + 0.798S_{t-1}^T,$$
$$\quad\quad (0.046) \quad\quad (0.062)$$
$$\quad\quad 5\% \quad\quad\quad 1\%$$

$$\overline{R}^2 = 0.942, \quad D = 1.889, \text{ autocorrelation: absent,}$$

(24.13)

where S_t^A denotes agriculture's share of non-oil GDP, S_t^I is industry's share and S_t^T is their combined share.[6]

These results confirm the Dutch Disease message in an interesting way. The Dutch Disease affects non-oil traded goods as a whole but its effect is significant only in agriculture. Manufacturing in particular was able to obtain import protection during the Dutch Disease decade which followed OPEC I. It should be noted that if the coefficient on R_t^* is denoted by a and the coefficient on the lagged dependent variable is denoted b, the long-run effect of petroleum revenue is given by $a(1-b)$. Thus, except for the industry case, the long-run coefficients are all significant and five to seven times as large as the short-run coefficients.

24.5.3. The Construction Sector

We now concentrate on the effects of petroleum revenue shocks on the construction sector's share of non-petroleum GDP. We ran the regression

$$C_t^* = 0.009 + 0.024R_t^* + 0.747C_{t-1}^*,$$
$$(0.015) \quad (0.077)$$
$$15\% \quad 1\% \tag{24.14}$$

$$\overline{R}^2 = 0.926, \quad D = 2.468, \text{ autocorrelation: inconclusive,}$$

where C_t^* denotes the construction sector's share of non-oil GDP. The results suggest that petroleum revenues affect the construction sector positively. Computing the long-run effect as above, the long-run effect is around four times as large as the short-run effect.

24.6. Counterfactual Macroeconomic Analysis

We now turn to Indonesia's macroeconomic adjustment to the three oil price shocks identified in Section 24.2. The analysis closely follows the method developed by Bevan *et al.* for the analysis of Kenya's adjustment to the 1976–79 coffee price boom (Chapter 2). The essence of the methodology is the comparison of Indonesia's observed macroeconomic performance with estimates of what that performance would have been in the absence of the particular trade shocks under discussion. This latter set of hypothetical macroeconomic outcomes is described as a 'counterfactual'.

24.6.1. Overview

The magnitude of the trade shock is estimated in Table 24.6. The method expresses the value of the trade shock as a sequence of lump-sum increases in national income at constant prices. This is done by construction of a sequence of counterfactual exports: estimates of what the value of exports would have been in the absence of the boom. The magnitude of the windfall is then estimated as the difference between the observed value of exports and this counterfactual value of exports.[7]

In the construction of counterfactual exports, the actual value of exports is divided by the barter terms of trade index and the resulting series is expressed in constant prices. This method thus assumes that the *volume* of exports was unaffected by the boom. Of course, some reallocation of resources towards the booming (petroleum) sector will have occurred in response to the boom and this reallocation will have increased national income. Insofar as our counterfactual does not allow for this fact, assuming the observed volume of exports to have been unaffected by the boom, it *overestimates* the counterfactual value of exports and thus *underestimates* the value of the windfall.

We now turn to the definition of the trade shocks. Indonesia's terms of trade series, shown in Figure 24.1, is reproduced schematically in Figure 24.8. It should be noted that Indonesia's price shock occurred in three distinct phases. Moreover, it was not really 'temporary'. By 1988 Indonesia's terms of trade had still not returned to their pre-1973 levels, although

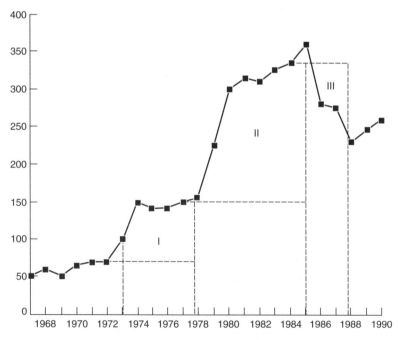

Figure 24.8. Schematic terms of trade, including oil and gas, 1967–88

Table 24.6. Magnitude of trade shock

A. *Single shock (1973–88)*

	Export price index (1970–72 = 1)	Import price index (1970–72 = 1)	Terms of trade (1970–72 = 1)	Counterfactual exports ($US m., current prices)	Windfall exports ($US m.)	
					Current prices	1972 price
1970	1	1	1	1,055	0	
1971	1	1	1	1,199	0	
1972	1	1	1	1,778	0	
1973	1.47	1.23	1.20	2,671	539	43
1974	4.00	1.64	2.44	3,041	4,384	2,67
1975	3.72	1.73	2.15	3,309	3,820	2,20
1976	4.13	1.76	2.34	3,654	4,901	2,77
1977	4.63	1.94	2.38	4,556	6,296	3,23
1978	4.70	2.21	2.12	5,491	6,151	2,77
1979	6.59	2.56	2.57	6,060	9,529	3,71
1980	9.45	2.99	3.15	6,941	14,967	4,99
1981	10.23	2.92	3.50	6,357	15,902	5,43
1982	9.52	2.88	3.30	5,976	13,770	4,77
1983	8.48	2.87	2.94	7,108	13,852	4,81
1984	8.23	2.71	3.03	6,698	13,646	5,03
1985	7.60	2.77	2.74	6,819	11,891	4,28
1986	5.32	2.69	1.97	7,490	7,296	2,70
1987	6.21	3.06	2.02	8,497	8,708	2,83
1988	6.66	3.34	1.99	9,775	9,728	2,91

the magnitude of the terms of trade increase had declined considerably since 1985.

The approach taken in our case study is to treat the Indonesian experience in two different ways. First, we treat the entire period from 1973 to 1988 as a single shock. The base period for construction of the counterfactual corresponding to this period is the average of the three-year period from 1970 to 1972. Second, we describe the 1973–88 period in terms of three distinct shocks. Referring to Figure 24.8, Shock I is treated as though it began in 1973, and the counterfactual for this shock has as its base period the average of the three years 1970–72. Shock II is treated as though it began in 1979 and ended in 1985. It must be stressed that the base period used in construction of the counterfactual for Shock II is the average of the three years 1976–78, and that this is different from the base period for Shock I. It follows that our estimates of the windfall effects of Shocks I and II *cannot be added together*, because they rest on different base periods. They must be treated separately. Shock III is again treated separately, as having begun in 1986 and having ended in 1988, with the base period being the average of the three years 1983–85.

Separate shocks (1973–78, 1979–85, 1986–88)

	Export price index (base period = 1)	Import price index (base period = 1)	Terms of trade (base period = 1)	Counterfactual exports ($US m., current prices)	Windfall exports ($US m.)	
					Current prices	Constant base-period prices
Shock I						
1970	1	1	1	1,055	0	0
1971	1	1	1	1,199	0	0
1972	1	1	1	1,778	0	0
1973	1.47	1.23	1.20	2,671	539	438
1974	4.00	1.64	2.44	3,041	4,384	2,671
1975	3.72	1.73	2.15	3,309	3,820	2,208
1976	4.13	1.76	2.34	3,654	4,901	2,774
1977	4.63	1.94	2.38	4,556	6,296	3,232
1978	4.70	2.21	2.12	5,491	6,151	2,773
Shock II						
1976	1	1	1	8,556	0	0
1977	1	1	1	10,853	0	0
1978	1	1	1	11,643	0	0
1979	1.40	1.15	1.21	12,849	2,740	2,370
1980	2.01	1.35	1.48	14,715	7,193	5,323
1981	2.17	1.31	1.65	13,477	8,782	6,662
1982	2.026	1.30	1.55	12,669	7,077	5,443
1983	1.80	1.29	1.39	15,070	5,890	4,540
1984	1.75	1.22	1.43	14,201	6,143	5,024
1985	1.61	1.25	1.29	14,457	4,253	3,402
Shock III						
1983	1	1	1	20,961	0	0
1984	1	1	1	20,345	0	0
1985	1	1	1	18,711	0	0
1986	0.69	0.97	0.71	20,552	−5,765	−5,929
1987	0.81	1.10	0.73	23,315	−6,109	−5,523
1988	0.87	1.20	0.72	26,823	−7,319	−6,076

24.6.2. Windfall Changes in Savings and Investment

We now estimate the degree to which the windfall increase in income estimated above was converted into changes in assets. We begin with an identity: the change in total savings is divided into three components: gross domestic investment, I^D, inventory accumulation, J, and foreign assets, F. Thus,

$$dS = dI^D + dJ + dF. \qquad (24.15)$$

The results are summarised in Table 24.7. All magnitudes are presented in millions of US dollars, expressed in present value, discounted at 10% to the base period indicated and measured in prices pertaining to that

Table 24.7. Summary of aggregate windfall income, investment and foreign savings

	Single shock (1973–88) 1973	Shock I (1973–78) 1973	Shock II (1979–85) 1979	Shock III (1986–88) 1986
1. Windfall income	27,144	10,705	22,596	−15,971
2. Windfall investment	7,876	3,427	8,670	−1,536
3. Windfall change in foreign assets	9,634	3,192	7,971	−6,847
4. Total windfall savings	17,510	6,619	16,641	−8,383
5. Windfall saving rate	0.65	0.62	0.74	0.53
Base year	1972	1972	1978	1985

Note: Rows (1)–(4) = net present value in $US m., discounted at 10% to base year as stated, in base-year prices; Row 4 = row 2 + row 3; row 5 = row 4/row 1

period. First, consider the 'single shock' results, pertaining to the terms of trade increase lasting from 1973 to 1988. The present value of the windfall increase in national income over the 1973 to 1988 period was US$27.1 billion. This was a large amount—equivalent to 185% of Indonesia's 1973 GDP. The income windfall produced additional investment worth US$7.9 billion (29% of the windfall income) and a windfall increase of foreign assets of US$9.6 billion (35% of the windfall and equivalent to increased reserves minus increased debt). It must be stressed that these calculations relate to *actual* outcomes relative to *counterfactual* outcomes. The increase of foreign assets must not be interpreted to mean that foreign debt *fell* relative to the base period. The reverse occurred. It means that the increase of debt was smaller than our estimates of what would *otherwise* have occurred, without the terms of trade shock—the counterfactual. Total savings increased by 64% of the windfall and consumption increased by 36% of the windfall.[8]

When the three shocks are considered separately, the patterns of response to each are quite different. These results are given in columns (2)–(4) of Table 24.7. Shock I was worth US$10.7 billion at 1973 prices. It provoked a US$3.4 billion increase in GFKF and a US$3.2 billion increase in foreign assets. Altogether, saving increased by US$6.6 billion, 62% of the windfall income. Shock II was larger and the proportion of the windfall that was saved—74%—was also larger. This result seems plausible and is consistent with the perception in Indonesia at the time that the windfall was temporary and should be invested wisely. Shortly before Shock II (November 1978) the government had devalued the currency for the explicit purpose of slowing the domestic absorption of the proceeds of Shock I. In this climate, a high rate of saving from Shock II is unsurprising.

Shock III reduced national income by US$16 billion in 1986 prices. The result was a contraction of GFKF, relative to the counterfactual, of US$1.5 billion and reduced foreign asset accumulation (primarily increased foreign debt) of US$6.8 billion, implying reduced total savings of US$8.4 billion, 52% of the windfall.

Tables 24.8 and 24.9 present these results in more detail. First, consider the change in domestic investment. Following Bevan *et al.* we express actual investment in units of GDP at pre-boom relative prices. This is done in Table 24.8. The computations take the observed ratio of gross domestic investment to GDP at current prices multiplied by an estimate of actual real income at constant pre-boom prices, constructed by adding observed GDP at pre-boom prices to the estimate of windfall income also at pre-boom prices shown in the final column of Table 24.6. The result is shown in column (1) of Table 24.8. It shows the value of expenditure on GDI expressed in units of GDP at pre-boom relative prices.

Counterfactual investment is estimated in columns (2) to (4) of Table 24.8. First we estimate counterfactual real income, Y_t^*, as GDP in constant pre-boom relative prices, Y_t^0, minus the assumed real return on cumulative windfall investment, lagged one year. We assume a real rate of return of 10%. Thus,

$$Y_t^* = Y_t^0 - 0.1\left(\sum_{t=t_0}^{t-1} dI_t\right),$$

where t_0 denotes the base year. The calculation of cumulative windfall investment up to year $(t-1)$ will be clear from the following discussion.

The counterfactual investment propensity shown in column (3) is equal to the pre-boom base period investment propensity. Thus for Shock I it is the average investment propensity for the years 1970–72, and so on. In the case of each of the three shocks, we thus assume the counterfactual investment propensity to be unchanged from the observed propensity in the base period. Clearly, for this method to be reliable we must assume that any change in the actual investment propensity during the period of the trade shock, relative to the base period, was *due to that shock* and not to any other factor. All of the observed difference between these two propensities is in effect being attributed to the trade shock and the domestic response to it.

Counterfactual investment (column 4) is now the product of columns (2) and (3). It is an estimate of what the value of real investment would have been in the absence of the boom. Annual windfall investment (column 5) is now the difference between actual investment at constant prices and column (6). The analysis proceeds year by year. The estimated 10%

Table 24.8. Counterfactual growth and capital formation

A. *Single shock (1973–88)*

	Actual GDP + windfall[a]	Counterfactual real income[a]	Counterfactual investment propensity	Counterfactual GFKF[a]	Windfall GFKF[a]
1970	9,142	9,142	0.167	1,528	0
1971	9,267	9,267	0.195	1,809	0
1972	11,036	11,036	0.229	2,534	0
1973	15,094	14,655	0.23	3,370	−78
1974	24,132	21,468	0.23	4,937	−32
1975	25,251	23,054	0.23	5,302	915
1976	29,286	26,431	0.23	6,079	1,265
1977	33,758	30,319	0.23	6,973	1,267
1978	34,658	31,551	0.23	7,256	2,148
1979	33,615	29,350	0.23	6,750	2,558
1980	43,954	38,155	0.23	8,775	2,282
1981	47,724	41,251	0.23	9,487	5,089
1982	45,272	38,955	0.23	8,959	3,938
1983	39,994	33,244	0.23	7,646	4,212
1984	40,943	33,554	0.23	7,717	3,006
1985	39,063	32,117	0.23	7,387	3,568
1986	33,794	28,073	0.23	6,456	3,095
1987	31,440	25,230	0.23	5,802	3,749
1988	33,632	26,974	0.23	6,204	4,387

rate of return on cumulative windfall investment in year $(t-1)$ is then used in the estimation of real income in year t, etc.

Table 24.9 applies a similar methodology to the acquisition of net foreign debt, defined as the difference between total foreign debt and total foreign exchange reserves, expressed in foreign exchange. Because the observed foreign savings propensity changed sharply from one year to the next, the base years in these calculations are the average of the *three* years prior to the boom. For example, the base for the 'Single shock' and the 'Shock I' results is the average of the three years 1970–72, etc. Clearly, the effects of windfall on foreign savings varied greatly from year to year, but during Shock I and Shock II the effects tended to be positive, whereas during Shock III they were negative.

24.6.3. Disaggregation into Public and Private Sectors

Indonesia's petroleum price boom accrued initially to the government. An increase in government spending resulted, but it is clear that much of this spending was productive (Warr 1992). Infrastructure was improved, especially the road transport system and public infrastructure affecting agriculture, such as irrigation facilities. Fertiliser imports were subsidised heavily, producing an impressive rate of increase in agricultural output.

Separate shocks (1973–78, 1979–85, 1986–88)

	Actual GDP + windfall[b]	Counterfactual real income[b]	Counterfactual investment propensity	Counterfactual GFKF[b]	Windfall GFKF[b]
Shock I					
70	9,142	9,142	0.167	1,528	0
71	9,267	9,267	0.195	1,809	0
72	11,036	11,036	0.229	2,534	0
73	15,094	14,655	0.23	3,370	−78
74	24,132	21,468	0.23	4,937	−32
75	25,251	23,054	0.23	5,302	915
76	29,286	26,431	0.23	6,079	1,265
77	33,758	30,319	0.23	6,973	1,267
78	34,658	31,551	0.23	7,256	2,148
Shock II					
76	37,797	37,797	0.250	9,479	0
77	46,356	46,356	0.244	11,315	0
78	51,975	51,975	0.271	14,104	0
79	47,960	45,590	0.27	12,309	972
80	64,729	59,308	0.27	16,013	270
81	71,136	64,349	0.27	17,374	4,353
82	67,192	61,188	0.27	16,520	2,622
83	58,182	52,820	0.27	14,261	2,990
84	59,781	53,635	0.27	14,481	1,176
85	56,426	51,785	0.27	13,982	1,843
Shock III					
83	82,564	82,564	0.296	24,481	0
84	87,616	87,616	0.261	22,948	0
85	87,337	87,337	0.280	24,494	0
86	69,700	75,629	0.28	21,176	−1,474
87	64,056	69,726	0.28	19,523	566
88	68,657	74,825	0.28	20,951	670

[a] US$ m., at constant 1972 prices
[b] $US m., at constant base-period prices: 1972, 1978 and 1985

Our results show, however, that government consumption also increased significantly as a consequence of the shocks.

Following Bevan *et al.*, we first construct a counterfactual estimate of how fiscal policy would have developed in the absence of the trade shocks. The analysis utilises the estimate of windfall income from Table 24.6 and counterfactual GDP from Table 24.8. As with Bevan *et al.*, the focus is on revenue and 'primary' or 'exhaustive' expenditure—government consumption plus government GFKF. The counterfactual analysis projects the base-period fiscal pattern into the future, when it is applied to counterfactual GDP. We then compare this outcome with the observed fiscal behaviour and the difference is attributed to the effects of the trade shock.

Table 24.9. Actual and counterfactual foreign savings (*FS*)

A. *Single shock (1973–88)*

	Actual FS[a]	Actual FS propensity	Counterfactual FS propensity	Counterfactual FS[a]	Windfa FS[a]
1970	−1,000	−0.109	−0.11	−1,000	0
1971	−1,124	−0.121	−0.12	−1,124	0
1972	−602	−0.054	−0.05	−602	0
1973	−974	−0.066	−0.08	−1,201	227
1974	−786	−0.036	−0.08	−1,760	973
1975	−2,288	−0.099	−0.08	−1,890	−398
1976	−946	−0.035	−0.08	−2,167	1,220
1977	−1,850	−0.06	−0.08	−2,486	635
1978	−880	−0.027	−0.08	−2,587	1,706
1979	535	0.017	−0.08	−2,406	2,942
1980	147	0.003	−0.08	−3,128	3,275
1981	−1,118	−0.026	−0.08	−3,382	2,263
1982	−2,313	−0.057	−0.08	−3,194	880
1983	−1,420	−0.04	−0.08	−2,725	1,305
1984	−432	−0.012	−0.08	−2,751	2,318
1985	−1,811	−0.052	−0.08	−2,633	821
1986	−2,774	−0.089	−0.08	−2,301	−472
1987	−2,843	−0.099	−0.08	−2,068	−774
1988	−402	−0.013	−0.08	−2,211	1,809

Table 24.10 reports the results, which are summarised in net present value form in Table 24.11. Our results suggest that of the estimated total change in GFKF over the period, 41% can be attributed to the government. Taking the shocks separately, Shock III differed from the previous two in that government investment increased owing to the shocks, even though total investment fell. Although government investment rose by an estimated US$7.2 billion owing to Shock III, total investment fell by US$1.5 billion, implying a decline in private investment of US$8.7 billion.

24.7. Conclusions

International petroleum price movements have a very significant effect on Indonesia. Our results confirm that Indonesia's adjustment to the impact of positive changes in petroleum prices broadly conforms to the predictions of economic theory. The predictions of both the Dutch Disease and the construction boom literature are confirmed. Positive trade shocks provoked government-led booms in investment. This produced increases in the ratios of the prices of non-traded goods to traded goods and also increases in the prices of construction materials relative to other non-traded goods.

B. *Separate shocks (1973–78, 1979–85, 1986–88)*

	Actual FS[b]	Actual FS propensity	Counterfactual FS propensity	Counterfactual FS[b]	Windfall FS[b]
Shock I					
1970	−1,000	−0.109	−0.11	9,142	0
1971	−1,124	−0.121	−0.12	9,267	0
1972	−602	−0.054	−0.05	11,036	0
1973	−974	−0.066	−0.08	14,655	227
1974	−786	−0.036	−0.08	21,468	973
1975	−2,288	−0.099	−0.08	23,054	−398
1976	−946	−0.035	−0.08	26,431	1,220
1977	−1,850	−0.060	−0.08	30,319	635
1978	−880	−0.027	−0.08	31,551	1,706
Shock II					
1976	−1,350	−0.035	−0.04	37,797	0
1977	−2,810	−0.060	−0.06	46,356	0
1978	−1,435	−0.027	−0.03	51,975	0
1979	817	0.017	−0.04	45,590	2,701
1980	224	0.003	−0.04	59,308	2,675
1981	−1,705	−0.026	−0.04	64,349	953
1982	−3,527	−0.057	−0.04	61,188	−999
1983	−2,166	−0.040	−0.04	52,820	16
1984	−659	−0.012	−0.04	53,635	1,556
1985	−2,762	−0.052	−0.04	51,785	−622
Shock III					
1983	−3,334	−0.040	−0.04	82,564	0
1984	−1,055	−0.012	−0.01	87,616	0
1985	−4,549	−0.052	−0.05	87,337	0
1986	−6,749	−0.089	−0.03	75,629	−4,114
1987	−6,916	−0.099	−0.03	69,727	−4,486
1988	−978	−0.013	−0.03	74,825	1,628

[a] US$ m., at constant 1972 prices
[b] $US m., at constant base-period prices: 1972, 1978 and 1985

The sectoral composition of Indonesian GDP was greatly affected by fluctuations in petroleum revenues. The Dutch Disease effects accelerated the relative decline of the agricultural sector within the Indonesian economy. Other traded goods sectors were affected less significantly, partly reflecting the effects of government investment from the proceeds of the boom. The construction sector expanded rapidly as a consequence of the petroleum price increases. The windfall increased domestic capital formation, a result which will not surprise observers of Indonesia. But our estimates also indicate that foreign liabilities—foreign debt minus international reserves—were also reduced by the shocks. This was true of both

Table 24.10. Counterfactual and windfall fiscal outcomes

A. *Single shock (1973–88)*[a]

	Counterfactual government revenue	Windfall government consumption	GFKF	Revenue	Consumption	GFKF	Primary surplus
1970	985	773	55	0	0	0	0
1971	1,125	835	76	0	0	0	0
1972	1,552	959	36	0	0	0	0
1973	2,061	1,274	48	245	282	−32	−4
1974	3,012	1,862	70	786	−184	911	60
1975	3,227	1,994	75	1,108	279	515	315
1976	3,692	2,281	86	1,569	430	409	730
1977	4,227	2,612	98	1,820	711	95	1,015
1978	4,387	2,711	102	1,985	1,009	−82	1,058
1979	4,204	2,598	98	2,487	512	549	1,426
1980	5,302	3,277	123	3,691	1,172	380	2,138
1981	5,720	3,535	133	5,063	1,520	204	3,339
1982	5,379	3,324	125	3,620	1,752	203	1,665
1983	4,558	2,817	106	3,066	1,153	59	1,855
1984	4,586	2,834	107	3,265	991	22	2,253
1985	4,368	2,700	102	3,286	1,398	99	1,789
1986	3,784	2,339	88	2,989	1,260	621	1,109
1987	3,368	2,082	78	2,581	747	1,296	539
1988	3,600	2,225	84	1,866	670	1,728	−531

B. *Separate shocks (1973–78, 1979–85, 1986–88)*[b]

	Counterfactual government revenue	Windfall government consumption	GFKF	Revenue	Consumption	GFKF	Primary surplus
Shock I							
1970	985	773	55	0	0	0	0
1971	1,125	835	76	0	0	0	0
1972	1,552	959	36	0	0	0	0
1973	2,061	1,274	48	245	282	−32	−4
1974	3,012	1,862	70	786	−184	911	60
1975	3,227	1,994	75	1,108	279	515	315
1976	3,692	2,281	86	1,569	430	409	730
1977	4,227	2,612	98	1,820	711	95	1,015
1978	4,387	2,711	102	1,985	1,009	−82	1,058
Shock II							
1978	9,905	5,783	32	0	0	0	0
1979	8,688	5,072	28	1,713	−238	978	972
1980	11,289	6,591	36	2,690	325	747	1,618
1981	12,230	7,140	39	4,531	717	485	3,329
1982	11,608	6,777	37	2,380	1,113	473	794
1983	9,993	5,834	32	1,859	337	224	1,297
1984	10,132	5,915	32	2,073	31	168	1,874
1985	9,761	5,699	31	2,136	671	280	1,185
Shock III							
1985	18,331	9,814	480	0	0	0	0
1986	15,873	8,498	416	349	120	1,281	−1,053
1987	14,642	7,839	384	−393	−1,065	2,908	−2,236
1988	15,720	8,416	412	−2,628	−1,483	3,926	−5,072

[a] US$ m., at constant 1972 prices
[b] $US m., at constant base-period prices: 1972, 1978 and 1985

Table 24.11. Summary of fiscal response to windfall income

	1972–88	1972–78	1978–85	1985–88
1. Change in total revenue	17,847	5,531	13,453	−2,181
2. Change in total government consumption	6,082	1,781	2,115	−2,074
3. Change in total government GFKF	3,224	1,542	2,829	7,170
4. Primary surplus	8,540	2,209	8,510	−7,277
5. Change in government GFKF/ total change in GFKF (%)	41	45	33	−467
6. Change in government consumption/total change in consumption (%)	63	44	36	27
Base year	1972	1972	1978	1985

Note: Rows (1)–(4) = net present value in $US m., discounted at 10% to base year as stated, in base-year prices; row 4 = row 1 − row 2 − row 3

the positive petroleum price shocks, 1973–74 and 1978–79. This result must not be interpreted to mean that the actual level of foreign debt fell over this period; in fact it rose very substantially. What it means is that, according to our estimates, foreign debt would have increased even more substantially over this same period if the trade shock had not occurred.

The petroleum price decline beginning in the mid-1980s produced a somewhat different pattern of adjustments. Private and public consumption declined, but government investment rose as a consequence of the negative trade shock. This result is somewhat surprising. The government's view of the price decline was apparently that it was more temporary than the private sector's view. Hence, the government considered it important to try to maintain the level of aggregate investment. This led to a substantial increase in public investment, which in turn greatly increased Indonesia's foreign debt. The strategy is risky. If the decline proves to be more long-lasting than the government's assessment, Indonesia will be left with an excessive, and possibly unmanageable, burden of foreign debt.

NOTES

This paper has benefited from the excellent research assistance of Cao Yong, Zhang Xiao Guang and Zita Albacea, and from helpful discussions with Will Martin, Anne Booth and Chris Manning.

1. GDP actually fell in 1982, but by less than 0.1%.
2. It should be emphasised that the index of traded goods prices used is a non-petroleum series—the price of non-petroleum imported commodities.
3. It is also consistent with the Dutch Disease theory, provided the theory is interpreted as applying to non-traded inputs, such as construction materials, as well as to non-traded consumption goods.
4. Quantity variables were not expressed as a proportion of GDP because the two variables 'non-petroleum contribution to GDP divided by GDP' and 'petroleum contribution to GDP divided by GDP' would then sum identically to unity.
5. The author acknowledges the kind assistance of Dr Will Martin of the World Bank in suggesting this methodology and in providing the capital stock series for Indonesia.
6. Note that these are shares of *non-petroleum* GDP and are thus free of the trivial effect of a petroleum boom in reducing other sectors' shares of *petroleum-inclusive* GDP.
7. The correspondence between the tables which follow and the tables reported by Bevan *et al.* in Chapter 2, with the Bevan *et al.* tables shown in parentheses is: 24.6(2.1); 24.8(2.2); 24.9(2.3); 24.10(2.8).
8. The above results include no allowance for changes in inventories, owing to the inadequacy of Indonesian data on this topic.

REFERENCES

Booth, A. and P. McCawley (eds) (1981) *The Indonesian Economy During the Soeharto Era*, Kuala Lumpur: Oxford University Press.

Corden, W.M. and P.G. Warr (1981) 'The Petroleum Boom and Exchange Rate Policy in Indonesia: A Theoretical Analysis', *Ekonomi dan Keuangan Indonesia/ Economics and Finance in Indonesia*, 29 (September): 335–59.

Martin, W. and P.G. Warr (1991) 'Agriculture's Decline in Indonesia: Supply or Demand Determined?', Policy Research Working Paper WPS 798, October, Washington DC: World Bank.

Warr, P.G. (1984) 'Exchange rate protection in Indonesia', *Bulletin of Indonesian Economic Studies*, 20 (August): 53–90.

——(1986) 'Indonesia's Other Dutch Disease: Economic Effects of the Petroleum Boom', in J.P. Neary and S. van Wijnbergen (eds), *Natural Resources and the Macroeconomy*, Oxford: Basil Blackwell, 288–320.

——(1992) 'Exchange Rate Policy, Petroleum Prices and the Balance of Payments', in A.E. Booth (ed.) *The Oil Boom and After: Indonesian Economic Policy and Performance in the Soeharto Era*, Singapore: Oxford University Press, 132–58.

Woo, W.T. and A. Nasution (1989) 'Indonesian Economic Policies and their Relation to External Debt Management' in J.D. Sachs and S.M. Collins (eds), *Developing Country Debt and Economic Performance*, vol. 3, Chicago: University of Chicago Press, 17–149.

Woo, W.T., B. Glassburner and A. Nasution (1989) 'Macroeconomic Policies, Crises and Long-Run Growth: The Case of Indonesia, 1965–85', unpublished manuscript, Washington DC: World Bank.

INDEX

Index